ARCHITECTURE NOW!
MUSEUMS

IMPRINT

PROJECT MANAGEMENT
Florian Kobler, Cologne

COLLABORATION
Sonja Altmeppen, Berlin
Christina Holona, Cologne

PRODUCTION
Ute Wachendorf, Cologne

DESIGN
Sense/Net, Andy Disl
and Birgit Eichwede, Cologne

GERMAN TRANSLATION
Nora von Mühlendahl, Ludwigsburg

FRENCH TRANSLATION
Jacques Bosser, Paris

© VG BILD-KUNST
Bonn 2010, for the works of
John Chamberlain, Alberto Giacometti,
Damien Hirst, Mario Merz, MVRDV,
Jean Nouvel, Pablo Picasso,
UNStudio/van Berkel & Bos,
and OMA/Rem Koolhaas

PRINTED IN ITALY
ISBN 978–3–8365–1224–4

© 2010 TASCHEN GMBH
Hohenzollernring 53
D–50672 Cologne
www.taschen.com

ARCHITECTURE NOW!
MUSEUMS

Architektur heute! MUSEEN
L'architecture d'aujourd'hui! MUSÉES

Philip Jodidio

TASCHEN

CONTENTS

6   INTRODUCTION   Einleitung / Introduction

48   HITOSHI ABE   Kanno Museum, Shiogama, Miyagi, Japan
56   ACEBO X ALONSO   National Museum of Science and Technology, MUNCYT, A Coruña, Spain
64   AIRES MATEUS   Santa Marta Lighthouse Museum, Cascais, Portugal
70   JUN AOKI   Aomori Museum of Art, Aomori, Aomori, Japan
80   ARM   Albury Library Museum, Albury, New South Wales, Australia
86   SHIGERU BAN   Centre Pompidou-Metz, Metz, France
92   BEHNISCH ARCHITEKTEN   Ozeaneum, German Oceanographic Museum, Stralsund, Germany
100 DAVID CHIPPERFIELD   Reconstruction of the Neues Museum, Museum Island, Berlin, Germany
                          Liangzhu Culture Museum, Hangzhou, China
112 PRESTON SCOTT COHEN   Taiyuan Museum of Art, Taiyuan, China
                          Tel Aviv Museum of Art, Tel Aviv, Israel
122 COOP HIMMELB(L)AU   Musée des Confluences, Lyon, France
126 DELUGAN MEISSL   Porsche Museum, Stuttgart, Germany
134 ELLIS WILLIAMS   Cornerstone Arts Centre, Didcot, Oxfordshire, UK
140 FRANK O. GEHRY   Art Gallery of Ontario Expansion, Toronto, Ontario, Canada
146 TEODORO GONZÁLEZ DE LEÓN   University Museum of Contemporary Art,
                          National Autonomous University of Mexico (UNAM), Mexico City, Mexico
154 GRAFT   Russian Jewish Museum of Tolerance, Moscow, Russia
160 NICHOLAS GRIMSHAW   Horno 3, Museo del Acero, Monterrey, Mexico
166 ZAHA HADID   Ordrupgaard Museum Extension, Copenhagen, Denmark
                          Mobile Art, Chanel Contemporary Art Container, various locations
                          MAXXI, National Museum of 21st-Century Arts, Rome, Italy
182 HERZOG & DE MEURON   TEA, Tenerife Espacio de las Artes, Santa Cruz de Tenerife, Canary Islands, Spain
192 HOK   Frost Art Museum, Miami, Florida, USA
198 ARATA ISOZAKI   Art Museum, Central Academy of Fine Arts, Beijing, China
206 KSV KRÜGER SCHUBERTH VANDREIKE   Museion, Museum of Modern and Contemporary Art, Bolzano, Italy
212 BRUNO MADER   Museum of the Landes de Gascogne, Sabres, France
218 FUMIHIKO MAKI   Shimane Museum of Ancient Izumo, Izumo, Shimane, Japan
224 FRANCISCO MANGADO   Archeology Museum of Álava, Vitoria, Spain

232	**RICHARD MEIER**	Arp Museum, Rolandseck, Germany
238	**PAULO MENDES DA ROCHA**	Portuguese Language Museum, São Paulo, São Paulo, Brazil
244	**RAFAEL MONEO**	Museum of the Roman Theater, Cartagena, Spain
252	**TOSHIKO MORI**	Visitor Center for Frank Lloyd Wright's Darwin D. Martin House, Buffalo, New York, USA
260	**MVRDV**	Matsudai Cultural Village Center, Matsudai, Niigata, Japan
266	**NIETO SOBEJANO**	Moritzburg Museum Extension, Halle, Saale, Germany
		Madinat al-Zahra Museum and Research Center, Córdoba, Spain
280	**RYUE NISHIZAWA**	Towada Art Center, Towada City, Aomori, Japan
286	**VALERIO OLGIATI**	Swiss National Park Visitor Center, Zernez, Switzerland
292	**I. M. PEI**	Museum of Islamic Art, Doha, Qatar
300	**RENZO PIANO**	Modern Wing of the Art Institute of Chicago, Chicago, Illinois, USA
308	**QUERKRAFT**	Liaunig Museum, Neuhaus/Suha, Carinthia, Austria
316	**SANAA / KAZUYO SEJIMA + RYUE NISHIZAWA**	Louvre-Lens, Lens, France
320	**SAUERBRUCH HUTTON**	Brandhorst Museum, Munich, Germany
328	**HARTWIG N. SCHNEIDER**	Stihl Art Gallery and Art School Waiblingen, Waiblingen, Germany
336	**ÁLVARO SIZA VIEIRA AND RUDOLF FINSTERWALDER**	Hombroich Museum, Neuss-Hombroich, Germany
342	**SNØHETTA**	Petter Dass Museum, Alstahaug, Sandnessjøen, Nordland, Norway
348	**EDUARDO SOUTO DE MOURA**	Bragança Contemporary Art Museum, Bragança, Portugal
354	**SSM ARCHITEKTEN**	Grenchen Art Museum Extension, Grenchen, Switzerland
360	**RANDALL STOUT**	Taubman Museum of Art, Roanoke, Virginia, USA
366	**BERNARD TSCHUMI**	New Acropolis Museum, Athens, Greece
376	**UNSTUDIO**	MOMEMA, Museum of Middle East Modern Art, Khor Dubai, United Arab Emirates
384	**URBANUS ARCHITECTURE & DESIGN**	Tangshan Urban Planning Museum, Tangshan, China
		OCT Art & Design Gallery, Shenzhen, China
396	**WANG SHU**	Ningbo History Museum, Ningbo, China
406	**ATELIER ZHANGLEI**	N4A Museum, Liyang, China
412	**INDEX**	
416	**CREDITS**	

INTRODUCTION

TO WISH UPON A STAR

As long as museums have existed, they have been associated with celebrated architects. The civic role of museums as symbols of local, regional, or national pride surely explains this ongoing relationship, as does the "value" placed on their contents. Architecture is called on to some extent to echo the significance of art, and, more frequently today, of the contents of other institutions, such as those devoted to science. Most museum-goers have heard of the so-called Bilbao effect which would have it that Frank O. Gehry's Guggenheim Bilbao (Bilbao, Spain, 1991–97; page 7) is responsible for the renewal of that Spanish city's center. Thus, calling on a "name" architect is seen as a way to draw in crowds—people with a penchant for culture, and surely for spending. Without contesting the drawing power of the Guggenheim Bilbao, it can be pointed out that Gehry's building was surely not the first instance of the successful combination of architecture and museums. Long before the modern era, buildings such as the Altes Museum, erected on Berlin's Museum Island from 1825 to 1828 by the famed architect Karl Friedrich Schinkel to house the Prussian royal family's art collection, firmly established this connection. And yet, for all his talent, Schinkel built in the Neoclassical style rather than affirming any astonishing new forms. Architecture was very much at the service of its patrons and its contents. One hundred and forty years later, Ludwig Mies van der Rohe completed the Neue Nationalgalerie in Berlin, in a decidedly different style that might be called classical Modernism. Here it is certain that the clarity and simplicity of the architecture carry the day, showing that modernity, too, could achieve the kind of *gravitas* required of institutions devoted to art.

THE BAUHAUS GOES WEST

So when did things go "wrong"—when did architecture take center stage and begin to allow individual architects to affirm their identity even as they gave shape to the ambitions of institutions and cities? One clear example slightly predates the Neue Nationalgalerie, but it was the work of another major Bauhaus architect, Marcel Breuer. The Whitney Museum of American Art, located on Madison Avenue in New York (1963–66), has an almost disturbing or blank presence that imposes itself on its surroundings, where traditional New York buildings are still the rule. It may well have been in New York that the rules of the museum game changed, beginning in the 1960s, allowing for significant works of contemporary architecture to signal that a new type of institution was emerging. Tom Hoving assumed the directorship of the Metropolitan Museum of Art in 1967 and, by the time he left, a decade later, the institution had been greatly expanded by the architect Kevin Roche (Roche Dinkeloo). Architecture itself was less the driving force of the expansion of the Met than the overall plan laid out by Hoving that included substantial gallery space, as well as infrastructure and such facilities as an expanded bookshop. Commerce entered the "temple" while brash new architecture began to play its role.

Often seeking to contest New York's role as America's cultural capital, Washington D.C. soon erected another monument intended to bring its premier art museum very much into the present. I. M. Pei, the architect of the East Building of the National Gallery of Art (1968–78), of the Grand Louvre project in Paris (1983–93; page 47), and the more recent Museum of Islamic Art in Doha (Qatar, 2003–08; page 293) has stated: "I have always been most interested in civic work, and in my opinion the best civic project is a museum. The museum has been my preference

because it sums up everything. The Louvre is about architecture, but, even more, it is the expression of a civilization. I learn a great deal when I build a museum, and if I don't learn, I can't design. From my first project in the studio of Gropius at Harvard, to my most recent work, the museum has been a constant and present reminder that art, history, and architecture are indeed one."[1] Pei's East Building is not a monument to the architect, but it does carry his distinctive geometric style and brought with it a constant flow of visitors, usually bound to see modern and contemporary art.

RENZO AND FRANK HIT THE TOWN

No, Gehry was by no means the inventor of the rather explosive cocktail of architecture, art, and big money that rules today's museum world, even as economies falter. The Centre Pompidou (Piano & Rogers, Paris, France, 1971–77; page 20) brought a new kind of cultural institution, modeled on André Malraux's *Maisons de la Culture*, into the heart of Paris with a bang that drew an average of 20 000 visitors a day for years. The tube-covered industrial look of the Centre Pompidou clearly played a role in the visitor numbers and thus the "success" of the venture. Yet barely 10 percent of visitors actually entered the Musée national d'art moderne, preferring in many cases to take in the spectacular view of Paris from the top floor. Virtually unknown prior to their selection for the Centre Pompidou, Richard Rogers and Renzo Piano became two of the leading lights of contemporary architecture, and Piano in particular has gone on to design a large number of museums, including the Modern Wing of the Art Institute of Chicago (Chicago, Illinois, USA, 2005–09; page 301). Piano is also the author of numerous other museum projects, to the extent that the respected US magazine *Architectural Record* recently asked if Piano had not become the country's "default architect." Nor are Piano's efforts devoted exclusively to art museums—his renovation and expansion of the California Academy of Sciences (San Francisco, California, USA, 2005–08; page 34) concerns a natural-history museum that was built to obtain a LEED Platinum rating reflecting its strategies to conserve energy and to use environmentally friendly building materials. The undulating roof of the structure, with a surface of over one hectare, is covered with 1.8 million native California plants. Careful study of the plants themselves, but also of the seismic implications of a planted roof, was part of the preparation of this aspect of the design that is open to visitors. It is calculated that the design of the roof reduces temperatures inside the museum by about 6°C. A rainwater collection system is designed to store and reuse about 13 500 cubic meters of water each year, reused for irrigation and gray water. The roof's shape and, indeed, the entire design of the museum were conceived to form a continuum with the surrounding park environment. Intended for schoolchildren and the general public, the Academy focuses on education and research on conserving natural environments and habitats. At a cost of $370 million, including the exhibition program and expenditures associated with the Academy's temporary housing, this project might not be the prototype of museums to come in the wake of the world's financial crisis, but its environmental concerns may well point the way forward.

The Guggenheim Bilbao (Bilbao, Spain, 1991–97; page 7) is without any doubt one of Frank O. Gehry's most spectacular architectural works. It is located in the center of the cultural district formed by the Museo de Bellas Artes, the University de Deusto, and the Opera House,

2

2
*Herzog & de Meuron, Transforming
Tate Modern, London, UK, 2008–12*

on a 32 700-square-meter site formerly occupied by a factory and parking lot. Three firms participated in an invited competition—Gehry, Arata Isozaki, and Coop Himmelb(l)au: a list that indicates the desire of the organizers of the project to produce a spectacular piece of architecture. Part of a $1.5 billion redevelopment for this industrial capital of the semiautonomous Basque region—which includes a subway line designed by Norman Foster, and a footbridge and airport by Santiago Calatrava—the new structure has a total floor area of 24 000 square meters with 10 600 square meters of exhibition space on three levels. Financed by the city, region, and Spanish government, the contents of the museum are in good part the responsibility of the Guggenheim Museum in New York, which made several attempts to expand in Europe under its dynamic former director Thomas Krens. The new museum is an eminently urban structure, located on the banks of the Nervion River and literally crossed through by the Puente de la Salve, which runs above part of the main exhibition gallery. From the outside, its most spectacular feature is the titanium cladding of its "metallic flower" shapes that were modeled by Gehry using the CATIA program developed by Dassault in France for fighter plane design. On the inside, visitors are greeted by a 55-meter-high atrium that cuts through the heart of the building. There are 18 galleries, but the most spectacular of these by far is the main exhibition space, which is free of structural columns and measures no less than 130 meters in length by 30 meters in width. Inevitably, such spaces invite comparison to the cathedrals of another era. Gehry also reaches the apogee here of his natural tendency to want to create buildings that are works of art—the museum as a work of art in and of itself. The success of the Guggenheim Bilbao in rejuvenating Bilbao and making it into a tourist destination has served Gehry well. He has built other museums since, the most recent of which is the Art Gallery of Ontario Expansion (Toronto, Canada, 2005–08; page 141).

BATMAN AND ROBIN TO THE RESCUE

Jacques Herzog and Pierre de Meuron were both born in Basel, Switzerland, in 1950. Although they are amongst the best-known of contemporary architects today and winners of the 2001 Pritzker Prize, it was their selection as designers of the Tate Gallery extension for contemporary art, situated in the Bankside Power Station on the Thames River (Tate Modern, London, UK, 1995–2000), that launched their international career. Their most recent museum project concerns a new building for the Tate (Transforming Tate Modern, 2008–12; page 8). The original Tate Modern was designed for 1.8 million visitors a year and it now receives over four million, a clear indication of its success. Like Piano, the Swiss architects have designed numerous museum projects since bursting onto the international scene. In 2005, they completed an expansion of the Walker Art Center (Minneapolis, Minnesota, USA, 2003–05; page 21) and a new building for the De Young Museum (San Francisco, California, USA, 2002–05; page 35). Herzog & de Meuron do not have an immediately definable style. Their work varies considerably and shows an uncommon inventiveness. Thus, more recently, they completed the CaixaForum (Madrid, Spain, 2001–08), which makes unusual use of the brick walls of the former Mediodía Power Station, lifted off the ground and internally rebuilt. Relatively small by the standards of other new cultural institutions designed by the Swiss architects, the CaixaForum proves that there is no set of standards. Another of the Swiss pair's outstanding projects is published in detail in this volume. The TEA (Tenerife Espacio de las Artes, Santa Cruz de Tenerife, Canary Islands, Spain, 2003–08; page 183) is in many respects typical of the newer type of multiuse cultural center that was invent-

3
Jean Nouvel, Quai Branly Museum,
Paris, France, 2001–06

3

ed by the *Maisons de la Culture* in France, and, above all, by the Centre Pompidou. The TEA includes exhibition zones, but also a library, an open-air event space, as well as the usual shop and restaurant. With its sliced, elongated forms, open courtyards, and punctured walls, the TEA is both autonomous in its setting and very much open to the city that surrounds it. This project places culture in a central position, a fact that has been emphasized throughout recent years in museums and cultural centers around the world. This is a place of gathering as much as it is a location for the exhibition of works of art for an educated elite.

BORDEAUX WINE OR SAKE?

Equally unpredictable in style and almost as prolific as Herzog & de Meuron, the French architect Jean Nouvel signed a very surprising museum of primitive art in Paris that participates in the increasing freedom given to (or taken by) architects. The Quai Branly Museum (Paris, France, 2001–06; page 9) is a 30 000-square-meter facility on the Seine River within sight of the Eiffel Tower. Jean Nouvel was chosen at the end of 1999 to build the museum from a field including Tadao Ando, Norman Foster, Renzo Piano, and MVRDV. As the architect says, the museum is intended to protect the works of art from harsh sunlight, and yet light is a key to its design. He says that his goal was to make the entire panoply of technical aspects, ranging from fire escapes to display cases, "disappear" in order to make the powerful objects visible. Working with the noted French landscape architect Gilles Clément, Nouvel created one of his most surprising buildings. Gardens flow under and around the building in such as way as to contribute to the feeling of "disappearance" imagined by Nouvel. The complex ebb and flow of the shapes of the new museum is one of Nouvel's strongest statements in favor of a new kind of architecture: neither specifically Modernist nor, indeed, directly linked to any other identifiable trend, it is an architecture of circumstances in the better sense of this affirmation. Today, Jean Nouvel is working on yet another expansion of the Louvre, this time in Abu Dhabi (United Arab Emirates; page 36). Construction there is due to be completed in 2012, and, unlike many other projects in the Persian Gulf, Abu Dhabi has expressed the clear desire to advance on this new outpost of the Paris institution.

Another star architect with a long list of museums to his credit is Tadao Ando. His culture-driven buildings include the Forest of Tombs Museum (Kumamoto, Japan, 1992), the Suntory Museum (Osaka, Japan, 1994), the Pulitzer Foundation for the Arts (Saint Louis, Missouri, USA, 1997–2000), the Modern Art Museum of Fort Worth (Fort Worth, Texas, USA, 1999–2002), the Chichu Art Museum on the Island of Naoshima (Japan, 2003; page 22), 21_21 Design Sight (Tokyo, Japan, 2004–07), an expansion of the Clark Art Institute (Williamstown, Massachusetts, USA, 2006–08), the renovation of Palazzo Grassi and the Punta della Dogana for the art patron François Pinault (Venice, Italy, 2003–09; page 37), and the Abu Dhabi Maritime Museum (Abu Dhabi, United Arab Emirates, 2006–). Though Ando's thick concrete walls and geometric vocabulary might well be more predicable than the latest designs by Herzog & de Meuron, the Japanese architect has such a mastery of quality and variety within his chosen style that he has most certainly marked the era of museum expansion more than almost any other architect.

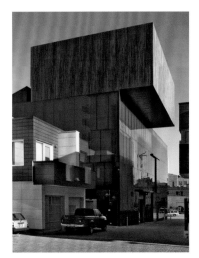

4

The number of new museum buildings designed by celebrated architects within the past 20 years almost defies listing. From the exten-sion of the Prado in Madrid by Rafael Moneo (Spain, 2001–07) to the UK star David Adjaye's Museum of Contemporary Art/Denver (Denver, Colorado, USA, 2004–07; page 10), architects have had a very good run with municipalities and museum trustees in developed countries. The latter project might give some hint of things to come, however, because the Denver Museum was built to obtain a LEED Gold Certifica-tion for environmental responsibility. It is also a somewhat smaller museum than many recently built institutions, a trend that is likely to be confirmed by restrictive economic conditions born of the recession that began in 2008. It is clear that the post-2008 world in museums and architecture will be radically changed for some time to come, with reduced donations and more careful spending all around. This is not to say that name architects will no longer build new museums, but rather that the scale and ambition of the projects will surely be reduced. Then, too, so many museums were built before the bubble burst that many cities no longer need a new Gehry, Piano, or Herzog creation.

CRASH AND BURN

The extent of difficulties engendered for museums by the economic crisis was underlined in an April 2009 publication: the Getty Trust in Los Angeles (with its well-known design by Richard Meier; page 45) lost $1.5 billion from its endowment in the second half of 2008; the Metropolitan Museum of Art in New York, which generates one-third of its operating budget from its endowment, saw those funds reduced from $2.9 billion to $2.1 billion in 2008, raising the specter of substantial deficits.[2] Questions are also being raised in the United States about the desirability of long-standing tax laws that permit donors to deduct museum gifts from their payments to the Internal Revenue Service. For some, however, it seems unfair that the United States government should thus indirectly finance museums when people are in need of med-ical care or food. Though this matter was far from being decided as this book went to press, it remains a fact that one of the main sources of the wealth of American museums, and hence their new construction, has been a steady and substantial flow of donations. Yoshio Taniguchi's renovation and expansion of New York's Museum of Modern Art (MoMA, 2002–04) had a total budget of $425 million, with con-struction alone costing $315 million, yet even these figures understate total expenses that rise to $858 million when the costs of MoMA Queens and moving back and forth are added to some acquisitions. Such substantial spending would be impossible in today's economic cli-mate, a fact that is of great importance in imagining where the museum boom of the early 21st century will go from here.

RUNNING INTO TURBULENCE

Although the museums of recent years have drawn a good deal of praise, and surely encouraged many new visitors to come forth, it often remains to be proven that the success sought by these institutions can be enduring. The graphic designer Ken Carbone, a founding partner of Carbone Smolan in New York, a noted "strategic design group that creates brand identities, exhibitions, and environmental graph-ics for cultural institutions," has lashed out more than once against the tendency of museums to consider name architects as saviors on white horses. Comments he wrote in 2004 in the magazine *I. D.* ring even more true in the light of recent economic upheavals. "Art museums con-tinue to rely on big architects to design spectacular buildings that become the most visible part of their institutional brand. These master-

5
*Santiago Calatrava, Milwaukee
Art Museum, Milwaukee, WI, USA,
1994–2001*

5

pieces rise from the earth like glimmering shards of ice, curving metal mountains, and soaring biomorphic creatures. They are magnificent, and they attract media attention and visitors from around the globe. Sounds like a winning formula? Far from it. Along with the high design, high finance, and high expectations, there's a high risk of failure…. The headlines speak for themselves. Last year, the Steven Holl-designed Bellevue Art Museum in Seattle closed after only two years of operation and an opening ceremony that rivaled the Oscars. The Milwaukee Art Museum is wrestling with a $25 million debt in the wake of its winged Calatrava addition (page 11). *The Hartford Courant* reported that the Wadsworth Atheneum's board decided to 'dump the design' for its planned expansion by Ben van Berkel of UNStudio after untold development costs. More recently, both the Whitney and the Los Angeles County Museum of Art pulled the plug on their Koolhaas-designed renovations. Costly but perhaps wise decisions."[3]

The museums published in this volume are all quite recent, but it cannot be said that any of them take into account the economic recession that began in 2008. It will be possible to better analyze the impact of these events within the normal time frame of design and construction, which implies periods ranging upwards of approximately three years. Some projects have clearly been put on hold or canceled already, but there have been such a significant number of new museums or extensions built across the world in the past three years that more than one book could be filled with their images. The selection for this book has been made on the basis of architectural interest, but also geographic spread and the very nature of the projects concerned, ranging from large institutional realizations, such as the expansion projects of the Louvre (Lens, 2009–12; page 317) or Centre Pompidou (Metz, 2006–10; page 87) in France, to small local projects like the Santa Marta Lighthouse Museum (Cascais, Portugal, 2003–07; page 65). The number of unbuilt or "virtual" projects has been limited in order to focus on "real" museums that are either already built or (hopefully) about to be. Nor is art the only subject of these museums—there is one devoted to steel (Horno 3, Museo del Acero, Monterrey, Mexico, 2006–07; page 161), another to the sea (Ozeaneum, German Oceanographic Museum, Stralsund, Germany, 2005–08; page 93), and another to a language (Portuguese Language Museum, São Paulo, São Paulo, Brazil, 2003–06; page 239). With Zaha Hadid's Mobile Art, Chanel Contemporary Art Container (various locations, 2007–; page 174), even handbags get star treatment.

DRIFTING BETWEEN HISTORY AND NATURE

Though the conservation of works of art might well imply a conservative approach, examples set by architects ranging from Piano & Rogers to Santiago Calatrava have surely freed museum trustees or political authorities from the fear of innovation. Rather, the "Bilbao effect" would seem to dictate the emergence of ever more surprising architecture. A number of the museums selected here do innovate in differing ways, though perhaps not always through spectacular architectural gestures. David Chipperfield's remake of the Neues Museum in Berlin (Germany, 1997–2009; page 101) stands out as a surprising approach to the difficulties posed by a wartime ruin. Bombed during World War II, and left in its ruined state by the East German regime, the Museum Island institution has been painstakingly restored to its original volumes by the English architect, with many of the scars of war visible in its walls. Other areas have been reconstituted using materials like

6
*Jean Nouvel, Museum of Human
Evolution, Burgos, Spain, 2000*

7
*Shigeru Ban, Centre Pompidou-Metz,
Metz, France, 2006–10*

6

concrete, a choice that has shocked some purists, and yet this is precisely what makes Chipperfield's intervention modern or timely. It should be pointed out that David Chipperfield is not the first British architect to confront the issue of Berlin war ruins. Norman Foster did so as well in the New German Parliament (Reichstag, 1995–99), about which he stated: "I have been at pains to retain and incorporate memories from the past in the fabric of the building—such as graffiti from the Russian occupation, the torching in the 1930s, the scars of war, original moldings and 1960s interventions."[4] The decidedly hybrid modernity introduced into the Neues Museum by David Chipperfield has nothing to do with pastiche. It is a sensitive and powerful effort to reconcile the present with the past in the charged context of German history, ranging from the original 19th-century building to its long history as a ruin, and on to 2009, when the return of museum objects signaled a healing continuity.

Zaha Hadid has made a career of shaking up expectations about the forms and function of architecture. Her latest museum (MAXXI, the National Museum of 21st-Century Arts, Rome, Italy, 1998–2009; page 178) is no exception. Rather than one or even several potential paths of discovery through the building, she speaks of drifting through space or "intertwining the circulation with the urban context." In clear terms, the unusual shape of the MAXXI building corresponds to a program that seeks to do nothing less than to rethink the museum experience. Far from the rectilinear model pioneered in New York's Museum of Modern Art (MoMA), even in its recent Yoshio Taniguchi intervention (page 23), Hadid thinks in three dimensions and all but banishes the straight line. This much architecture may well challenge curators. Come to think of it, parts of the Guggenheim Bilbao, such as its long "snake" gallery, might be described less as a challenge than as a sort of "mission impossible." Where Gehry has made clear his desire to embody the same sort of freedom as contemporary art, Hadid appears to focus more on issues of function and the flow of space. In her object design as well as in her architecture, Zaha Hadid has emphasized a continuous, almost liquid approach to volumes and forms, implying a challenge to the established order of just about everything, from the plan to the wall. It remains to be seen if this challenge will be perceived in the future as a personal expression of aesthetics or as a revolution in architecture. The MAXXI will play an important role in answering that question.

An important source of innovation in recent architecture has been the emergence of talents from China. Modifications in Chinese laws have permitted individual architects to make their mark as opposed to the monolithic "institutes" that dominated the profession for decades. A good deal of the new Chinese architecture may have a somewhat difficult or even "disturbing" appearance to Western eyes, but its strength is obvious. This is surely the case of Wang Shu's Ningbo History Museum (Ningbo, China, 2003–08; page 397), which assumes the shape of an artificial mountain. A number of Western architects, such as Jean Nouvel (Museum of Human Evolution, Burgos, Spain, 2000; page 12), have experimented with similarly inspired concepts, but Wang Shu has actually built his great mountain of a museum. Describing the project in terms not only of the mountain but also of valleys and tunnels, the architect states: "The interior and exterior of the building were covered with bamboo-plate-modeled concrete and more than 20 kinds of recycled bricks, which is like a magnificent and thrifty substance existing between artificiality and nature."

7

VIRTUALLY THERE

Despite the emphasis in this book on "real" museums, a few unbuilt works have been selected because of their significance, and because they are likely, given promised government funding, to see the light of day. Three of these new institutions are located in France, and are by well-known architects. Perhaps following the lead of the Guggenheim Bilbao, but also the Tate Gallery's early efforts to spread to other locations, both the Centre Pompidou and the Louvre in Paris have announced expansion plans in the French provinces. The Louvre is, of course, also involved in a plan to build a museum with Jean Nouvel in Abu Dhabi. The Centre Pompidou-Metz by Shigeru Ban is the furthest along of these endeavors, due to be inaugurated in 2010 (page 87). Ban is, of course, known for his innovative designs and use of materials, such as structural paper tubes. The Metz facility has an unexpected roof, modeled on a Chinese hat the architect bought in Paris. The ample spaces of the new Pompidou are in part inspired by the Forum in the original Piano & Rogers building, and in part by the need to make room for increasingly large works of contemporary art. It is interesting to note that Ban's involvement in the competition for this project was largely due to his admiration for the audacity of the original Centre. "When I heard about the competition," says Shigeru Ban, "I thought that it would be a very appropriate project for me to participate in. I respect Renzo Piano and Richard Rogers, and I like architecture that is innovative. I saw that the Centre Pompidou was the client and I was sure that they would accept an innovative proposal. I thought that this was a competition that I had to win. I knew that the building was to be in Metz, and I must admit that I did not know much about the city. It is not very important where it is since the Centre Pompidou is involved."[5]

Shigeru Ban's own description of the project gives an interesting insight into the way contemporary museums are conceived, and how his own approach has been influenced by other recent museums. When asked if the roof or the contents of the building came first in his mind, Shigeru Ban responds: "The two came together. Many architects make buildings that are difficult to use as museums. Museum people and artists always say that they don't need architects. They prefer industrial spaces such as the ones used at DIA Beacon (OpenOffice, Beacon, New York, USA, 2004), or Tate Modern (Herzog & de Meuron, London, UK, 2000). They say that architects design museums more for themselves than for the art. I wanted to design something that would be a good museum, but also send a strong message. In the original program, it was requested of the architects that they design gallery spaces in modules 15 meters wide with different lengths. I thought that a useful gallery should have as much wall space as possible, with the best climate control available. I thought of tubes because they have a maximum amount of wall surface—they are in boxes that are very easy to control in terms of climate. Another characteristic of the program is the Grand Nef (nave) space with a very high ceiling. Because the Centre Pompidou in Paris does not have sufficient high-ceilinged space, there are parts of the collection that cannot be shown to the public, so the Grand Nef is important to the museum. I decided to place the galleries in the form of rectangular tubes, stacked above the Grand Nef. The Forum and Grand Nef spaces are thus created by the hanging tubes and the roof. The roof is not symmetrical like the hat because of the content of the building. If you see the roof from above, however, the basic shape is still a symmetrical hexagon pattern."[6]

Heneghan.Peng.Architects, Grand
Egyptian Museum, Giza, Egypt,
2007–14

8

Surprisingly, the Louvre also selected Japanese architects to design their extension in the city of Lens (France, 2009–12; page 317). Ryue Nishizawa and Kazuyo Sejima (SANAA) have experience in museum design, but more specifically in the area of contemporary art. The skewed, angular forms selected by the architects for Lens with the kind of broad, open glazing that is seen in their other work might seem contradictory with the rather closed, stone architecture of the original Louvre. The goal here, however, is to bring something of the wealth of the Paris institution to the provinces and to do so in an open, generous way. Indeed, both Metz and Lens are located in areas of France that have economic difficulties related to the long decline of their industrial base. It will, of course, remain to be seen if either Shigeru Ban or SANAA can generate the kind of architectural excitement that followed the opening of Frank Gehry's Guggenheim Bilbao, but the Spanish initiative with the New York museum surely inspired these ambitious expansion plans.

The city of Lyon is the venue of another museum that remains virtual for the moment, although opening is scheduled for 2013. The Musée des Confluences (France, 2001–13; page 123) has been designed by Coop Himmelb(l)au. Called the "Crystal Cloud of Knowledge" by its Austrian architects, this piece of architecture might be seen as having its aesthetic or formal origins closer to the time when "deconstructivism" was all the rage. This is an interesting aspect of certain large projects that are the visible aspect of conceptual advances in architecture. The architects won the competition for the project in 2001, but it should be noted that three of their earlier projects were included in the 1988 exhibition *Deconstructivst Architecture* at New York's Museum of Modern Art (MoMA). This is not meant to be a critique of the Lyon project, but rather an indication that a great deal of patience and persistence is required on the part of architects who challenge convention, as Wolf D. Prix and his team have done with the Musée des Confluences.

Almost as unusual as the choice of Japanese architects for two significant cultural institutions located in France, the Grand Egyptian Museum (Giza, Egypt, 2007–14; page 14), located on the plateau of the Pyramids near Cairo, is being designed by an Irish woman (Roisin Heneghan) and a man of Chinese origin, Shih-Fu Peng (Heneghan.Peng.Architects), together with a reputed Dutch landscape architecture firm (West8). Due for completion in 2014, the 100 000-square-meter facility is to cost no less than 350 million. The very fact of building near the Pyramids is a considerable gamble, but it is clear that the Egyptian Museum in Cairo is outdated by the flow of tourists and the age of the building, while coordinating the museum with the actual site in Giza is both logical and more efficient. Under the leadership of Egyptian Minister of Culture Farouk Hosni, this project has been in gestation for a long period, but it now appears ready to advance. In describing their project, the architects state: "The Grand Egyptian Museum is not a singular museum in the traditional sense of the museum. It is constructed as a complex of different activities which contribute to a cultural environment that is centered around Egyptology. By weaving different navigation routes through the complex, the world of ancient Egypt can be explored in different modes and levels. The museum is both a repository of cultural artifacts and an interactive cultural resource."

9
Delugan Meissl, Porsche Museum,
Stuttgart, Germany, 2006–08

9

SIXTEEN TONS OF NUMBER NINE COAL

Although art remains by far the favored content of new museums, a number of other subjects have been at the origin of the institutions featured here. Francisco Aires Mateus created one of the smaller museums in this book (Santa Marta Lighthouse Museum, Cascais, Portugal, 2003–07; page 65) around the subject of the neighboring 1868 lighthouse, but also of lighthouses in general. The Portuguese architect made a coherent whole out of what was a rather heterogeneous site and allowed for its conversion to a new use. This is reasoning that might correspond on a small scale to the frequently expressed hope of municipal authorities that a museum will regenerate a given area that has fallen into disrepair or even abandonment. The Ozeaneum (German Oceanographic Museum, Stralsund, Germany, 2005–08; page 93) by Behnisch Architekten also makes use of existing architecture to some extent, in this case a converted historic warehouse, but it also relates directly to its waterside site, featuring exhibitions on the Baltic and North Seas. With a total area of 60 000 square meters, the Ozeaneum is in a different league than the Santa Marta Lighthouse Museum, of course, but it also participates in an urban regeneration program for Quartier 66.

The Austrian architects Delugan Meissl have recently completed the new Porsche Museum (Stuttgart, Germany, 2006–08; page 127), one of a series of such structures designed in Germany by well-known architects, such as UNStudio (Mercedes-Benz Museum, Stuttgart, 2003–06; page 29), or Coop Himmelb(l)au (BMW Welt, Munich, 2001–07; page 42). Here the goal is to evoke the distinctive style of the car brand and also to fit into a notably industrial site. The result is both spectacular and dynamic in form, as might well have been hoped given the subject matter of the museum and the 100 million budget.

Nicholas Grimshaw has delved into an even more unusual type of new museum, one centered around a 70-meter-high furnace building in a former steel-producing facility in Mexico—Horno 3, Museo del Acero (Monterrey, Mexico, 2006–07; page 161). The rehabilitation and reuse of industrial facilities has, of course, been undertaken in numerous other locations, seeking to give value to structures that may well have an aesthetic appeal, but which otherwise would face demolition. There is an authenticity in a rehabilitated industrial building that no amount of architectural creativity can imitate or re-create, and the 145 000 visitors to the Museo del Acero in its first six months of operation testify to the level of public interest in this type of museum. Paulo Mendes da Rocha, 2006 winner of the Pritzker Prize, has designed museums dedicated to art such as the Brazilian Museum of Sculpture (São Paulo, São Paulo, Brazil, 1987–92; page 43), but his latest venture into this area deals with a more unexpected content. The Portuguese Language Museum (São Paulo, São Paulo, Brazil, 2003–06; page 239) is set in the late 19th-century Neoclassical Luz Railway Station. The museum actually occupies a little more than half of what remains an operating station, creating challenges that were both technical and aesthetic for the strongly Modernist architect. Even more unexpected as a subject for a museum, Zhang Lei's N4A Museum (Liyang, China, 2006–07; page 407) sings the praises of the New 4th Army. Established in 1937, the N4A was one of the main forces of the Chinese Communist Party, active south of the Yangtze River from the 1930s on. Powerful and perhaps more than a little enigmatic, the structure again highlights the inventiveness of contemporary Chinese architects, and their aesthetic sense, which stands somewhat apart from that of design in Europe, or even the rest of Asia.

10

FROM SOUTHIE TO THE BOWERY

Art-museum expansions have been led by institutions ranging from the Metropolitan to the Louvre that rarely, if ever, show contemporary art. Other museums, such as the Centre Pompidou (Musée national d'art moderne), Tate Gallery, or Museum of Modern Art (MoMA) do show contemporary art, but their major attractions are more in the category generally called "modern," ranging from late 19th-century art to the work of the postwar period. It is only recently that institutions exclusively devoted to contemporary art have joined the march toward striking new buildings designed by celebrated architects. An example in this area is the Institute of Contemporary Art (Boston, Massachusetts, USA, 2004–06; page 16), by the New York architects Diller Scofidio + Renfro. This $41 million, 5760-square-meter facility is located at the water's edge on Fan Pier in South Boston, a highly visible and successful indication of the inroads that contemporary art has made in the museum-going population. The arrival of really contemporary art and architecture in South Boston (referred to as Southie by its residents) is no small event. Although the Institute is close to South Station, Government Center, and the well-known Anthony's Pier Four restaurant, it is also in an area once known for its rough manners, and poor, largely Irish population.

The New Museum of Contemporary Art (New York, New York, USA, 2005–07; page 31) by Ryue Nishizawa and Kazuyo Sejima of SANAA is a second example of the new link between contemporary art and talented architects. Located on the Bowery, a Lower East Side avenue that has recently undergone a process of gentrification, the New Museum is one of the most remarked upon new buildings to rise in Manhattan in a number of years. The oldest road in Manhattan, the Bowery was the most elegant street of the city at the end of the 18th century, but in the 1920s and 1930s it became an impoverished area. A series of films featuring the *Dead End Kids* or *The Bowery Boys* gave the area a reputation far beyond New York City. From the 1940s until the end of the 1970s, the Bowery was known mostly for its population of alcoholics and homeless people. Even today, some minor remnants of this atmosphere exist in the area, although chic cafés and hotels are more the rule. Consisting essentially in a series of apparently blank, randomly stacked boxes, the New Museum represents an intelligent and economical solution to problems posed by its narrow site (21 meters wide by 34 meters deep for a height of 52 meters). By displacing the boxes that form the essentially neutral and high gallery spaces, the architects managed to bring light in where it was desired and to create outdoor terraces with views of downtown New York. Their aluminum cladding material (expanded aluminum mesh, with a bright anodized finish) gives the structure a constantly changing shimmer that certainly sets it apart from more staid neighbors. The New Museum architectural initiative is "the centerpiece of a $64 million capital project that included construction of the new building, expansion of the museum's endowment, and other costs related to planned growth, financed entirely by a fundraising campaign and sale of the museum's previous site on Broadway in SoHo."

EAST OF EDEN

Aside from the Louvre-Lens, Sejima and Nishizawa are also the authors of the 21st-Century Museum of Contemporary Art (Kanazawa, Ishikawa, Japan, 2002–04; page 44). This innovative structure, in the form of a fully glazed 112.5-diameter circle, combines cutting-edge

10
Diller Scofidio + Renfro, Institute of
Contemporary Art, Boston, MA, USA,
2004–06

11
Teodoro González de León, University
Museum for Contemporary Art,
National Autonomous University of
Mexico (UNAM), Mexico City, Mexico,
2006–08

11

architecture with a very high level of contemporary art. With an advisory committee originally including Lars Nittve (Director of the Moderna Museet), Alfred Pacquement (Director of the Musée national d'art moderne at the Centre Pompidou), and Neil Benezra (Director of SFMoMA), the 21st-Century Museum makes a clear statement in favor of bringing contemporary art and architecture into the heart of even such a traditional city as Kanazawa. Close to a number of government buildings, the museum is directly opposite the famous Kenroku-en gardens. Completed over a period of 200 years, from the 17th to the 19th century, Kenroku-en was the outer garden of Kanazawa Castle. The garden, one of the most famous in Japan, was designated as a National Site of Scenic Beauty in 1922 and as a National Site of Special Scenic Beauty in 1985. With its full-height windows, low profile, and pure geometric form, the 21st-Century Museum is not in contradiction with its prestigious neighbor, quite the contrary, actually.

The angular, white University Museum for Contemporary Art (National Autonomous University of Mexicom—UNAM, Mexico City, Mexico, 2006–08; page 147) by Teodoro González de León is another proof of the spreading tendency to give a new place to contemporary art, beyond the gallery and fair circuit that it has long inhabited more easily than the museum world. The museum is located at one end of a new plaza that serves as an entrance to the Cultural Center of the University. The museum is laid out on two levels: the plaza level including exhibition galleries, reception area, store, and bookshop, as well as educational areas; and a lower level, partially excavated from volcanic rock, where the 300-seat auditorium, offices, storerooms, a cafeteria, restaurant, and mediatheque are located. The architect states that the proportions of the structure "were carefully chosen after visiting 35 contemporary art museums and galleries around the world." In this remark there is a sense that new locations for contemporary art have much in common, in particular the aim of bringing the creativity of today to the attention of a broader public.

CULTURE FOR THE PEOPLE

Whatever the future may hold, it seems clear that recent years have seen an accelerating trend toward the construction of more and more museums. The success of talented architects, from I. M. Pei to Renzo Piano, Frank Gehry and the younger generation, in making museums into architectural events, or perhaps works of art in themselves, needs to be observed from a certain distance. There are many reasons for which the "Bilbao effect" may not take hold in given cases. In fact, the success of Gehry's Guggenheim Bilbao has proven rather difficult to repeat. And yet the fact that 8.2 million visitors passed beneath I. M. Pei's glass Pyramid in the Cour Napoléon of the Louvre in 2008 does show that intelligently conceived architecture can play a role in bringing the public into museums. The Louvre is now confronted with the problem of having too many visitors—roughly five million admissions were projected as a maximum when Pei finished his work there in 1993. By multiplying ancillary activities from auditorium events to restaurants, shops, and libraries, museums have become tourist attractions of course, but also, frequently, a kind of culturally oriented community center, a place of gathering and meeting. The relationship of today's museums to the churches of the past has often been pointed out, and yet the museum as a sanctuary, a sort of humanist temple, is now a thing of the past. Much discussion of the "democratization" of art and culture has fueled political initiatives in countries such as France, for example under the presidency of François Mitterrand with Jack Lang as Minister of Culture. The widespread construction of museums, limited not only to art, nor indeed to the more traditional sorts of art, has finally begun to have an impact on a more general public. Once reserved for a moneyed elite, the appreciation of art has indeed spread to a wider base of visitors. Despite the legitimate reservations raised by such commentators as Ken Carbone about the ultimate viability of many expensive museum extensions, visitor numbers confirm that museums now represent an important proportion of leisure time in many countries.

The current economic situation will surely have an effect on many existing institutions, and even more certainly on future projects. Smaller, more ecologically responsible museums may well profit from the downturn, but it may be safe to say that the close relationship between "quality" architecture and the museum world is here to stay. Though a stellar reputation may be no guarantee that an architect knows how to design the right museum in the right circumstances, there is a clearly established correlation between the world of culture and that of the higher end of architectural design. A famous architect has rarely hurt the reputation and visitor numbers of a museum, even if cost overruns and occasional impractical solutions do plague some recent projects. Museums have opened a whole new world for many tourists and residents of cities fortunate enough to have interesting buildings and collections. More than private houses or even office buildings, museums have done a great deal to bring the general public closer not only to art, of course, but also to contemporary architecture. That is the most enduring legacy of the boom times that cultural institutions have recently gone through. With that assurance, those who decide on museum projects in the future, and their architects, will surely find solutions to overcome the problems posed by less abundant funding. The stars of art and the stars of architecture are bound together.

Philip Jodidio, Grimentz, May 1, 2009

1   I. M. Pei, preface to the book *I. M. Pei, Architect*, New York, 2008.
2   "Troubles deepen for museums: layoffs, budget cuts and cancelled shows," *The Art Newspaper*, April 2009.
3   Ken Carbone, "The Shell Game: Too many museums are investing in star architecture at the expense of art," *I. D.* magazine, May 2004.
4   Fax from Norman Foster to the author, November 1, 1996.
5   Interview of Shigeru Ban by the author, July 23, 2008, Paris.
6   Ibid.

EINLEITUNG

MAN WÜNSCHT SICH EINEN STAR

Seitdem Museen existieren, verbindet man sie auch mit berühmten Architekten. Die gesellschaftliche Rolle von Museen als Symbole lokalen, regionalen oder nationalen Selbstbewusstseins erklärt diese anhaltende Beziehung gewiss ebenso wie der „Wert", den man ihren Inhalten beimisst. Ihre Architektur soll gewissermaßen die Bedeutung der Kunst und heutzutage noch öfter auch die anderer Bereiche widerspiegeln – wenn sie z. B. der Wissenschaft gewidmet sind. Die meisten Museumsbesucher haben schon vom sogenannten Bilbao-Effekt gehört, der besagt, dass Frank O. Gehrys Guggenheim Museum in Bilbao (1991–97, Seite 7) die Erneuerung des Zentrums dieser spanischen Stadt ausgelöst hat. So betrachtet man die Berufung eines „namhaften" Architekten als Mittel, um Menschenmassen anzuziehen – Leute mit einer Vorliebe für Kultur und sicherlich auch zum Geldausgeben. Ohne die Anziehungskraft des Guggenheim Museums in Bilbao bestreiten zu wollen, ist doch darauf hinzuweisen, dass Gehrys Bauwerk nicht das erste Beispiel einer gelungenen Verbindung von Architektur und Museum darstellt. Schon lange vor der Moderne begründeten Bauten wie das Alte Museum, das der berühmte Architekt Karl Friedrich Schinkel 1825 bis 1828 auf der Berliner Museumsinsel zur Unterbringung der königlich-preußischen Kunstsammlungen errichtete, dieses Verhältnis. Allerdings baute Schinkel, bei all seiner Begabung, im klassizistischen Stil, anstatt irgendwelche überraschenden neuen Formen zu präsentieren. Die Architektur stand in erster Linie im Dienst ihrer Bauherren und ihrer Inhalte. 140 Jahre später vollendete Ludwig Mies van der Rohe die Neue Nationalgalerie in Berlin in einem völlig anderen Stil, den man als klassische Moderne bezeichnen könnte. Hier ist es eindeutig, dass Klarheit und Schlichtheit der Architektur den Sieg davongetragen und gezeigt haben, dass auch mit den Mitteln der Moderne die für Kunstinstitutionen erforderliche Form der *gravitas* zu erreichen war.

DAS BAUHAUS *GOES WEST*

Wann also liefen die Dinge „aus dem Ruder" – wann stellte sich das Bauwerk in den Mittelpunkt und begann, einzelnen Architekten die Darstellung ihrer Identität zu ermöglichen, auch wenn sie den Wünschen von Institutionen und Städten Gestalt verliehen? Ein eindeutiges Beispiel dafür ging der Neuen Nationalgalerie voraus, das Werk eines anderen Bauhaus-Architekten: Marcel Breuers Whitney Museum of American Art an der Madison Avenue in New York (1963–66) zeigt eine fast störende oder beunruhigende Präsenz, die sich ihrer Umgebung aufdrängt, in der noch traditionelle New Yorker Bauten vorherrschen. Es war wohl auch in New York, wo sich die Spielregeln für Museen Anfang der 1960er-Jahre veränderten, als eindrucksvolle Bauten zeitgenössischer Architektur einen neuen Typus dieser Institution begründeten. Tom Hoving übernahm 1967 die Leitung des Metropolitan Museum of Art, und als er es zehn Jahre später verließ, war es von dem Architekten Kevin Roche (Büro Roche Dinkeloo) wesentlich erweitert worden. Die treibende Kraft dahinter war weniger die Architektur als die Gesamtplanung von Hoving, die erheblich mehr Ausstellungsfläche sowie Infrastruktureinrichtungen, z. B. die Erweiterung der Buchhandlung, vorsah. Sogar der Kommerz fand also Eingang in den „Tempel", als eine spektakuläre neue Architektur ins Spiel kam.

Die Stadt Washington D. C., die oft New York die Rolle als kulturelle Hauptstadt Amerikas streitig macht, errichtete bald darauf ein anderes Baudenkmal, das sein bedeutendstes Kunstmuseum in die Gegenwart führen sollte. I. M. Pei, der Architekt des East Building der

12

National Gallery of Art (1968–78), des Grand Louvre in Paris (1983–93, Seite 47) und des kürzlich errichteten Museums für islamische Kunst in Doha (Katar, 2003–08, Seite 293), hat erklärt: „Ich war immer eher an städtischen Bauten interessiert, und meiner Meinung nach ist ein Museum das beste aller städtischen Projekte. Meine Vorliebe gilt dem Museum, weil es alles zusammenfasst. Der Louvre ist Architektur, aber darüber hinaus ist er Ausdruck einer Zivilisation. Ich lerne sehr viel, wenn ich ein Museum baue, und wenn ich nicht lerne, kann ich nicht planen. Von meinem ersten Entwurf im Atelier von Gropius in Harvard bis zu meinen neuesten Bauten hat mich das Museum stets daran erinnert, dass Kunst, Geschichte und Architektur tatsächlich eins sind."[1] Peis East Building ist kein Denkmal für den Architekten, aber es zeigt seinen eigenen geometrischen Stil und zieht ständig Besucher an, die normalerweise nur kommen, um moderne und zeitgenössische Kunst zu betrachten.

RENZO UND FRANK SIND IN DER STADT ANGEKOMMEN

Gehry war also keineswegs der Erfinder des reichlich explosiven Cocktails aus Architektur, Kunst und großem Geld, der heute die Welt der Museen regiert – trotz aller Wirtschaftskrisen. Mit dem Centre Pompidou in Paris (Piano & Rogers, 1971–77, Seite 20) entstand im Herzen von Paris auf einen Schlag eine neue Form von Kulturinstitution nach dem Vorbild von André Malrauxs *Maisons de la Culture*, die jahrelang durchschnittlich 20 000 Besucher pro Tag anlockte. Das mit Rohren überzogene, industrielle Erscheinungsbild spielte eindeutig eine Rolle bei den Besucherzahlen und damit für den „Erfolg" des Unternehmens. Doch kaum 10 % der Besucher betraten das Musée national d'art moderne wirklich, vielmehr beschränkten sie sich auf den spektakulären Blick auf Paris vom obersten Geschoss. Die vor ihrer Beauftragung mit dem Centre Pompidou praktisch völlig unbekannten Richard Rogers und Renzo Piano wurden zu Leitfiguren unter den zeitgenössischen Architekten, und vor allem Piano hat danach eine große Zahl von Museen gebaut, u. a. den Modern Wing des Art Institute in Chicago (Chicago, Illinois, 2005–09, Seite 301). Piano hat derart viele andere Museen geplant, dass die angesehene nordamerikanische Zeitschrift *Architectural Record* kürzlich die Frage stellte, ob er nicht zum „Standardarchitekten" des Landes avanciert sei. Und nicht nur den Kunstmuseen hat sich Piano gewidmet – seine Erneuerung und Erweiterung der California Academy of Sciences (San Francisco, Kalifornien, 2005–08, Seite 34) betrifft ein naturhistorisches Museum, das eine LEED-Platin-Auszeichnung für die Maßnahmen zur Energieeinsparung und die Nutzung umweltfreundlicher Materialien erhielt. Das wellenförmige Dach des Gebäudes mit einer Fläche von mehr als 1 ha ist mit 1,8 Millionen einheimischen Pflanzen bedeckt. Gründliches Studium dieser Pflanzen, aber auch der seismischen Auswirkungen eines begrünten Dachs gehörten zu den Vorbereitungen für diesen Aspekt des Gebäudes, der für Besucher zugänglich ist. Man hat berechnet, dass die Art des Dachs die Temperatur im Innern des Museums um etwa 6 °C reduziert. Ein System zum Auffangen des Regenwassers speichert etwa 13 500 m³ Wasser jährlich, das zur Bewässerung und als Brauchwasser genutzt wird. Die Form des Dachs und das ganze Erscheinungsbild des Gebäudes bilden eine Einheit mit der umgebenden Parklandschaft. Die auf die Information von Schülern und des allgemeinen Publikums ausgerichtete Akademie konzentriert sich auf Weiterbildung und Forschung zur Erhaltung natürlicher Landschafts- und Lebensräume. Dieses 370-Millionen-Dollar-Projekt (einschließlich Ausstellungsprogramm und Kosten für die vorübergehende Unterbringung der Akademie) ist wegen der Weltwirtschaftskrise vielleicht nicht der Prototyp für künftige Museen, aber seine umweltfreundliche Zielsetzung ist durchaus zukunftsweisend.

13

Das Guggenheim Museum in Bilbao (1991–97, Seite 7) ist zweifellos eines der spektakulärsten Bauwerke von Frank O. Gehry. Es liegt im Zentrum des 32 700 m² großen Kulturbezirks, der vom Museo de Bellas Artes, der Universidad de Deusto und dem Opernhaus gebildet wird und früher von einer Fabrik und einem Parkplatz eingenommen wurde. Zu dem Wettbewerb waren drei Büros geladen: Gehry, Arata Isozaki und Coop Himmelb(l)au – Namen, die vom Wunsch der Auslober nach einem spektakulären Bauwerk zeugen. Das neue Gebäude ist Teil eines 1,5 Milliarden Dollar umfassenden Sanierungskonzepts der Industriemetropole in der halbautonomen baskischen Region, zu dem auch eine von Norman Foster geplante U-Bahn sowie eine Fußgängerbrücke und ein Flughafengebäude von Santiago Calatrava gehören. Das Museum hat eine Gesamtgeschossfläche von 24 000 m²; davon verteilen sich 10 600 m² Ausstellungsfläche auf drei Ebenen. Die Verantwortung für die Exponate des von der Stadt, der Region und der spanischen Regierung finanzierten Museums liegt überwiegend beim Guggenheim Museum in New York, das unter seinem dynamischen früheren Leiter Thomas Krens mehrere Versuche unternommen hat, sich auch in Europa niederzulassen. Das neue Museum ist ein in hohem Maß urbanes Bauwerk, am Ufer des Flusses Nervion gelegen und buchstäblich durchschnitten von der Brücke Puente de la Salve, die oberhalb eines Teils des großen Ausstellungssaals verläuft. Das spektakulärste Merkmal der Außenform aus „Metallblüten" ist die Titanverkleidung, die von Gehry mit dem Programm CATIA gestaltet wurde, das die Rüstungsfirma Dassault in Frankreich für den Entwurf von Kampfflugzeugen entwickelt hat. Innen werden die Besucher von einem 55 m hohen Atrium im Zentrum des Gebäudes empfangen. Es gibt 18 Ausstellungsräume; bei weitem der spektakulärste von allen ist jedoch der größte, 130 m lange und 30 m breite stützenfreie Saal. Derartige Räume legen unweigerlich den Vergleich mit den Kathedralen früherer Zeitalter nahe. Gehry erreicht hier auch den Höhepunkt seiner Bemühungen, Bauten zu schaffen, die Kunstwerke sind – das Museum als Kunstwerk an sich und für sich allein betrachtet. Der Erfolg des Guggenheim Museums bei der Verjüngung Bilbaos und als Touristenattraktion ist Gehry gut bekommen. Er hat seither weitere Museen entworfen, zuletzt den Erweiterungsbau der Art Gallery of Ontario (Toronto, Kanada, 2005–08, Seite 141).

BATMAN UND ROBIN ALS RETTER

Jacques Herzog und Pierre de Meuron wurden beide 1950 im schweizerischen Basel geboren. Obgleich sie heute zu den bekanntesten zeitgenössischen Architekten gehören und 2001 den Pritzker-Preis erhielten, verdanken sie ihre internationale Karriere dem Auftrag für die Erweiterung der Tate Gallery für Gegenwartskunst im alten Bankside-Kraftwerk an der Themse (Tate Modern, London, 1995–2000). Ihr jüngstes Museumsprojekt ist ein Neubau für die Tate (Transforming Tate Modern, 2008–12, Seite 8). Die ursprüngliche Tate Modern war für 1,8 Millionen Besucher jährlich konzipiert und zählt jetzt über 4 Millionen – ein überzeugender Beleg für ihren Erfolg. Ebenso wie Piano haben auch die Schweizer Architekten zahlreiche Museumsprojekte realisiert, seitdem sie die internationale Szene betraten. 2005 vollendeten sie eine Erweiterung des Walker Art Center (Minneapolis, Minnesota, 2003–05, Seite 21) und einen Neubau für das Museum De Young (San Francisco, Kalifornien, 2002–05, Seite 35). Herzog & de Meuron haben keinen unmittelbar ablesbaren Stil. Ihre Bauten variieren stark und zeugen von ihrem ungewöhnlichen Einfallsreichtum. Erst vor kurzem vollendeten sie das CaixaForum (Madrid, 2001–08), bei dem die Backsteinwände des früheren Kraftwerks Mediodía vom Boden angehoben und innen eingebaut wurden. Dieses im Vergleich zu den anderen neuen, von diesen

14

Schweizer Architekten geplanten Kultureinrichtungen kleine Gebäude beweist, dass sie keinen vorgegebenen Regeln folgen. Ein anderes ihrer bemerkenswerten Projekte wird ausführlich in diesem Buch vorgestellt. Das TEA (Tenerife Espacio de las Artes, Santa Cruz de Tenerife, Kanarische Inseln, 2003–08, Seite 183) ist in vielerlei Hinsicht typisch für die neue Art der Mehrzweckkulturzentren, die auf die französischen *Maisons de la Culture* zurückgehen, in erster Linie auf das Centre Pompidou. Das TEA enthält Ausstellungsflächen, aber auch eine Bibliothek, einen Veranstaltungsbereich im Freien und wie üblich einen Shop und ein Restaurant. Mit seinen klaren, langgezogenen Formen, offenen Höfen und durchbrochenen Wänden ist das TEA sowohl ein Solitärbau als auch zur umgebenden Stadt geöffnet. Dieses Projekt versetzt die Kultur in eine zentrale Position – eine Tatsache, die in den letzten Jahren vermehrt für Museen und Kulturzentren in aller Welt zutrifft. Dies ist sowohl ein Ort der Begegnung als auch zur Ausstellung von Kunstwerken für eine gebildete Elite.

BORDEAUX ODER SAKE?

Der französische Architekt Jean Nouvel, dessen Stil ebenso wenig berechenbar und fast so vielfältig wie der von Herzog & de Meuron ist, plante in Paris ein höchst erstaunliches Museum für primitive Kunst im Rahmen der zunehmenden Freiheit, die Architekten gewährt wird (oder die sie sich nehmen). Das Museum Quai Branly (Paris, 2001–06, Seite 9) ist ein 30 000 m^2 großes Gebäude am Ufer der Seine mit Blick auf den Eiffelturm. Jean Nouvel wurde Ende 1999 aus einer Gruppe, zu der außerdem Tadao Ando, Norman Foster, Renzo Piano und MVRDV gehörten, ausgewählt und mit dem Bau des Museums beauftragt. Laut Aussage des Architekten soll das Museum die Kunstwerke vor grellem Sonnenlicht schützen, und dennoch ist Licht ein Schlüsselelement dieses Entwurfs. Sein Ziel, sagt Nouvel, sei es gewesen, alle erforderlichen technischen Einrichtungen, von Notausgängen bis zu Ausstellungsvitrinen, „verschwinden" zu lassen, um die eindrucksvollen Exponate herauszustellen. In Zusammenarbeit mit dem bekannten französischen Landschaftsarchitekten Gilles Clément hat Nouvel hier eines seiner erstaunlichsten Bauwerke geschaffen. Gärten fließen unter dem Gebäude entlang und um es herum und tragen zum Eindruck des von Nouvel erwünschten „Verschwindens" bei. Die komplexen auf- und absteigenden Formen dieses neuen Museums gehören zu den stärksten Bekenntnissen Nouvels zu einer neuen Art der Architektur, die weder spezifisch modernistisch ist, noch irgendeinem anderen identifizierbaren Trend zuzuordnen ist. Es handelt sich um eine den Bedingungen entsprechende Architektur im wahrsten Sinn des Worts. Gegenwärtig arbeitet Nouvel an einer neuen Niederlassung des Louvre, diesmal in Abu Dhabi (Vereinigte Arabische Emirate, Seite 36). Sie soll 2012 fertiggestellt werden, und im Gegensatz zu vielen anderen Projekten am Persischen Golf besteht man in Abu Dhabi auf der Realisierung dieser neuen Außenstelle des Pariser Louvre.

Ein weiterer Architekt mit einer langen Liste von Museumsbauten ist Tadao Ando. Zu den von ihm geplanten Kultureinrichtungen gehören das Museum Forest of Tombs (Kumamoto, Japan, 1992), das Suntory Museum (Osaka, Japan, 1994), die Pulitzer Foundation for the Arts (Saint Louis, Missouri, 1997–2000), das Modern Art Museum of Fort Worth (Fort Worth, Texas, 1999–2000), das Kunstmuseum Chichu auf der Insel Naoshima (Japan, 2003, Seite 22), 21_21 Design Sight (Tokio, 2004–07), ein Erweiterungsbau des Clark Art Institute (Williamstown, Massachusetts, 2006–08), der Umbau des Palazzo Grassi und der Punta della Dogana für den Kunstmäzen François Pinault (Venedig, 2003–

14
Tadao Ando, Chichu Art Museum,
Naoshima, Japan, 2003

15
Yoshio Taniguchi, Renovation and
Expansion of the Museum of Modern
Art, New York, NY, USA, 2002–04

15

09, Seite 37) und das Abu Dhabi Maritime Museum (Abu Dhabi, Vereinigte Arabische Emirate, 2006–). Obgleich sich die starken Betonwände und das geometrische Vokabular dieses Museums Ando eindeutiger zuschreiben lassen als Herzog & de Meuron ihre jüngsten Bauten, zeigen Andos Gebäude in dem von ihm gewählten Stil eine derart meisterhafte Qualität und Vielfalt, dass er die Ära der Museumsneubauten wohl stärker geprägt hat als irgendein anderer Architekt.

Die Zahl der von berühmten Architekten in den letzten 20 Jahren neu geplanten Museen ist nahezu unüberschaubar. Von der Erweiterung des Prado in Madrid von Rafael Moneo (2001–07) bis zum Museum of Contemporary Art/Denver (Denver, Colorado, 2004–07, Seite 10) des britischen Stararchitekten David Adjaye waren die Architekten bei den Stadtverwaltungen und Museumsdirektoren in Industrieländern sehr gefragt. Das Museum in Denver, das für seine Umweltqualität mit einem LEED-Zertifikat in Gold ausgezeichnet wurde, könnte jedoch einen Hinweis auf die Zukunft geben. Es ist auch etwas kleiner als viele der vorher errichteten Museen – ein Trend, der sich vermutlich angesichts der 2008 begonnenen wirtschaftlichen Rezession fortsetzen wird. Mit Sicherheit wird sich in naher Zukunft die Welt der Museumsarchitektur radikal verändern, weil Fördermittel ausbleiben und die Ausgaben überall gekürzt werden. Das bedeutet nicht, dass bekannte Architekten keine neuen Museen mehr bauen werden, aber der Maßstab und die Ansprüche werden sicher abnehmen. Außerdem wurden so viele Museen vor Ausbruch der Krise errichtet, dass viele Städte keine neuen Schöpfungen von Gehry, Piano oder Herzog & de Meuron mehr benötigen.

DER CRASH UND DIE FOLGEN

Das Ausmaß der durch die Wirtschaftskrise ausgelösten Probleme der Museen ist in einer Publikation vom April 2009 nachzulesen: Der Getty Trust in Los Angeles (mit seinem bekannten Bau von Richard Meier, Seite 45) verzeichnete im zweiten Halbjahr 2008 einen Verlust seiner Stiftungsgelder von 1,5 Milliarden Dollar; beim Metropolitan Museum of Art in New York, das ein Drittel der Unterhaltskosten aus seinen Stiftungsgeldern bestreitet, reduzierten sich die Gelder 2008 von 2,9 Milliarden auf 2,1 Milliarden Dollar, und es fürchtet erhebliche Defizite.[2] In den Vereinigten Staaten wird auch die Frage aufgeworfen, ob die seit langem bestehenden Steuergesetze noch zeitgemäß seien, nach denen Spenden an Museen abzugsfähig sind. Manchen erscheint es durchaus unfair, dass die US-Regierung indirekt Museen finanziert, während es der Bevölkerung an medizinischer Versorgung oder Nahrung mangelt. Obgleich dies bei Drucklegung des vorliegenden Buchs noch längst nicht entschieden war, sind stetige und umfangreiche Spenden nach wie vor wichtige Einnahmequellen amerikanischer Museen, und ihre Neubauten waren stets darauf angewiesen. Yoshio Taniguchis Erneuerung und Erweiterung des New Yorker Museum of Modern Art (MoMA, 2002–04) hatte einen Gesamtetat von 425 Millionen Dollar, wobei allein der Bau 315 Millionen Dollar kostete. Doch auch diese Zahlen waren nicht die Gesamtkosten, die sich auf 858 Millionen Dollar beliefen, wenn man dazu die Ausgaben für das MoMA in Queens und den Hin- und Hertransport sowie einige Neuerwerbungen mit einrechnet. Im heutigen Wirtschaftsklima wären solche Ausgaben vollkommen unmöglich – eine Tatsache, die von großer Bedeutung für die Einschätzung der Zukunft des Museums nach dem großen Boom zu Beginn des 21. Jahrhunderts ist.

16

AUF DEM WEG IN SCHWIERIGKEITEN

Obgleich die neuen Museen der letzten Jahre hoch gelobt wurden und zweifellos viele neue Besucher angelockt haben, steht der Beweis noch aus, dass der Erfolg dieser Einrichtungen von Dauer sein wird. Der Grafiker Ken Carbone, Mitbegründer von Carbone Smolan in New York, einem bekannten „strategischen Designteam, das Corporate Identities, Ausstellungen und Umweltgrafiken für kulturelle Institutionen" erarbeitet, hat mehr als einmal gegen die Tendenz gewettert, dass Museen namhafte Architekten als Retter in der Not betrachten. Die Kommentare, die er 2004 in der Zeitschrift *I. D.* schrieb, klingen angesichts der gegenwärtigen Wirtschaftskrise noch zutreffender: „Kunstmuseen verlassen sich weiterhin auf große Architekten, die spektakuläre Bauten planen, welche zu ihren Markenzeichen werden. Diese Meisterwerke ragen aus dem Boden wie schimmernde Eisbrocken, gekrümmte Metallberge und aufsteigende biomorphe Kreaturen. Sie sind großartig und erregen die Aufmerksamkeit der Medien und Besucher aus aller Welt. Klingt dies nach einem Rezept für Gewinner? Weit gefehlt! Diese hochwertige Gestaltung, die hohen Kosten und die damit verbundenen hohen Erwartungen bergen auch ein hohes Risiko zu scheitern … Die Schlagzeilen sprechen für sich. Im vorigen Jahr schloss das von Steven Holl geplante Bellevue Art Museum in Seattle nach nur zwei Betriebsjahren und einer Eröffnungszeremonie, die der Oscar-Verleihung würdig gewesen wäre. Das Milwaukee Art Museum kämpft mit Schulden von 25 Millionen Dollar als Folge seines schwungvollen Calatrava-Anbaus (Seite 11). Der *Hartford Courant* berichtete, dass der Vorstand des Wadsworth Atheneum beschlossen hat, den Entwurf für die geplante Erweiterung von Ben van Berkel von UNStudio zu ‚kippen‘, da die Kosten nicht vorhersehbar waren. Kürzlich haben sowohl das Whitney als auch das Los Angeles County Museum ihre von Koolhaas geplanten Umbauten aufgegeben. Kostspielige, aber vermutlich kluge Entscheidungen!"[3]

Die in diesem Band vorgestellten Museen stammen alle aus jüngerer Zeit, aber man kann nicht sagen, dass auch nur eines davon die 2008 begonnene wirtschaftliche Rezession berücksichtigt habe. Deren Auswirkungen werden sich im normalen Zeitrahmen zwischen Planung und Ausführung, der etwa drei Jahre und mehr beträgt, besser beurteilen lassen. Einige Projekte sind bereits zurückgestellt oder storniert worden, aber in den vergangenen drei Jahren sind in aller Welt so viele neue Museen oder Erweiterungen entstanden, dass mehr als ein Buch damit gefüllt werden könnte. Die Auswahl für den vorliegenden Band erfolgte aufgrund der architektonischen Bedeutung, aber auch nach der geografischen Verteilung und der Art der betreffenden Projekte, die von großen Institutionen wie den Erweiterungsplanungen des Louvre (Lens, 2009–12, Seite 317) oder des Centre Pompidou (Metz, 2006–10, Seite 87) in Frankreich bis zu kleinen örtlichen Planungen wie dem Leuchtturmmuseum Santa Marta (Cascais, Portugal, 2003–07, Seite 65) reichen. Die Zahl der ungebauten oder „virtuellen" Projekte wurde beschränkt, um die Aufmerksamkeit auf „reale" Museen zu lenken, die entweder schon gebaut sind oder es (hoffentlich) noch werden. Auch ist Kunst nicht das einzige Thema dieser Museen – es gibt eins, das dem Stahl gewidmet ist (Horno 3, Museo del Acero, Monterrey, Mexiko, 2006–07, Seite 161), ein weiteres dem Meer (Ozeaneum, Deutsches Meeresmuseum, Stralsund, 2005–08, Seite 93) und wieder ein anderes einer Sprache (Museu da Lingua Portuguesa, São Paulo, Brasilien, 2003–06, Seite 239). In Zaha Hadids Projekt Mobile Art, Chanel Contemporary Art Container (verschiedene Standorte, 2007–, Seite 174) werden sogar Handtaschen wie Stars behandelt.

16
Behnisch Architekten, Ozeaneum,
German Oceanographic Museum,
Stralsund, Germany, 2005–08

17
Photo of the Neues Museum ruins
taken in 1985

18
David Chipperfield, Neues Museum,
Berlin, Germany, 1997–2009

17

18

SICH TREIBEN LASSEN ZWISCHEN GESCHICHTE UND NATUR

Obgleich die Konservierung von Kunstwerken auch konservative Lösungen erwarten lässt, haben Architekten von Piano & Rogers bis Santiago Calatrava durch die von ihnen konzipierten Vorbilder Museumsvorstände und Politiker von der Furcht vor Innovationen befreit. Vielmehr scheint der „Bilbao-Effekt" die Entstehung immer erstaunlicherer Architekturen zu verlangen. Einige für dieses Buch ausgewählte Museen zeigen unterschiedliche Arten von Innovation, wenn auch nicht immer durch spektakuläre Architekturformen. David Chipperfields Rekonstruktion des Neuen Museums in Berlin (1997–2009, Seite 101) ist eine hervorragende Lösung für eine Kriegsruine. Dieses im Zweiten Weltkrieg durch Bomben zerstörte und vom DDR-Regime in diesem Zustand belassene Bauwerk auf der Museumsinsel ist von dem britischen Architekten sorgfältig in seinem ursprünglichen Umfang wiederhergestellt worden, wobei viele Spuren der Kriegseinwirkungen sichtbar geblieben sind. Einige Teile sind wiederaufgebaut worden, z.B. in Beton – eine Entscheidung, die einige Puristen schockiert hat – und dennoch ist es genau dies, was Chipperfields Eingriffe modern oder zeitgemäß macht. Übrigens ist David Chipperfield nicht der erste britische Architekt, der sich mit Berliner Kriegsruinen auseinandergesetzt hat. Norman Foster ging beim Reichstagsgebäude in Berlin (1995–99) ähnlich vor und erklärte: „Ich habe mich bemüht, Reminiszenzen an die Vergangenheit zu bewahren und in das Gebäude zu integrieren – z.B. die Beschriftungen von russischen Besatzern, Spuren von der Brandstiftung in den 1930er-Jahren, die Beschädigungen aus dem Krieg, alte Mauerwerksteile und Eingriffe aus den 1960er-Jahren."[4] Die von David Chipperfield dem Neuen Museum verliehene, bewusst hybride Modernität hat nichts mit Pastiche zu tun. Es ist ein sensibler und eindrucksvoller Versuch, Gegenwart und Vergangenheit im belasteten Kontext deutscher Geschichte miteinander zu versöhnen – der hier vom ursprünglichen Bauwerk aus dem 19. Jahrhundert über seinen langen Zustand als Ruine bis zum Jahr 2009 reicht, in dem die Rückkehr der Exponate eine heilende Kontinuität signalisiert.

Zaha Hadid hat in ihrer Laufbahn alle Vorstellungen über Formen und Funktion von Architektur auf den Kopf gestellt. Ihr neuestes Museum (MAXXI, Museo nazionale delle arti del XXI secolo, Rom, Italien, 1998–2009, Seite 178) bildet darin keine Ausnahme. Anstelle eines oder gar mehrerer Rundgänge durch das Museum spricht sie von „sich durch den Raum treiben lassen" oder einer „Verflechtung des Durchlaufs mit dem städtischen Kontext". Genauer gesagt, die ungewöhnliche Form des MAXXI-Gebäudes entspricht einem Programm, das nichts weniger zum Ziel hat als ein Umdenken im Erleben eines Museums. Weit entfernt vom rechtwinkligen Vorbild des New Yorker Museum of Modern Art (MoMA), sogar seiner Erneuerung durch Yoshio Taniguchi (Seite 23), denkt Zaha Hadid dreidimensional und verbannt die gerade Linie. So viel Architektur kann auch eine Herausforderung für Kuratoren bedeuten. So gesehen, ließen sich Teile des Guggenheim Museums Bilbao, z.B. dessen lange „Schlangen"-Galerie, weniger als Herausforderung denn als eine Art „unmögliche Aufgabe" auffassen. Während Gehry klar formuliert hat, mit seiner Architektur die gleiche Art von Freiheit ausdrücken zu wollen wie die zeitgenössische Kunst, scheint Hadid sich mehr auf Aspekte der Funktion und den Raumfluss zu konzentrieren. In ihrer Objektgestaltung wie auch ihrer Architektur betont sie eine kontinuierliche, beinahe fließende Behandlung von Volumen und Formen, die eine totale Herausforderung der etablierten Ordnung, vom Grundriss bis zur Wand, darstellt. Es bleibt abzuwarten, ob diese Herausforderung künftig als persönliche ästhetische Ausdrucksform oder als Revolution der Architektur betrachtet werden wird. Das MAXXI wird eine wichtige Rolle bei der Beantwortung dieser Frage spielen.

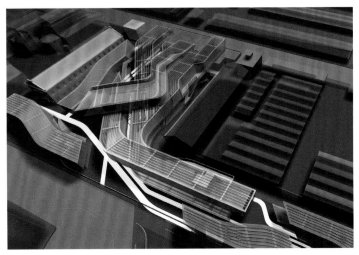

19
*Zaha Hadid, MAXXI: National Museum
of 21st-Century Arts, Rome, Italy,
1998–2009*

19

Einen wichtigen Innovationsschub für die neueste Architektur leistet das Auftreten von Talenten aus China. Die Lockerung der chinesischen Gesetzgebung ermöglicht es selbstständigen Architekten, gegenüber den monolithischen „Instituten", die den Berufsstand über Jahrzehnte beherrschten, Zeichen zu setzen. Viele der neuen chinesischen Bauten mögen für westliche Augen schwierig oder gar „verwirrend" erscheinen, aber ihre Ausdruckskraft ist eindeutig. Dies trifft zweifellos auf Wang Shus Historisches Museum in Ningbo (China, 2003–08, Seite 397) zu, das die Form eines künstlichen Bergs aufweist. Mehrere westliche Architekten, wie z. B. Jean Nouvel, haben mit ähnlich inspirierten Konzepten (Museo de la Evolución Humana, Burgos, 2000, Seite 12) experimentiert, aber Wang Shu hat seinen Museumsberg auch tatsächlich gebaut. Der Architekt verwendet für die Beschreibung seines Projekts nicht nur den Begriff „Berg", sondern auch die Ausdrücke „Täler" und „Tunnel": „Das Gebäude wurde innen und außen mit Beton verkleidet, der Bambusplatten nachgebildet ist, sowie mit über 20 Arten von recycelten Backsteinen überzogen, die ein großartiges und sparsames, zwischen künstlich und natürlich angesiedeltes Volumen bilden."

VIRTUELL VORHANDEN

Obgleich der Schwerpunkt dieses Buchs auf „realen" Museen liegt, wurden auch einige ungebaute, aber bedeutende Entwürfe ausgewählt, weil die von den Behörden zugesagte Finanzierung ihre Ausführung realistisch erscheinen lässt. Drei dieser neuen Projekte liegen in Frankreich und stammen von angesehenen Architekten. Möglicherweise den frühen Vorbildern von Guggenheim Bilbao und der Tate Gallery folgend, sich auch an anderen Orten anzusiedeln, haben sowohl das Centre Pompidou als auch der Louvre Erweiterungspläne in der französischen Provinz angekündigt. Der Louvre ist bekanntlich auch an der Planung eines Museumsbaus von Jean Nouvel in Abu Dhabi beteiligt. Das Centre Pompidou-Metz von Shigeru Ban ist das am weitesten fortgeschrittene dieser Projekte und soll 2010 eröffnet werden (Seite 87). Ban ist durch seine innovativen Entwürfe und die Verwendung besonderer Materialien, wie z. B. Papppröhren, bekannt geworden. Das Gebäude in Metz hat ein ungewöhnliches, nach dem Vorbild eines chinesischen Huts geformtes Dach, den der Architekt in Paris gekauft hatte. Die großzügigen Räume des neuen Centre Pompidou sind auch vom Forum im ursprünglichen Gebäude von Piano & Rogers inspiriert sowie von der Notwendigkeit bestimmt, Raum für die immer größer werdenden Werke der zeitgenössischen Kunst zu schaffen. Es ist interessant, dass der Architekt hauptsächlich deshalb an dem Wettbewerb für dieses Projekt teilgenommen hat, weil er die Kühnheit des Originalgebäudes bewundert. „Als ich vom Wettbewerb erfuhr", sagt Shigeru Ban, „dachte ich, das sei ein geeignetes Projekt, an dem ich teilnehmen möchte. Ich habe Respekt vor Renzo Piano und Richard Rogers, und ich liebe innovative Architektur. Ich sah, dass das Centre Pompidou der Auslober war, und ich war sicher, dass man einen innovativen Vorschlag akzeptieren würde. Ich dachte, dies wäre ein Wettbewerb, den ich gewinnen müsste. Ich wusste, dass das Gebäude für Metz vorgesehen war, und muss zugeben, dass ich nicht viel über diese Stadt wusste. Es ist auch nicht sehr wichtig, wo sie liegt, weil das Centre Pompidou beteiligt ist."[5]

Shigeru Bans eigene Beschreibung dieses Projekts gibt einen interessanten Einblick in die Art und Weise, wie moderne Museen konzipiert werden und wie sein Vorgehen von anderen neuen Museen beeinflusst wurde. Auf die Frage, ob er zuerst an das Dach oder den Inhalt des Gebäudes gedacht habe, antwortete Shigeru Ban: „Beides traf zusammen. Viele Architekten entwerfen Gebäude, die sich nur schwer als

20
Coop Himmelb(l)au, Musée des
Confluences, Lyon, France, 2001–13

20

Museen nutzen lassen. Museumsleute und Künstler sagen immer, dass sie keine Architekten brauchen. Sie bevorzugen Industriebauten wie diejenigen, welche DIA Beacon (OpenOffice, Beacon, New York, 2004) oder Tate Modern (Herzog & de Meuron, London, 2000) nutzen. Sie sagen, dass Architekten Museen eher für sich selbst als für die Kunst entwerfen. Ich wollte ein gutes Museum planen, aber auch eine wichtige Botschaft verkünden. Die ursprüngliche Ausschreibung forderte von den Architekten, Ausstellungsräume unterschiedlicher Länge in 15 m breiten Modulen zu planen. Ich dachte, eine brauchbare Galerie sollte so viel Wandfläche wie möglich und die bestmöglichen Klimaanlagen haben. Ich dachte an Rohre, weil sie die meiste Wandfläche besitzen – sie befinden sich in Kisten, deren Klima sehr einfach zu kontrollieren ist. Ein weiteres Merkmal der Ausschreibung ist der Grand Nef (das Hauptschiff) mit einer sehr hohen Decke. Weil das Centre Pompidou in Paris nicht genügend Räume mit hohen Decken hat, können Teile der Sammlung dem Publikum nicht gezeigt werden, daher ist der Grand Nef wichtig für das Museum. Ich beschloss, die Ausstellungsräume in Form rechtwinkliger Rohre über dem Grand Nef zu stapeln. Das Forum und der Grand Nef werden daher von den hängenden Rohren und dem Dach gebildet. Das Dach ist aufgrund des Gebäudeinhalts nicht symmetrisch wie der Hut. Von oben gesehen, ist die Grundform des Dachs jedoch trotzdem ein symmetrisches, aus Sechsecken gebildetes System."[6]

Erstaunlicherweise wählte der Louvre ebenfalls japanische Architekten für seinen Neubau in Lens (Frankreich, 2009–12, Seite 317). Ryue Nishizawa und Kazuyo Sejima (SANAA) haben Erfahrung in der Museumsplanung, aber vor allem im Bereich der zeitgenössischen Kunst. Die von den Architekten für Lens vorgesehenen eckigen Formen mit der für ihre Bauten typischen großzügigen, offenen Verglasung mögen im Widerspruch zur geschlossenen Natursteinarchitektur des originalen Louvre stehen. Hier bestand das Ziel jedoch darin, etwas vom Reichtum der Pariser Einrichtung in die Provinz zu bringen, und das auf großzügige, offene Weise. Tatsächlich liegen sowohl Metz als auch Lens in Regionen Frankreichs, die aufgrund des lang anhaltenden Verfalls ihrer Industrien wirtschaftliche Probleme haben. Es bleibt natürlich abzuwarten, ob Shigeru Ban oder SANAA mit ihren Bauten eine ähnliche architektonische Anziehungskraft entfalten wie Gehry mit seinem Guggenheim Museum in Bilbao, aber zweifellos hat die spanische Initiative des New Yorker Museums die ehrgeizigen Erweiterungspläne inspiriert.

Die Stadt Lyon ist der geplante Standort eines weiteren Museums, das gegenwärtig nur virtuell existiert, obgleich seine Eröffnung für 2013 vorgesehen ist. Das Musée des Confluences (Frankreich, 2001–13, Seite 123) wird von Coop Himmelb(l)au geplant. Die ästhetischen oder formalen Ursprünge dieses von seinen österreichischen Architekten „Kristallwolke des Wissens" genannten Bauwerks scheinen auf die Zeit zurückzugehen, als der „Dekonstruktivismus" noch in Mode war. Es ist ein interessanter Aspekt mancher großer Projekte, dass sie sichtbar Zeugnis von der konzeptuellen Entwicklung der Architektur ablegen. Die Architekten gewannen den Wettbewerb für dieses Museum im Jahr 2001, aber es ist zu erwähnen, dass drei frühere Projekte von ihnen in der Ausstellung *Deconstructivist Architecture* 1988 im New Yorker Museum of Modern Art (MoMA) enthalten waren. Dies ist nicht als Kritik am Lyoner Entwurf gemeint, vielmehr als Hinweis darauf, dass viel Geduld und Beharrungsvermögen seitens der Architekten erforderlich ist, wenn sie neue Wege beschreiten wie Wolf Prix und sein Team beim Musée des Confluences.

21
Aires Mateus, Santa Marta Lighthouse
Museum, Cascais, Portugal, 2003–07

22
UNStudio, Mercedes-Benz Museum,
Stuttgart, Germany, 2003–06

21

Fast ebenso ungewöhnlich wie die Wahl japanischer Architekten für zwei bedeutende Kultureinrichtungen in Frankreich ist die Tatsache, dass das Große Ägyptische Museum in Gise (2007–14, Seite 14) auf dem Plateau der Pyramiden bei Kairo von einer irischen Architektin (Roisin Heneghan) und einem Architekten chinesischer Herkunft, Shih-Fu Peng (Heneghan.Peng.Architects), in Zusammenarbeit mit bekannten niederländischen Landschaftsarchitekten (West8) geplant wird. Das 100 000 m² große Museum soll 2014 eröffnet werden und wird mindestens 350 Millionen Euro kosten. Das Bauen nahe den Pyramiden ist natürlich mit großen Risiken verbunden, aber das Ägyptische Museum in Kairo ist wegen seines Alters und des Touristenstroms eindeutig überholt und die Verbindung des Museums mit dem eigentlichen Gräberfeld in Gise sowohl logisch als auch effizient. Dieses unter der Leitung des ägyptischen Kulturministers Farouk Hosni stehende Projekt hat eine lange Vorgeschichte, aber jetzt scheint seine Realisierung voranzukommen. Die Architekten beschreiben ihren Entwurf wie folgt: „Das Große Ägyptische Museum ist kein spezielles Museum im üblichen Sinn des Worts. Es wird als Komplex für verschiedene Aktivitäten errichtet, die ihren Beitrag zu einer auf Ägyptologie konzentrierten Kultur leisten. Durch die Anlage verschiedener Rundgänge kann die Welt des alten Ägyptens auf verschiedene Weisen und unterschiedlichen Ebenen erfahren werden. Das Museum ist sowohl ein Ort zur Bewahrung kultureller Artefakte als auch eine interaktive Kulturinstitution."

„SIXTEEN TONS OF NUMBER NINE COAL"

Obgleich die Kunst nach wie vor den bevorzugten Inhalt neuer Museen bildet, sind auch andere Themen für die Entstehung von hier dargestellten Einrichtungen verantwortlich. Francisco Aires Mateus entwarf eines der kleineren in diesem Buch veröffentlichten Museen, das Leuchtturmmuseum Santa Marta (Cascais, Portugal, 2003–07, Seite 65), das sich mit dem benachbarten Leuchtturm von 1868, aber auch allgemein mit dem Thema „Leuchttürme" befasst. Der portugiesische Architekt schuf ein zusammenhängendes Ganzes aus einem eher heterogenen Gelände und führte es einer neuen Nutzung zu. Es folgt derselben Idee, die in kleinem Maßstab der von kommunalen Behörden häufig geäußerten Hoffnung entspricht, dass ein Museum einen heruntergekommenen oder gar aufgegebenen Bereich regenerieren werde. Das Ozeaneum (Deutsches Meeresmuseum, Stralsund, 2005–08, Seite 93) von Behnisch Architekten nutzt ebenfalls z.T. die bestehende Architektur, in diesem Fall ein historisches Lagerhaus. Aber es nimmt auch unmittelbar Bezug auf die Lage am Meer und zeigt Ausstellungen über die Ost- und Nordsee. Mit 60 000 m² Fläche spielt das Ozeaneum natürlich in einer anderen Liga als das Leuchtturmmuseum Santa Marta, aber es ist auch Teil eines städtischen Sanierungsprogramms namens Quartier 66.

Die österreichischen Architekten Delugan Meissl haben vor kurzem das neue Porsche Museum (Stuttgart, 2006–08, Seite 127) gebaut, eines von mehreren derartiger Projekte in Deutschland von bekannten Architekten wie z.B. UNStudio (Mercedes-Benz Museum, Stuttgart, 2003–06, Seite 29) oder Coop Himmelb(l)au (BMW Welt, München, 2001–07, Seite 42). Hier bestand das Ziel darin, das besondere Flair der Automarke einzufangen und zugleich den Bau gut in das Industriegelände einzupassen. Das Ergebnis ist eine spektakuläre und dynamische Form, was bei diesem Thema und einem Etat von 100 Millionen Euro auch zu erwarten war.

Nicholas Grimshaw hat sich mit einem noch ungewöhnlicheren Museumstyp auseinandergesetzt, der um einen 70 m hohen Hochofen eines früheren Stahlwerks in Mexiko errichtet wurde – Horno 3, Museo del Acero (Monterrey, Mexiko, 2006–07, Seite 161). Die Sanierung und Umnutzung von Industriebauten ist natürlich auch an zahlreichen anderen Standorten erfolgt, um Gebäude mit ästhetischem Anspruch aufzuwerten, die anderenfalls abgerissen worden wären. Ein sanierter Industriebau besitzt eine Authentizität, wie sie kein noch so kreativer Architekt erschaffen oder imitieren könnte, und die 145 000 Besucher, die das Museo del Acero in den ersten sechs Monaten besichtigt haben, sind ein Beleg für das Interesse des Publikums an einem derartigen Museumstyp. Paulo Mendes da Rocha, der 2006 den Pritzker-Preis erhielt, hat Kunstmuseen wie z. B. das Brasilianische Skulpturenmuseum (São Paulo, Brasilien, 1987–92, Seite 43) gebaut, aber sein jüngstes Projekt auf diesem Gebiet hat einen unerwarteten Inhalt. Das Museu da Lingua Portuguesa (São Paulo, 2003–06, Seite 239) wurde in den neoklassizistischen Bahnhof Luz aus dem späten 19. Jahrhundert gesetzt. Das Museum nimmt etwas mehr als die Hälfte des noch betriebenen Bahnhofs ein und war eine sowohl technische als auch ästhetische Herausforderung für den entschieden modernistischen Architekten. Einem noch ungewöhnlicheren Thema widmet sich das N4A Museum (Liyang, China, 2006–07, Seite 407) von Zhang Lei zu Ehren der Neuen 4. Armee. Die 1937 gegründete N4A gehörte zu den wichtigsten Streitkräften der Kommunistischen Partei Chinas und kämpfte seit den 1930er-Jahren am südlichen Ufer des Jangtse. Auch dieses eindrucksvolle und höchst rätselhafte Gebäude ist ein Beweis für den Einfallsreichtum und das ästhetische Empfinden zeitgenössischer chinesischer Architekten, die sie von ihren Kollegen in Europa und sogar im übrigen Teil Asiens unterscheiden.

VON SOUTHIE ZUR BOWERY

Die großen Institutionen, die Neubauten von Kunstmuseen initiiert haben, vom Metropolitan bis zum Louvre, waren selten, wenn überhaupt, der Gegenwartskunst gewidmet. Andere, z. B. das Centre Pompidou (Musée national d'art moderne), die Tate Gallery oder das Museum of Modern Art (MoMA) zeigen zwar zeitgenössische Kunstwerke, aber ihre Hauptattraktionen liegen eher im Bereich dessen, was man als „moderne" Kunst bezeichnet – vom Ende des 19. Jahrhunderts bis zur Nachkriegszeit. Erst in jüngster Zeit haben sich ausschließlich der zeitgenössischen Kunst gewidmete Museen auf den Weg zu Neubauten von berühmten Architekten begeben. Ein Beispiel dafür ist das Institute of Contemporary Art (Boston, Massachusetts, 2004–06, Seite 16) der New Yorker Architekten Diller Scofidio + Renfro. Dieses 41 Millionen Dollar teure, 5760 m² große Gebäude liegt am Fan Pier in South Boston und ist ein weithin sichtbares und erfolgreiches Zeichen dafür, dass die Gegenwartskunst im Bewusstsein der Museumsbesucher angekommen ist. Das Auftreten von wirklich zeitgenössischer Kunst und Architektur in South Boston (das von seinen Bewohnern Southie genannt wird) ist kein unbedeutendes Ereignis. Obgleich das Museum nahe der South Station, dem Regierungszentrum und dem bekannten Restaurant Anthony's Pier Four liegt, ist dies auch ein Viertel, das einst für seine rauen Sitten und seine armen, überwiegend irischen Bewohner bekannt war.

Das New Museum of Contemporary Art (New York, 2005–07, Seite 31) von Ryue Nishizawa und Kazuyo Sejima von SANAA ist ein weiteres Beispiel für die neue Beziehung zwischen zeitgenössischer Kunst und talentierten Architekten. Das Museum an der Bowery, einer

23

23
Ateleir Zhanglei, N4A Museum,
Liyang, China, 2006–07

24
Kazuyo Sejima + Ryue Nishizawa /
SANAA, New Museum of Contempo-
rary Art New York, NY, USA, 2005–07

Avenue in der Lower East Side, die in letzter Zeit eine Aufwertung erfahren hat, ist einer der bemerkenswertesten Neubauten der vergangenen Jahre in Manhattan. Die Bowery, die älteste Straße Manhattans, war Ende des 18. Jahrhunderts die eleganteste Straße der Stadt, galt aber in den 1920er- und 1930er-Jahren als Armenbezirk. Eine Reihe von Filmen über die „Dead End Kids" („Kinder der Sackgasse") oder die „Bowery Boys" machte das Gebiet weit über New York City hinaus bekannt. Von den 1940er-Jahren bis Ende der 1970er-Jahre kannte man die Bowery vorwiegend wegen der dort beheimateten Alkoholiker und Obdachlosen. Noch heute sind geringe Spuren dieser Atmosphäre erkennbar, obgleich schicke Cafés und Hotels vorherrschen. Das New Museum besteht im Wesentlichen aus einer Reihe scheinbar beliebig gestapelter Kisten und ist (mit 21 m Breite, 34 m Tiefe und 52 m Höhe) eine intelligente und wirtschaftliche Lösung für das problematische, enge Grundstück. Durch Verschiebung der Kisten, die vorwiegend neutrale und hohe Ausstellungsräume enthalten, ist es den Architekten gelungen, Licht nach Bedarf einzulassen und Außenterrassen mit Blick auf Downtown New York zu bilden. Die Aluminiumverkleidung (ein glänzend eloxiertes Geflecht aus Streckmetall) verleiht dem Gebäude einen ständig wechselnden Schimmer, der es deutlich von seinen eher nüchternen Nachbarn abhebt. Die Baumaßnahme wurde beschrieben „als zentrales Element eines Projekts mit einem Etat von 64 Millionen Dollar, das den Neubau, die Erhöhung des Stiftungskapitals und weitere Aufwendungen für geplantes Wachstum umfasste und ausschließlich durch eine Spendenaktion und den Verkauf des früheren Grundstücks am Broadway in SoHo finanziert wurde".

JENSEITS VON EDEN

Außer dem Louvre-Lens haben Sejima und Nishizawa auch das Museum für die Kunst des 21. Jahrhunderts in Kanazawa (Ishikawa, Japan, 2002–04, Seite 44) gebaut. Dieses innovative, vollverglaste Gebäude in Kreisform mit einem Durchmesser von 112,5 m verbindet hochmoderne Architektur mit zeitgenössischer Kunst auf höchstem Niveau. Mit einer Beraterkommission, zu der ursprünglich Lars Nittve (Direktor des Moderna Museet), Alfred Pacquement (Direktor des Musée national d'art im Centre Pompidou) und Neil Benezra (Direktor des SFMoMA) gehörten, ist das Museum eine klare Aussage zugunsten der Einführung von Kunst und Architektur in das Herz einer derart traditionellen Stadt wie Kanazawa. Das Gebäude liegt in der Nähe mehrerer Verwaltungsbauten und direkt gegenüber dem berühmten Garten Kenroku-en. Dieser entstand über einen Zeitraum von 200 Jahren vom 17. bis zum 19. Jahrhundert und war der äußere Garten der Burg von Kanazawa. Er gehört zu den berühmtesten Gärten Japans und wurde 1922 zum National Site of Scenic Beauty und 1985 zum National Site of Special Scenic Beauty erklärt. Mit seiner vollen Verglasung, der niedrigen Silhouette und klaren geometrischen Form steht das Museum in keinem Widerspruch zu diesem renommierten Nachbarn, ganz im Gegenteil.

Das scharfkantige, weiße Museo Universitario de Arte Contemporáneo (Universidad Nacional Autónoma de Mexico – UNAM, Mexiko-Stadt, 2006–08, Seite 147) von Teodoro González de León ist ein weiterer Beweis für die zunehmende Tendenz, der zeitgenössischen Kunst außerhalb von Galerien und Kunsthandel, die sich ihrer bisher eher angenommen haben als die Museen, einen neuen Standort zu geben. Dieses Museum liegt an einer großen Plaza, die als Eingang zum Kulturzentrum der Universität dient. Es verfügt über zwei Geschosse: Auf der Ebene des Platzes liegen Ausstellungsräume, Empfang, Lager und Buchhandlung sowie Lehrbereiche, eine untere, in den vulkanischen Fels

24

geschlagene Ebene enthält das Auditorium mit 300 Plätzen, Büro- und Lagerräume, eine Cafeteria, ein Restaurant und eine Mediathek. Der Architekt erklärt, dass die Proportionen des Gebäudes „nach dem Besuch von 35 Museen und Galerien für zeitgenössische Kunst in aller Welt" sehr sorgfältig erwogen wurden. Aus dieser Bemerkung lässt sich entnehmen, dass die neuen Standorte für Gegenwartskunst viel gemeinsam haben, vor allem das Anliegen, die aktuelle Kreativität einem breiteren Publikum nahezubringen.

KULTUR FÜR DAS VOLK

Was auch immer die Zukunft für uns bereithält, es scheint klar zu sein, dass in den letzten Jahren ein Trend zum Bau von immer mehr Museen herrschte. Der Erfolg begabter Architekten von I. M. Pei bis zu Renzo Piano, Frank O. Gehry und der jüngeren Generation, Museen als architektonische Events oder vielleicht sogar eigenständige Kunstwerke zu gestalten, muss jedoch aus einer gewissen Distanz betrachtet werden. Es gibt viele Gründe dafür, dass der „Bilbao-Effekt" in bestimmten Fällen nicht eintreten wird. In der Tat hat sich gezeigt, dass der Erfolg von Gehrys Guggenheim in Bilbao sich nur schwer wiederholen lässt. Und doch ist die Tatsache, dass 8,2 Millionen Besucher im Jahr 2008 unter Peis gläserner Pyramide im Cour Napoléon den Louvre durchquert haben, ein Beweis dafür, dass intelligent konzipierte Architektur das Publikum ins Museum führen kann. Der Louvre steht jetzt vor dem Problem, zu viele Besucher zu haben – etwa 5 Millionen waren vorgesehen, als Pei sein Bauwerk 1993 vollendete. Durch die Zunahme von Nebenaktivitäten, von Veranstaltungen im Auditorium bis zu Restaurants, Läden und Bibliotheken sind Museen natürlich zu Touristenattraktionen geworden, aber häufig auch zu städtischen Kulturzentren, zu Orten der Versammlung und Begegnung. Auf das Verhältnis heutiger Museen zu den Kirchen früherer Jahrhunderte ist oft hingewiesen worden, aber das Museum als weihevolle Stätte, als eine Art humanistischer Tempel, gehört heute trotzdem der Vergangenheit an. Die vielen Diskussionen über die „Demokratisierung" von Kunst und Kultur haben politische Initiativen wie z. B. in Frankreich unter der Präsidentschaft von François Mitterrand und dessen Kulturminister Jack Lang ausgelöst. Der verbreitete Bau von nicht nur auf moderne oder auch traditionelle Kunst beschränkte Museen hat schließlich auch Wirkung auf das allgemeinere Publikum ausgeübt. Die Vorliebe für Kunst, die einst einer wohlhabenden Elite vorbehalten war, hat sich in der Tat auf eine breitere Basis verlagert. Trotz der berechtigten, durch Kommentatoren wie Ken Carbone geäußerten Bedenken über die Lebensfähigkeit vieler teurer Museumsneubauten bestätigen die Besucherzahlen, dass Museen heute in vielen Ländern einen großen Beitrag zur Freizeitgestaltung leisten.

Die wirtschaftliche Situation wird sicher Auswirkungen auf viele bestehende Einrichtungen und zweifellos auf künftige Projekte haben. Kleinere, stärker ökologisch orientierte Museen könnten von der Krise profitieren. Man kann aber mit einiger Sicherheit sagen, dass die enge Beziehung zwischen „qualitativ hochwertiger" Architektur und der Museumswelt Bestand haben wird. Obgleich die Berufung eines Stararchitekten keine Garantie dafür ist, dass er das richtige Museum für die gegebenen Bedingungen zu bauen weiß, besteht eindeutig ein Zusammenhang zwischen der Welt der Kultur und den hohen Ansprüchen der Architektur. Ein berühmter Architekt hat selten dem Ruf und den Besucherzahlen eines Museums geschadet, auch wenn Kostenüberziehung und gelegentlich unpraktische Lösungen einigen neueren Museen zu schaffen machen. Museen haben eine neue Welt für viele Touristen und Bewohner der Städte eröffnet, die das Glück haben, interessante

Bauten und Sammlungen zu besitzen. Museen haben mehr als Privathäuser oder Bürobauten dazu beigetragen, den Menschen nicht nur die Kunst, sondern auch moderne Architektur nahezubringen. Dies ist das bleibende Vermächtnis des Booms der Kultureinrichtungen der vergangenen Jahren. Mit dieser Gewissheit werden diejenigen, die künftig über Museumsprojekte zu entscheiden haben, und ihre Architekten bestimmt Lösungen finden, um die Probleme der Etatkürzungen zu überwinden. Die Stars der Kunst und die Stars der Architektur bleiben einander verbunden.

Philip Jodidio, Grimentz, 1. Mai 2009

[1]   I. M. Pei, Vorwort zum Buch: *I. M. Pei, Architect*, New York 2008.
[2]   „Troubles deepen for museums: layoffs, budget cuts and cancelled shows", *The Art Newspaper*, April 2009.
[3]   Ken Carbone, „The Shell Game: Too many museums are investing in star architecture at the expense of art", *I. D.*, Mai 2004.
[4]   Fax von Norman Foster an den Autor, 1. November 1996.
[5]   Interview des Autors mit Shigeru Ban in Paris, 23. Juli 2008.
[6]   Ebd.

INTRODUCTION

PARIER SUR LES STARS

Depuis qu'ils existent, les musées ont souvent vu leur nom associé à celui d'architectes célèbres. Le rôle civique des musées comme symbole de fierté locale, régionale ou nationale explique certainement la pérennité de cette relation, ainsi que la « valeur ajoutée » qu'elle apporte aux collections. L'architecture est invitée d'une certaine manière à venir en écho aux œuvres d'art ou, plus fréquemment de nos jours, à d'autres thématiques, les sciences par exemple. La plupart des visiteurs de musées ont entendu parler du fameux « effet Bilbao » selon lequel le Guggenheim Bilbao, édifié par Frank O. Gehry en Espagne (1991–97, page 7), est à l'origine du renouveau du centre de cette ville. Faire appel à un grand nom de l'architecture, à une star, serait ainsi une façon d'attirer les foules, en tout cas celles qui ont le goût de la culture ou du moins pour la consommation culturelle. Sans contester le pouvoir d'attraction du Guggenheim Bilbao, il faut noter que le bâtiment de Gehry n'est pas le premier exemple d'association réussie entre architecture et musées. Longtemps avant le modernisme, des institutions comme l'Altes Museum, édifié sur l'Île aux musées à Berlin entre 1825 et 1828 par le fameux architecte Karl Friedrich Schinkel pour accueillir les collections d'art de la famille royale de Prusse, avaient déjà fermement noué ce lien. Quel qu'ait été son talent, Schinkel avait néanmoins construit dans le style néoclassique plutôt que d'inventer une forme nouvelle et étonnante. Cent quarante ans plus tard, toujours à Berlin, Ludwig Mies van der Rohe achevait la Neue Nationalgalerie dans un style très différent, qualifiable de modernisme classique. Il est certain que là aussi, la clarté et la simplicité de l'architecture ont rempli leur tâche et montré que la modernité pouvait atteindre au niveau de *gravitas* attendu des institutions consacrées à l'art.

QUAND LE BAUHAUS PASSE À L'OUEST

Quand les choses ont-elles « dérapé » ? À quel moment l'architecture s'est-elle emparée du devant de la scène et a-t-elle commencé à offrir à certains architectes l'occasion d'affirmer leur identité, tout en mettant en forme les ambitions d'institutions et de villes ? Un exemple éclairant, qui précède de peu la Neue Nationalgalerie, est également l'œuvre d'un autre acteur majeur du Bauhaus, Marcel Breuer. Le Whitney Museum of American Art, situé sur Madison Avenue à New York (1963–66) impose sa présence massive et presque dérangeante dans un environnement où le style traditionnel new-yorkais reste de règle. C'est peut-être bien en effet à New York que les règles du jeu ont changé à partir du début des années 1960, ce qui a permis à des réalisations significatives de l'architecture contemporaine de faire naître un nouveau type de construction. Tom Hoving était directeur du Metropolitan Museum of Art en 1967 et, au moment de son départ, une décennie plus tard, les installations de son musée avaient été généreusement agrandies par l'architecte Kevin Roche (Roche Dinkeloo). Mais c'était moins l'architecture qui avait propulsé l'extension de ce musée que le plan d'ensemble établi par Hoving. Il comprenait en effet des espaces d'exposition substantiellement plus vastes, des infrastructures nouvelles et des équipements développés comme la librairie, elle aussi agrandie. Le commerce faisait son entrée dans le « temple » et une nouvelle architecture provocatrice entrait dans le jeu.

Cherchant souvent à remettre en cause le rang de capitale culturelle de l'Amérique détenu par New York, Washington allait bientôt se lancer elle aussi dans la construction de nouvelles installations qui allaient propulser son plus important musée d'art dans la modernité. I. M.

25

25
*Renzo Piano, California Academy of
Sciences, San Francisco, CA, USA,
2005–08*

25 + 26
*Herzog & de Meuron, De Young
Museum, San Francisco, CA, USA,
2002–05*

Pei, architecte du nouveau bâtiment est de la National Gallery of Art (1968–78), du projet du Grand Louvre à Paris (1983–93, page 47), et du très récent musée d'Art islamique à Doha (Qatar, 2003–08, page 293) déclarait en 2008 : « J'ai toujours été très intéressé par le secteur public et, à mon avis, le projet le plus emblématique dans ce domaine est le musée. Le musée a ma préférence parce qu'il résume tout. Le Louvre est un problème d'architecture, mais est encore plus l'expression d'une civilisation. J'apprends beaucoup lorsque je construis un musée, et, si je n'apprends pas, je ne peux créer. Dès mon premier projet, réalisé à l'atelier de Gropius à Harvard, jusqu'à mon œuvre la plus récente, le musée a été pour moi un rappel, constamment présent, que l'art, l'histoire et l'architecture ne font qu'un. »[1] Le bâtiment est de Pei n'est pas un monument à sa propre gloire, mais il exprime néanmoins son style personnel géométrique, et attire depuis son ouverture un flux constant de visiteurs plutôt sensibles à l'art moderne et contemporain.

QUAND RENZO ET FRANK FONT LEUR ENTRÉE

Non, Gehry n'est en rien l'inventeur du cocktail assez explosif d'architecture, d'art et d'argent qui régit aujourd'hui le monde des musées, même encore dans nos économies en crise. Le Centre Pompidou (Piano & Rogers, Paris, 1971–77, page 20) a inventé en plein cœur de Paris un nouveau type d'institution culturelle modelé sur le concept des Maisons de la culture d'André Malraux, et son succès attire en moyenne 20 000 visiteurs par jour depuis des années. Le style industriel à tuyauterie apparente du Centre a certainement joué un rôle dans ce record d'influence et forgé la « réussite » de l'entreprise. Néanmoins à peine 10 % des visiteurs pénétraient au départ dans les salles du Musée national d'art moderne, préférant admirer la vue spectaculaire que l'on a sur Paris du sommet du bâtiment. Pratiquement inconnus avant d'avoir remporté ce concours, Richard Rogers et Renzo Piano sont devenus depuis deux des plus grandes célébrités de l'architecture contemporaine, et Piano en particulier a conçu un grand nombre de musées, dont le Modern Wing de l'Art Institute de Chicago (Chicago, Illinois, États-Unis, 2005–09, page 301). Il a été responsable de tant de projets dans ce domaine que le très respecté magazine professionnel américain *Architectural Record* s'est récemment demandé s'il n'était pas devenu « l'architecte par défaut » de ce pays. Les entreprises de Piano ne se limitent pas au domaine de l'art, comme le montrent la rénovation et l'extension des installations de l'Académie des sciences de Californie (San Francisco, Californie, États-Unis, 2005–08, page 34), un musée des sciences naturelles qui visait l'habilitation « LEED Platine » accordée en fonction de la réduction de la consommation d'énergie et de l'utilisation de matériaux écologiques. La toiture ondulée de plus d'un hectare de surface est recouverte de 1,8 million de plants de végétaux d'origine californienne. L'étude approfondie de ces plantes, mais aussi des qualités antisismiques de ce toit végétalisé, faisaient partie intégrante de ce projet de couverture accessible aux visiteurs. On a calculé que ce toit réduisait la température à l'intérieur du musée de six degrés. Un système de collecte des eaux de pluie devrait permettre de stocker et de réutiliser environ 13 500 mètres cubes d'eau chaque année pour l'irrigation et divers usages techniques. Le profil de la toiture et la conception du musée tout entier forment un *continuum* avec le parc qui l'entoure. Orientée vers le grand public et les écoliers, l'Académie se consacre à l'éducation et aux recherches sur la préservation des environnements et habitats naturels. Représentant un investissement de 370 millions de dollars, y compris le programme d'expositions et les installations temporaires pendant la durée des travaux, ce projet peut sembler d'un montant élevé en cette période de crise financière mondiale, mais, par ses préoccupations environnementales, montre certainement la voie.

Le musée Guggenheim de Bilbao (Bilbao, Espagne, 1991–97, page 7) est sans aucun doute l'une des œuvres architecturales de Frank O. Gehry les plus spectaculaires. Il se dresse au centre du quartier culturel formé par le Museo de Bellas Artes, l'université de Deusto, et l'Opéra sur un terrain de 32 700 mètres carrés jadis occupé par une usine et un parking. Trois agences avaient participé au concours sur invitation – Gehry, Arata Isozaki et Coop Himmelb(l)au –, dont les noms manifestaient le désir des organisateurs d'une architecture spectaculaire. Faisant partie d'un projet de rénovation urbaine de la capitale industrielle de la région basque semi-autonome de 1,5 milliard de dollars (comprenant également une ligne de métro aux stations dessinées par Norman Foster, une passerelle piétonnière et un aéroport confiés à Santiago Calatrava), le nouveau bâtiment compte 24 000 mètres carrés, dont 10 600 consacrés aux salles d'exposition réparties sur trois niveaux. Financé par la ville, la région et le gouvernement espagnol, le pilotage du projet a été confié en grande partie au musée Guggenheim de New York, qui avait tenté à plusieurs reprises de se développer en Europe sous la direction dynamique de son ancien directeur, Thomas Krens. Le nouveau musée est une structure éminemment urbaine, édifiée sur la rive d'un fleuve, le Nervion, et pratiquement traversé par le pont de La Salve, qui surmonte une partie de la galerie principale. Vu de l'extérieur, sa caractéristique la plus étonnante tient à ses formes de « fleur métallique » habillées de titane et modelées par Gehry à partir du logiciel français CATIA mis au point par Dassault pour la conception d'avions de chasse. Les visiteurs sont accueillis à l'intérieur par un atrium de 55 mètres de haut découpé au cœur du bâtiment. Des dix-huit galeries, la plus spectaculaire est de loin l'espace d'exposition principal dégagé de toute colonne qui ne mesure pas moins de 130 mètres de long par 30 de large. Inévitablement, un tel espace incite à la comparaison avec les cathédrales d'une autre ère. Gehry a atteint ici le sommet de sa tendance naturelle à créer des bâtiments qui sont aussi des œuvres d'art, ce musée étant une œuvre d'art en soi. Le succès du Guggenheim Bilbao, qui a contribué à la revitalisation de la ville et est même devenu une destination touristique, a beaucoup apporté à l'architecte. Il a depuis construit d'autres musées, dont le plus récent est son extension de l'Art Gallery de l'Ontario (Toronto, Canada, 2005–08, page 141).

BATMAN ET ROBIN À LA RESCOUSSE

Jacques Herzog et Pierre de Meuron sont tous deux nés à Bâle (Suisse) en 1950. Ils comptent parmi les plus célèbres architectes actuels, ont remporté le prix Pritzker en 2001, et c'est leur sélection pour l'extension de la Tate Gallery, dans une ancienne centrale thermique en bordure de la Tamise (Tate Modern, Londres, Royaume-Uni, 1995–2000), qui a lancé leur carrière internationale. Leur plus récent projet de musée est celui d'un nouveau bâtiment pour la Tate (Transforming Tate Modern, 2008–12, page 8). La Tate Modern, conçue pour accueillir 1,8 million de visiteurs par an, en reçoit aujourd'hui quatre millions, confirmation incontestable de sa réussite. Comme Renzo Piano, les deux architectes suisses ont réalisé de nombreux musées depuis ce premier succès. En 2005, ils ont achevé une extension du Walker Art Center (Minneapolis, Minnesota, États-Unis, 2003–05, page 21) et un nouveau bâtiment pour le De Young Museum (San Francisco, Californie, États-Unis, 2002–05, page 35). Leur style n'est pas de ceux qui se reconnaissent au premier regard. Leurs réalisations varient considérablement, mais témoignent à chaque fois d'une inventivité assez rare. Ainsi, ont-ils récemment achevé le CaixaForum à Madrid (2001–08), qui réutilise les murs de brique de l'ancienne centrale électrique de Mediodía, surélevée et entièrement reconstruite de l'intérieur. De dimensions relative-

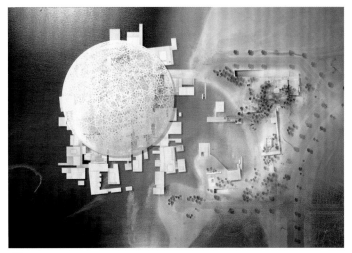

27
*Jean Nouvel, Louvre Abu Dhabi, Abu
Dhabi, UAE, 2007–12*

ment réduites selon les critères habituels des nouvelles institutions culturelles, le CaixaForum prouve qu'ils n'appliquent pas de règles fixes. Un autre de leurs projets remarquables est également publié en détails dans ce volume : le TEA (Tenerife Espacio de la Artes, Santa Cruz de Tenerife, Iles Canaries, Espagne, 2003–08, page 183) est à de nombreux égards caractéristique d'un type plus récent de centre culturel polyvalent inventé à partir de l'expérience des Maisons de la culture françaises, et surtout par le Centre Pompidou. Le TEA comprend des salles d'exposition, mais aussi une bibliothèque, un lieu pour des manifestations en plein air et les restaurant et boutique habituels. Ses formes découpées et allongées, ses cours ouvertes et ses murs percés rendent le TEA à la fois indépendant de son cadre et très ouvert sur la ville qui l'entoure. Ce projet place la culture en position centrale, un concept qui s'est développé au cours de ces dernières années dans de nombreux musées et centres culturels à travers le monde. Ils sont aussi bien des lieux d'échanges où l'on se donne rendez-vous, que des sites d'expositions d'art destinées à une élite cultivée.

BORDEAUX OU SAKÉ ?

De style tout aussi imprévisible et presque aussi prolifique qu'Herzog & de Meuron, l'architecte français Jean Nouvel a signé un très surprenant musée consacré aux arts primitifs qui illustre la liberté de plus en plus grande accordée aux architectes (ou conquise par eux). Le musée du quai Branly à Paris (2001–06, page 9) est un bâtiment de 30 000 mètres carrés en bordure de la Seine, à quelques pas de la tour Eiffel. Jean Nouvel a été choisi à la fin de l'année 1999 pour construire ce musée à l'issue d'un concours qui réunissait Tadao Ando, Norman Foster, Renzo Piano et MVRDV. Comme il l'explique, le bâtiment veut protéger les œuvres de la lumière du soleil, mais, dans le même temps, celle-ci est la clé même du projet. Son but a été de faire « disparaître » toute la panoplie des aspects techniques, des sorties de secours aux vitrines de présentations, pour rendre encore mieux perceptible la force des objets exposés. Collaborant avec le célèbre paysagiste français Gilles Clément, Nouvel a ainsi proposé à Paris l'une de ses créations les plus surprenantes. Des jardins courent tout autour du musée, se glissent même sous sa masse et contribuent ainsi à cet effet de « disparition » recherché par l'architecte. Le jeu complexe de flux et de reflux des formes du bâtiment est l'un de ses manifestes les plus provocants en faveur d'une architecture d'un type nouveau. Ni moderniste ni directement liée à aucune tendance connue, c'est une architecture de circonstances au meilleur sens du terme. Aujourd'hui, Nouvel travaille sur le projet du Louvre à Abou Dhabi (Émirats arabes unis, page 36), dont la construction devrait être achevée en 2012. À la différence de ce qui arrive à de nombreux projets programmés dans le Golfe persique, l'émirat d'Abou Dhabi a clairement exprimé son désir de poursuivre activement la construction de cet avant-poste de l'institution française.

Tadao Ando est une autre de ces stars de l'architecture à posséder une longue liste de musées à son actif. Ses interventions dans le domaine culturel comprennent le musée de la Forêt des tombes (Kumamoto, Japon, 1992), le musée Suntory (Osaka, Japon, 1994), la Pulitzer Foundation for the Arts (Saint Louis, Missouri, États-Unis, 1997–2000), le Modern Art Museum of Fort Worth (Fort Worth, Texas, États-Unis, 1992–2002), le musée d'art Chichu sur l'île de Naoshima (Japon, 2003, page 22), 21_21 Design Sight (Tokyo, Japon, 2004–07), une extension du Clark Art Institute (Williamstown, Massachusetts, États-Unis, 2006–08), la rénovation du Palazzo Grassi et de la Punta della

28
Tadao Ando, Punta della Dogana,
Venice, Italy, 2003–09

28

Dogana pour le mécène François Pinault (Venise, Italie, 2003–09, page 37) et le Musée maritime d'Abou Dhabi (Émirats arabes unis, 2006–). Si le strict vocabulaire géométrique et les épais murs de béton d'Ando sont généralement plus attendus que les dernières créations d'Herzog & de Meuron, l'architecte japonais possède une telle maîtrise de la qualité et de la variété au sein du style qu'il s'est choisi, qu'il a certainement davantage marqué l'ère de l'extension de musées que la plupart de ses confrères.

Le nombre de musées nouveaux conçus par des architectes célèbres au cours des vingt dernières années rend l'établissement d'une liste pratiquement impossible. De l'extension du Prado à Madrid par Rafael Moneo (2001–07) au Museum of Contemporary Art / Denver de la star britannique David Adjaye (Denver, Colorado, États-Unis, 2004–07, page 10), les architectes se sont taillé un franc succès auprès des municipalités et des conseils d'administration de musées des pays développés. Le dernier projet cité pourrait cependant indiquer une nouvelle tendance, car le musée de Denver a été conçu sous condition qu'il obtienne la certification «LEED Gold» pour le développement durable. C'est également un musée un peu plus petit que beaucoup d'institutions récentes, une orientation qui pourrait bien se confirmer au vu de la dépression économique actuelle. Il est clair que les rapports entre les musées et l'architecture de l'après 2008 seront radicalement modifiés pour un certain temps au fil des diminutions des donations et des restrictions de dépenses en général. Ceci ne veut pas dire que les grands architectes ne construiront plus de nouveaux musées, mais plutôt que l'échelle et les ambitions de leurs projets seront certainement réduites. Par ailleurs, tant d'établissements ont été édifiés avant l'éclatement de la bulle financière, que beaucoup de villes n'ont plus besoin des services de Gehry, Piano ou Herzog & de Meuron.

CRASH EN VUE ?
L'étendue des difficultés provoquées par la crise économique dans le secteur des musées a été soulignée dans une publication d'avril 2009 : le Getty Trust de Los Angeles (au fameux design de Richard Meier, page 45) a perdu 1,5 milliard de dollars de son capital au cours de la seconde moitié de 2008. Le Metropolitan Museum of Art de New York, qui tire un tiers de son budget de fonctionnement de ses placements, a vu ces fonds réduits de 2,9 milliards de dollars à 2,1 milliards, ce qui n'a pas manqué de faire évoquer le spectre d'un prochain déficit. [2] Des interrogations sont également posées, toujours aux États-Unis, sur l'opportunité de lois fiscales anciennes qui permettent aux mécènes de déduire des impôts les dons aux musées. Pour certains, il semble injuste que le gouvernement des États-Unis finance indirectement les musées, alors que tant d'administrés ont besoin de soins médicaux ou même d'aide alimentaire. Bien que ce sujet soit loin d'avoir fait l'objet de décisions à l'heure où ce livre est mis sous presse, il reste que l'une des principales sources de richesse des musées américains, et donc par contrecoup leurs programmes de constructions nouvelles, tient au flux substantiel et régulier de donations. Le budget total de la rénovation et de l'extension du Museum of Modern Art de New York (MoMA, 2002–04) par Yoshio Taniguchi s'est élevé à 425 millions de dollars, dont 315 pour la seule construction, des chiffres qui grimpent à 858 millions si l'on y ajoute les coûts du MoMA Queens, des déménagements et réemménagements et de quelques acquisitions. Des dépenses aussi importantes seraient quasi impossibles dans le climat économique actuel, et il est difficile d'établir des projections sur ce que deviendra le «boom» des musées du début du XXIe siècle.

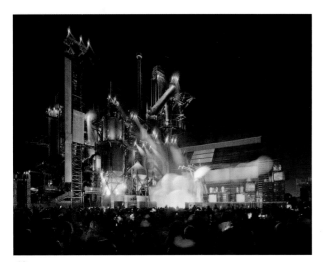

29

ZONE DE TURBULENCES

Bien que les nouveaux musées récemment édifiés aient été beaucoup applaudis, et aient certainement incité les visiteurs à les découvrir, il reste souvent à prouver que le succès recherché par ces institutions soit durable. Le graphiste Ken Carbone, associé fondateur de Carbone Smolan à New York, «groupe de design stratégique créant des identités de marque, des expositions et des programmes graphiques d'environnement pour des institutions culturelles», s'est élevé plus d'une fois contre la tendance des musées à considérer les grands noms de l'architecture comme des chevaliers blancs. Ses commentaires, publiés en 2004 dans le magazine *I. D.* sonnent encore plus juste à la lumière des récentes turbulences économiques. «Les musées d'art continuent à se reposer sur les grands architectes pour concevoir des bâtiments spectaculaires qui deviendront l'élément le plus visible de leur marque institutionnelle. Ces chefs-d'œuvre jaillissent du sol sous forme d'éclats de glace scintillants, de montagnes aux courbes métalliques ou de créatures biomorphiques. Serait-ce la formule gagnante? On en est loin. Parallèlement à la haute architecture, la haute finance et les attentes ambitieuses des commanditaires, est apparu un risque d'échec élevé… Les titres de la presse parlent d'eux-mêmes. L'an dernier le Bellevue Art Museum de Seattle, conçu par Steven Holl, a fermé à l'issue de deux années seulement de fonctionnement. Sa cérémonie d'inauguration avait rivalisé avec celle des Oscars. Le Milwaukee Art Museum bataille avec une dette de 25 millions de dollars consécutive à la construction de sa nouvelle aile due à Calatrava (page 11). *The Hartford Courant* rapporte que le conseil d'administration du Wadsworth Atheneum a décidé de "jeter à la corbeille" le projet de son extension signé Ben van Berkel d'UNStudio, après la révélation de coûts non prévus. Plus récemment, le Whitney et le Los Angeles County Museum of Art ont abandonné leur projet de rénovation par Koolhaas. Des décisions coûteuses, mais peut-être sages… »[3]

Les musées publiés dans cet ouvrage sont tous assez récents, mais aucun d'eux n'a encore pris en compte la récession économique entamée en 2008. Il sera possible de mieux analyser son impact dans un laps de temps normal de conception et de construction, soit trois ans environ. Certains projets sont déjà mis en attente ou annulés, mais pour le moment on a construit tant de nouveaux musées ou extensions à travers le monde au cours de ces trois dernières années qu'il faudrait plus d'un seul livre pour les recenser. La sélection présentée dans les pages qui suivent a été établie sur la base de l'intérêt architectural des projets, mais également sur celle de leur répartition géographique et de leur nature qui va d'importantes réalisations institutionnelles, comme les programmes d'extension du Louvre (Lens, 2009–12, page 317) ou du Centre Pompidou (Metz, 2006–10, page 87), à de petites opérations locales comme le musée du Phare de Santa Marta (Cascais, Portugal, 2003–07, page 65). Le nombre de projets non réalisés ou «virtuels» a été limité afin de mettre l'accent sur les «vrais» musées, soit déjà construits soit, espérons-le, en voie de l'être. L'art n'est pas le seul thème de ces musées. L'un d'eux est consacré à l'acier (Horno 3, Museo del Acero, Monterrey, Mexique, 2006–07, page 161), un autre à la mer (Ozeanum, Musée océanographique allemand, Stralsund, Allemagne, 2005–08, page 93) et un autre encore au langage (musée de la Langue portugaise, Sao Paulo, Brésil, 2003–06, page 239). Avec le Mobile Art, Chanel Contemporary Art Container de Zaha Hadid (divers lieux, 2007–, page 174), même les sacs à main ont reçu un traitement royal.

30
Paulo Mendes da Rocha, Portuguese Language Museum, São Paulo, SP, Brazil, 2003–06

30

AU FIL DU COURANT, ENTRE HISTOIRE ET NATURE

Si la fonction naturelle de protection des œuvres d'art peut favoriser une approche conservatrice, les exemples d'architectes choisis, de Piano & Rogers à Santiago Calatrava, montrent que les décideurs ou les autorités politiques se sont libérés des craintes de l'innovation. « L'effet Bilbao » semble avoir favorisé l'émergence d'une architecture sans cesse plus étonnante. Un certain nombre de musées sélectionnés ici innovent concrètement et de différentes façons, même si ce n'est pas toujours à travers des gestes architecturaux spectaculaires. La rénovation du Neues Museum à Berlin (1997–2009, page 101) par David Chipperfield s'illustre par une approche surprenante des difficultés posées par la réhabilitation de quasi-ruines. Bombardée à la fin de la Seconde Guerre mondiale et laissée à l'état de vestiges par le régime est-allemand, la grande institution de l'Île aux musées a été restaurée avec beaucoup de soins dans ses volumes originaux par l'architecte britannique qui a tenu à laisser visibles de nombreuses cicatrices de la guerre. D'autres parties ont été reconstituées en utilisant des matériaux comme le béton, choix qui a pu choquer certains puristes, mais qui est précisément ce qui rend l'intervention de Chipperfield moderne ou de son temps. Il faut noter que l'architecte n'est pas le premier Britannique à être confronté au défi des ruines berlinoises. Norman Foster avait connu cette situation lors de sa restauration du nouveau Parlement allemand, le Reichstag (1995–99) au sujet duquel il expliquait s'être : « …efforcé de conserver et d'incorporer des souvenirs du passé dans le tissu du bâtiment, comme les graffitis de l'occupation russe, l'incendie des années 1930, les cicatrices de la guerre, certaines moulures originales et les interventions des années 1960. » [4] La modernité résolument hybride introduite dans le Neues Museum par David Chipperfield n'a rien à voir avec un pastiche. C'est une tentative sensible de réconcilier le présent avec le passé dans le contexte chargé de l'histoire allemande, couvrant une période qui part de la construction du bâtiment au XIXe siècle, se poursuit par une longue période à l'état de ruines et s'achève provisoirement en 2009 avec la réinstallation des œuvres.

Zaha Hadid a consacré sa carrière à la remise en cause des a priori sur les formes et les fonctions en architecture. Son dernier musée, le MAXXI (musée national des Arts du XXIe siècle, Rome, Italie, 1998–2009, page 178) n'y fait pas exception. Plutôt que de cheminements de découverte à travers son bâtiment, elle préfère parler de « flotter à travers l'espace » ou d'un « entrelacement des circulations avec le contexte urbain ». En termes clairs, la forme inhabituelle du MAXXI correspond à un programme qui ne cherche rien moins qu'à repenser l'expérience muséale. Loin du modèle orthogonal, encore récemment illustré au Museum of Modern Art (MoMA) de New York par Yoshio Taniguchi (page 23), Hadid pense en trois dimensions et bannit avant tout la ligne droite. Une si forte présence de l'architecture est un défi pour les conservateurs. Si l'on y pense bien, une partie du Guggenheim de Bilbao, comme la longue galerie « serpentine » est moins une gageure qu'une « mission impossible ». Alors que Gehry exprimait clairement le désir de bénéficier de la même liberté que les artistes contemporains, Hadid paraît se concentrer davantage sur les enjeux de la fonction et les flux d'espace. Dans ses créations d'objets et d'architectures, elle a mis en œuvre une approche continue, quasi liquide, des volumes et des formes, remettant en cause l'ordre « établi » d'à peu près tout ce qui est structure, du sol au plafond. Il reste à vérifier si ce défi sera perçu dans le futur comme l'expression d'une esthétique personnelle ou comme une révolution architecturale. Le MAXXI constituera sans doute un élément important de réponse à cette interrogation.

31
Wang Shu, Ningbo History Museum,
Ningbo, China, 2003–08

L'émergence de nouveaux talents en Chine représente par ailleurs une importante source d'innovation en architecture récente. Des modifications de l'appareil législatif chinois ont permis à des individualités de faire leur apparition face aux « instituts » monolithiques qui dominaient la profession depuis des décennies. Une bonne part de la nouvelle architecture de ce pays peut sembler un peu difficile ou même « dérangeante » pour un regard occidental, mais sa puissance est évidente. C'est certainement le cas du musée d'Histoire de Ningbo de Wang Shu (Ningbo, Chine, 2003–08, page 397), qui se présente sous la forme d'une montagne artificielle. Un certain nombre d'architectes occidentaux, dont Jean Nouvel (musée de l'Évolution humaine, Burgos, Espagne, 2000, page 12), ont expérimenté des concepts similaires, mais Wang Shu a réellement construit ce grand musée montagne. Décrivant lui-même son projet en termes de montagne, mais aussi de vallées et de tunnels, l'architecte précise : « L'intérieur et l'extérieur du bâtiment ont été recouverts de panneaux de ciment à motif de bambou et de plus de vingt types de briques recyclées – une substance aussi magnifique qu'économique entre artifice et nature. »

VIRTUELLEMENT BIEN LÀ

Bien que l'accent ait été mis dans ce livre sur les musées « réels », quelques œuvres encore sur plans ont été retenues pour leur importance, et parce qu'elles seront probablement réalisées dans la mesure où les financements publics promis seront débloqués. Trois de ces nouvelles institutions sont situées en France et signées d'architectes connus. Suivant peut-être la voie du Guggenheim Bilbao, mais aussi des projets d'extension de la Tate Gallery à d'autres lieux, le Centre Pompidou et le Louvre ont annoncé des programmes d'extension en régions. Le Louvre s'est par ailleurs engagé dans la création d'un nouveau musée à Abou Dhabi qui a été confié à Jean Nouvel. Le Centre Pompidou-Metz de Shigeru Ban est le plus avancé de ces projets puisqu'il doit être inauguré en 2010 (page 87). Ban est bien connu pour ses projets novateurs et son utilisation de matériaux comme les tubes de carton structurels. Les installations de Metz seront regroupées sous une curieuse toiture inspirée d'un chapeau chinois acheté à Paris par l'architecte. Les amples espaces de ce nouveau Centre Pompidou sont en partie inspirés de l'atrium du bâtiment parisien de Piano & Rogers, et en partie du besoin d'espaces suffisant pour accueillir les œuvres souvent imposantes des artistes contemporains. Il est intéressant de noter que la participation de Ban au concours organisé pour Metz a été largement due à son admiration pour l'audace du Centre Beaubourg : « Dès que j'ai entendu parler de ce concours, j'ai pensé que ce type de projet me correspondait bien. Je respecte Renzo Piano et Richard Rogers et j'aime l'architecture qui innove. J'ai vu que le client était le Centre Pompidou et j'étais certain qu'il était prêt à accepter une proposition novatrice. J'ai aussi pensé que c'était un concours que je me devais de remporter. Je savais que le bâtiment était prévu pour Metz, et je dois admettre que je ne connaissais pas grand-chose de cette ville. Mais le lieu n'était pas très important dans la mesure où le Centre Pompidou participait à la décision. » [5]

La description de ce projet par son architecte donne une vision intéressante de la façon dont sont conçus les musées contemporains, et précise en quoi son approche a pu être influencée par d'autres musées récents. À la question de savoir ce qui lui est venu en premier à l'esprit, le toit ou le contenu, Ban répond : « Les deux, simultanément. De nombreux architectes proposent des constructions difficiles à utiliser en tant que musées. Les responsables culturels et les artistes répètent qu'ils n'ont pas besoin des architectes. Ils préfèrent des espaces industriels

32
*Kazuyo Sejima + Ryue Nishizawa /
SANAA, Louvre-Lens, Lens, France,
2009–12*

comme ceux du Dia Beacon (OpenOffice, Beacon, New York, États-Unis, 2004) ou de la Tate Modern (Herzog & de Meuron, Londres, Royaume-Uni, 2000), et disent que les architectes construisent des musées plus pour eux-mêmes que pour l'art. Je voulais créer quelque chose qui soit un non-musée, mais qui envoie aussi un message fort. Dans le programme, on demandait aux architectes de concevoir des galeries modulaires de quinze mètres de large de différentes longueurs. Je pense que pour être pratique, une galerie doit posséder d'aussi grands murs que possible et la meilleure climatisation imaginable. J'ai pensé à la forme tubulaire parce qu'elle offre le maximum de surface de murs dans une "boîte" qui permet un contrôle aisé de la climatisation. Une autre caractéristique du programme est la grande nef, de grande hauteur de plafond. Parce que le Centre Pompidou parisien ne dispose pas d'espaces suffisamment hauts, certaines pièces de sa collection ne peuvent être présentées au public, et cette nef est donc importante pour le musée de Metz. J'ai décidé que les galeries en forme de tubes rectangulaires seraient empilées au-dessus de la nef. Le forum et la grande nef sont ainsi générés par la présence de ces tubes suspendus et de la toiture. Le toit n'est pas aussi symétrique que le chapeau chinois, du fait du contenu du bâtiment. Cependant, si vous le regardez de dessus, vous voyez que sa forme reste un hexagone symétrique. »[6]

Curieusement, le Louvre a également choisi une agence japonaise pour concevoir son extension à Lens (France, 2009–12, page 317). Ryue Nizhizawa et Kazuyo Sejima (SANAA) ont l'expérience de la conception de musées, mais plus spécifiquement de ceux consacrés à l'art contemporain. Les formes en biais anguleuses, retenues pour Lens, et les immenses parois transparentes déjà aperçues dans leurs autres réalisations peuvent sembler en contradiction avec l'architecture de pierre et fermée du Louvre. L'objectif ici est de décentraliser une partie de la richesse de l'institution parisienne dans un esprit ouvert et généreux. Metz et Lens sont deux villes situées dans des régions qui connaissent de grandes difficultés économiques liées au déclin de leur industrie. Il reste à voir si Shigeru Ban ou SANAA pourront faire naître cette sorte d'excitation architecturale qui avait suivi l'ouverture du Guggenheim Bilbao de Frank O. Gehry, mais il n'en demeure pas moins que l'initiative espagnole en collaboration avec le musée new-yorkais a certainement inspiré ces plans ambitieux.

La ville de Lyon comptera sans doute dans un proche avenir un nouveau musée, mais qui reste virtuel pour l'instant, bien que son inauguration soit prévue pour 2013. Le musée des Confluences (2001–13, page 123) a été conçu par Coop Himmelb(l)au. Appelé « Nuage de cristal de la connaissance » par ses architectes autrichiens, cette œuvre semble tirer son esthétique ou ses origines formelles de l'époque ou le « déconstructivisme » faisait rage. Certains grands projets reflètent ainsi les progrès conceptuels de l'architecture. L'agence viennoise avait remporté le concours organisé en 2001, mais il faut savoir que trois de leurs précédents projets figuraient dans l'exposition *Deconstructivist Architecture*, organisée en 1988, au Museum of Modern Art de New York. Ceci n'est pas une critique du projet lyonnais, mais plutôt l'indication que beaucoup de patience et de persistance sont demandées aux architectes qui défient les conventions, comme Wolf D. Prix et son équipe dans ce musée des Confluences.

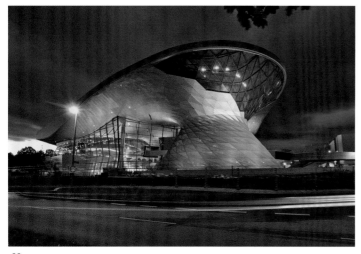

33

Choix presque aussi curieux que les Japonais des deux grandes institutions françaises citées plus haut, le Grand Musée égyptien (Gizeh, Égypte, 2007–14, page 14), prévu sur le plateau des Pyramides près du Caire, a été conçu par une Irlandaise, Roisin Heneghan et son partenaire d'origine chinoise, Shih-Fu Peng (Heneghan.Peng.Architects), tous deux associés à une agence de paysagisme néerlandaise réputée (West8). Prévu pour être achevé en 2014, cet équipement culturel de 100 000 mètres carrés ne devrait pas coûter moins de trois cent cinquante millions d'euros. Le fait même de construire à proximité des pyramides est un pari considérable, mais il est évident que le Musée égyptien du Caire est dépassé aussi bien par le flux de touristes que par son âge. La coordination du musée et du site de Gizeh est à la fois logique et plus efficace. Sous la direction du ministre égyptien de la Culture, Farouk Hosni, ce projet resté en gestation pendant longtemps, semble avoir maintenant démarré. Pour décrire leur proposition, les architectes précisent que « Le Grand Musée égyptien n'est pas un pur musée au sens traditionnel du terme. Il est conçu comme un complexe de différentes activités qui contribuent à un environnement culturel centré sur l'égyptologie. Par le tissage de différents cheminements à travers le complexe, le monde de l'ancienne Égypte pourra être exploré à différents niveaux et selon divers modes. Le musée sera à la fois un conservatoire d'artefacts culturels et un centre de documentation culturelle interactif ».

MUSÉES POUR TOUS, ET POUR TOUT

Bien que l'art reste le domaine principal des nouveaux musées, un certain nombre d'autres thématiques sont traitées par les institutions présentées dans ces pages. Francisco Aires Mateus a créé l'un des plus petits musées de ce livre (musée du Phare de Santa Marta, Cascais, Portugal, 2003–07, page 65) sur un phare datant de 1868, mais aussi sur les phares en général. L'architecte portugais a réussi à faire un tout cohérent d'un lieu assez hétérogène et à imaginer sa reconversion. Cette démarche correspond à petite échelle à l'espoir fréquemment émis par les municipalités qu'un musée puisse régénérer une zone en déclin, voire même abandonnée. L'Ozeaneum (Musée océanographique allemand, Stralsund, Allemagne, 2005–08, page 93) de Behnisch Architekten utilise, dans une certaine mesure, une architecture existante – des entrepôts qui ont une valeur historique – en lien direct avec leur site en bord de mer pour présenter des expositions sur la Baltique et la mer du Nord. Avec ses 60 000 mètres carrés, l'Ozeaneum joue dans une ligue différente de celle du musée du Phare de Santa Marta, bien sûr, mais participe également à un programme de rénovation urbaine appelé « Quartier 66 ».

Les architectes autrichiens Delugan Meissl ont récemment achevé le nouveau musée Porsche (Stuttgart, Allemagne, 2006–08, page 127) qui fait partie d'une série d'institutions de ce type conçues par UNStudio (Mercedes-Benz Museum, Stuttgart, Allemagne, 2003–06, page 29) ou Coop Himmelb(l)au (BMW Welt, Munich, Allemagne, 2001–07, page 42). L'objectif était d'évoquer le style si personnel du constructeur automobile et de s'intégrer à un site essentiellement industriel. Le résultat est à la fois dynamique et spectaculaire, comme on pouvait s'y attendre pour un tel thème et un budget de cent millions d'euros.

33
*Coop Himmelb(l)au, BMW Welt,
Munich, Germany, 2001–07*

34
*Paulo Mendes da Rocha, Brazilian
Museum of Sculpture, São Paulo, SP,
Brazil, 1987–92*

34

Nicholas Grimshaw s'est plongé dans un type de musée encore plus particulier, centré autour d'un ancien haut-fourneau dans une aciérie mexicaine désaffectée (Horno 3, Museo del Acero, Monterrey, Mexique, 2006–07, page 161). La réhabilitation et le réemploi d'installations industrielles ont été entreprises dans de nombreux sites pour tenter de redonner de la valeur à des constructions qui peuvent encore exercer un attrait esthétique, mais qui étaient condamnées à la démolition. On observe dans ces bâtiments industriels réhabilités une authenticité qu'aucune forme de créativité architecturale ne peut imiter ou recréer. Les 145 000 visiteurs du Museo del Acero pour les six premiers mois de son existence témoignent de l'intérêt que le public porte à ce type de présentation. Paulo Mendes da Rocha, prix Pritzker 2006, a conçu des musées d'art comme le musée brésilien de la Sculpture (São Paulo, Brésil, 1987–92, page 43), mais sa dernière incursion dans le domaine muséal abordait un thème moins courant. Le musée de la Langue portugaise (São Paulo, Brésil, 2003–06, page 239) est installé dans la gare de chemin de fer de style néoclassique de Luz, datant de la fin du XIXᵉ siècle. Il occupe en fait un peu plus de la moitié de cette gare toujours en fonctionnement, ce qui posait des défis à la fois techniques et esthétiques à cet architecte au style moderniste marqué. Thème encore plus inattendu, le N4A Museum de Zhang Lei (Liyang, Chine, 2006–07, page 407) chante les louanges de la Nouvelle 4ᵉᵐᵉ Armée. Créée en 1937, elle était l'une des principales forces militaires du Parti communiste chinois et intervenait au sud du Yang-Tsé-Kiang. D'aspect puissant et un peu plus qu'énigmatique, cette construction met en valeur l'inventivité des architectes chinois contemporains et leur sens esthétique, qui se démarquent en quelque sorte de la création européenne, voire même du reste de l'Asie.

DU SOUTHIE AU BOWERY

Les extensions de musées d'art ont été initiées par des institutions qui, du Metropolitan au Louvre, présentent rarement, voire jamais, de l'art contemporain. D'autres musées, comme le Centre Pompidou (Musée national d'art moderne), la Tate Gallery ou le Museum of Modern Art (MoMA) de New York se consacrent à l'art d'aujourd'hui, mais ce qui attire le plus les visiteurs est la catégorie appelée « moderne » qui va de la fin du XIXᵉ siècle aux lendemains de la Seconde Guerre mondiale. Ce n'est que récemment que des institutions entièrement consacrées à l'art contemporain ont rejoint le mouvement des nouvelles constructions spectaculaires conçues par des architectes célèbres. Un exemple en est l'Institute of Contemporary Art de Boston (Boston, Massachusetts, États-Unis, 2004–06, page 16) dû aux architectes new-yorkais Diller Scofidio + Renfro. Ce bâtiment de 5760 mètres carrés, qui a coûté quarante et un millions de dollars, se dresse en bordure de l'Océan, à Fan Pier, dans le quartier de South Boston, témoignage hautement visible et réussi de la percée de l'art contemporain auprès du public des amateurs de musées. L'arrivée d'un art et d'une architecture réellement actuels à South Boston (appelé *Southie* par ses habitants) est un événement d'importance. L'Institut se trouve à proximité de la gare Sud, de Government Center et du restaurant très connu, *Anthony's Pier Four*, mais il se situe aussi dans un quartier naguère réputé pour sa brutalité et sa population pauvre, en grande partie d'origine irlandaise.

Le New Museum of Contemporary Art (New York, États-Unis, 2005–07, page 31) par Ryue Nishizawa et Kazuyo Sejima de SANAA offre un second exemple de ces nouveaux liens entre l'art contemporain et les architectes de grand talent. Situé sur le Bowery, une avenue du Lower East Side qui s'embourgeoise depuis peu, le New Museum est l'un des immeubles de Manhattan les plus commentés parmi ceux appa-

35
*Kazuyo Sejima + Ryue Nishizawa /
SANAA, 21st-Century Museum of
Contemporary Art, Kanazawa, Ishi-
kawa, Japan, 2002–04*

35

rus depuis quelques années. Plus ancienne artère de Manhattan, le Bowery était la plus élégante rue de la ville à la fin du XVIIIe siècle, mais se paupérisa dans les années 1920 et 1930. Une série de films sur les *Dead End Kids* ou les *Bowery Boys* lui donna une réputation qui dépassa largement les limites de New York. Des années 1940 à la fin des années 1970, le quartier était surtout connu pour sa population d'alcooliques et de sans-abri. Aujourd'hui encore, quelques vestiges de cette atmosphère subsistent, bien que les cafés et les hôtels chics soient davantage la règle. Composé essentiellement d'une série de boîtes aveugles empilées un peu comme au hasard, le New Museum est une solution intelligente et économique aux problèmes posés par l'étroitesse de son terrain (21 mètres de large par 34 mètres de profondeur pour une hauteur du bâti de 52 mètres). En décalant légèrement ces boîtes qui correspondent à des espaces d'exposition neutres de grande hauteur de plafond, les architectes ont réussi à faire pénétrer la lumière naturelle là où elle était nécessaire, et à créer des terrasses offrant des vues sur le centre de New York. Le matériau d'habillage (treillis d'aluminium déployé à finition anodisée brillante) crée une vibration lumineuse qui se modifie en permanence et distingue radicalement l'immeuble de ses voisins. Cette nouvelle initiative architecturale est le « point central d'un projet de soixante-quatre millions de dollars d'investissement qui comprend la construction du bâtiment, l'extension du capital du musée et d'autres coûts de développement entièrement financés par une campagne de levée de fonds et la vente du précédent site du musée sur Broadway à SoHo ».

À L'EST D'ÉDEN

En dehors du Louvre-Lens, Kazuyo Sejima et Ryue Nishizawa sont également les auteurs du musée d'Art contemporain du XXIe siècle (Kanazawa, Ishikawa, Japon, 2002–04, page 44). Cette construction novatrice, en forme de tambour entièrement vitré de 112,5 mètres de diamètre, associe une architecture d'avant-garde à une collection d'art contemporain de très haut niveau. Conseillé par un comité qui comprenait à l'origine Lars Nittve (directeur du Moderna Museet), d'Alfred Pacquement (directeur du Musée national d'art moderne au Centre Pompidou) et Neil Benezra (directeur du MoMA de San Francisco), ce musée est un geste volontariste en faveur de l'insertion de l'art et de l'architecture contemporains dans une ville particulièrement traditionnelle, Kanazawa. Au voisinage d'un certain nombre de bâtiments officiels, le musée fait directement face aux fameux jardins de Kenroku-en. Réalisé au cours d'une période de deux cents ans du XVIIe au XIXe siècle, Kenroku-en était le jardin extérieur du château de Kanazawa. Ce jardin est l'un des plus célèbres du Japon, classé « Site national de beauté spectaculaire » en 1922 et « Site national de beauté spectaculaire spéciale » en 1985. Par ses immenses ouvertures, son profil surbaissé et la pureté de sa forme géométrique, le Musée du XXIe siècle n'entre pas en contradiction avec son prestigieux voisin. C'est même le contraire.

L'anguleux et immaculé musée universitaire d'Art contemporain (Université autonome nationale du Mexique – UNAM, Mexico, Mexique, 2006–08, page 147) de Teodoro González de León est une nouvelle preuve de la tendance de plus en plus répandue à donner une visibilité nouvelle à l'art contemporain, au-delà du circuit des galeries et des foires où il était naguère mieux accueilli que dans les musées. Ce musée se trouve sur le côté d'une nouvelle place qui sert d'entrée au centre culturel de l'Université, et s'organise sur deux niveaux : celui de la

36
*Richard Meier, The Getty Center,
Los Angeles, CA, USA, 1984-97*

36

place, qui comprend l'accueil, les galeries d'exposition, une boutique, une librairie et des équipements éducatifs, et un niveau inférieur, en partie creusé dans la roche volcanique, où sont logés un auditorium de trois cents sièges, des bureaux, des réserves, une cafétéria, un restaurant et une médiathèque. L'architecte a précisé que les proportions du bâtiment « avaient été soigneusement calculées après avoir visité trente-cinq musées et galeries d'art contemporain à travers le monde ». À travers cette remarque, se dessine le sentiment que les nouveaux lieux de l'art contemporain ont beaucoup en commun et qu'ils ont, avant tout, apporté à un public plus vaste la connaissance de la créativité du monde d'aujourd'hui.

LA CULTURE POUR LE PEUPLE

Quel que soit ce que le futur nous réserve, il semble que les années récentes aient été témoin d'une tendance accélérée à la construction de musées de plus en plus nombreux. La capacité d'architectes de talent, de I. M. Pei à Renzo Piano et Frank O. Gehry, mais aussi d'une génération plus jeune, à faire de leurs musées des événements architecturaux ou peut-être même des œuvres d'art en soi, doit être regardée d'une certaine distance. De multiples raisons font que « l'effet Bilbao » ne fonctionne pas dans tous les cas. En fait, le succès du musée de Gehry s'est avéré assez difficile à répéter. Que 8,2 millions de visiteurs soient passés sous la Pyramide de verre de I. M. Pei dans la cour Napoléon du Louvre en 2008 montre qu'une architecture de conception rationnelle peut elle aussi jouer un rôle pour attirer de nouveaux visiteurs dans un musée. Le Louvre est aujourd'hui confronté au problème d'avoir trop de visiteurs : lors de l'achèvement de ses travaux en 1993, on en prévoyait environ cinq millions seulement ! En multipliant les activités annexes, que ce soit des manifestations en auditorium, les restaurants, les boutiques, les librairies, les musées sont devenus des attractions touristiques bien sûr, mais également des sortes de centres culturels, de lieux de rassemblement et de rencontre. La relation entre les musées actuels et les églises du passé a souvent été notée, mais le musée sanctuaire, temple humaniste, appartient déjà au passé. De nombreux débats sur la « démocratisation » de l'art et de la culture ont alimenté les initiatives politiques locales dans des pays comme la France, par exemple sous la présidence de François Mitterrand lorsque Jack Lang était ministre de la culture. L'extension de la construction de musées, qui ne se limitent ni à l'art ni aux formes traditionnelles de l'art, a finalement commencé à exercer un impact sur un plus vaste public. Jadis réservée à une élite aisée, l'appréciation de l'art s'est étendue à une masse plus nombreuse de visiteurs. Malgré les réserves légitimes émises par des commentateurs comme Ken Carbone sur la viabilité ultime de tant d'extensions coûteuses, le nombre grandissant des visiteurs confirme que le musée représente une proportion de plus en plus importante du temps de loisirs dans de nombreux pays.

La situation économique exercera certainement son effet sur de nombreuses institutions actuelles, et plus encore sur les projets à venir. Des musées moins grands, davantage respectueux du développement durable, pourraient profiter d'un renversement de tendance, mais on peut dire sans trop de risque que la relation étroite entre une architecture « de qualité » et le monde muséal est vouée à durer. Même si sa réputation internationale ne garantit pas qu'un architecte sache concevoir un musée adapté aux circonstances, il existe une corrélation clairement établie entre le monde de la culture et celui de la conception architecturale de haut niveau. Un architecte célèbre a rarement porté atteinte à la réputation et au nombre de visiteurs d'un musée, même si certains dépassements budgétaires et solutions peu pratiques ont posé récemment quelques problèmes. Les musées ont ouvert les portes d'un monde nouveau à de nombreux touristes et résidents de villes disposant par bonheur de bâtiments et de collections intéressantes. Plus que les résidences privées ou même les immeubles de bureaux, les musées ont fait beaucoup pour rapprocher le grand public non seulement de l'art bien sûr, mais aussi de l'architecture contemporaine. C'est l'héritage le plus durable des années de frénésie d'expansion qu'ils viennent de traverser. Armés de cette assurance, ceux qui décideront des projets muséaux à venir, et leurs architectes, trouveront certainement des solutions pour dépasser les problèmes posés par une diminution des financements. Les stars de l'art et les stars de l'architecture ont partie liée.

Philip Jodidio, Grimentz, 1er mai 2009

[1]   I. M. Pei, préface au livre *I. M. Pei, Architect*, New York, 2008.
[2]   «Les problèmes des musées s'intensifient: licenciements, coupes budgétaires et expositions annulées», *The Art Newspaper*, avril 2009
[3]   Ken Carbone, «The Shell Game: Too many museums are investing in star architecture at the expense of art», *I. D. magazine*, mai 2004.
[4]   Fax de Norman Foster à l'auteur, 1er novembre 1996.
[5]   Entretien entre Shigeru Ban et l'auteur, 23 juillet 2008, Paris.
[6]   Ibid.

HITOSHI ABE

Atelier Hitoshi Abe
3–3–16 Oroshimachi
Wakabayashi-ku
Sendai, Miyagi 984–0015
Japan

Tel: +81 22 784 3411
Fax: +81 22 782 1233
E-mail: contact@a-slash.jp
Web: www.a-slash.jp

HITOSHI ABE was born in 1962 in Sendai, Japan. He worked from 1988 to 1992 in the office of Coop Himmelb(l)au and obtained his M.Arch degree from SCI-Arc in 1989. He created his own firm, Atelier Hitoshi Abe, in 1992. Beginning in 1994, he directed the Hitoshi Abe Architectural Design Laboratory at the Tohoku Institute of Technology. He has been a Professor at Tohoku University since 2002, and, since 2007, Chair and Professor at the Department of Architecture and Urban Design, School of Arts and Architecture at UCLA, Los Angeles, California. He won the 2003 Architectural Institute of Japan Award, for the Reihoku Community Hall. His work includes the Miyagi Water Tower (Rifu, Miyagi, 1994); the Gravel-2 House (Sendai, Miyagi, 1998); the Neige Lune Fleur Restaurant (Sendai, Miyagi, 1999); the Miyagi Stadium (Rifu, Miyagi, 2000); the Michinoku Folklore Museum (Kurikoma, Miyagi, 2000); and the A-House (Sendai, Miyagi, 2000). More recently, he completed the Kanno Museum (Shiogama, Miyagi, 2004–05, published here); the KCH / Whopper Clinic and Residence (Saitama, Saitama, 2006); and the FRP Ftown Building (Sendai, Miyagi, 2007), all in Japan.

HITOSHI ABE wurde 1962 in Sendai, Japan, geboren. Von 1988 bis 1992 arbeitete er im Büro Coop Himmelb(l)au und erhielt 1989 seinen M. Arch. am Southern California Institute of Architecture – SCI-Arc. 1992 gründete er seine eigene Firma, Atelier Hitoshi Abe. Ab 1994 leitete er das Hitoshi Abe Architectural Design Laboratory am Tohoku Institute of Technology. Seit 2002 ist er Professor an der Tohoku University und seit 2007 Lehrstuhlinhaber und Professor am Department of Architecture and Urban Design, School of Arts and Architecture an der University of California, Los Angeles. 2003 gewann er den Architectural Institute of Japan Award für die Stadthalle Reihoku. Zu seinen Werken gehören der Wasserturm Miyagi (Rifu, Miyagi, 1994), das Haus Gravel-2 (Sendai, Miyagi, 1998), das Restaurant Neige Lune Fleur (Sendai, Miyagi, 1999), das Stadion von Miyagi (Rifu, Miyagi, 2000), das Volkskundemuseum Michinoku (Kurikoma, Miyagi, 2000) und das Haus A (Sendai, Miyagi, 2000). In jüngster Zeit stellte er das Kanno Museum fertig (Shiogama, Miyagi, 2004–05, hier veröffentlicht), die Klinik und das Wohnhaus KCH / Whopper (Saitama, Saitama, 2006) und das FRP Ftown Building (Sendai, Miyagi, 2007), alle in Japan.

HITOSHI ABE, né en 1962 à Sendai (Japon), a travaillé de 1988 à 1992 dans l'agence Coop Himmelb(l)au et a obtenu son M.Arch de SCI-Arc en 1989. Il a créé sa propre structure, Atelier Hitoshi Abe, en 1992. À partir de 1994, il a dirigé le Laboratoire de conception architecturale Hitoshi Abe à l'Institut de technologie de Tohoku. Il est professeur à l'université de Tohoku depuis 2002 et, depuis 2007, est président et professeur au Département d'architecture et d'urbanisme de la School of Arts and Architecture à l'UCLA (Los Angeles, Californie). En 2003, il a remporté le prix de l'Institut d'architecture du Japon pour la salle communale de Reihoku. Parmi ses réalisations, toutes au Japon : le château d'eau de Miyagi (Rifu, Miyagi, 1994) ; la maison Gravel-2 (Sendai, Miyagi, 1998) ; le restaurant Neige Lune Fleur (Sendai, Miyagi, 1999) ; le stade de Miyagi (Rifu, Miyagi, 2000) ; le musée du folklore Michinoku (Kurikoma, Miyagi, 2000) et la maison A (Sendai, Miyagi, 2000). Plus récemment, il a achevé le musée Kanno (Shiogama, Miyagi, 2004–05) publié ici ; la clinique et résidence KCH / Whopper (Saitama, Saitama, 2006) et l'immeuble urbain FRP Ftown (Sendai, Miyagi, 2007).

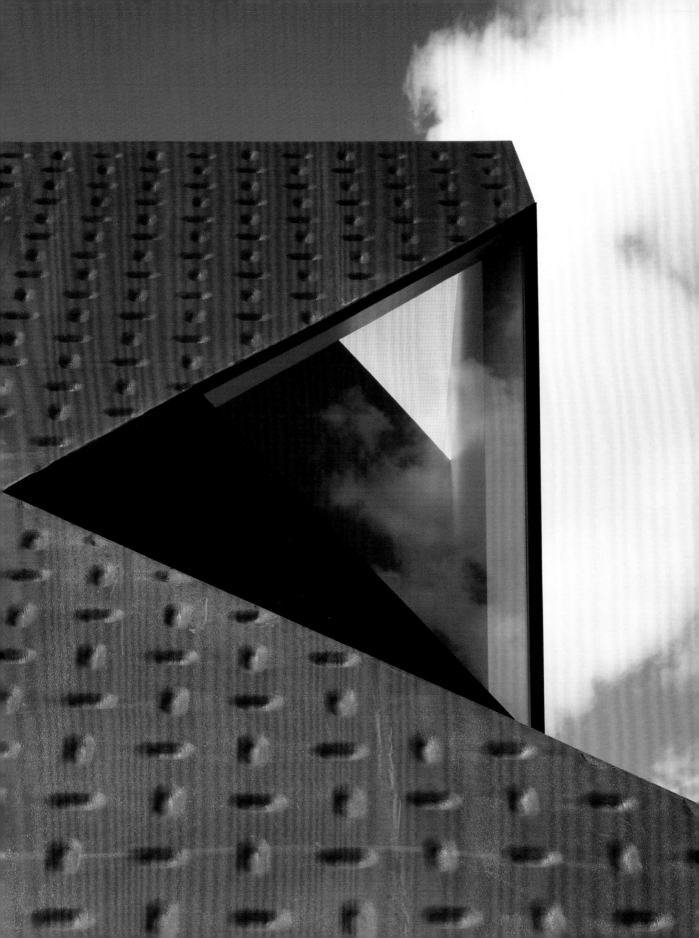

KANNO MUSEUM
Shiogama, Miyagi, Japan, 2004–05

Address: 3-4-15 Tamagawa, Shiogama, Miyagi, Japan, +81 22 361 1222, www.kanno-museum.jp
Area: 220 m². Client: not disclosed. Cost: not disclosed
Collaboration: Structural Design Office OAK, Sogo Consultants, Kajima Corporation

The closed, metallic forms of the Kanno Museum and its small scale put it immediately in a category apart—destined to surprise any visitor.

Die geschlossenen, metallischen Formen des Kanno Museums und sein kleiner Maßstab versetzen es auf den ersten Blick in eine besondere Kategorie – und bringen alle Besucher zum Staunen.

La forme métallique fermée du musée Kanno et son échelle réduite le placent dans une catégorie à part et ne peuvent que surprendre le visiteur.

Built on a 638-square-meter site overlooking the Pacific Ocean, this is a private museum for the display of just eight sculptures owned by the client. The architect created eight spaces for the works, "inflating them like soap bubbles." These interior spaces are generated by the "boundary conditions of each cell," as though they were cut out of foam within the 10 x 12 x 10-meter exterior frame. The cells are made of 3.2-millimeter-thick steel plates with 25 embossed protuberances per square meter. The architect explains: "Honeycomb panels are formed by welding the embossed protuberances of a cell to those of the adjoining cell, resulting in an unusual structure like an aggregation of soap bubbles." The surprising Cor-ten steel exterior of the building, itself quite sculptural, was chosen so that the Kanno Museum would be "potent enough to stimulate local artistic activities."

Dieses auf einem 638 m² großen Grundstück errichtete Gebäude mit Blick auf den Pazifischen Ozean ist ein privates Museum zur Ausstellung von nur acht Skulpturen, die dem Bauherrn gehören. Der Architekt schuf acht Räume für die Kunstwerke, „aufgebläht wie Seifenblasen". Diese Innenräume werden durch die „Grenzbedingungen jeder Zelle" gebildet, als wären sie innerhalb eines 10 x 12 x 10 m großen äußeren Rahmens aus Schaum geschnitten. Die Zellen bestehen aus 3,2 mm starken Stahlplatten mit 25 Ausstanzungen pro Quadratmeter. Der Architekt erläutert: „Verbundplatten mit Wabenkern entstehen durch Schweißen der Ausbuchtungen einer Zelle an die der Nachbarzelle, wodurch eine ungewöhnliche Struktur, ähnlich einer Anhäufung von Seifenblasen, entsteht." Das erstaunliche äußere Erscheinungsbild des Gebäudes aus Cor-Ten-Stahl, selbst eine Skulptur, wurde gewählt, „um durch seine Wirkung vor Ort Kunstaktivitäten anzuregen".

Édifié sur un terrain de 638 mètres carrés dominant l'océan Pacifique, ce musée privé a été conçu pour accueillir huit sculptures seulement, propriété du client. L'architecte a créé huit volumes « qu'il a gonflés comme des bulles de savon ». Ces espaces sont générés à partir de « la condition de la limite de chaque cellule », comme s'ils étaient découpés dans de la mousse dans la structure extérieure de 10 x 12 x 10 mètres. Les cellules en tôle d'acier de 3,2 millimètres d'épaisseur présentent vingt-cinq protubérances estampées par mètre carré. « Les panneaux en nid d'abeille sont formés par la soudure des protubérances d'une cellule à celles de la cellule adjacente, ce qui permet d'obtenir une structure étrange évoquant un agrégat de bulles de savon », explique l'architecte. Elle aussi très sculpturale, l'étonnante façade en acier Cor-ten a été dessinée pour que l'aspect du musée Kanno soit « suffisamment marquant pour stimuler les activités artistiques locales ».

The largely rectangular form of the structure contrasts with the complex folding of its interior spaces, visible in these photos and in the drawings below.

Die überwiegend rechtwinklige Form des Gebäudes bildet einen Kontrast zu den komplex gestalteten Innenräumen, wie aus diesen Fotos und den Zeichnungen unten ersichtlich ist.

La forme essentiellement rectangulaire du bâtiment contraste avec le déploiement complexe de ses espaces intérieurs, visibles dans ces photos et dans les plans ci-dessous.

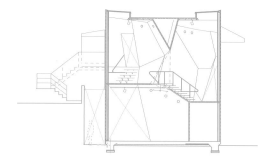

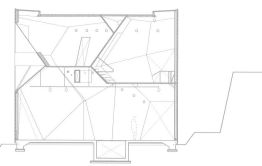

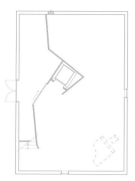  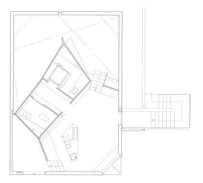

The use of white, typical in modern museums, clashes here with the textures and shapes that the architect introduces into the rectangular floor plans (above).

Die für moderne Museen typische Verwendung der Farbe Weiß kollidiert hier mit den Strukturen und Formen, die der Architekt in die rechtwinkligen Grundrisse eingefügt hat (oben).

Typique des musées modernes, l'utilisation de la couleur blanche entre ici en collision avec les textures et les formes introduites par l'architecte sur un plan au sol rectangulaire (ci-dessus).

ACEBO X ALONSO

Victoria Acebo y Ángel Alonso Arquitectos
C/ Martin Soler 6
28045 Madrid
Spain

Tel: +34 91 506 05 04
Fax: +34 91 506 13 60
E-mail: x@aceboxalonso.com
Web: www.aceboxalonso.blogspot.com

Victoria Acebo was born in Ponferrada, Spain, in 1969. She received her degree as an architect from ETSA Madrid, 1995. She has been a Professor at the European University of Madrid since 2003. This is also the case of Ángel Alonso, born in Santander, Spain, in 1966, who also obtained his degree from ETSAM in 1995. They created **ACEBO X ALONSO** in 1995. Aside from the National Museum of Science and Technology, MUNCYT (A Coruña, 2004–07, published here), they have worked on the Varsavsky House (Madrid, 2003–07); and a Fair Complex (Palma de Mallorca, 2007) and Biodiesel Factory (2007), which have not yet been built. Earlier work includes the Terzagui House (Salamanca, 1996–98); the L-C House (Santander, 1997–99); and the M-U Houses (Guipúzcoa, 1999–2002), all in Spain.

Victoria Acebo wurde 1969 in Ponferrada, Spanien, geboren. Sie schloss ihr Architekturstudium 1995 an der ETSA in Madrid ab. Seit 2003 ist sie Professorin an der Europäischen Universität in Madrid. Dies trifft auch auf Ángel Alonso zu, der 1966 in Santander, Spanien, geboren wurde und seinen Abschluss ebenfalls 1995 an der ETSA Madrid machte. 1995 gründeten sie das Büro **ACEBO X ALONSO**. Außer dem Kunstzentrum A Coruña (A Coruña, 2004–07, hier veröffentlicht) haben sie das Haus Varsavsky (Madrid, 2003–07) gebaut sowie einen Messekomplex (Palma de Mallorca, 2007) und eine Biodieselfabrik (2007) geplant, die noch nicht ausgeführt wurden. Zu ihren früheren Werken zählen das Haus Terzagui (Salamanca, 1996–98), das Haus L-C (Santander, 1997–99) und die Häuser M-U (Guipúzcoa, 1999–2002), alle in Spanien.

Victoria Acebo, née à Ponferrada (Espagne) en 1969, a reçu son diplôme d'architecture de l'ETSA Madrid en 1995. Elle est professeure à l'Université européenne de Madrid depuis 2003. C'est aussi le cas d'Ángel Alonso, né à Santander (Espagne) en 1966, également diplômé de l'ETSAM en 1995. Ils ont fondé **ACEBO X ALONSO** en 1995. En dehors du Centre des arts de La Corogne (La Corogne, 2004–07) publié ici, ils ont travaillé sur les projets de la maison Varsavsky (Madrid, 2003–07) et sur un complexe de foires-expositions (Palma de Majorque, 2007) et une usine de biodiesel (2007), non encore construits. Parmi leurs réalisations antérieures, toutes en Espagne : la maison Terzagui (Salamanque, 1996–98) ; la maison L-C (Santander, 1997–99) et les maisons M-U (Guipúzcoa, 1999–2002).

NATIONAL MUSEUM OF SCIENCE AND TECHNOLOGY, MUNCYT

A Coruña, Spain, 2004–07

Address: Avenida Labañou, 15011 A Coruña, Spain
Area: 6034 m². Client: Diputacion A Coruña. Cost: € 9 million

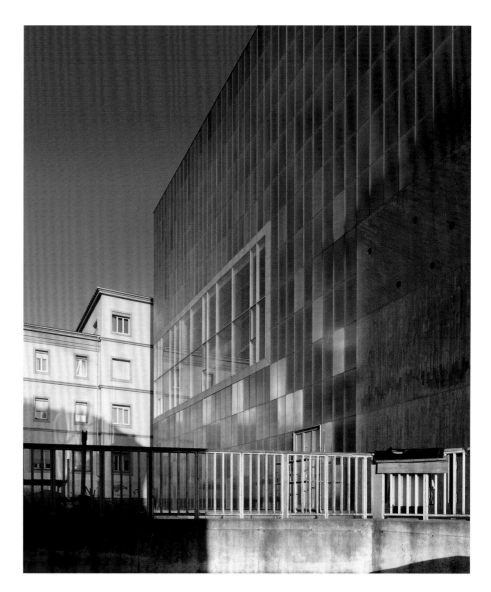

The full, cubic volume of the structure is enlivened by various, sometimes irregular, surface treatments.

Das gewaltige kubische Volumen des Gebäudes wird durch die unterschiedliche, manchmal auch ungleichmäßige Oberflächenbehandlung belebt.

Le volume entièrement cubique du bâtiment s'anime de divers traitements de surface, de nature parfois irrégulière.

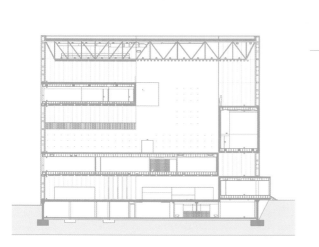

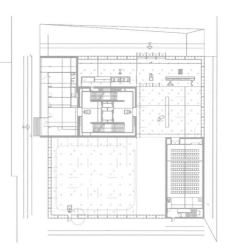

The architects were the winners of an international competition, whose original program included a dance school and a museum on the same site. They proposed a single volume, but with differentiated space. They explain: "We had the chance to add, subtract, divide, but we chose to multiply. The strange concrete form contains the school, while the outer surface, the space between the form and the limit, contains the museum." A series of concrete boxes contains the functions of the school, while the museum is set around these concrete volumes, with six different height spaces, forming a continuous space. Outer refracting glass panels are attached to aluminum frames using structural silicone in a system that was tested to withstand winds of 200 kilometers per hour. The architects used 1000 colored cylinders made of glass wool, a material sometimes employed in industrial spaces with significant mechanical noise levels. They explain: "We disposed them with four different colors to provoke some kind of vibrating topography. They hide the different layers that compose the technical floor: air conditioning, maintenance paths, lighting." For complex reasons, not linked to the work of the architects, this building, originally called the A Coruña Arts Center, has now become the new National Museum of Science and Technology, or MUNCYT, due to open to the public in June 2010.

Die Architekten hatten einen internationalen Wettbewerb gewonnen, dessen ursprüngliches Programm eine Tanzschule und ein Museum auf demselben Grundstück vorsah. Sie schlugen ein zusammenhängendes Volumen vor, jedoch mit getrennten Bereichen. Dazu ihre Erklärung: „Wir hatten die Chance zu addieren, zu subtrahieren, zu dividieren, aber wir beschlossen zu multiplizieren. Die fremdartige Betonform enthält die Schule, während das Museum die Außenfläche, den Raum zwischen der Form und der Begrenzung, einnimmt." Die Schule ist in mehreren Betonkisten untergebracht; das Museum ist um diese herum angeordnet und besteht aus sechs Räumen unterschiedlicher Höhe, die einen zusammenhängenden Bereich bilden. Die äußeren lichtbrechenden Glastafeln sind an Aluminiumrahmen befestigt, wobei konstruktives Silikon in einem System verwendet wurde, das Windstärken von 200 km/h widerstehen kann. Die Architekten benutzten 1000 farbige Zylinder aus Glaswolle, einem Material, das gelegentlich für Industrieräume mit hohem Lärmpegel verwendet wird. Sie erklären: „Wir legten sie in vier verschiedenen Farben an, um eine quasi vibrierende Topografie zu erzielen. Sie verbergen die verschiedenen Schichten, die im Technikgeschoss enthalten sind: Klimaanlage, Wartungsgänge, Beleuchtung." Aus verschiedenen Gründen, die nichts mit der Arbeit der Architekten zu tun haben, wurde aus dem ursprünglich als Kunstzentrum von A Coruña bezeichneten Gebäude das neue Nationalmuseum für Wissenschaft und Technologie (MUNCYT), das im Juni 2010 eröffnet werden soll.

Ce projet est l'aboutissement d'un concours dont le programme original comprenait une école de danse et un musée. Les architectes ont proposé un volume unique, mais différencié. « Nous avions la possibilité d'ajouter, de soustraire, de diviser, mais avons décidé de multiplier. L'étrange forme en béton contient l'école, tandis que l'espace supérieur, situé entre la base et le sommet du bâtiment, contient le musée », expliquent-ils. Une série de boîtes en béton accueille les diverses fonctions de l'école, tandis que le musée qui s'organise autour d'elles comprend six volumes de hauteurs différentes, mais formant un espace continu. Les panneaux de verre réfléchissants des façades sont fixés sur des cadres d'aluminium par un silicone structurel, selon une technique qui les rend capables de résister à des vents de 200 km/h. Les architectes ont par ailleurs mis en place mille cylindres en laine de verre – matériau habituellement utilisé dans les environnements industriels à haut niveau sonore. Ils expliquent : « Nous avons disposé de quatre couleurs différentes pour créer une sorte de topographie vibrante. Ils dissimulent les différentes strates des plafonds techniques : climatisation, coursives de maintenance, éclairage ». Pour des raisons complexes, non liées à l'intervention des architectes, ce bâtiment, appelé à l'origine le Centre des Arts de La Corogne, est devenu le nouveau musée national de la Science et de la Technologie (MUNCYT), qui devrait ouvrir en juin 2010.

The broad, open interior spaces seen here before the installation of the Science Museum facilitated the transition from the earlier scheme that called for a dance school and museum.

Die weiten, offenen Innenräume, hier vor der Einrichtung des Wissenschaftsmuseums, erleichterten die Umplanung des ursprünglichen Entwurfs für eine Tanzschule und ein Museum.

Les vastes volumes intérieurs ouverts – vus ici avant l'installation du musée de la Science – ont facilité l'adaptation des plans prévus antérieurement pour une école de danse et un musée.

AIRES MATEUS

Francisco Aires Mateus Arquitectos
Rua de Campolide 62
1070–037 Lisbon
Portugal

Tel: +351 21 382 75 00
Fax: +351 21 382 75 09
E-mail: f@airesmateus.com
Web: www.airesmateus.com

MANUEL ROCHA DE AIRES MATEUS was born in Lisbon in 1963. He graduated as an architect from the Faculty of Architecture at the Technical University of Lisbon (FA-UTL; 1986). He worked with Gonçalo Byrne beginning in 1983 and with his brother **FRANCISCO XAVIER ROCHA DE AIRES MATEUS** beginning in 1988. He has taught at the Harvard GSD (2002, 2005), and the Accademia di Architettura (Mendrisio, Switzerland) since 2001. Francisco Aires Mateus was born in Lisbon in 1964. He likewise graduated from the FA-UTL (1987). He also began working with Gonçalo Byrne beginning in 1983, before his collaboration with his brother. He, too, has taught at Harvard and in Mendrisio. Their work includes the Sines Cultural Center (Sines, 2000); the Casa No Litoral (Litoral Alentejano, 2000); the Alenquer House (Alenquer, 2002); a plan for the Park Hyatt Hotel (Dublin, Ireland, 2003); and the Santa Marta Lighthouse Museum (Cascais, 2003–07, published here), all in Portugal unless otherwise stated.

MANUEL ROCHA DE AIRES MATEUS wurde 1963 in Lissabon geboren. 1986 schloss er sein Architekturstudium an der Universidade Técnica de Lisboa (FA-UTL) ab. Er arbeitete ab 1983 bei Gonçalo Byrne und ab 1988 mit seinem Bruder **FRANCISCO XAVIER ROCHA DE AIRES MATEUS** zusammen. Er hat an der Harvard Graduate School of Design (2002, 2005) unterrichtet und lehrt seit 2001 an der Accademia di Architettura in Mendrisio in der Schweiz. Francisco Aires Mateus wurde 1964 in Lissabon geboren. Auch er studierte ab 1987 an der FA-UTL und war vor der Zusammenarbeit mit seinem Bruder ab 1983 bei Gonçalo Byrne tätig. Er lehrte ebenfalls in Harvard und Mendrisio. Zu ihren Werken zählen das Kulturzentrum in Sines (2000), die Casa No Litoral (Litoral Alentejano, 2000), das Haus in Alenquer (2002), eine Planung für das Park Hyatt Hotel (Dublin, Irland, 2003) und das Leuchtturmmuseum Santa Marta (Cascais, 2003–07, hier veröffentlicht), alle in Portugal, sofern nicht anders angegeben.

MANUEL ROCHA DE AIRES MATEUS est né à Lisbonne en 1963. Diplômé de la Faculté d'architecture de l'Universidade Técnica de Lisboa (FA-UTL, Lisbonne, 1986), il a travaillé avec Gonçalo Byrne, à partir de 1983, et avec son frère, **FRANCISCO XAVIER ROCHA DE AIRES MATEUS**, à partir de 1988. Il a enseigné à l'Harvard GSD (2002 et 2005) et à l'Accademia di Architettura (Mendrisio, Suisse, depuis 2001). Francisco Aires Mateus, né à Lisbonne en 1964, est également diplômé de la FA-UTL (1987) et a commencé à travailler avec Gonçalo Byrne en 1983, avant de collaborer avec son frère. Il a lui aussi enseigné à Harvard et à Mendrisio. Parmi leurs réalisations, essentiellement au Portugal : le centre culturel Sines (Sines, 2000) ; la Casa No Litoral (Litoral Alentejano, 2000) ; la maison d'Alenquer (Alenquer, 2002) ; un plan pour le Park Hyatt Hotel (Dublin, Irlande, 2003) et le musée du Phare de Santa Marta (Cascais, 2003–07), publié ici.

SANTA MARTA LIGHTHOUSE MUSEUM

Cascais, Portugal, 2003–07

Address: Forte de Santa Marta, 2750-342 Cascais, Portugal
Area: 435 m². Client: Câmara Municipal de Cascais. Cost: € 1.95 million
Collaborators: Sofia Chinita Janeiro, Filipe Boím

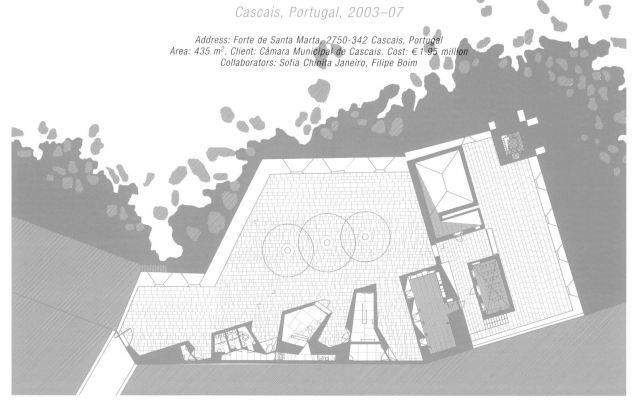

Built in 1868, the Santa Marta lighthouse has a 25-meter-high masonry tower painted in blue and white horizontal bands with a red lantern. It is adjacent to the ruins of the 17th-century Santa Marta fort. The lighthouse authority of Portugal turned the facility over to the City of Cascais for the creation of a museum dedicated to both the fort and the lighthouse, in 2000. It is set to the west of the Tagus Estuary on the Estoril coast near Lisbon. The museum is dedicated to four basic themes: the lighthouses of Portugal; the Santa Marta fort and lighthouse; lighthouses and navigation in general; and the functions of the lighthouse keeper. The architects state: "From the 17th century onwards the amassing of different plans for this place, the material and technological resources employed during each period, and the use of the existing heritage combined to create a series of conversions and extensions. Nevertheless, the site features architectonic units of unequivocal reading, disposed according to organizational principles that remain quite clear. The alteration and decay of some of its parts is the outcome of a process of natural selection that the project seeks to use to its benefit. Singling out the elements of greater permanence and poetic value, the proposal rebuilds a founding order with them and from them, encapsulating the memory of the elapsed time, and allowing for its new use as a museum of the lighthouse."

Der 1868 errichtete Leuchtturm Santa Marta ist ein 25 m hoher Mauerwerksbau mit weißen und blauen Querstreifen und einer roten Laterne. Er steht neben den Ruinen der Festung Santa Marta aus dem 17. Jahrhundert. Die für die Leuchttürme in Portugal zuständige Behörde überließ das Gebäude 2000 der Stadt Cascais für die Errichtung eines dem Fort und dem Leuchtturm gewidmeten Museums. Es steht westlich der Mündung des Tejo an der Costa do Estoril bei Lissabon. Das Museum ist vier Hauptthemen gewidmet: den Leuchttürmen Portugals, der Festung und dem Leuchtturm Santa Marta, Leuchttürmen und Navigation allgemein und den Aufgaben eines Leuchtturmwärters. Die Architekten erklären: „Bis ins 17. Jahrhundert zurückgehend, haben viele Planungen für diesen Standort, die in den verschiedenen Perioden verwendeten materiellen und technischen Ressourcen und die Nutzung des baulichen Bestands zu zahlreichen Umbauten und Erweiterungen geführt. Dennoch sind auf dem Gelände noch einzigartige, nach klaren Prinzipien angeordnete Architekturelemente erhalten geblieben. Veränderung und Verfall einiger Teile sind das Ergebnis eines natürlichen Selektionsprozesses, den die Planung positiv nutzen will. Der Entwurf stellt mit diesen Teilen eine bauliche Ordnung wieder her, indem er Elemente von bleibendem, poetischem Wert hervorhebt. Damit soll die Vergangenheit bewahrt werden und die neue Nutzung als Museum des Leuchtturms ermöglicht werden."

Construit en 1868, à l'ouest de l'estuaire du Tage sur la côte d'Estoril près de Lisbonne, le phare de Santa Marta se présente sous la forme d'une tour en maçonnerie de 25 mètres de haut, peinte de bandes horizontales bleues et blanches et surmontée d'une lanterne rouge. Il se dresse à proximité immédiate du fort de Santa Marta (XVIIe siècle). L'Autorité des phares portugais l'a confié à la ville de Cascais, en 2000, pour y créer un musée consacré à la fois au phare et au fort. La programmation se décline sur quatre thèmes : les phares portugais, le fort et le phare de Santa Marta, les phares et la navigation en général, ainsi que les fonctions du gardien de phare. « Depuis le XVIIe siècle, la multiplication des plans mis en œuvre pour ce lieu, les matériaux et les ressources technologiques utilisées à chaque période, et l'utilisation du patrimoine existant se sont combinés dans une succession de transformations et d'extensions. Néanmoins, le site présente des éléments architectoniques de lecture univoque, répartis selon des principes d'organisation qui restent assez clairs. L'altération et le délabrement de certaines parties est l'aboutissement d'un processus de sélection naturelle dont le projet s'est proposé de tirer profit. Faisant ressortir les éléments de permanence et de valeur poétique les plus marquants, la proposition reconstruit à partir d'eux un nouvel ordre fondateur, qui intègre la mémoire du temps écoulé et permet un nouvel usage : celui du musée du Phare », expliquent les architectes.

The existing lighthouse is seamlessly integrated into the new design, which stands out with its crisp, white lines from the rocky shoreline.

Der alte Leuchtturm wurde nahtlos in den neuen Entwurf integriert, der sich mit seinen scharfkantigen, weißen Formen von der felsigen Küste abhebt.

Le phare existant s'est intégré sans rupture dans le nouveau projet qui se détache de la côte rocheuse par son profil tendu d'un blanc éclatant.

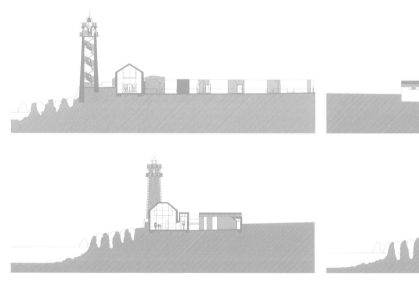

The architects have created essentially geometric volumes with few visible openings: because of their cladding and scale, these structures do not compete with the lighthouse, but rather draw attention to it.

Die Architekten entschieden sich für überwiegend geometrische Formen mit wenigen sichtbaren Öffnungen – durch ihre Verkleidung und ihren Maßstab konkurrieren die Neubauten nicht mit dem Leuchtturm, sondern machen vielmehr auf ihn aufmerksam.

Les architectes ont créé des volumes géométriques ponctués de quelques rares ouvertures. Conséquence de leur échelle et de leur habillage, ces constructions n'entrent pas en concurrence avec le phare, mais attirent plutôt l'attention sur lui.

JUN AOKI

Jun Aoki & Associates
#701 Harajuku New Royal Building
3–38–11 Jingumae
Shibuya-ku
Tokyo 150–0001
Japan

Fax: +81 3 3478 0508
Web: www.aokijun.com

Born in 1956 in Yokohama, Japan, **JUN AOKI** graduated from the University of Tokyo in 1980, completed the Master Course in Architecture two years later, and became a registered architect in 1986. He worked in the office of Arata Isozaki (1983–90) and created his own firm, Jun Aoki & Associates, in 1991. He has lectured at Tokyo University (1995–98), the Tokyo Institute of Technology (1998–2000), and the Tokyo National University of Fine Arts and Music (1999–2001). He won the Tokyo House Prize in 1994 for the H House, and the 1999 Architectural Institute of Japan Annual Award for the Fukushima Lagoon Museum. Jun Aoki has also worked actively as an artist, winning the Minister of Education's Art Encouragement Prize in 2005. His built work includes the H House (Katsuura, Chiba 1994); the O House (Setagaya, Tokyo, 1996); Yusuikan (swimming pool, Toyosaka, Niigata, 1997); the Fukushima Lagoon Museum (Toyosaka, Niigata, 1997); Louis Vuitton Nagoya (Nagoya, Aichi, 1999); Louis Vuitton Ginza (exterior design, Ginza, Tokyo, 2000); and Louis Vuitton New York (exterior design, New York, 2001), all in Japan unless stated otherwise. His Aomori Museum of Art (Aomori, Aomori, 2004–05, published here) opened in 2006.

Der 1956 in Yokohama, Japan, geborene **JUN AOKI** schloss 1980 sein Studium an der Universität von Tokio ab und absolvierte zwei Jahre später einen Masterkurs. 1986 wurde er als Architekt registriert. Er arbeitete im Büro von Arata Isozaki (1983–90) und gründete 1991 seine eigene Firma, Jun Aoki & Associates. Er hat an der Tokyo University (1995–98), dem Tokyo Institute of Technology (1998–2000) und der Tokyo National University of Fine Arts and Music (1999–2001) gelehrt. Er gewann 1994 den Tokyo House Prize für das Haus H und 1999 den Architectural Institute of Japan Annual Award für das Lagunen-Museum Fukushima. Jun Aoki arbeitet auch als freischaffender Künstler und wurde 2005 mit dem Minister of Education's Art Encouragement Prize ausgezeichnet. Zu seinen ausgeführten Bauten zählen das Haus H (Katsuura, Chiba, 1994), das Haus O (Setagaya, Tokio, 1996), Yusuikan (ein Schwimmbad, Toyosaka, Niigata, 1997), das Lagunen-Museum Fukushima (Toyosaka, Niigata, 1997), Louis Vuitton Nagoya (Nagoya, Aichi, 1999), Louis Vuitton Ginza (Außengestaltung, Ginza, Tokio, 2000) und Louis Vuitton New York (Außengestaltung, New York, 2001), alle in Japan, sofern nicht anders angegeben. Sein Kunstmuseum Aomori (Aomori, 2004–05, hier veröffentlicht) wurde 2006 eröffnet.

Né en 1956 à Yokohama (Japon), **JUN AOKI**, diplômé de l'université de Tokyo en 1980, a achevé son mastère en architecture deux ans plus tard, et a commencé à exercer en 1986. Il a travaillé dans l'agence d'Arata Isozaki (1983–90), puis a créé sa propre structure, Jun Aoki & Associates, en 1991. Il a enseigné à l'université de Tokyo (1995–98), à l'Institut de technologie de Tokyo (1998–2000) et à l'Université nationale des Beaux-arts et de la Musique (Tokyo, 1999–2001). Il a remporté le Tokyo House Prize en 1994 pour la maison H, et le Prix annuel de l'Institut d'architecture du Japon 1999 pour le musée du Lagon de Fukushima. Aoki a également mené une carrière d'artiste, remportant le Prix d'encouragement à l'art du ministère de l'Éducation en 2005. Parmi ses réalisations, pour la plupart au Japon : la maison H (Katsuura, Chiba 1994) ; la maison O (Setagaya, Tokyo, 1996) ; la piscine Yusuikan (Toyosaka, Niigata, 1997) ; le musée du Lagon de Fukushima (Toyosaka, Niigata, 1997) ; le magasin Louis Vuitton Nagoya (Nagoya, Aichi, 1999) ; le magasin Louis Vuitton Ginza (extérieur, Ginza, Tokyo, 2000) et le magasin Louis Vuitton New York (extérieur, New York, 2001). Son musée d'Art d'Aomori (Aomori, 2004–05), publié ici, a ouvert en 2006.

AOMORI MUSEUM OF ART

Aomori, Aomori, Japan, 2004–05

Address: 185 Chikano, Yasuta, Aomori City 038–0021, Japan, Tel: +81 17 783 3000, www.aomori-museum.jp
Area: 21 133 m². Client: Aomori Prefecture. Cost: not disclosed
Collaborators: Hisashi Houjin, Tetsuo Nishizawa, Kuniatsu Nemoto, Toru Murayama, Hiroaki Namba,
Shinichi Tokuda, Yuko Nagayama, Takayoshi Nagaishi, Daisuke Narushima

Within apparently modern volumes, the architect introduces continual surprises that give the building a decidedly contemporary feel. Here, otherwise blank walls are penetrated in several different ways.

In die eindeutig modernen Volumen hat der Architekt immer neue Überraschungsmomente eingefügt, die das Gebäude entschieden zeitgenössisch erscheinen lassen. Hier wurden die ansonsten nackten Wände in unterschiedlicher Weise durchbrochen.

Dans des volumes d'aspect moderniste, l'architecte a introduit de multiples surprises qui confèrent une présence résolument contemporaine. Ici, des murs neutres ponctués de différents types d'ouvertures.

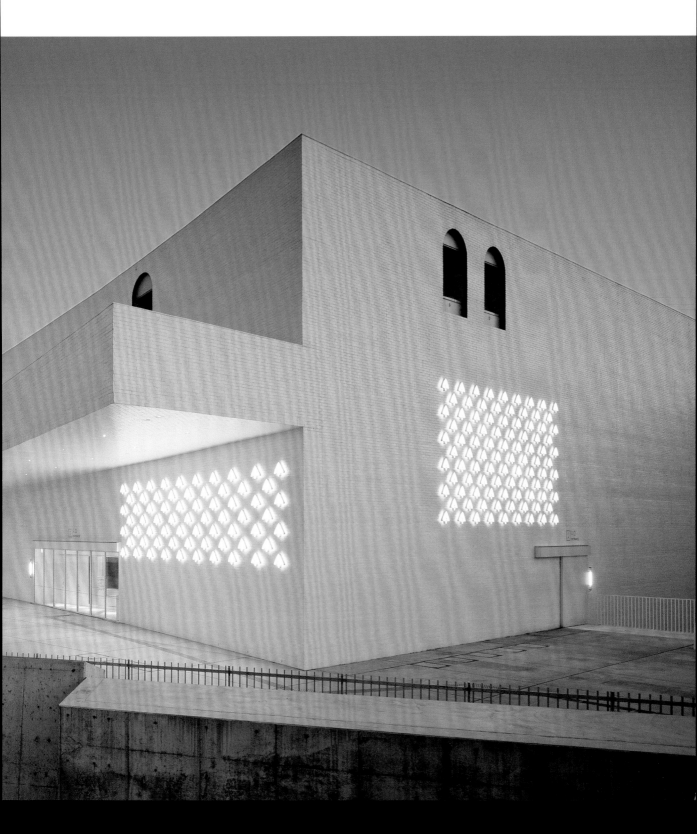

The Aomori Museum of Art is located near the archeological site of the Sannai Maruyama ruins, regarded as an important vestige of the Jomon Period (10 000–300 BC). The Aomori Prefecture government decided to use these ruins as the starting point of cultural development for the city. Jun Aoki's project was selected over 393 others in an international design competition held in 1999 and 2000. The architect states: "We suggested digging trenches horizontally and vertically into the ground as if they were ruins of an excavation site and defined geometric positive-negative profiles of the ground as the fundamental space of the museum." Construction of the museum was completed in September 2005, and it opened to the public in the summer of 2006. Jun Aoki describes the building as having "an even roof and an irregular bottom," covering the furrowed surface and facing upward. Jun Aoki has made extensive use here of brick and earth-based materials. The architect explains: "Applying a single rule, namely employing this positive-negative form, two kinds of exhibition rooms with completely different qualities of space are obtained: one is a white cube space built into the structure and one is between the ground surface and the bottom of the structure."

Das Kunstmuseum Aomori liegt nahe dem archäologischen Gelände der Ruinen von Sannai Maruyama, die als wichtige Überreste aus der Jomon-Periode (10 000–300 v. Chr.) gelten. Die Verwaltung der Präfektur Aomori beschloss, diese Ruinen als Ausgangspunkt für die kulturelle Entwicklung der Stadt zu nutzen. Jun Aokis Entwurf wurde aus über 393 eingereichten Projekten eines internationalen Wettbewerbs von 1999/2000 ausgewählt. Der Architekt erläutert: „Wir schlugen vor, horizontale und vertikale Gräben auszuheben, als wären es Reste einer Ausgrabungsstätte, und bestimmten geometrische positiv-negative Formen als wesentlichen Raum des Museums." Das Gebäude wurde im September 2005 fertiggestellt und im Sommer 2006 eröffnet. Jun Aoki schildert es als einen Bau „mit einem geraden Dach und einem ungeraden Unterteil", das die zerfurchte Außenfläche bedeckt und nach oben weist. Jun Aoki hat hierfür viel Backstein und Materialien aus Erde verwendet. Er erklärt dazu: „Indem wir nur einer Regel folgten, nämlich der Anwendung dieser positiv-negativen Form, erhielten wir zwei Arten von Ausstellungsbereichen mit völlig unterschiedlichen Qualitäten: einen weißen, kubischen Raum, der in die Struktur eingefügt wurde, und einen, der zwischen der Erdoberfläche und dem Unterteil der Konstruktion liegt."

Le musée d'Art d'Aomori est implanté à proximité du site archéologique des ruines de Sannai Maruyama, importants vestiges datant de la période Jomon (10 000–300 av. J.-C.). L'administration de la préfecture d'Aomori a décidé de faire de ce site le point de départ d'un projet de développement culturel de la ville. La proposition de Jun Aoki a été choisie parmi celles des 393 participants à un concours international organisé en 1999 et 2000. L'architecte a ainsi expliqué son projet : « Nous avons proposé de creuser dans le sol des tranchées horizontales et verticales, comme si c'étaient les ruines d'un site de fouille, et nous avons défini des profils géométriques positifs-négatifs du sol comme éléments fondateurs de ce musée ». La brique et les matériaux à base de terre ont également été abondamment utilisés. La construction s'est achevée en septembre 2005, et le bâtiment a été ouvert au public pendant l'été 2006. Jun Aoki parle d'un « toit régulier et une base irrégulière », recouvrant la surface égalisée et regardant vers le haut. Les architectes expliquent : « Par l'application d'une règle simple – l'emploi de la forme négative-positive –, nous avons obtenu deux types de salles d'exposition aux qualités spatiales complètement différentes. L'une est un volume cubique blanc intégré dans la structure, et l'autre se trouve entre la surface du sol et la base de la structure ».

With gestures such as the long stair-way that appears to go up through the ceiling of a generous space (above), the architect plays on space and volume in unexpected ways.

Mit Einfällen wie der langen Treppe, die scheinbar durch die Decke eines großzügigen Raumes stößt (oben), spielt der Architekt auf unerwartete Weise mit Raum und Volumen.

À travers des gestes comme ce grand escalier qui semble traverser le plafond d'une salle de proportions généreuses (ci-dessus), l'architecte joue sur l'espace et le volume de façons inattendues.

The Aomori Museum of Art is situated
next to an excavation site—the
Sannai Maruyama ruins (Jomon
Period, 10 000–300 BC), right—contrasting sharply with the museum's
contemporary collections (above).

Das Kunstmuseum Aomori befindet
sich neben einer Ausgrabungsstätte –
den Ruinen von Sannai Maruyama
(aus der Jomon-Periode, 10 000–300
v. Chr.), rechts –, die in starkem
Gegensatz zu den zeitgenössischen
Sammlungen des Museums (oben)
steht.

Le musée d'Art Aomori est adjacent
au site de fouilles des ruines de
Sannai Maruyama (période Jomon,
10 000–300 av. J.-C.), à droite, qui
contrastent fortement avec les collections d'art contemporain du musée
(ci-dessus).

Jun Aoki takes obvious pleasure in generating seemingly massive, opaque volumes that float in space, allowing visitors to pass through their solid mass.

Jun Aoki bildet offenbar gern scheinbar massive, lichtundurchlässige Volumen, die im Raum schweben und den Besuchern ermöglichen, diese zu durchschreiten.

Jun Aoki prend un plaisir évident à créer des volumes opaques d'apparence massive qui flottent dans l'espace, tout en faisant en sorte que les visiteurs puissent les franchir.

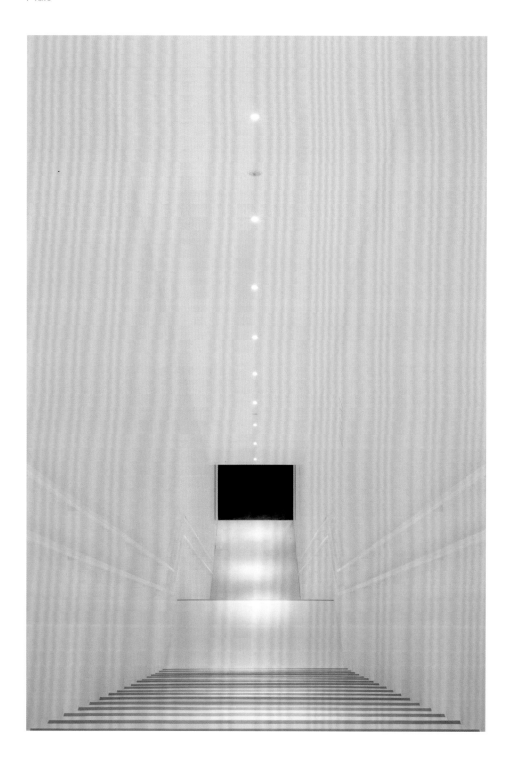

The extreme simplicity of Aoki as seen here is not really as close to minimalism as it might appear, instead generating feelings of disorientation or surprise.

Aokis hier erkennbare extreme Schlichtheit ist dem Minimalismus nicht so eng verwandt, wie es den Anschein hat. Vielmehr erzeugt sie das Gefühl von Desorientiertheit oder Überraschungsmomente.

L'extrême simplicité du langage d'Aoki qu'expriment ces images n'est pas vraiment aussi proche du minimalisme que l'on pourrait croire, mais génère plutôt des sentiments de désorientation ou de surprise.

The architect makes frequent use of
hovering masses that are, of course,
not as heavy as they might seem.
Light passes through and around
these blocks, making way for
generous exhibition areas.

Der Architekt arbeitet häufig mit
schwebenden Massen, die natürlich
nicht so schwer sind, wie sie wirken.
Das Licht dringt durch und führt um
diese Blocks, die großzügigen Ausstellungsbereichen Platz machen.

L'architecte utilise fréquemment des
masses suspendues qui ne sont pas
aussi lourdes qu'elles le paraissent.
La lumière traverse ou contourne ces
blocs qui laissent place à de généreux espaces d'exposition.

ARM

ARM
Level 11, 522 Flinders Lane
Melbourne, Victoria 3000
Australia

Tel: +61 3 8613 1888
Fax: +61 3 8613 1889
E-mail: arm.melb@a-r-m.com.au
Web: www.a-r-m.com.au

ARM, created in 1988, is named after its three founding directors, Stephen Ashton, Howard Raggatt, and Ian McDougall. They have since been joined by a fourth director, Tony Allen, while Neil Masterton was appointed Design Director in 2007. Stephen Ashton has degrees in architecture (B.Arch) and in business administration. Howard Raggatt received his M.Arch degree from RMIT University in Melbourne. He was appointed the first Adjunct Professor of Architecture at RMIT in 1993, where he and Ian McDougall developed the Master's course in Urban Design. Ian McDougall also received his architectural training at RMIT (B.Arch, M.Arch). He is Adjunct Professor of Architecture at RMIT and a Professor of Architecture and Urban Design at the University of Adelaide. Tony Allen received his B.Arch degree from the University of New South Wales. Their work includes Storey Hall, RMIT (Melbourne, 1996); the National Museum of Australia (Canberra, 2001); master planning for the Melbourne Docklands (1996–2004); the remodeling of the Melbourne Central Shopping Centre (2005); Albury Library Museum (Albury, New South Wales, 2006–07, published here); the Melbourne Recital Centre and MTC Theatre (2008); Perth Arena (Western Australia, under construction); and the Southbank Cultural Precinct Redevelopment (Melbourne, 2009–), all in Australia.

Der Name des 1988 gegründeten Büros **ARM** geht auf seine drei Gründer zurück: Stephen Ashton, Howard Raggatt und Ian McDougall. Inzwischen gibt es einen vierten Leiter, Tony Allen, und Neil Masterton ist seit 2007 Entwurfsdirektor. Stephen Ashton hat Studienabschlüsse in Architektur (B. Arch.) und Betriebswirtschaft. Howard Raggatt machte seinen M. Arch. an der Universität RMIT in Melbourne. 1993 wurde er zum ersten außerordentlichen Professor für Architektur am RMIT ernannt, wo er mit Ian McDougall den neuen Masterstudiengang für Städtebau begründete. Ian McDougall studierte ebenfalls am RMIT (B. Arch., M. Arch.). Er ist außerordentlicher Architekturprofessor am RMIT und Professor für Architektur und Städtebau an der University of Adelaide. Tony Allen erhielt den B. Arch. an der University of New South Wales. Zu den Bauten von ARM zählen die Storey Hall am RMIT (Melbourne, 1996), das National Museum of Australia (Canberra, 2001), der Masterplan für die Hafenanlagen von Melbourne (1996–2004), die Umgestaltung des Melbourne Central Shopping Centre (2005), das Albury Library Museum (Albury, New South Wales, 2006–07, hier veröffentlicht), das Recital Centre und MTC Theatre von Melbourne (2008), die Perth Arena (Westaustralien, im Bau) und die Sanierung des Kulturbezirks Southbank (Melbourne, 2009–), alle in Australien.

Le nom de l'agence **ARM**, créée en 1988, correspond à celui de ses trois directeurs fondateurs, Stephen Ashton, Howard Raggatt et Ian McDougall. Ils ont été rejoints par un quatrième directeur, Tony Allen, tandis que Neil Masterton était désigné directeur de conception en 2007. Stephen Ashton est diplômé en architecture (B.Arch) et en administration des affaires. Howard Raggatt est M.Arch de la RMIT University à Melbourne. Il a été le premier à être nommé professeur adjoint d'architecture à RMIT en 1993, où il a mis au point, avec Ian McDougall, le nouveau cours de mastère en urbanisme. Ian McDougall tient également sa formation architecturale de RMIT (B.Arch, M.Arch). Il a récemment été nommé professeur d'architecture et d'urbanisme à l'université d'Adelaide. Tony Allen est B.Arch (University of New South Wales). Parmi leurs réalisations, toutes en Australie: le Storey Hall, RMIT (Melbourne, 1996); le National Museum of Australia (Canberra, 2001); le plan directeur du Melbourne Docklands (1996–2004); la rénovation du centre commercial central de Melbourne (2005); le Albury Library Museum (Albury, Nouvelle-Galles du Sud, 2006–07), publié ici; le Melbourne Recital Centre et le MTC Theatre (2008); le Perth Arena (Australie-Occidentale, en construction) et la Southbank Cultural Precinct Redevelopment (Melbourne, 2009–).

ALBURY LIBRARY MUSEUM

Albury, New South Wales, Australia, 2006–07

Address: PO Box 323, Albury, NSW 2640, Australia, +61 2 6023 8333, www.alburycity.nsw.gov.au/librarymuseum
Area: 2890 m². Client: Albury City. Cost: €4 million
Collaborators: Ian McDougall, William Pritchard, Rhonda Mitchell, Andrew Lilleyman

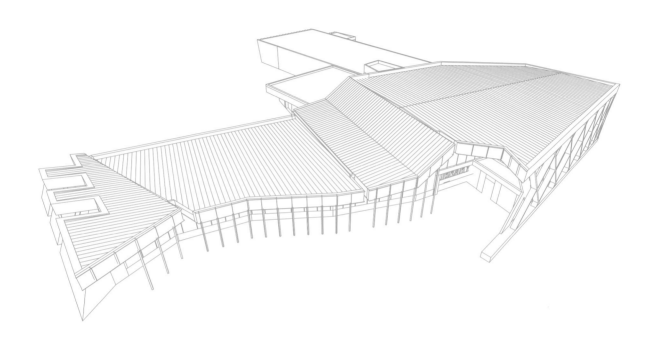

Selected by Albury City Council in 2003 to create a combined facility for the Albury Public Library and Albury Museum, the architects also took on the task of making this "a new type of public building," also providing community and IT facilities for the region. The structure has two wings, one for the library and one for the museum, as well as a common area "that houses staff, community, and the collaborative information hub." The architects state: "Our architectural vision for the building was to bring together reminiscences and almost familiar elements from the Albury region: the giant webbing of the railway bridge over the Murray, the banks, levees and trees of the surrounding landscape, the river course itself, the streetscape of the civic precinct, the coved cornices of a railway carriage, even the types of materials that one sees on the buildings in Albury. The scale of the building responds to its civic significance and draws from the adjacent existing street façades. All this is the palette through which we create the building."

Die vom Rat der Stadt Albury 2003 zur Planung eines gemeinsamen Gebäudes für die Stadtbücherei und das Museum ausgewählten Architekten sahen darin auch die Aufgabe, „ein öffentliches Gebäude neuen Typs" und zugleich Gemeinschafts- und IT-Einrichtungen für die Region zu errichten. Der Bau besteht aus zwei Trakten, einem für die Bibliothek und einem für das Museum, sowie einem gemeinschaftlichen Bereich, „der Mitarbeitern, der Gemeinde und als allgemeine Informationszentrale dient". Die Architekten erklären: „Wir stellten uns vor, dass das Gebäude Erinnerungen und vertraute Elemente aus der Region Albury zusammenführen sollte – das gewaltige Gitterwerk der Eisenbahnbrücke über den Murray, die Ufer, die Dämme und die Bäume der umgebenden Landschaft, den Flusslauf und das Straßennetz des Stadtbezirks, die gewölbten Dächer der Eisenbahnwaggons und sogar die verschiedenen Materialien der Bauten in Albury. Der Maßstab des Neubaus entspricht seiner städtischen Bedeutung und übernimmt Elemente der Fassadengestaltung benachbarter Bauten. Aus all diesen Elementen gestalteten wir das Gebäude."

Choisis par le conseil municipal d'Albury en 2003 pour créer un établissement commun à la bibliothèque publique et au musée de la ville, les architectes se sont également efforcés d'en faire « un nouveau type de bâtiment public », qui offre également à la région divers services communautaires, en particulier dans le domaine des technologies de l'information. Le bâtiment possède deux ailes, l'une pour la bibliothèque la seconde pour le musée, ainsi qu'une partie commune « qui abrite le personnel, les installations communales et la plate-forme d'information participative… Pour cette réalisation, notre vision architecturale a été de rapprocher des souvenirs et des éléments presque familiers de la région d'Albury : le maillage géant du pont de chemin de fer sur la Murray, les rives, les digues et les arbres du paysage environnant, le cours de la rivière, le paysage urbain du centre administratif, les corniches en queue d'aronde d'un wagon, et même le type de matériaux que l'on observe dans les constructions d'Albury. L'échelle du musée répond à sa signification civique et s'inspire des façades adjacentes. Tout cela constitue la palette à partir de laquelle nous avons créé ce bâtiment », expliquent les architectes.

The volumes of the museum are folded into a flowing continuity that can be seen clearly in the image to the right and the drawing on the left page. The interior view below betrays a rather surprising complexity.

Die Bereiche des Museums bilden einen fließenden Übergang, wie das Bild rechts und die Zeichnung auf der linken Seite deutlich machen. Die Innenaufnahme unten verrät dagegen eine überraschende räumliche Vielfalt.

Les volumes du musée sont pliés en un flux continu, clairement observable dans les images de droite et le dessin de la page de gauche. La vue intérieure, en bas, traduit une complexité assez surprenante.

Library areas, such as the "kidspace" above, are cheerful and bright, while the entrance zone (above, right) is high and generous.

Die Bibliotheksräume, zum Beispiel der „kidspace" oben, sind fröhlich und hell gestaltet, der Eingangsbereich dagegen (oben, rechts) ist großzügig und hoch.

La zone de la librairie comme le « kidspace » (espace des enfants) ci-dessus sont chaleureux et lumineux tandis que l'entrée (ci-dessus, à droite) affiche son ampleur par la hauteur de ses plafonds.

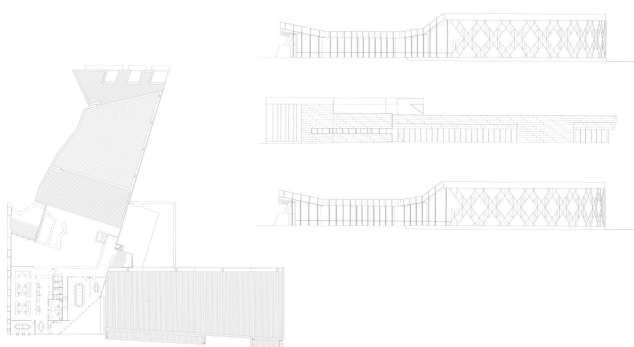

SHIGERU BAN

Shigeru Ban Architects
5–2–4 Matsubara
Setagaya-ku
Tokyo 156–0043
Japan

Tel: +81 3 3324 6760
Fax: +81 3 3324 6789
E-mail: tokyo@shigerubanarchitects.com
Web: www.shigerubanarchitects.com

Born in 1957 in Tokyo, **SHIGERU BAN** studied at SCI-Arc from 1977 to 1980. He then attended the Cooper Union School of Architecture, where he studied under John Hejduk (1980–82). He worked in the office of Arata Isozaki (1982–83), before founding his own firm in Tokyo in 1985. His work includes numerous exhibition designs (such as those for the Alvar Aalto show at the Axis Gallery, Tokyo, 1986). His buildings include the Odawara Pavilion (Kanagawa, 1990); the Paper Gallery (Tokyo, 1994); the Paper House (Lake Yamanaka, 1995); and the Paper Church (Takatori, Hyogo, 1995), all in Japan. He has also designed ephemeral structures such as his Paper Refugee Shelter made with plastic sheets and paper tubes for the United Nations High Commissioner for Refugees (UNHCR). He designed the Japanese Pavilion at Expo 2000 in Hanover. He installed his Paper Temporary Studio on top of the Centre Pompidou in Paris to work on the new Centre Pompidou-Metz (Metz, France, 2006–10, published here). Other recent work includes the Papertainer Museum (Seoul Olympic Park, Songpa-Gu, South Korea, 2003–06); the Nicolas G. Hayek Center (Tokyo, 2005–07); the Takatori Church (Kobe, Hyogo, 2005–07), the last two in Japan; and the disaster relief Post-Tsunami Rehabilitation Houses (Kirinda, Hambantota, Sri Lanka, 2005–07). Recent work includes Hanegi Forest Annex (Setagaya, Tokyo, 2004); Mul(ti)houses (Mulhouse, France, 2001–05); and the Metal Shutter Houses on West 19th Street in New York (New York, 2009).

Der 1957 in Tokio geborene **SHIGERU BAN** studierte von 1977 bis 1980 am Southern California Institute of Architecture (SCI-Arc) und anschließend bis 1982 bei John Hejduk an der Cooper Union School of Architecture. Bevor er 1985 in Tokio ein eigenes Büro gründete, arbeitete er bei Arata Isozaki (1982–83). Zu seinen Werken zählen viele Ausstellungsarchitekturen (über Alvar Aalto in der Galerie Axis, Tokio, 1986) und u. a. folgende Bauwerke: der Odawara-Pavillon (Kanagawa, 1990), eine Galerie aus Papier (Tokio, 1994), ein Haus aus Papier (Yamanaka-See, 1995) und eine Kirche aus Papier (Takatori, Hyogo, 1995), alle in Japan. Er hat auch temporäre Bauten geplant, z. B. für den Hohen Flüchtlingskommissar der Vereinten Nationen (UNHCR) einen Schutzbau für Flüchtlinge, der aus Plastikfolie und Papprohren besteht. Er entwarf den japanischen Pavillon für die Expo 2000 in Hannover und installierte auf dem Centre Pompidou in Paris aus Papier sein temporäres Atelier, um dort am neuen Centre Pompidou-Metz (Metz, 2006–10, hier veröffentlicht) zu arbeiten. Zu seinen neueren Werken zählen das Papertainer Museum (Olympiapark Seoul, Songpa-Gu, Südkorea, 2003–06), das Nicolas G. Hayek Center (Tokio, 2005–07), die Kirche in Takatori (Kobe, Hyogo, 2005–07), beide in Japan, sowie Einrichtungen für die Katastrophenhilfe nach der Tsunami-Katastrophe (Kirinda, Hambantota, Sri Lanka, 2005–07). Neuere Bauwerke sind auch ein Anbau im Hanegi-Wald (Setagaya, Tokio, 2004), die Mul(ti)houses (Mulhouse, Frankreich, 2001–05) und das Metal Shutter House in der West 19th Street in New York (2009).

Né en 1957 à Tokyo, **SHIGERU BAN** a étudié à SCI-Arc de 1977 à 1980 et à la Cooper Union School of Architecture, auprès de John Hejduk (1980–82). Il a travaillé dans l'agence d'Arata Isozaki (1982–83), avant de fonder la sienne à Tokyo en 1985. Son œuvre comprend de nombreuses installations d'expositions (Alvar Aalto Show à la galérie Axis, Tokyo, 1986) et des bâtiments comme le pavillon Odawara (Kanagawa, 1990) ; une galerie de papier (Tokyo, 1994) ; une maison de papier (lac Yamanaka, 1995) et une église de papier (Takatori, Hyogo, 1995), tous au Japon. Il a également conçu des structures éphémères comme son abri en papier pour réfugiés fait de film plastique et tubes de carton pour le Haut Commissariat des Nations Unies pour les réfugiés (UNHCR). Il a dessiné le pavillon japonais pour Expo 2000 à Hanovre. Son atelier temporaire en tubes de carton a été installé au sommet du Centre Pompidou à Paris, annexe de son agence pendant le chantier du nouveau Centre Pompidou-Metz (Metz, France, 2006–10), publié ici. Parmi ses autres réalisations récentes : Le musée Papertainer (Parc olympique de Séoul, Singpa-Gu, Corée du Sud, 2003–06) ; le Centre Nicolas G. Hayek (Tokyo, 2005–07) ; l'église de Takatori (Kobe, Hyogo, 2005–07) et les maisons de la reconstruction après le tsunami (Kirinda, Hambantota, Sri Lanka, 2005–07) ; l'annexe de la forêt d'Hanegi (Setagaya, Tokyo, 2004) ; les Mul(ti)houses (Mulhouse, France, 2001–05) et les Metal Shutter Houses sur West 19th Street à New York (2009).

CENTRE POMPIDOU-METZ

Metz, France, 2006–10

*Address: Avenue de l'Amphithéâtre, 57000 Metz, France, +33 3 8756 5524, www.centrepompidou-metz.fr
Area: 11 176 m². Client: City of Metz. Cost: not disclosed
Collaboration: Jean de Gastines, Philip Gumuchdjian*

Shigeru Ban Architects (Tokyo) in association with Jean de Gastines (Paris) and Philip Gumuchdjian (London) won the design competition to build a new Centre Pompidou in the city of Metz on November 26, 2003. In this instance, Ban's surprising woven timber roof, based on a hexagonal pattern, was the most visible innovation, but his proposal to suspend three 90 x 15-meter gallery "tubes" above the required Grand Nef (nave) and Forum spaces was also unexpected and inventive. Working at the time of the competition on the Japan Pavilion (Expo 2000, Hanover, Germany, 1999–2000), Shigeru Ban purchased a Chinese hat in a crafts shop in Paris in 1998. "I was astonished at how architectonic it was," says Shigeru Ban. "The structure is made of bamboo, and there is a layer of oil-paper for waterproofing. There is also a layer of dry leaves for insulation. It is just like a roof for a building. Since I bought this hat, I wanted to design a roof in a similar manner." Ban was anxious to participate in the original competition because of the involvement of the Centre Pompidou, whose architecture he had admired as being audacious for its time. Aside from its spectacular interior spaces, the Centre Pompidou-Metz is intended to open broadly onto its surrounding piazza, echoing the architect's frequent interest in the ambiguity of interior and exterior.

Shigeru Ban Architects (Tokio) in Zusammenarbeit mit Jean de Gastines (Paris) und Philip Gumuchdjian (London) gewannen am 26. November 2003 den Wettbewerb für ein neues Centre Pompidou in der Stadt Metz. In diesem Fall war Bans erstaunliches geflochtenes Holzdach, das auf einem sechseckigen System basiert, die auffallendste Innovation. Doch auch sein Vorschlag, drei 90 x 15 m große Galerie-„Röhren" über dem geforderten Grand Nef (Schiff) und dem Forum aufzuhängen, war überraschend und einfallsreich. Shigeru Ban, der damals am Wettbewerb für den japanischen Pavillon (Expo 2000, Hannover, 1999–2000) arbeitete, kaufte 1998 in einem Pariser Kunstgewerbegeschäft einen chinesischen Hut: „Ich war erstaunt, wie architektonisch er war", sagt der Architekt. „Er besteht aus Bambus, mit einer wasserdichten Schicht aus Ölpapier darüber. Zur Isolierung hat er auch eine Schicht aus getrockneten Blättern. Das ist genauso wie bei einem Hausdach. Seit ich diesen Hut gekauft habe, wollte ich ein Dach auf ähnliche Weise planen." Ban wollte unbedingt an dem Wettbewerb teilnehmen, weil er vom Centre Pompidou ausgelobt worden war, das er für seine damals kühne Architektur bewunderte. Von seinen spektakulären Innenräumen abgesehen, soll das Centre Pompidou-Metz sich weit zur umgebenden Piazza öffnen und die anhaltende Auseinandersetzung des Architekten mit der Doppeldeutigkeit von Innen- und Außenraum spiegeln.

Shigeru Ban Architects (Tokyo) en association avec Jean de Gastines (Paris) et Philip Gumuchdjian (Londres) a remporté le concours pour la construction d'une antenne du Centre Pompidou à Metz le 26 novembre 2003. Si sa surprenante couverture en entrelacs de bois de forme hexagonale est l'innovation la plus perceptible, la suspension des trois galeries tubulaires de 90 x 15 mètres au-dessus de la grande nef et du forum prévus par le programme est une solution tout aussi novatrice et inattendue. Travaillant au moment du concours sur le projet du Pavillon japonais d'Expo 2000 (Hanovre, Allemagne, 1999–2000), Ban avait acheté un chapeau de paille dans une boutique d'artisanat chinois : « …Ce chapeau m'a surpris par son caractère architectonique. C'est une structure en bambou, sur laquelle vient se tendre une feuille de papier huilé imperméable. Des feuilles séchées renforcent également l'isolation. C'est exactement comme un toit pour le bâtiment. Depuis cet achat, j'ai eu envie de construire un toit de nature similaire. » Ban avait envie de participer à ce concours parce qu'il appréciait l'implication du Centre Pompidou dont il avait admiré l'architecture, si audacieuse pour son temps. Le Centre Pompidou-Metz, aux volumes intérieurs spectaculaires, devrait s'ouvrir sur une place qui illustre l'intérêt que porte souvent Ban aux ambiguïtés entre intérieur et extérieur.

Drawings above show the suspended exhibition "tubes."

Die Zeichnungen oben zeigen die aufgehängten Ausstellungs-„Rohre".

Les plans ci-dessous illustrent les « tubes » d'exposition suspendus.

The roof of the Centre Pompidou-Metz, inspired by a Chinese hat bought by the architect, is seen in a virtual view (above) and under construction in 2009 (below).

Das Dach des Centre Pompidou-Metz, inspiriert von einem chinesischen Hut, den der Architekt sich gekauft hatte, wird hier als virtuelle Ansicht (oben) und im Bau 2009 (unten) gezeigt.

La toiture du Centre Pompidou-Metz, inspirée d'un chapeau chinois acheté un jour par l'architecte, vue ici en image virtuelle (ci-dessus) et en construction en 2009 (ci-dessous).

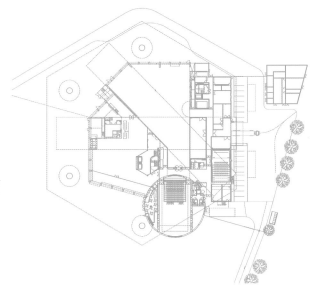

The architect's idea was to have generous spaces that would be covered and yet open out onto the surrounding square. Exhibition areas allow for large-scale works of art to be installed.

Das Ziel des Architekten war es, großzügige Räume zu schaffen, die sowohl überdacht als auch zum benachbarten Platz geöffnet sind. Die Ausstellungsbereiche bieten Platz zur Installation großmaßstäblicher Kunstwerke.

L'idée de l'architecte était de créer de généreux volumes qui soient à la fois couverts et ouverts sur la place entourant le bâtiment. Les espaces d'exposition permettent de présenter des œuvres d'art de grandes dimensions.

The wooden pattern of the museum's roof is visible in these images, soaring above a restaurant space. Despite its apparent irregularity, the roof design is generated from a repetitive pattern.

Die hölzerne Struktur des Museumsdachs über dem Restaurantbereich ist auf diesen Bildern sichtbar. Trotz seiner scheinbaren Unregelmäßigkeit liegt ihm ein gleichmäßiges System zugrunde.

La structure en bois de la couverture visible au-dessus du restaurant. Malgré l'irrégularité apparente de sa forme, la toiture suit un motif répétitif.

Ozeaneum ▶

BEHNISCH ARCHITEKTEN

Behnisch Architekten / Rotebühlstr. 163 A
70197 Stuttgart / Germany
Tel: +49 711 60 77 20 / Fax: +49 711 607 72 99
E-mail: ba@behnisch.com / Web: www.behnisch.com

Born in 1922 in Dresden, Germany, Günter Behnisch grew up in Dresden and in Chemnitz. He studied architecture at the Technical University of Stuttgart (1947–51, Dipl.-Ing.), before setting up his own office in 1952. In 1966, he created the firm of Behnisch & Partner, and from 1967 to 1987, he was a Professor for Design, Industrial Buildings and Planning, and Director of the Institute for Building Standardization at the Technical University, Darmstadt. In 1989, he established an office in Stuttgart with his son Stefan. This office became independent in 1991 and is now called **BEHNISCH ARCHITEKTEN**, with partners Stefan Behnisch, David Cook, and Martin Haas. Stefan Behnisch was born in 1957 in Stuttgart. He studied philosophy at the Philosophische Hochschule der Jesuiten, Munich (1976–79), economics at the Ludwig Maximilian University, Munich, and architecture in Karlsruhe (1979–87). He worked at Stephen Woolley & Associates (Venice, California, 1984–85), and has been a principal partner at Behnisch since 1992. Born in Manchester in 1966, David Cook studied architecture at the Polytechnic in Manchester and obtained his diploma at the University of East London in 1992. From 1993, he has worked with Behnisch Architekten and, since 2006, has been a partner in the office. Together with Stefan Behnisch and Martin Haas, he has been heading the practice Behnisch Architekten since 2006. Martin Haas was born in 1967 in Waldshut. After working as a cameraman, he began studying architecture at the Technical University of Stuttgart in 1988, where he obtained his diploma in 1995. He studied at South Bank University, London, worked with Alan Brookes Assoc. in London, and produced advertising films. In 1995, he started working with Behnisch Architekten and has been a partner in the firm since 2006.

Dipl.-Ing. Günter Behnisch, 1922 in Dresden geboren, wuchs in Dresden und Chemnitz auf. Er studierte von 1947 bis 1951 Architektur an der Technischen Hochschule Stuttgart und eröffnete 1952 sein eigenes Büro. 1966 gründete er die Firma Behnisch & Partner und war von 1967 bis 1987 Professor für Entwurf, Industriebau und Baugestaltung sowie Leiter des Instituts für Standardisierung im Bauen an der Technischen Universität Darmstadt. 1989 gründete er mit seinem Sohn Stefan ein Zweigbüro in Stuttgart. Es wurde 1991 unabhängig und heißt heute **BEHNISCH ARCHITEKTEN** mit den Partnern Stefan Behnisch, David Cook und Martin Haas. Stefan Behnisch wurde 1957 in Stuttgart geboren. Er studierte Philosophie an der Philosophischen Hochschule der Jesuiten in München (1976–79), Volkswirtschaft an der Ludwig-Maximilians-Universität in München und Architektur in Karlsruhe (1979–87). Er arbeitete bei Stephen Woolley & Associates (Venice, Kalifornien, 1984–85) und ist seit 1992 leitender Partner bei Behnisch Architekten. Der 1966 in Manchester geborene David Cook studierte Architektur am Polytechnic in Manchester und machte 1992 sein Diplom an der University of East London. Seit 1993 arbeitet er bei Behnisch Architekten. Mit Stefan Behnisch und Martin Haas leitet er Behnisch Architekten seit 2006. Martin Haas wurde 1967 in Waldshut geboren. Nach seiner Tätigkeit als Kameramann studierte er ab 1988 Architektur an der Technischen Universität Stuttgart, wo er 1995 sein Diplom erhielt. Er studierte außerdem an der South Bank University in London, war bei Alan Brookes Assoc. in London tätig und produzierte Werbefilme. Seit 1995 arbeitet er bei Behnisch Architekten und ist seit 2006 Teilhaber des Büros.

Né en 1922 à Dresde (Allemagne), Günter Behnisch a été élevé dans cette ville et à Chemnitz. Il a étudié l'architecture de 1947 à 1951 à l'Université polytechnique de Stuttgart (Dipl.-Ing.), avant de créer son agence en 1952. En 1966, il fonde Behnisch & Partner et, de 1967 à 1987, est professeur de conception, de conception d'immeubles industriels et d'urbanisme, ainsi que directeur de l'Institut de standardisation de la construction à l'Université polytechnique de Darmstadt. En 1989, il ouvre une agence à Stuttgart, avec son fils Stefan. Ce bureau, indépendant en 1991, s'appelle aujourd'hui **BEHNISCH ARCHITEKTEN**, et compte trois associés, Stefan Behnisch, David Cook, et Martin Haas. Stefan Behnisch, né en 1957 à Stuttgart, a étudié la philosophie à la Philosophische Hochschule der Jesuiten à Munich (1976–79), l'économie à l'université Ludwig Maximilian, également à Munich, et l'architecture à Karlsruhe (1979–87), et est partenaire principal de Behnisch depuis 1992. Né à Manchester en 1966, David Cook a étudié l'architecture à Manchester Polytechnic et obtenu son diplôme de l'université d'East London en 1992. Depuis 1993 il travaille pour Behnisch Architekten dont il est devenu partenaire en 2006. Avec Stefan Behnisch et Martin Haas, il dirige l'agence Behnisch Architekten depuis 2006. Martin Haas est né en 1967 à Waldshut. Après avoir travaillé comme cameraman, il a commencé à étudier l'architecture à l'Université technique de Stuttgart en 1988, dont il est sorti diplômé en 1995. Il a également étudié à la South Bank University (Londres), travaillé pour Alan Brookes Assoc. à Londres, et produit des films publicitaires. Il a débuté chez Behnisch Architekten en 1995, dont il est devenu partenaire en 2006.

OZEANEUM

German Oceanographic Museum, Stralsund, Germany, 2005–08

Hafenstraße 11, 18439 Stralsund, +49 3831 2650-610, www.ozeaneum.de
Area: 8700 m². Client: Deutsches Meeresmuseum Stralsund. Cost: €60 million

This museum complex includes aquariums, exhibitions about the Baltic Sea, the world's oceans and marine research, as well as a special display on "Giants of the Sea." Günter Behnisch's practice Behnisch & Partner was responsible for the competition entry for the Ozeaneum, then the project was developed further by Behnisch Architekten. The architects describe their task: "The competition brief posed a diverse range of challenges: this was to be a technically and architecturally ambitious natural history museum complex incorporating large aquaria; a modern landmark facility that was to be integrated in the largely intact urban environment of a traditional Hanseatic city, and optimally aligned with warehouses and granaries built in the course of the port island site's development in the 19th century. Design proposals were also to take into account the German Oceanographic Museum's educational remit, namely to familiarize visitors with underwater flora and fauna and the importance of conserving their natural habitats." The site is on the northern port island of Stralsund, in an area called Quartier 66, and the project clearly "relates to the sea, rather than to the buildings of the old town." The museum is entered through a new harbor promenade, with a ground-level foyer containing a shop, a café, and services. The three main exhibition spaces are located above ground level, reached via a 30-meter-high suspended escalator that crosses the foyer. Two aquariums on the inland side of the site are devoted to the Baltic and North Seas. The exterior is marked by steel "ribbons reminiscent of sails." One of three historic warehouses on the site has been incorporated into the complex and houses multipurpose space and the museum administration.

Dieser Museumskomplex enthält Aquarien, Ausstellungen über die Ostsee, die Weltmeere und Meeresforschung sowie eine besondere Schau über die „Riesen der Meere". Günter Behnischs Büro Behnisch & Partner war für den Wettbewerbsbeitrag verantwortlich, danach wurde das Projekt von Behnisch Architekten weiterentwickelt. Die Architekten beschreiben ihre Aufgabe wie folgt: „Die Wettbewerbsausschreibung stellte verschiedene Herausforderungen: Man wünschte ein technisch und architektonisch anspruchsvolles naturgeschichtliches Museum mit großen Aquarien – eine moderne Anlage, die als Wahrzeichen dienen sollte und sich sowohl in die weitgehend intakte Struktur der historischen Hansestadt als auch optimal in die Bebauung der Hafeninsel mit Speichern und Lagerhäusern aus dem 19. Jahrhundert einfügen sollte. Die Entwürfe sollten auch die pädagogische Aufgabe des Deutschen Meeresmuseums berücksichtigen, das heißt die Besucher mit der Unterwasserflora und -fauna und der Notwendigkeit, diese natürlichen Lebensräume zu erhalten, vertraut machen." Das Grundstück liegt auf der nördlichen Hafeninsel von Stralsund, im sogenannten Quartier 66, und der Entwurf bezieht sich eindeutig „auf die See und nicht auf die Bauten der Altstadt". Das Museum wird von einer neuen Hafenpromenade erschlossen. Das Foyer im Erdgeschoss enthält einen Laden, ein Café und Dienstleistungsbereiche. Die drei großen Ausstellungsräume liegen darüber und werden über eine 30 m lange, aufgehängte Rolltreppe erreicht, die das Foyer durchquert. Zwei Aquarien auf der Landseite des Grundstücks sind der Ost- bzw. der Nordsee gewidmet. Das Äußere kennzeichnen stählerne „Bänder, die an Segel erinnern". Eins der drei historischen Lagerhäuser auf dem Gelände wurde in die Anlage integriert und enthält Mehrzweckbereiche und Räume für die Museumsverwaltung.

Ce complexe muséal comprend des aquariums, des salles d'exposition sur la mer Baltique, le monde des océans et la recherche marine, ainsi qu'une présentation spéciale sur le thème des « géants de la mer ». L'agence de Günther Behnisch, Behnisch & Partner, a été l'auteur de la proposition pour le concours de l'Ozeaneum, mais le projet a été développé par Behnisch Architekten. Les architectes décrivent ainsi leur intervention : « Le programme du concours posait différents types de défis. Ce devait être un complexe de musée d'histoire naturelle techniquement et architecturalement ambitieux, intégrant de vastes aquariums, une installation monumentale moderne intégrée dans l'environnement urbain en grande partie intact d'une ville hanséatique traditionnelle, et le tout harmonieusement aligné sur les entrepôts et greniers datant du développement du port au XIXe siècle. Nos propositions devaient également prendre en compte la fonction éducative du Musée océanographique, et, en particulier, la familiarisation des visiteurs avec la flore et la faune aquatiques, ainsi que l'importance de la sauvegarde des habitats naturels ». Le site se trouve sur l'île nord du port de Stralsund dans une zone appelée « Quartier 66 » et le projet est donc nettement « plus en relation avec la mer qu'avec les constructions de la vieille ville ». On pénètre dans le musée par une nouvelle promenade portuaire. Le rez-de-chaussée contient un hall d'accueil, une boutique, un café et des installations de service. Les trois volumes d'exposition principaux, situés en étage, sont accessibles par un escalier mécanique suspendu de 30 mètres de long, qui traverse le hall. Les deux aquariums du côté du continent sont consacrés à la mer Baltique et à la mer du Nord. L'extérieur se caractérise par la présence de « rubans (d'acier) rappelant des voiles ». L'un des trois entrepôts présents sur le site a été incorporé dans le complexe et abrite à la fois un espace polyvalent et l'administration du musée.

With its sweeping white curves, the Ozeaneum stands out sharply from the older buildings that surround it, and yet the new architecture seems to enfold the existing structures.

Mit seinen schwungvollen, weißen Kurven hebt sich das Ozeaneum deutlich von den Altbauten seiner Umgebung ab; dennoch scheint die neue Architektur den baulichen Bestand zu umfassen.

Les amples courbes blanches de l'Ozeaneum se détachent avec force des constructions anciennes qui l'entourent. Dans le même temps cette architecture nouvelle semble presque engober les bâtiments existants.

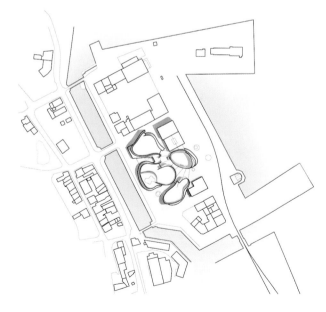

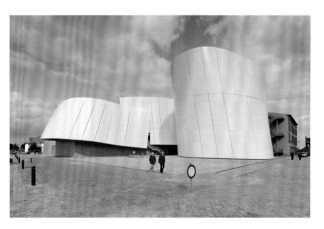

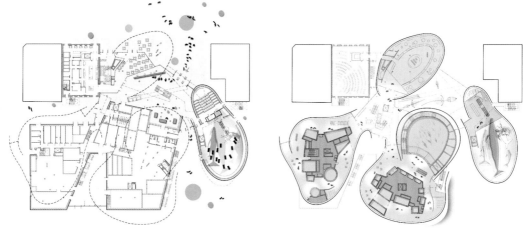

The amoeboid forms of the plan (left page, bottom) allow for different environments, ranging from darker, more intimate spaces, such as the ones above, to soaring, bright areas, which were logically placed in the visitor's path.

Die amöbenartigen Formen des Grundrisses (linke Seite unten) lassen unterschiedliche Bereiche entstehen, von dunkleren, intimeren Räumen wie den oben gezeigten bis zu den groß-zügigen, hellen, die logischerweise am Besucherweg liegen.

Les formes amibiennes du plan (page de gauche, en bas) se prêtent à dif-férents environnements, allant d'es-paces assez sombres et plus intimes, comme ceux présentés ci-dessus, à d'amples volumes lumineux qui ryth-ment rationnellement les déplace-ments du visiteur (page de gauche).

Part of the exhibition space of the Ozeaneum is devoted to "giants of the sea," seen here as if swimming in their natural environment above visitors who can lie down as they observe.

Einige Ausstellungsbereiche des Ozeaneums sind, wie hier gezeigt, den „Riesen der Meere" gewidmet, als würden sie in ihrer natürlichen Umgebung über den Besuchern schwimmen, die sich zu deren Beobachtung hinlegen können.

Une partie des expositions de l'Ozeaneum est consacrée aux « géants de la mer », immobilisés ici dans leur environnement naturel au-dessus des visiteurs qui peuvent même les observer couchés.

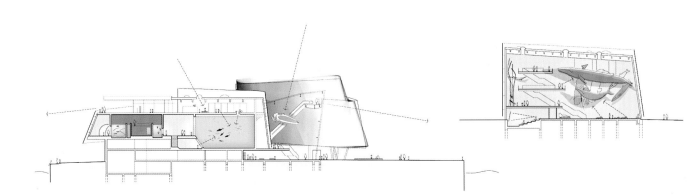

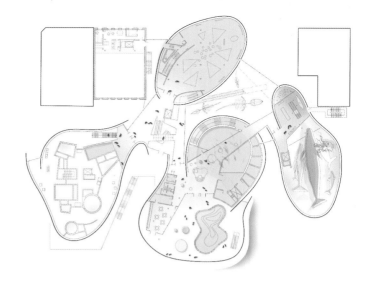

DAVID CHIPPERFIELD

David Chipperfield Architects Ltd.
1A Cobham Mews / Agar Grove / London NW1 9SB / UK
Tel: +44 207 267 94 22 / Fax: +44 207 172 67 93 47
E-mail: info@davidchipperfield.co.uk / Web: www.davidchipperfield.com

David Chipperfield Architects, Gesellschaft von Architekten mbH
Joachimstr. 11 / 10119 Berlin / Germany
Tel: +49 30 280 170 0 / Fax: +49 30 280 170 15
E-mail: info@davidchipperfield.de

Born in London in 1953, **DAVID CHIPPERFIELD** obtained his Diploma in Architecture from the Architectural Association (AA, London, 1977). He worked in the offices of Norman Foster and Richard Rogers, before establishing David Chipperfield Architects (London, 1984). Built work includes the Arnolfini Arts Center (Bristol, 1987); the Plant Gallery and Central Hall of the Natural History Museum (London, 1993); the River and Rowing Museum (Henley-on-Thames, 1996), all in the UK. His recent work includes the Landeszentralbank (Gera, Germany, 1994–2001); the Figge Art Museum (Davenport, Iowa, USA, 2005); the Museum of Modern Literature (Marbach, Germany, 2006); the America's Cup Building "Veles et Vents" (Valencia, Spain, 2006); and the Ansaldo City of Cultures (Milan, Italy, 2000–07). Recently he has completed the Liangzhu Culture Museum (Hangzhou, China, 2003–08, published here); the Kivik Art Centre Pavilion (Kivik, Sweden, 2007–08, with Antony Gormley); the reconstruction of the Neues Museum (Berlin, Germany, 1997–2009, published here); the Anchorage Museum at Rasmuson Center (Anchorage, Alaska, USA, 2003–09); and the design of numerous Dolce & Gabbana shops beginning in 1999. Current works include the San Michele Cemetery (Venice, Italy, 1998–2013); a new entrance building to Berlin's Museum Island (Germany); the Palace of Justice in Salerno (Italy); the Hepworth Wakefield (UK); the Turner Contemporary Gallery in Margate (UK); the expansion of the Saint Louis Art Museum (USA); the Aust-Agder Cultural Historic Centre in Arendal (Norway); and a new MBA building for the HEC Paris School of Management (France).

Der 1953 in London geborene **DAVID CHIPPERFIELD** erhielt sein Architekturdiplom 1977 an der Architectural Association (AA, London). Er arbeitete in den Büros von Norman Foster und Richard Rogers, bevor er 1984 in London David Chipperfield Architects gründete. Zu seinen ausgeführten Bauten zählen das Arnolfini Arts Center (Bristol, 1987), die Plant Gallery und zentrale Halle des Natural History Museum (London, 1993), das River and Rowing Museum (Henley-on-Thames, 1996), alle in Großbritannien. Seine neueren Bauten sind die Landeszentralbank (Gera, Deutschland, 1994–2001), das Figge Art Museum (Davenport, Iowa, 2005), das Literaturmuseum der Moderne (Marbach, Deutschland, 2006), das America's Cup Building „Veles et Vents" (Valencia, 2006) und die Stadt der Kulturen Ansaldo (Mailand, 2000–07). In jüngster Zeit wurden fertiggestellt: das Kulturmuseum Liangzhu (Hangzhou, China, 2003–08, hier veröffentlicht), der Pavillon des Kivik Arts Centre (Kivik, Schweden, 2007–08, mit Antony Gormley), die Rekonstruktion des Neuen Museums (Berlin, 1997–2009, hier veröffentlicht), das Anchorage Museum im Rasmuson Center (Anchorage, Alaska, 2003–09) und seit 1999 zahlreiche Läden für Dolce & Gabbana. In Arbeit befinden sich derzeit der Friedhof San Michele (Venedig, 1998–2013), ein neues Eingangsgebäude für die Museumsinsel in Berlin, der Justizpalast in Salerno (Italien), das Kunstmuseum Hepworth in Wakefield (Großbritannien), die Turner Contemporary Gallery in Margate (Großbritannien), die Erweiterung des Saint Louis Art Museum (USA), das Kulturhistorische Zentrum Aust-Agder in Arendal (Norwegen) und ein neues Gebäude für die Betriebswirtschaftslehre der Managementschule HEC in Paris.

Né à Londres en 1953, **DAVID CHIPPERFIELD** est diplômé en architecture de l'Architectural Association (Londres, 1977). Il travaille chez Norman Foster et Richard Rogers avant de créer David Chipperfield Architects en 1984 à Londres. Parmi ses réalisations : l'Arnolfini Arts Center (Bristol, 1987) ; la galerie des plantes et le hall central du Natural History Museum (Londres, 1993) et le River and Rowing Museum (Henley-on-Thames, 1996). Plus récemment, il a réalisé la Landeszentralbank (Gera, Allemagne, 1994–2001) ; le Figge Art Museum (Davenport, Iowa, 2005) ; le musée de la Littérature moderne (Marbach, Allemagne, 2006) ; le bâtiment « Veles et Vents » pour l'America's Cup (Valencia, Espagne, 2006) et la Cité des cultures Ansaldo (Milan, 2000–07). Récemment, il a achevé le musée de la Culture liangzhu (Hangzhou, Chine, 2003–08), publié ici ; le Pavillon des arts de Kivik (Kivik, Suède, 2007–08, avec Antony Gormley) ; la reconstruction du Neues Museum (Berlin, 1997–2009, publié ici) ; l'Anchorage Museum au Rasmuson Center (Anchorage, Alaska, États-Unis, 2003–09) et de nombreux magasins Dolce & Gabbana depuis 1999. Il travaille actuellement au projet du cimetière de San Michele à Venise (1998–2013) ; à un nouveau bâtiment d'entrée pour la Museuminsel à Berlin ; au palais de justice de Salerne (Italie) ; à la galerie d'art Hepworth Wakefield (G.-B.) ; à la galerie d'art Turner Contemporary à Margate (G.-B.) ; à l'extension du Saint-Louis Art Museum (États-Unis) ; au Centre culturel historique Aus-Agder à Arendal (Norvège) et à un nouveau bâtiment de MBA pour l'école HEC à Paris.

RECONSTRUCTION OF THE NEUES MUSEUM

Museum Island, Berlin, Germany, 1997–2009

Address: Bodestraße 3, 10178 Mitte, Berlin, +49 30 266 424 242, www.neues-museum.de
Gross floor area: 20 500 m². Client: Stiftung Preussischer Kulturbesitz represented by the Bundesamt für Bauwesen und Raumordnung.
Cost: not disclosed

The audacity of David Chipperfield has consisted in introducing a new stairway within the restored but bare brick walls of the old museum. No imitation of an old décor is attempted, yet the spirit of the building has been preserved.

Die Kühnheit von David Chipperfields Planung bestand in der Einfügung einer neuen Treppe in die restaurierten, aber nackten Backsteinwände des alten Museumsgebäudes. Er hat keine Imitation des alten Dekors versucht und dennoch den Geist des Bauwerks bewahrt.

L'audace de David Chipperfield se manifeste ici dans l'introduction d'un nouvel escalier entre les murs de briques nus mais restaurés de l'ancien musée. L'esprit du bâtiment a été conservé, sans tentative d'imiter le décor disparu.

In 1997, David Chipperfield (with Julian Harrap) won the international competition to rebuild the Neues Museum on Berlin's Museum Island. Designed by Friedrich August Stüler (1841–59), the structure was heavily damaged during World War II. The architect states: "The key aim of the project was to recomplete the original volume, and encompassed the repair and restoration of the parts that remained after the destruction of the Second World War. The original sequence of rooms was restored with new building sections that create continuity with the existing structure." Chipperfield conscientiously filled the gaps left by war but followed the guidelines of the Charter of Venice, "respecting the historical structure in its different states of preservation." Prefabricated concrete elements were used to create new exhibition rooms, while a concrete staircase replaces the original. Recycled, handmade bricks were used in other, new volumes, including the Northwest Wing, and the South Dome. Though somewhat controversial, partly because it renders permanent certain scars of the war, Chipperfield's approach to this museum intended, amongst other things, to display Egyptian antiquities, seems to be very appropriate and successful. A new building, the James Simon Gallery (2007–13), will be built between the Neues Museum and the Spree, "echoing the urban situation of the site pre-1938." The new building seeks to extend and amplify the idea of a colonnade that existed on Museum Island, while permitting the creation of proper facilities for visitors. An ongoing master plan for the island that Chipperfield is also involved with will surely go on far beyond 2013.

1997 gewann David Chipperfield (mit Julian Harrap) den internationalen Wettbewerb für die Rekonstruktion des Neuen Museums auf der Berliner Museumsinsel. Das von Friedrich August Stüler geplante Bauwerk (1841–59) wurde im Zweiten Weltkrieg schwer beschädigt. Der Architekt erläutert: „Das Hauptziel des Projekts war die Wiederherstellung des ursprünglichen Umfangs und bedeutete die Reparatur und Restaurierung der nach der Zerstörung im Zweiten Weltkrieg erhaltenen Teile. Die originale Raumfolge wurde wiederhergestellt, neue Bauteile wurden hinzugefügt, die einen Zusammenhang mit dem Bestand bilden." Chipperfield füllte die im Krieg entstandenen Lücken gewissenhaft aus, folgte jedoch den Richtlinien der Charta von Venedig, „das historische Bauwerk in den verschiedenen Stadien seiner Erhaltung zu respektieren". Vorfabrizierte Betonelemente dienten der Schaffung neuer Ausstellungsräume, während eine Betontreppe die ursprüngliche ersetzte. In anderen neuen Bereichen, z.B. im Nordwestflügel, und für die südliche Kuppel wurden recycelte, handgefertigte Ziegel verwendet. Obgleich Chipperfields Lösung für dieses Museum, das u.a. die ägyptische Sammlung aufnehmen soll, in mancher Hinsicht umstritten ist, auch weil sie einige Wunden aus dem Krieg sichtbar lässt, erscheint sie durchaus angemessen und erfolgreich. Ein Neubau, die James-Simon-Galerie (2007–13), entsteht zwischen dem Neuen Museum und der Spree und „stellt die städtische Situation des Geländes vor 1938" wieder her. Das Gebäude soll die Kolonnaden auf der Museumsinsel wieder aufnehmen und erweitern sowie Einrichtungen für Besucher bieten. Der aktuelle Masterplan für die Museumsinsel, an dem auch Chipperfield beteiligt war, wird sicher weit über 2013 hinaus fortgeführt werden.

C'est en 1997 que David Chipperfield (avec Julian Harrap) a remporté le concours international pour la reconstruction du Neues Museum, en partie consacré aux antiquités égyptiennes, installé sur la Museumsinsel à Berlin. Conçus par Friedrich August Stüler (1841–59), les bâtiments avaient été en partie détruits pendant la Seconde Guerre mondiale. « L'objectif essentiel du projet était de compléter le volume original et de réparer et restaurer des parties qui avaient subsisté après les destructions de la guerre. La séquence originale des salles a été rétablie dans les nouveaux bâtiments, ce qui permet de créer une continuité avec l'existant », explique Chipperfield. L'architecte à rempli les vides béants laissés par la guerre, mais selon l'un des principes de la Charte de Venise qui est de « respecter la structure historique dans ses différents états de conservation ». Des éléments en béton préfabriqués ont été utilisés pour les nouvelles salles d'expositions et des degrés en béton ont remplacé l'escalier d'origine. La brique recyclée de fabrication artisanale est le matériau retenu pour d'autres volumes, dont l'aile nord-ouest et la coupole sud. Bien que controversée, en partie parce qu'elle fige certaines cicatrices de la guerre, l'approche de Chipperfield semble particulièrement appropriée et réussie. Un nouveau bâtiment, la galerie James Simon, sera construit (2007–13) entre le Neues Museum et la Spree « en rappel de la situation urbaine du site avant 1938 ». Le nouveau bâtiment développe et amplifie l'idée de colonnade qui existait jadis sur l'île des musées tout en facilitant la création d'installations destinées aux visiteurs. La réalisation du plan directeur de l'île, auquel participe également Chipperfield, devrait se poursuivre bien au-delà de 2013.

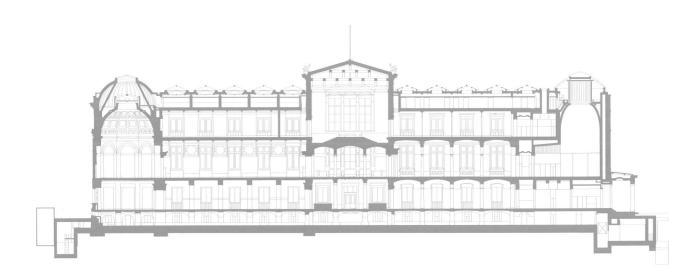

The basic volumes of the original building have emerged after years of standing in ruins. In a sense, the architect has allowed the greatly respected old building to come to life in the 21st century.

Die Grundformen des ursprünglichen Gebäudes sind nach Jahren in ruinösem Zustand wieder auferstanden. In gewissem Sinne hat der Architekt den hochgeschätzten Altbau im 21. Jahrhundert zu neuem Leben erweckt.

Les volumes de base du bâtiment d'origine sont réapparus après avoir été laissés à l'état de ruines pendant des décennies. En un sens, l'architecte a ressuscité pour le XXIe siècle un prestigieux bâtiment ancien.

Chipperfield has struck a delicate balance between renovating existing space and updating it while retaining its original feeling. Here, he reconciles modernity with a venerable building long in ruins.

Chipperfield hat eine feinfühlige Balance zwischen Renovierung und Modernisierung gewahrt, welche die ursprüngliche Ausstrahlung wahrt. Hier versöhnt er die Moderne mit einem ehrwürdigen Gebäude, das lange in Trümmern lag.

Chipperfield a installé un équilibre délicat entre la rénovation d'un espace existant et sa modernisation, tout en conservant son esprit d'origine. Ici, il concilie la modernité avec un bâtiment historique en ruines depuis longtemps.

Where walls or spaces could be recovered, they have been, allowing the irregularity of the ruin to emerge. New spaces are generated within the overall envelope of the original building.

Wo Wände oder Räume wiederhergestellt werden konnten, wurden ihnen die Unregelmäßigkeiten der Ruine belassen. Innerhalb der Gesamthülle des Altbaus entstanden neue Bereiche.

A chaque fois que c'était possible, les murs ou les volumes ont été restitués en conservant des traces de leur état passager de ruine. De nouveaux espaces ont été aménagés à l'intérieur de l'enveloppe du bâtiment ancien.

LIANGZHU CULTURE MUSEUM

Hangzhou, China, 2003–08

Address: Meilizhou Road 1, Liangzhu, Hangzhou, Zhejiang, 311113 China
Gross floor area: 9500 m². Client: Zhejiang Vanke Narada Real Estate Group Co., Ltd. Cost: not disclosed

This new museum is located in a park near the city of Hangzhou. It is dedicated to objects from the Jade or Liangzhu culture (*c.* 3000 BC). The architect states: "The building is set on a lake and connected via bridges to the park. The sculptural quality of the building ensemble reveals itself gradually as the visitor approaches the museum through the park landscape." Four linear exhibition halls make up the museum. Each is 18 meters wide and has an interior courtyard, but their height differs. The museum is clad in Iranian travertine. The entrance to the museum, with its ipe wood reception desk, is reached through a courtyard. The museum possesses all the rigor of David Chipperfield's architecture, tempered here by the green surroundings and courtyard plantings, but also by the slightly varied tones of the travertine cladding. The whole gives an impression of a structure that is made to last, with its choice of materials and its understated elegance.

Dieses neue Museum steht in einem Park in der Nähe der Stadt Hangzhou und enthält Exponate aus der Jade- oder Liangzhu-Kultur (ca. 3000 v. Chr.). Der Architekt erklärt: „Das Gebäude steht in einem See und ist durch Brücken mit dem Park verbunden. Die plastische Qualität der Anlage erschließt sich nach und nach, wenn der Besucher sich durch den Park dem Museum nähert." Es besteht aus vier horizontalen Ausstellungshallen, die jeweils 18 m breit, jedoch unterschiedlich in der Höhe sind und einen Innenhof haben. Der Bau ist mit persischem Travertin verkleidet. Der Eingangsbereich mit einer Empfangstheke aus Ipe-Tropenholz wird über einen Hof erreicht. Das Museum zeigt die ganze Strenge von Chipperfields Architektur, die hier jedoch durch die grüne Umgebung und die Bepflanzung des Hofs sowie die leicht unterschiedlichen Farbtöne der Travertinverkleidung gemildert wird. Insgesamt ist es ein Gebäude, das durch die Wahl der Materialien und seine zurückhaltende Eleganz Dauerhaftigkeit ausstrahlt.

Ce nouveau musée, consacré à des objets (principalement en jade) de la culture liangzhu (env. 3000 av. J.-C.), est situé dans un parc près de la ville de Hangzhou. «Le bâtiment est implanté dans un lac et relié au parc par des passerelles. La qualité sculpturale de l'ensemble se révèle au visiteur au fur et à mesure qu'il approche du musée à travers le parc», explique l'architecte. Le musée se compose de quatre salles d'exposition rectangulaires. De 18 mètres de large chacune et de hauteurs de plafonds variables, elles sont complétées par une cour intérieure. Les façades sont habillées de travertin iranien. L'entrée, dont la banque d'accueil est en bois d'ipé, est aménagée à l'extrémité d'une cour. Le musée offre toute la rigueur de l'architecture de David Chipperfield tempérée par l'environnement de verdure et les plantations dans les cours, mais aussi par les légères variations de teinte du travertin. Par ses choix de matériaux et son élégance discrète, l'ensemble donne le sentiment d'une structure faite pour durer.

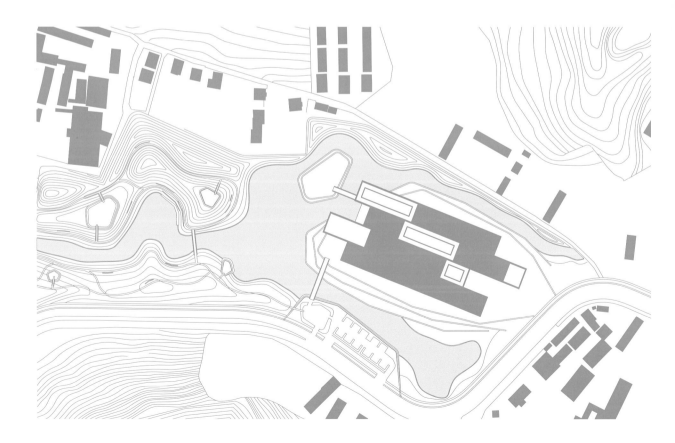

With a plan made up of four, staggered, rectangular volumes (see plan, left page), the museum is seen with its stone-clad simplicity in the images on this page.

Auf den Abbildungen dieser Seite zeigt sich das Museum mit seinem Grundriss aus vier gestaffelten, rechteckigen Volumen (siehe links) in seiner mit Naturstein verkleideten Schlichtheit.

Composé de quatre volumes rectangulaires décalés (plan de la page de gauche), le musée habillé de pierre se singularise par sa simplicité.

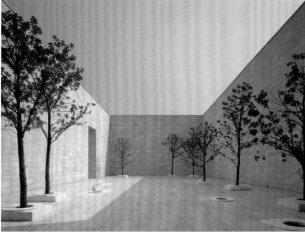

The largely blank, stone clad façades of the museum lift up and open out into courtyard areas, contrasting opacity with an almost unexpected lightness.

Die überwiegend freien, mit Naturstein verkleideten Fassaden erheben und öffnen sich zu den Hofräumen; Undurchsichtigkeit kontrastiert mit fast unerwarteter Helligkeit.

En grande partie aveugles, les façades parées de pierre se soulèvent et s'ouvrent sur des cours dans un contraste surprenant entre opacité apparente et légèreté.

The rectilinear volumes of the architecture affirm their presence while allowing light, air, and above all the passage of visitors in generous, open, spaces.

Die geradlinigen Formen der Architektur betonen ihre Präsenz; die großzügigen, offenen Räume lassen Licht und Luft ein und bieten vor allem Platz für den Rundgang der Besucher.

Les volumes rectilignes affirment leur présence tout en facilitant la circulation de la lumière, de l'air et des visiteurs dans des espaces généreux et ouverts.

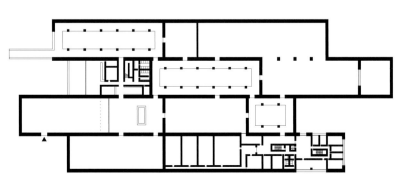

PRESTON SCOTT COHEN

Preston Scott Cohen, Inc.
675 Massachusetts Avenue
Cambridge, MA 02139
USA

Tel: +1 617 441 2110
Fax: +1 617 441 2113
E-mail: info@pscohen.com
Web: www.pscohen.com

PRESTON SCOTT COHEN received his B.F.A. (1982) and B.Arch (1983) degrees from the Rhode Island School of Design. In 1985, he earned his M.Arch degree from the Harvard GSD. Cohen was awarded First Prize in the international competitions for the Robbins Elementary School in Trenton (New Jersey, 2006), and for two museums: the Taiyuan Art Museum in Taiyuan (China, 2007–10, published here) and the Tel Aviv Museum of Art, Amir Building (Israel, 2007–10, also published here). Cohen is the Chair of the Department of Architecture at Harvard GSD, where he is the coordinator of the first year design studios and teaches the foundation course in Projective and Topological Geometry, Advanced Studios and Design Thesis. He was the Perloff Professor at UCLA (2002) and the Frank Gehry International Chair at the University of Toronto (2004). He has held faculty positions at Princeton, the Rhode Island School of Design, and Ohio State University. The firm's work includes the Goodman House (Pine Plains, New York, 2004); the Nanjing University Performing Arts Center (Nanjing, China, 2007–09); the Fahmy House (Los Gatos, California, 2007–09); and a Public Arcade in New York City (New York, 2007–09).

PRESTON SCOTT COHEN machte den B.F.A. (1982) und den B.Arch. (1983) an der Rhode Island School of Design, 1985 den M.Arch. an der Harvard Graduate School of Design (GSD). Er erhielt erste Preise in den internationalen Wettbewerben für die Robbins Elementary School in Trenton (New Jersey, 2006) und für zwei Museen: das Kunstmuseum in Taiyuan (China, 2007–10, hier veröffentlicht) und das Amir-Gebäude des Kunstmuseums in Tel Aviv (Israel, 2007–10, ebenfalls hier veröffentlicht). Cohen ist Lehrstuhlinhaber im Fachbereich Architektur der Harvard GSD, wo er die Studienanfänger im Grundkurs für projektive und topologische Geometrie unterrichtet sowie für die Bereiche Advanced Studies und Design Thesis zuständig ist. Er war Inhaber der Perloff-Professur an der UCLA (2002) und des Lehrstuhls Frank Gehry an der University of Toronto (2004). Darüber hinaus hat er an der Princeton University, der Rhode Island School of Design und der Ohio State University gelehrt. Zu den Bauten des Büros zählen das Haus Goodman (Pine Plains, New York, 2004), das Zentrum für darstellende Künste der Universität Nanjing (Nanjing, China, 2007–09), das Haus Fahmy (Los Gatos, Kalifornien, 2007–09) und eine öffentliche Arkade in New York City (2007–09).

PRESTON SCOTT COHEN est B.F.A. (1982) et B.Arch (1983) de la Rhode Island School of Design et M.Arch de l'Harvard GSD (1985). Il a reçu le Premier prix du concours international pour la Robbins Elementary School à Trenton (New Jersey, 2006) et pour deux musées : le musée d'Art de Taiyuan (Chine, 2007–10), publié ici, et le bâtiment Amir du musée d'Art de Tel Aviv (Israël, 2007–10), également publié ici. Cohen préside le Département d'architecture de l'Harvard GSD où il est également coordinateur des ateliers de projets de première année, et enseignant pour le cours de base de géométrie projective et topologique, les ateliers avancés et les projets de thèse. Il a été Perloff Professor à l'UCLA (2002) et a occupé la Frank Gehry International Chair à l'université de Toronto (2004). Il a également enseigné à Princeton, à la Rhode Island School of Design et à l'Ohio State University. Parmi ses réalisations : la maison Goodman (Pine Plains, New York, 2004) ; le centre des arts du spectacle de l'université de Nankin (Nankin, Chine, 2007–09) ; la maison Fahmy (Los Gatos, Californie, 2007–09) et un auvent de galerie commerciale à New York (2007–09).

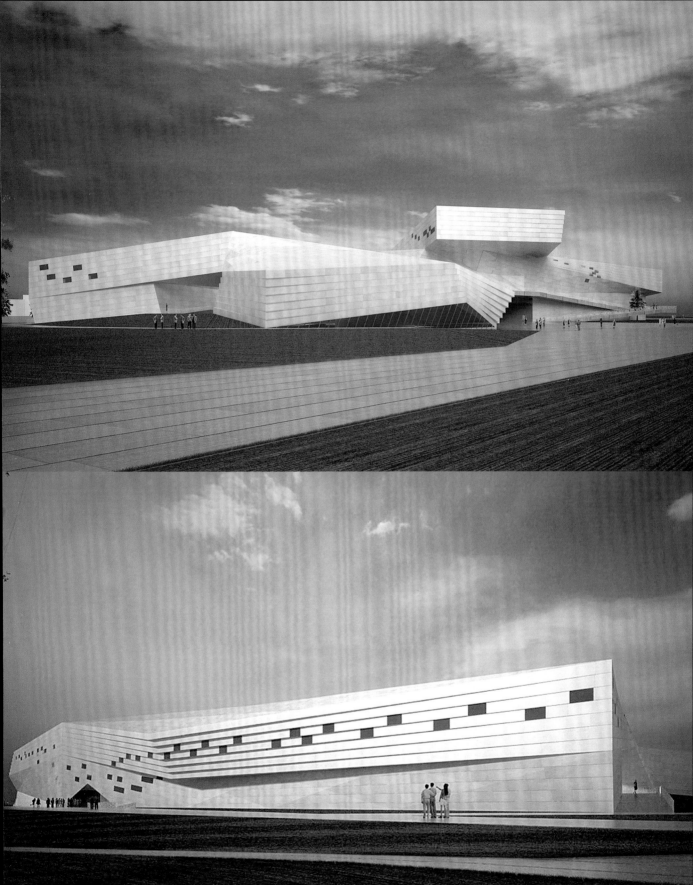

TAIYUAN MUSEUM OF ART

Taiyuan, China, 2007–10

Address: Chang Feng Culture and Business District, Taiyuan, Shanxi, China
Area: 32 000 m². Client: Taiyuan City Government. Cost: $47 million

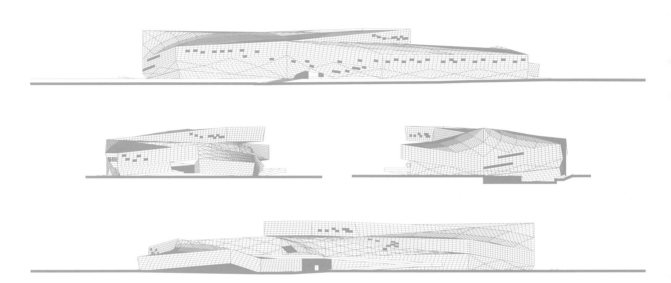

This is a competition-winning proposal. The architect relates the design to the agricultural landscapes of Shanxi Province. "Just as the landscapes of curved terraces in Shanxi respond to the laws of irrigation and topography, the curved and tessellated surfaces of the Taiyuan Museum of Art respond to contemporary technologies for controlling natural and artificial light," he says. He also relates the design to the multiple vanishing points that are typical of Chinese painting. The galleries are designed to allow visitors either to follow a predetermined path or to make their own way according to their tastes. Three main architectural elements are identified: the museum entrance, the sculpture garden entrance, and the entrance to the educational programs. The differing needs that correspond to the museum's functions are allowed for in the design. Ecological concerns, a rising issue in China, are responded to through the collection of rainwater to irrigate the surrounding landscape, and careful examination of available glass technologies, such as the use of embedded photovoltaics.

Dieses Projekt ist das Ergebnis eines Wettbewerbs. Der Architekt nimmt mit seinem Entwurf Bezug auf die bäuerliche Landschaft der Provinz Shanxi: „Wie die Landschaft der geschwungenen Terrassen in Shanxi den Gesetzen der Bewässerung und der Topografie folgt, so entsprechen die gekrümmten und kleinteiligen Flächen des Kunstmuseums von Taiyuan den modernen Technologien zur Kontrolle des natürlichen und künstlichen Lichts." Er bezieht sich auch auf die vielfältigen Fluchtpunkte, die typisch für die chinesische Malerei sind. Die Ausstellungsbereiche sind so angeordnet, dass Besucher entweder einem vorgegebenen Rundgang folgen oder auf Wunsch auch ihren eigenen Weg suchen können. Drei Hauptelemente der Architektur sind ablesbar: der Eingang zum Museum, der Eingang zum Skulpturengarten und der Zugang zu den pädagogischen Programmen. Die unterschiedlichen Funktionen des Museums sind im Entwurf berücksichtigt. Ökologische Belange werden in China ein immer wichtigeres Thema. Durch das Speichern des Regenwassers zur Bewässerung der umgebenden Landschaft und eine sorgfältige Prüfung der verfügbaren Verglasungstechniken, z. B. mit eingefügten Fotovoltaikelementen, wurde dem Rechnung getragen.

Ce projet, choisi à l'issue d'un concours, est en lien avec les paysages agricoles de la région du Shanxi. « De même que le paysage de terrasses en courbes du Shanxi répond aux lois de l'irrigation et de la topographie, les plans incurvés recouverts de mosaïque du musée d'Art de Taiyuan répondent aux technologies actuelles de contrôle de la lumière naturelle ou artificielle », précise l'architecte qui relie également son projet aux points de fuite multiples typiques de la peinture chinoise. Les galeries sont disposées de façon à permettre aux visiteurs de suivre un cheminement prédéterminé ou de choisir leur itinéraire selon leurs goûts. La composition s'organise autour de trois éléments principaux : l'entrée du musée, l'entrée du jardin de sculpture et celle des services éducatifs. Les différents besoins des différentes fonctions du musée sont prisent en compte. Les préoccupations écologiques, sujet de plus en plus brûlant en Chine, sont traitées par la collecte des eaux de pluie pour irriguer le jardin paysager environnant et la mise en œuvre de technologies d'utilisation du verre, à travers des cellules photovoltaïques intégrées par exemple.

The folding lines of the museum as a whole (seen above) are closely echoed in the interior design visible in the rendering on this page.

Die schrägen Umrisse der Gesamt-form des Museums (siehe oben) wiederholen sich in der Innenraum-gestaltung, wie die Darstellungen auf dieser Seite zeigen.

Le principe de plis des façades du musée (ci-dessus) se retrouve en écho fidèle dans la disposition des espaces intérieurs.

Plans that show interrelated, irregular
forms where straight lines are the
rule generate spectacular interior
spaces, such as the one seen in the
rendering below, where natural light
predominates.

Die Grundrisse zeigen ineinander
übergehende, unregelmäßige Formen,
wobei gerade Linien die Regel sind.
Dadurch entstehen spektakuläre
Innenräume, wie zum Beispiel auf der
unteren Abbildung zu sehen, in denen
natürliches Licht vorherrscht.

Les plans composés de formes irré-
gulières imbriquées à base de lignes
droites, génèrent de spectaculaires
espaces intérieurs, comme celui
figurant dans le rendu ci-dessous,
baigné de lumière naturelle.

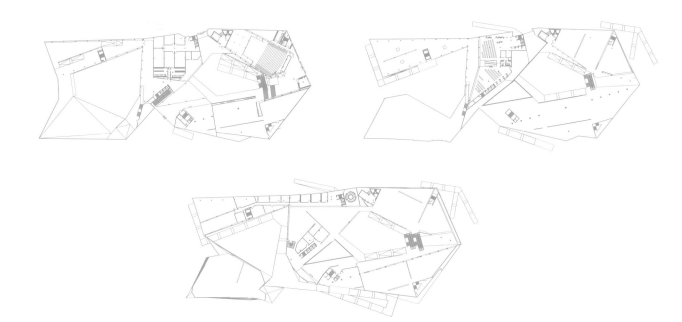

Further renderings of interior spaces
demonstrate a careful attention to
the walls where works of art can be
shown, making paintings stand out
in spite of the fairly complex play of
architectural elements.

Weitere Darstellungen der Innenräume zeigen, welche Aufmerksamkeit den Wänden gewidmet wurde,
an denen Kunstwerke ausgestellt
sind. Dadurch werden die Gemälde
hervorgehoben, ungeachtet des sehr
komplexen Spiels der architektonischen Elemente.

D'autres perspectives des espaces
intérieurs illustrent l'attention
portée aux murs sur lesquels seront
présentées les œuvres. Ils font ressortir l'impact des peintures malgré
le jeu assez complexe des éléments
architecturaux.

TEL AVIV MUSEUM OF ART

Tel Aviv, Israel, 2007–10

Address: 27 Shaul Hamelech Blvd., Tel Aviv 64329, Israel, + 972 607 7020, www.tamuseum.com
Area: 20 000 m². Client: Motti Omer, Director and Chief Curator, Tel Aviv Museum of Art. Cost: $45 million

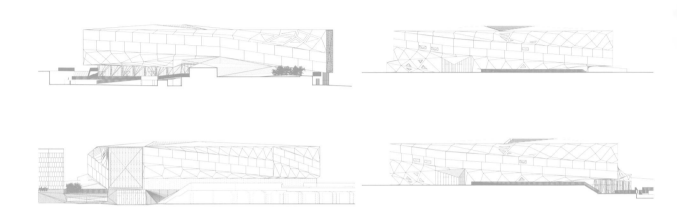

Elevation drawings of the building show its forward leaning, faceted shape. The cladding covers most of the visible surfaces of the imposing structure.

Aufrisszeichnungen des Gebäudes zeigen seine geneigte, facettierte Form. Die Verkleidung bedeckt den Großteil der sichtbaren Oberflächen dieses eindrucksvollen Bauwerks.

Des plans d'élévation montrent l'inclinaison du musée vers l'avant et sa forme facettée. L'habillage recouvre la plupart des surfaces visibles de l'imposante construction.

This project was the winner of a 2003 international competition. The building is to include galleries for Israeli art, architecture and design, drawings and prints, temporary exhibitions, a photography study center and archives, a multidisciplinary auditorium, seminar and conference rooms, an art library, restaurant, administrative offices, and storage facilities. The museum is located in the middle of Tel Aviv's cultural area on a triangular site. The architect states: "The building represents an unusual synthesis of two opposing paradigms of contemporary museum architecture; the museum of neutral white boxes and the museum of architectural spectacle." A 26-meter-high atrium is the central element around which galleries are organized. Given the nature of the site and the program, the architect uses a system of divergent axes that change from floor to floor. Preston Scott Cohen insists, however, that the new structure has a "family resemblance" to the original museum building and also that it makes reference to local Mendelsohn and Bauhaus Modernism.

Auch dieser Entwurf ist der Gewinner eines internationalen Wettbewerbs aus dem Jahr 2003. Das Gebäude soll Galerien für israelische Kunst, Architektur und Design, Zeichnungen und Drucke, Wechselausstellungen, ein Fotozentrum und Archive, ein interdisziplinäres Auditorium, Seminar- und Konferenzräume, eine Kunstbibliothek, ein Restaurant, Büro- und Lagerräume enthalten. Das Museum steht mitten in Tel Avivs Kulturbezirk auf einem dreieckigen Grundstück. Der Architekt erklärt: „Das Gebäude repräsentiert eine ungewöhnliche Synthese zweier gegensätzlicher Paradigmen gegenwärtiger Museumsarchitektur: das Museum aus neutralen, weißen Kisten und das Museum als architektonisches Spektakel." Ein 26 m hohes Atrium ist das zentrale Element, um das herum die Ausstellungsräume angeordnet sind. Angesichts der Bedingungen des Grundstücks und des Programms entschied sich der Architekt für ein System divergierender Achsen, die sich von Geschoss zu Geschoss ändern. Preston Scott Cohen betont jedoch, dass der Neubau eine „Familienähnlichkeit" mit dem alten Museumsgebäude habe und auch auf die örtliche Architektur von Mendelsohn und der Bauhaus-Moderne Bezug nehme.

Ce projet a remporté un concours international organisé en 2003. Le bâtiment comprendra des galeries d'art, d'architecture, de design israélien, également de dessins et d'estampes, des salles d'expositions temporaires, un centre d'étude et des archives de photographie, un auditorium polyvalent, des salles de séminaires et de conférences, une bibliothèque d'art, un restaurant, des bureaux administratifs et des réserves. Le musée se dresse au centre du quartier culturel de Tel Aviv sur un terrain de forme triangulaire. « Ce bâtiment représente une synthèse inhabituelle de deux paradigmes contradictoires de l'architecture muséale contemporaine : le musée composé de boîtes blanches neutres et le *musée-spectacle architectural* », précise l'architecte. L'élément central est un atrium de 26 mètres de haut autour duquel viennent se greffer les galeries. Étant donné la nature du site et le contenu du programme, l'architecte a mis au point un système d'axes divergents qui change de niveau en niveau. Preston Scott Cohen insiste cependant sur la « ressemblance de famille » de cette nouvelle construction avec le bâtiment d'origine du musée et sa référence au modernisme de Mendelsohn et du Bauhaus.

A rendering shows the entrance area of the museum. Below, a plan with the truncated triangular form of the building and the angled placement of interior elements.

Cette image de synthèse montre la zone de l'accès. Ci-dessous, un plan décrit la forme triangulaire tronquée du musée et l'implantation en biais des éléments intérieurs.

Ein Rendering zeigt den Eingangsbereich des Museums. Unten: Ein Grundriss zeigt die kegelstumpfartige Form des Gebäudes und die verwinkelte Anordnung der inneren Räume.

Bending and folding volumes create spaces where views open from one area onto another. The design is dynamic and unexpected.

Durch gebogene und gefaltete Volumen entstehen Bereiche, in denen man von einem Raum zum anderen durchblicken kann. Der Entwurf ist dynamisch und überraschend.

Les volumes repliés ou courbés créent des espaces qui offrent au visiteur des perspectives transversales, et créent une surprenante dynamique d'ensemble.

COOP HIMMELB(L)AU

Coop Himmelb(l)au
Wolf D. Prix / W. Dreibholz & Partner ZT GmbH
Spengergasse 37
1050 Vienna
Austria

Tel: +43 1 546 60
Fax: +43 1 546 60-600
E-mail: office@coop-himmelblau.at
Web: www.coop-himmelblau.at

Wolf D. Prix, Helmut Swiczinsky, and Michael Holzer founded **COOP HIMMELB(L)AU** in 1968 in Vienna, Austria. In 1988, a second office was opened in Los Angeles. Wolf D. Prix was born in 1942 in Vienna, and educated at the Technical University, Vienna, at SCI-Arc, and at the Architectural Association (AA), London. Since 2003, he has been Head of the Institute for Architecture, the Head of Studio Prix, and serves as Vice-Rector of the university. Wolfdieter Dreibholz was born in Vienna in 1941 and received a degree in engineering and architecture from the Technical University, Vienna, in 1966. He became CEO of Coop Himmelb(l)au Wolf D. Prix / W. Dreibholz & Partner ZT GmbH in 2004. Completed projects of the group include the Rooftop Remodeling Falkestraße (Vienna, Austria, 1983/1987–88); remodeling of the Austrian Pavilion in the Giardini (Venice, Italy, 1995); the UFA Cinema Center (Dresden, Germany, 1993–98); the SEG Apartment Tower (Vienna, Austria, 1994–98); and Expo '02, Forum Arteplage (Biel, Switzerland, 1999–2002). Recent work includes the Academy of Fine Arts (Munich, Germany, 1992/2002–05); the Akron Art Museum (Akron, Ohio, USA, 2001–07); BMW Welt (Munich, Germany, 2001–07); the Central Los Angeles Area High School #9 for the Visual and Performing Arts (Los Angeles, 2002–08); the Dalian International Conference Center (Dalian, China, 2008–10); the Musée des Confluences (Lyon, France, 2001–13, published here); the Busan Cinema Center (Busan, South Korea, 2005–11); and the European Central Bank (Frankfurt, Germany, 2003–14).

Wolf D. Prix, Helmut Swiczinsky und Michael Holzer gründeten **COOP HIMMELB(L)AU** 1968 in Wien. 1988 wurde ein weiteres Büro in Los Angeles eröffnet. Wolf D. Prix wurde 1942 in Wien geboren und studierte an der Wiener Technischen Universität, am Southern California Institute of Architecture – SCI-Arc und an der Architectural Association (AA) in London. Seit 2003 ist Prix Vizerektor der Universität für angewandte Kunst in Wien sowie Leiter des Instituts für Architektur und des Studio Prix. Wolfdieter Dreibholz wurde 1941 in Wien geboren und schloss 1966 sein Studium der Architektur und des Ingenieurwesens an der Wiener Technischen Universität ab. Er wurde 2004 Geschäftsführer von Coop Himmelb(l)au Wolf D. Prix / W. Dreibholz & Partner ZT GmbH. Zu den ausgeführten Projekten des Büros zählen der Dachausbau in der Falkestraße in Wien (1983/87–88), der Umbau des österreichischen Pavillons in den Giardini in Venedig (1995), das UFA-Kinozentrum (Dresden, 1993–98), das SEG-Wohnhochhaus (Wien, 1994–98) und das Forum Arteplage, Expo '02 (Biel, Schweiz, 1999–2002). Neuere Bauten sind die Akademie der bildenden Künste (München, 1992/2002–05), das Akron Art Museum (Akron, Ohio, 2001–07), die BMW Welt (München, 2001–07), die High School #9 for the Visual and Performing Arts (Los Angeles, Kalifornien, 2002–08), das internationale Konferenzzentrum von Dalian (China, 2008–10), das Musée des Confluences (Lyon, 2001–13, hier vorgestellt), das Kinocenter von Busan (Südkorea, 2005–11) und die Europäische Zentralbank (Frankfurt am Main, 2003–14).

Wolf D. Prix, Helmut Swiczinsky et Michael Holzer ont fondé **COOP HIMMELB(L)AU** à Vienne (Autriche) en 1968 et ont ouvert une seconde agence à Los Angeles en 1988. Wolf D. Prix est né à Vienne en 1942 et a étudié à la Technische Universität de Vienne, au Southern Califonia Institute of Architecture (SCI-Arc) et à l'Architectural Association de Londres (AA). Depuis 2003, il est à la tête de l'Institut pour l'architecture et du Studio Prix, et occupe la fonction de vice-recteur de la TU de Vienne. Wolfdieter Dreibholz, né à Vienne en 1941, est diplômé en ingénierie et architecture de la TU de Vienne (1966). Il a pris la direction de Coop Himmelb(l)au Wolf D. Prix / W. Dreibholz & Partner ZT GmbH en 2004. Parmi les réalisations du groupe : le remodellage du toit de la Falkestraße (Vienne, 1983/1987–88) ; la rénovation du Pavillon autrichien dans les Giardini (Venise, 1995) ; le UFA Cinema Center (Dresde, 1993–98) ; la tour d'appartements SEG (Vienne, 1994–98) et le Forum Arteplage d'Expo '02 (Bienne, Suisse, 1999–2002). Les projets plus récents comprennent : l'Académie des Beaux-arts (Munich, Allemagne, 1992/2002–05) ; l'Akron Art Museum (Akron, Ohio, 2001–07) ; BMW Welt (Munich, 2001–07) ; le Central Los Angeles Area High School #9 pour les arts visuels et du spectacle (Los Angeles, États-Unis, 2002–08) ; le Centre de conférences international Dalian (Dalian, Chine, 2008–10) et le musée des Confluences (Lyon, France, 2001–13), publié ici ; le complexe de cinéma de Busan (Busan, Corée du Sud, 2005–11) et la Banque centrale européenne (Francfort, Allemagne, 2003–14).

MUSÉE DES CONFLUENCES

Lyon, France, 2001–13

Address: 86, quai Perrache, 69002 Lyon, France, +33 4 78 37 3000, www.museedesconfluences.fr
Area: 26 700 m². Client: Département du Rhône, Lyon, France.
Cost: € 100 million. Team: Wolf D. Prix (Design Principal), Markus Prossnigg (Project Partner),
Angus Schoenberger (Project Architect)

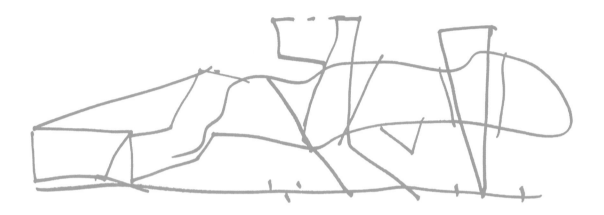

Christened the "Crystal Cloud of Knowledge" by the winning Austrian architects, this 20 000-square-meter facility is sponsored by the Conseil Général du Rhône and the City of Lyon. The museum is intended as the centerpiece of the redevelopment of a former industrial site set at the confluence of the Rhône und Saône rivers. The amorphous, cloud-like exhibition structure is intended to give the impression that it is floating over an angled glass base. According to the architects: "The crystal rising toward the side of the town is conceived as an urban forum and entrance hall for visitors. Its shape, which can be read clearly, stands for the everyday world. In contrast to this the cloud hides the knowledge about the future; it is a soft space of hidden streams and countless transitions." With a predicted flow of some 500 000 visitors a year, the museum is meant to be an "urban leisure space," according to the architects, who were selected over Peter Eisenman, Steven Holl, and François Seigneur in the 2001 competition. The most spectacular gesture within the structure appears to be the "Gravity Well," an interior patio tilted at a 23.5° angle, like the earth itself, and lined with a spiral staircase. Coop Himmelb(l)au, in descriptive texts for their project, seek to obviate the question of style, preferring to claim that their design is an exercise in "simultaneity" and the result of a "profound negotiation of differences." Equally unclear is the actual function of the institution, which is apparently intended to take on not only cultural but also scientific issues.

Diese von den österreichischen Architekten „Kristallwolke des Wissens" genannte, über 20 000 m² große Institution wird vom Conseil Général du Rhône und der Stadt Lyon finanziert. Das Museum ist als Mittelpunkt der Sanierung eines früheren Industriegeländes am Zusammenfluss von Rhône und Saône geplant. Das amorphe, wolkenähnliche Gebilde soll den Eindruck vermitteln, als schwebe es über einer eckigen, gläsernen Basis. Die Architekten erläutern: „Der sich zur Stadtseite erhebende Kristall ist als städtisches Forum und Eingangshalle für Besucher konzipiert. Seine klar ablesbare Form steht für die Alltagswelt. Im Gegensatz dazu verbirgt die Wolke das Wissen über die Zukunft; sie bildet einen sanften Raum mit verborgenen Strömungen und zahllosen Übergängen." Mit einer prognostizierten Besucherzahl von etwa 500 000 pro Jahr soll das Museum – nach dem Wunsch der Architekten, die 2001 den Wettbewerb vor Peter Eisenman, Steven Holl und François Seigneur gewannen – zu einem „städtischen Freizeitbereich" werden. Das spektakulärste Element des Gebäudes ist die sogenannte Quelle der Schwerkraft, ein wie die Erde im Winkel von 23,5 Grad gekippter Innenhof, um den eine Wendeltreppe führt. Coop Himmelb(l)au suchen in ihrem beschreibenden Text die Frage des Stils zu vermeiden und behaupten lieber, dass ihr Entwurf eine Übung in „Gleichzeitigkeit" und das Ergebnis einer „gründlichen Auseinandersetzung mit den Unterschieden" sei. Ebenso unklar ist die eigentliche Funktion der Einrichtung, die offenbar nicht nur kulturelle, sondern auch wissenschaftliche Aufgaben übernehmen soll.

Baptisé « nuage de cristal de la connaissance » par les architectes autrichiens qui en ont remporté le concours, ce bâtiment de 20 000 mètres carrés est financé par le Conseil général du Rhône et la ville de Lyon. Ce musée est l'élément central d'un vaste plan de rénovation d'un site industriel déclassé au confluent du Rhône et de la Saône. La structure de forme libre évoquant un nuage donne l'impression qu'il flotte au-dessus d'un socle facetté en verre. Selon les architectes : « Le cristal qui s'élève vers la ville est conçu comme un forum urbain qui sert de hall d'entrée pour les visiteurs. Sa forme, de lecture aisée, exprime le quotidien. Par contraste, le nuage cache la connaissance du futur. C'est un espace lisse de flux et de transitions multiples. » Attendant quelque 500 000 visiteurs par an, ce musée est aussi un « espace de loisirs urbains », selon les termes des architectes, dont la proposition a été choisie face à celles de Peter Eisenman, Steven Holl et François Seigneur en 2001. Le geste le plus spectaculaire devrait être le Puits de pesanteur (« Gravity Well »), un patio intérieur incliné à 23,5 degrés (l'axe de la terre) dans lequel vient s'enrouler un escalier en spirale. Dans ses présentations du projet, Coop Himmelb(l)au contourne la question du style, préférant affirmer que le projet est un exercice de « simultanéité » et le résultat d'une « négociation approfondie des différences ». La fonction réelle de cette institution, axée autour d'objectifs tant culturels que scientifiques, ne semble guère plus claire.

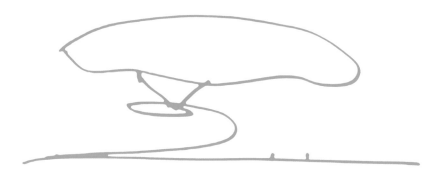

Simple line sketches lay out the lines of force that run through the kind of complex structure seen in the rendering above.

Die einfachen Strichzeichnungen zeigen den Verlauf der Kräfte durch das komplexe, im Rendering oben dargestellte Gebäude.

De simples croquis au trait installent les lignes de force qui traversent la complexité de la structure présentée ci-dessus en image de synthèse.

DELUGAN MEISSL

Delugan Meissl Associated Architects
Mittersteig 13/4
1040 Vienna
Austria

Tel: +43 1 585 36 90
Fax: +43 1 585 36 90 11
E-mail: office@deluganmeissl.at
Web: www.deluganmeissl.at

Delugan-Meissl ZT GmbH was jointly founded by Elke Delugan-Meissl and Roman Delugan in 1993. In 2004, they changed the name of the firm to **DELUGAN MEISSL ASSOCIATED ARCHITECTS**. Elke Delugan-Meissl was born in Linz, Austria, and studied at the University in Innsbruck. She worked in several offices in Innsbruck and Vienna before creating Delugan Meissl. Roman Delugan was born in Merano, Italy, and studied at the University of Applied Arts in Vienna. Dietmar Feistel was born in Bregenz, Austria, and studied at the University of Technology in Vienna. He became an associate partner at Delugan Meissl Associated Architects in 2004. Martin Josst was born in Hamburg, Germany, and studied at the Muthesius Academy of Art and Design in Kiel, Germany, before working in the office of Morphosis in Los Angeles and becoming an associate partner at Delugan Meissl Associated Architects in 2004. Christopher Schweiger was born in Salzburg, Austria, studied at the Universities of Applied Arts in Vienna and Berlin, and was a collaborator and project manager at Delugan Meissl beginning in 1996, before becoming an associate partner in 2004. Aside from the Porsche Museum (Stuttgart, Germany, 2006–08, published here)—competition (2005)—they have recently completed a number of residential projects in Vienna. They were the ex aequo First Prize winners for the Darat King Abdullah II Cultural Center (Amman, Jordan, 2008), and are currently working on the Filmmuseum in Amsterdam (to be completed in 2010).

Die Firma Delugan-Meissl ZT GmbH wurde 1993 von Elke Delugan-Meissl und Roman Delugan gegründet. 2004 änderten sie den Namen des Büros in **DELUGAN MEISSL ASSOCIATED ARCHITECTS**. Elke Delugan-Meissl wurde im österreichischen Linz geboren und studierte an der Universität Innsbruck. Sie arbeitete in verschiedenen Büros in Innsbruck und Wien, bevor sie mit Roman Delugan die gemeinsame Firma gründete. Roman Delugan wurde in Meran, Italien, geboren und studierte an der Universität für angewandte Kunst in Wien. Dietmar Feistel stammt aus Bregenz, Österreich, und studierte an der Technischen Universität Wien. Er wurde 2004 Partner von Delugan Meissl Associated Architects. Der Hamburger Martin Josst studierte an der Muthesius-Akademie für Kunst und Design in Kiel, bevor er im Büro von Morphosis in Los Angeles arbeitete und 2004 Partner von Delugan Meissl Associated Architects wurde. Christopher Schweiger wurde in Salzburg geboren, studierte an der Universität für angewandte Kunst in Wien sowie in Berlin und war seit 1996 Mitarbeiter und Projektmanager bei Delugan Meissl, wo er 2004 Partner wurde. Außer dem Porsche Museum (Stuttgart, Wettbewerb 2005, Ausführung 2006–08, hier veröffentlicht) hat das Büro in jüngster Zeit verschiedene Wohnbauten in Wien realisiert. Es gewann ex aequo den ersten Preis im Wettbewerb für das Kulturzentrum Darat King Abdullah II (Amman, Jordanien, 2008) und arbeitet zurzeit am Filmmuseum in Amsterdam (geplante Fertigstellung 2010).

L'agence Delugan-Meissl ZT GmbH a été fondée par Elke Delugan-Meissl et Roman Delugan en 1993. En 2004, elle a pris le nom de **DELUGAN MEISSL ASSOCIATED ARCHITECTS**. Elke Delugan-Meissl, née à Linz (Autriche), a étudié à l'université d'Innsbruck. Elle a travaillé dans plusieurs agences d'Innsbruck et de Vienne avant de créer la structure actuelle. Roman Delugan, né à Merano (Italie), a étudié à l'université des Arts appliqués de Vienne. Dietmar Feistel, né à Bregenz (Autriche), a étudié à la Technische Universität de Vienne. Il est partenaire associé de l'agence Delugan Meissl Associated Architects depuis 2004. Martin Josst, né à Hambourg, a étudié à l'académie Muthesius d'art et de design de Kiel (Allemagne), avant de travailler pour Morphosis à Los Angeles et de devenir partenaire associé de Delugan Meissl Associated Architects en 2004. Christopher Schweiger, né à Salzbourg, a étudié à l'université des Arts appliqués de Vienne, et de Berlin, et été collaborateur, puis responsable de projet chez Delugan Meissl Associated Architects à partir de 1996, avant d'en devenir partenaire associé en 2004. En dehors du musée Porsche (Stuttgart, Allemagne, 2006–08, concours en 2005), publié ici, l'agence a récemment réalisé un certain nombre de projets résidentiels à Vienne. Elle a remporté le premier prix ex aequo pour le centre culturel Darat King Abdullah II (Amman, Jordanie, 2008) et travaille actuellement au projet du Filmmuseum d'Amsterdam qui devrait être achevé en 2010.

PORSCHE MUSEUM

Stuttgart, Germany, 2006–08

Address: Porscheplatz 1, 70435 Stuttgart-Zuffenhausen, Germany, + 49 711 911 20 911,
www.porsche.com/germany/aboutporsche/porschemuseum. Area: 13 333 m². Client: Dr. Ing. h. c. Ferdinand Porsche.
Cost: € 100 million. Collaboration: HG Merz (Exhibition Concept), Wenzel & Wenzel Architects (Realization),
Gassmann & Grossman (Site Management), L. A. P. (Structural Engineering)

The architects have resolved the complex issue of giving an impression of movement and quality to a fixed structure. Lifting off the ground, the museum opens onto the street in front of it.

Die Architekten lösten die komplexe Aufgabe, einem feststehenden Gebäude den Eindruck von Bewegung und Qualität zu verleihen. Das vom Boden abgehobene Museum öffnet sich zur davor liegenden Straße.

Les architectes ont résolu le défi complexe de donner une impression de mouvement à une structure fixe. Comme suspendu au-dessus du sol, le musée s'ouvre sur la rue qui le longe.

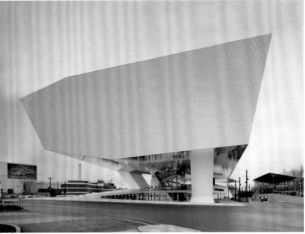

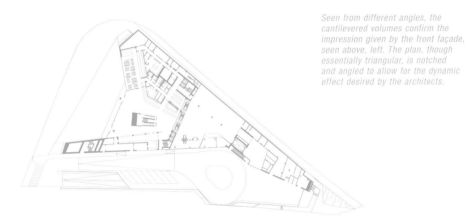

Seen from different angles, the cantilevered volumes confirm the impression given by the front façade, seen above, left. The plan, though essentially triangular, is notched and angled to allow for the dynamic effect desired by the architects.

Aus verschiedenen Winkeln gesehen, bestätigen die auskragenden Volumen den Eindruck der vorderen Fassade (links oben). Der im Wesentlichen dreieckige Grundriss ist eingeschnitten und verschoben, um die von den Architekten angestrebte dynamische Wirkung zu erreichen.

Vus sous différents angles, les volumes en porte-à-faux confirment l'impression donnée par la façade principale (page de gauche, en haut). Le plan, de forme à peu près triangulaire, est indenté et incliné pour assurer l'impression de dynamisme souhaitée par les architectes.

Although economic circumstances may mean that the trend will end for a time, German automobile manufacturers, such as Mercedes-Benz and BMW, have engaged in a notable surge of museum construction in recent years. The Porsche Museum is the most recent of these ambitious ventures. Delugan Meissl, winners of a 2005 competition, explain: "The central draft concept was the translation of the versatile and vivid brand into the language of architecture." Expected to attract more than 200 000 visitors each year, the monolithic structure is 160 meters long, 70 meters wide, and 28 meters high. The 35 000-ton "floating" superstructure of the museum, with its three-dimensional lattice formwork, rests on only three pylons, with 60-meter spans between these supports. A foyer greets visitors, with a restaurant and a museum shop. The exhibition pattern leads visitors on a spiraling visit of the vehicles that have made Porsche one of the most prestigious automobile brands. Like the Mercedes-Benz Museum by UNStudio (Stuttgart, Germany, 2003–06), the Porsche Museum has a rather "difficult" site with nearby roads and rail lines complicating the task of the architects, but also stimulating them apparently. With its leaning, powerful form, the Porsche Museum embodies not only the idea of the brand, but also the sense of movement that might well be expected of fast cars.

Obgleich die wirtschaftlichen Rahmenbedingungen für ein Ende dieses Trends sprechen, haben deutsche Automobilhersteller wie Mercedes-Benz und BMW sich in den vergangenen Jahren in hohem Maß im Museumsbau engagiert. Das Porsche Museum ist das neueste dieser ehrgeizigen Vorhaben. Die Gewinner des Wettbewerbs von 2005, die Architekten Delugan Meissl, erklären: „Zentrales Anliegen des Entwurfskonzepts war die Übertragung der vielseitigen und erfolgreichen Marke in die Sprache der Architektur." Das monolithische Bauwerk, das für mehr als 200 000 Besucher jährlich konzipiert wurde, ist 160 m lang, 70 m breit und 28 m hoch. Der 35 000 t schwere, „schwebende" Aufbau des Museums mit seiner dreidimensionalen Fachwerkkonstruktion ruht auf nur drei Pylonen mit einer Spannweite von 60 m zwischen diesen Stützen. Im Foyer, das auch einen Museumsshop und ein Restaurant enthält, werden die Besucher empfangen. Das Ausstellungsdesign führt sie auf einem spiralförmigen Weg zu den Fahrzeugen, die Porsche zu einer der renommiertesten Automarken gemacht haben. Ebenso wie das Mercedes-Benz Museum von UNStudio (Stuttgart, 2003–06) steht das Porsche Museum auf einem verhältnismäßig „schwierigen" Grundstück mit benachbarten Straßen und Eisenbahnlinien, was die Aufgabe der Architekten erschwert, sie aber offensichtlich auch stimuliert hat. Mit seiner kraftvollen, aufstrebenden Form verkörpert das Porsche Museum nicht nur die Idee dieser Marke, sondern auch das Gefühl von Bewegung, wie man es von schnellen Autos erwarten kann.

Si la conjoncture économique peut freiner pour un temps cette tendance, les constructeurs automobiles allemands comme Mercedes-Benz et BMW se sont engagés depuis quelques années dans la construction de musées. Le musée Porsche est la plus récente de ces ambitieuses entreprises. Les architectes associés de l'agence Delugan Meissl, qui en ont remporté le concours en 2005, expliquent que « le concept central de départ était la traduction de cette marque dynamique et versatile dans le langage de l'architecture ». La construction monolithique de 160 mètres de long par 70 de large et 28 de haut devrait accueillir deux cent mille visiteurs par an. La superstructure « flottante » de 35 000 tonnes, au coffrage en lattis tridimensionnel ne repose que sur trois poteaux chacun séparés de 60 mètres. Les visiteurs sont accueillis dans un atrium au sein duquel se trouvent également un restaurant et une boutique. L'exposition consiste en un circuit en spirale parmi les voitures qui ont fait de Porsche l'une des plus prestigieuses marques automobiles. Comme le Mercedes-Benz Museum d'UNStudio (Stuttgart, Allemagne, 2003–06), le musée Porsche occupe un terrain assez difficile à proximité de routes et de voies de chemin de fer qui ont compliqué la tâche des architectes, mais les ont apparemment stimulés. Par son profil incliné et plein de force, le musée incarne non seulement l'idée que l'on se fait de la marque, mais aussi la symbolique de mouvement que l'on attend de ces voitures rapides.

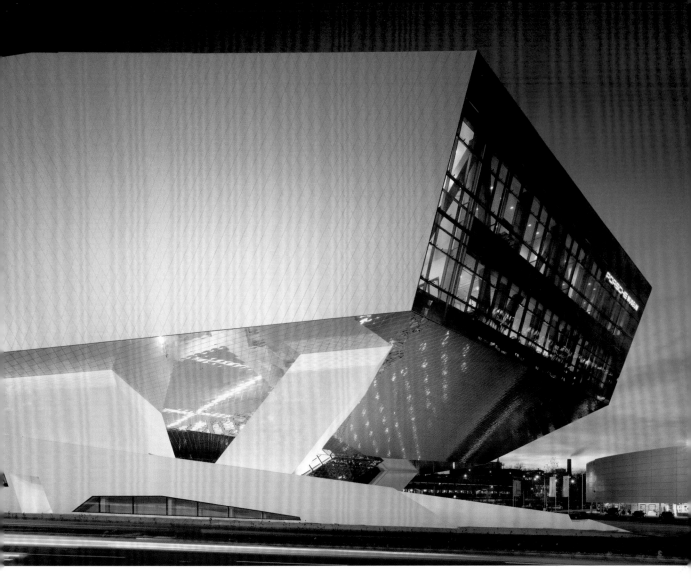

Alternating smooth, closed façades with largely glazed ones, the building looks almost completely transparent from certain angles, such as the view on the left page.

Aus bestimmten Richtungen gesehen, wirkt das Gebäude mit seinen glatten, geschlossenen Fassaden im Wechsel mit großzügig verglasten Flächen fast vollständig transparent, wie die Ansicht auf der linken Seite zeigt.

Alternant des façades fermées et lisses à d'autres généreusement vitrées, le bâtiment semble presque complètement transparent sous certains angles, comme le montre la vue de la page de gauche.

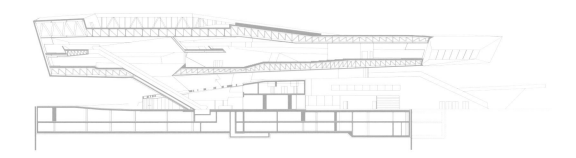

The architects also alternate opaque
surfaces with broad glazing inside
the museum, affording views of
cars exhibited some distance from
the visitor.

Auch im Innern des Museums gestalteten die Architekten undurchsichtige
Flächen im Wechsel mit großzügig
verglasten, die dem Besucher Durch-
blicke zu den entfernter gelegenen
Wagen ermöglichen.

Les architectes ont également alterné
les surfaces opaques et largement
vitrées à l'intérieur du musée, pour
ouvrir des perspectives sur l'exposition des voitures.

There is an obvious aesthetic continuity between the exterior and the interior of the museum, where, in the image above, an escalator allows visitors to move along the axis of some of the cars on display, heightening the dynamic image of the cars themselves.

Es besteht eine deutliche Kontinuität zwischen dem Äußeren und dem Innern des Museums, in dem (siehe Bild oben) eine Rolltreppe die Besucher entlang der Achse führt, an der verschiedene Wagen ausgestellt sind. Dadurch wird auch die dynamische Wirkung der Exponate betont.

La continuité esthétique entre l'extérieur et l'intérieur du musée est évidente. Dans l'image ci-dessus, des escaliers mécaniques permettent aux visiteurs de se déplacer dans l'axe d'exposition des voitures, renforçant ainsi l'impression de dynamisme donnée par celles-ci.

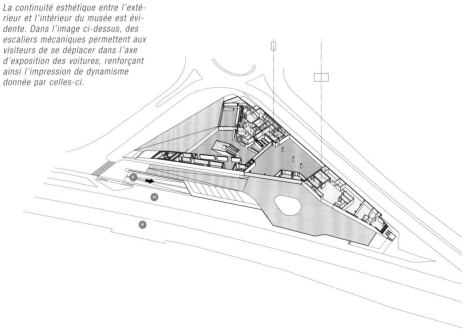

ELLIS WILLIAMS

Ellis Williams Architects
Exmouth House
Pine Street
London EC1R OJH
UK

Tel: +44 207 841 72 00 / Fax: +44 207 833 38 50
E-mail: info@ewa.co.uk / Web: www.ewa.co.uk

ELLIS WILLIAMS is an architecture practice with studios in London, Cheshire, and Berlin. There are three directors in the London studio: Dominic Williams, Lester Korzelius, and Paul Deanus, all architects who have a wide range of experience in many different building typologies. The art team in London is led by Dominic Williams, who has a particular interest and experience in working on arts projects and directly with artists. Born in 1965 in Manchester, he studied Art at Manchester, Architecture at Sheffield Architectural School in the late 1980s, and "life on the road" as a guitarist with the band Junk. He then worked at Skidmore, Owings & Merrill (1991–94), before joining the Ellis Williams Partnership in 1994. Rob Freeman joined Ellis Williams Architects in 1998 after studying at Sheffield University, and was a member of the team that realized the BALTIC Centre for Contemporary Art. Past projects by Dominic Williams have included a virtual mausoleum, an experimental technology college, and an art and music urban box thesis in Manchester, his hometown. The BALTIC Centre for Contemporary Art (Gateshead, Tyneside, UK, 1999–2002) was his first major completed work, which was won in competition when he was 28 years old. Williams headed the London office team (with Rob Freeman, Project Architect) for the Cornerstone Arts Centre in Didcot (Oxfordshire, UK, 2006–08, published here). He is currently involved in a performance centre in a Design Academy in Birmingham and the Oriel Mostyn Art Gallery in north Wales, both in the UK.

ELLIS WILLIAMS ist ein Architekturbüro mit Niederlassungen in London, Cheshire und Berlin. Das Londoner Atelier wird von Dominic Williams, Lester Korzelius und Paul Deanus geleitet – alles Architekten, die große Erfahrung mit den verschiedensten Bautypen haben. Das Team für Kunst in London leitet Dominic Williams, der besonderes Interesse an und Erfahrungen mit Kunstprojekten und der direkten Arbeit mit Künstlern hat. Er wurde 1965 in Manchester geboren, studierte Ende der 1980er-Jahre Kunst in Manchester, Architektur an der Sheffield Architectural School und als Gitarrist mit der Band Junk „das Leben auf der Straße". Danach arbeitete er bei Skidmore, Owings & Merrill (1991–94) und schloss sich 1994 Ellis Williams Architects an. Rob Freeman trat 1998 nach dem Studium an der Universität Sheffield bei Ellis Williams Architects ein und gehörte zum Team, welches das BALTIC Centre for Contemporary Art realisierte. Zu den Projekten von Dominic Williams zählen ein virtuelles Mausoleum, ein experimentelles Technikcollege und eine Dissertation über eine städtische Kunst- und Musikbox in seiner Heimatstadt Manchester. Das BALTIC Centre for Contemporary Art (Gateshead, Tyneside, Großbritannien, 1999–2002) war sein erster großer ausgeführter Entwurf, mit dem er im Alter von 28 Jahren den Wettbewerb gewann. Dominic Williams leitete auch das Team des Londoner Büros (mit Rob Freeman als Projektarchitekt) für das Cornerstone Arts Centre in Didcot (Oxfordshire, Großbritannien, 2006–08, hier veröffentlicht). Zurzeit arbeitet er an einem Theater für die Design Academy in Birmingham und die Kunstgalerie Oriel Mostyn in Nordwales (beide in Großbritannien).

ELLIS WILLIAMS est une agence d'architecture possédant des bureaux à Londres, dans le Cheshire et à Berlin. L'agence londonienne compte trois directeurs : Dominic Williams, Lester Korzelius et Paul Deanus, tous architectes possédant l'expérience de différentes typologies de bâtiments. L'équipe de Londres est dirigée par Dominic Williams qui s'intéresse particulièrement aux projets artistiques et travaille souvent directement avec des artistes. Né en 1965 à Manchester, il a étudié l'art dans cette ville et l'architecture à la Sheffield Architectural School à la fin des années 1980 avant de « vivre sur la route » comme guitariste du groupe Junk. Il a ensuite travaillé chez Skidmore, Owings & Merrill (1991–94), avant de rejoindre Ellis Williams Architects en 1994. Rob Freeman est arrivé chez Ellis Williams Architects en 1998, après des études à l'université de Sheffield. Il a participé au projet du BALTIC Centre for Contemporary Art. Les projets de Dominic Williams comprennent un musée virtuel, un collège de technologies expérimentales, la « Music urban box thesis » pour Manchester, sa ville natale. Le BALTIC Centre for Contemporary Art (Gateshead, Tyneside, Royaume-Uni, 1999–2002) a été sa première œuvre d'importance, dont il a remporté le concours à l'âge de 28 ans. Dominic Williams a dirigé l'équipe de Londres (avec Rob Freeman, architecte de projet) pour le Cornerstone Arts Centre de Didcot (Oxfordshire, Royaume-Uni, 2006–08), publié ici. Il travaille actuellement à un centre de spectacles pour une académie de Design à Birmingham et pour la galerie d'art Oriel Mostyn au Nord du Pays de Galles, les deux en Royaume-Uni.

CORNERSTONE ARTS CENTRE

Didcot, Oxfordshire, UK, 2006–08

Address: 25 Station Road, Didcot, Oxon, OX11 7NE, United Kingdom, +44 1235 515 144, www.cornerstone-arts.org
Area: 1900 m². Client: South Oxfordshire District Council. Cost: € 6.05 million
Collaborating Artists: Jacqui Poncelet, Richard Layzell

Dominic Williams states: "Didcot was a town perceived without a centre or much cultural focus. Hence, South Oxfordshire District Council's plan was to address this issue by creating a new pedestrian area linking a retail area with an arts centre and cinema. Ellis Williams Architects were selected by competition to design a new art centre on a cleared site that faced north onto a new town square within the new development. It is also important to note that an earlier demographic study highlighted that there was also a rapidly growing younger population and hence the design needed to be inclusive to a wide range of activities for all ages." Although the architects had a client, they had no "end-user" as such to interact with. Programmatic space requirements included a "flexible performance venue for 240 seated people, a dance rehearsal space, three visual and media arts workshops, a gallery space, and associated social, administrative and back-of-house spaces." A central foyer links all the interior spaces, leading the architect to state that the scheme revolves around a series of "interlocking forms." The project involved collaboration with two artists: Jacqui Poncelet who worked with the team on cladding and internal acoustic panels, and Richard Layzell who developed the shop window display on Market Place. A number of passive systems and orientations ensure that the building is environmentally responsible.

Dominic Williams erklärt: „Didcot war eine Stadt ohne wahrnehmbares Zentrum und mit nur bescheidenem kulturellem Leben. Der South Oxfordshire District Council wollte diesen Mangel durch die Schaffung einer neuen Fußgängerzone beheben, die die Einkaufsgegend mit einem Kunstzentrum und einem Kino verbindet. Ellis Williams Architects gewannen den Wettbewerb und wurden mit dem Bau des Kunstzentrums auf einem freigelegten Gelände beauftragt, das im Norden zu einem neuen Platz im Neubaugebiet orientiert ist. Außerdem ist erwähnenswert, dass in einer früheren demografischen Untersuchung darauf hingewiesen wurde, dass es eine schnell wachsende junge Bevölkerung gebe. Der Entwurf sollte daher Aktivitäten für alle Altersstufen einbeziehen." Die Architekten hatten es zwar mit einem Bauherrn zu tun, doch mit keinem beteiligten „Endnutzer". Das Raumprogramm umfasst „einen flexiblen Theaterbereich mit 240 Plätzen, einen Raum für Tanzproben, drei Werkstätten für bildende und Medienkunst, einen Ausstellungsbereich und zugehörige Verwaltungs- und Versorgungsräume". Ein zentral angeordnetes Foyer verbindet sämtliche Innenbereiche und veranlasste den Architekten zu der Aussage, dass der Entwurf um eine Reihe „ineinander verzahnter Formen" kreist". In die Planung wurden zwei Künstler einbezogen: Jacqui Poncelet arbeitete bei der Verkleidung und inneren Akustik mit dem Team zuammen, Richard Layzell gestaltete das Schaufenster am Market Place. Verschiedene passive Energiesysteme stellen die Umweltfreundlichkeit des Gebäudes sicher.

« Didcot était une ville dont on ne percevait pas le centre et qui n'exerçait pas le moindre attrait culturel. L'objectif du conseil du district de l'Oxfordshire-Sud était de répondre à cette problématique par la création d'une nouvelle zone piétonnière reliant une zone commerciale à un centre artistique et un cinéma. Ellis Williams Architects a été choisi à l'issue du concours organisé pour le centre artistique prévu sur un terrain dégagé donnant au nord sur une nouvelle place prévue dans le périmètre de rénovation. Il est également important de noter qu'une étude démographique soulignait la présence d'une population jeune croissante et que le projet devait donc inclure une large gamme d'activités ouvertes à toutes les classes d'âge », explique Dominic Williams. Si les architectes avaient bien face à eux un client, ils n'avaient pas le contact avec les utilisateurs finaux. La programmation comprenait « un lieu de spectacles polyvalent de deux cent quarante places, une salle de répétition de danse, trois ateliers d'arts plastiques ou médiatiques, une galerie et les installations nécessaires pour l'administration, la réception du public, la maintenance ». Un atrium central fait le lien entre les divers volumes intérieurs, ce qui fait dire aux architectes que le plan est constitué d'une série de « formes imbriquées ». Le projet a fait appel à deux artistes : Jacqui Poncelet qui a travaillé sur l'habillage des murs et les panneaux acoustiques intérieurs, et Richard Layzell qui a mis au point la vitrine sur Market Place. Divers dispositifs passifs ou orientables confirment la nature durable du projet.

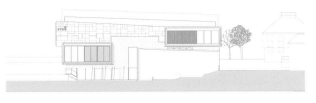

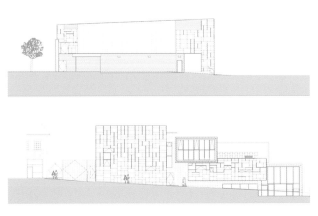

The architecture evokes an accumulation of boxes, partially transparent, but benefiting from large glazed areas seen above and in elevation drawings.

Die Architektur wirkt wie eine Anhäufung von teilweise transparenten Kisten, profitiert jedoch von den großen, verglasten Flächen, die oben und auf den Ansichtszeichnungen zu sehen sind.

L'architecture fait penser à une accumulation de boîtes partiellement transparentes qui bénéficient de zones largement vitrées (ci-dessus et dans les élévations).

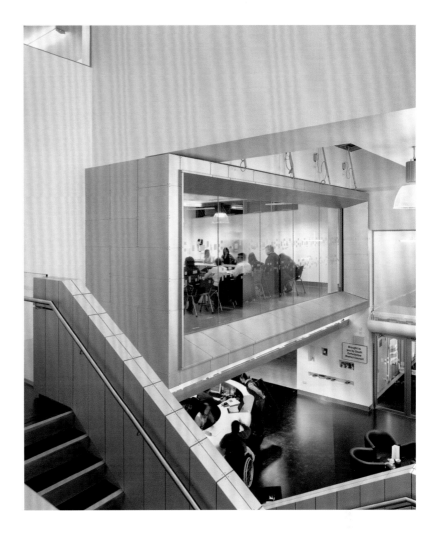

The accumulation of rectangular
volumes that characterizes the architecture is echoed in these interior
views, including the theater space
seen below.

Die für diese Architektur charakteristische Anhäufung rechtwinkliger
Volumen wiederholt sich auch in
den Innenräumen, sogar im unten
abgebildeten Theaterbereich.

L'accumulation de volumes rectangulaires qui caractérise cette
architecture se retrouve en écho
à l'intérieur, y compris dans l'auditorium (ci-dessous).

FRANK O. GEHRY

Gehry Partners, LLP
12541 Beatrice Street
Los Angeles, CA 90066
USA

Tel: +1 310 482 3000
Fax: +1 310 482 3006
Web: www.foga.com

Born in Toronto, Canada, in 1929, **FRANK O. GEHRY** studied at the University of Southern California, Los Angeles (1951–54), and at Harvard (1956–57). Princi-pal of Gehry Partners, LLP, Los Angeles, since 1962, he received the Pritzker Prize in 1989. Some of his notable projects are the Loyola Law School (Los Angeles, 1981–84); the Norton Residence (Venice, California, 1983); the California Aerospace Museum (Los Angeles, 1982–84); the Schnabel Residence (Brentwood, California, 1989); the "Dancing House", office building (Prague, Czech Republic, 1996); the Guggenheim Museum (Bilbao, Spain, 1991–97); the DG Bank Headquarters (Berlin, Ger-many, 2001); the Fisher Center for the Performing Arts at Bard College (Annandale-on-Hudson, New York, 2002); the Walt Disney Concert Hall (Los Angeles, 2003); and the Massachusetts Institute of Technology Stata Complex (Cambridge, Massachusetts, 2003). Recent completed work includes the Jay Pritzker Pavilion at Millennium Park (Chicago, Illinois 1999–2004); the Hotel Marques de Riscal (Elciego, Spain, 2003–06); the Art Gallery of Ontario Expansion (Toronto, Canada, 2005–08, published here); InterActiveCorpHeadquarters (New York, New York 2003–07); The Lewis Library (Princeton, New Jersey, 2002–08); and the Serpentine Pavilion (London, UK, 2008). Recent and current work includes the Guggenheim Abu Dhabi (UAE); Beekman Tower (New York, New York); the Museum of Tolerance (Jerusalem); the Ohr-O'Keefe Muse-ums (Biloxi, Mississippi); the New World Symphony (Miami, Florida); and the Lou Ruvo/Cleveland Clinic Brain Institute (Las Vegas, Nevada).

Der 1929 im kanadischen Toronto geborene **FRANK O. GEHRY** studierte an der University of Southern California, Los Angeles (1951–54), und in Harvard (1956–57). Seit 1962 ist er Chef von Gehry Partners, LLP, Los Angeles; 1989 erhielt er den Pritzker-Preis. Zu seinen bekannten Projekten gehören u. a. die Loyola Law School (Los Angeles, 1981–84), das Wohnhaus Norton (Venice, Kalifornien, 1983), das California Aerospace Museum (Los Angeles, 1982–84), das Wohnhaus Schnabel (Brent-wood, Kalifornien, 1989), das „Tanzende Haus", ein Bürogebäude in Prag (1996), das Guggenheim Museum in Bilbao (1991–97), die Hauptverwaltung der DG Bank (Berlin, 2001), das Fisher Center for the Performing Arts am Bard College (Annandale-on-Hudson, New York, 2002), die Walt Disney Concert Hall (Los Angeles, 2003) und der Stata Complex des Massachusetts Institute of Technology (Cambridge, Massachusetts, 2003). Neue Projekte sind der Jay Pritzker Pavillon im Millennium Park in Chicago (1999–2004), das Hotel Marqués de Riscal (Elciego, Spanien, 2003–06), der Erweiterungsbau für die Art Gallery of Ontario (Toronto, 2005–08, hier veröffent-licht), die Hauptverwaltung der InterActiveCorp (New York, 2003–07), die Lewis Library (Princeton, New Jersey, 2002–08) und der Serpentine Pavilion (London, 2008). Zu den jüngsten Arbeiten gehören Guggenheim Abu Dhabi (Vereinigte Arabische Emirate), der Beekman Tower (New York), das Museum der Toleranz in Jerusalem, die Ohr-O'Keefe-Museen (Biloxi, Mississippi), die New World Symphony (Miami, Florida) und das Lou Ruvo/Cleveland Clinic Brain Institute (Las Vegas, Nevada).

Né à Toronto, Canada, en 1929, **FRANK O. GEHRY** a étudie à l'University of Southern California, Los Angeles (1951–54), puis à Harvard (1956–57). Il dirige l'agence Gehry Partners, LLP, Los Angeles, depuis 1962, et a reçu en 1989 le prix Pritzker. Parmi ses projets les plus remarqués : la Loyola Law School (Los Angeles, 1981–84) ; la résidence Norton (Venice, Californie, 1983) ; le California Aerospace Museum (Los Angeles, 1982–84) ; la résidence Schnabel (Brentwood, Californie, 1989) ; la « maison dansante », immeuble de bureaux (Prague, République tchèque, 1996) ; le musée Guggenheim (Bilbao, Espagne, 1991–97) ; le siège de la DG Bank (Berlin, 2001) ; le Fisher Center for the Performing Arts de Bard College (Annandale-on-Hudson, New York, 2002) ; le Walt Disney Concert Hall (Los Angeles, 2003) et le complexe Stata du Massachusetts Institute of Technology (Cambridge, Massachusetts, 2003). Parmi ses réalisations récentes : le pavillon Jay Pritzker dans le Millennium Park (Chicago, 1999–2004) ; l'hôtel Marques de Riscal (Elciego, Espagne, 2003–06) ; l'extension de l'Art Gallery of Ontario (Toronto, Canada, 2005–08, publiée ici ; le siège d'InterActiveCorp (New York, 2003–07) ; la bibliothèque Lewis (Princeton, New Jersey, 2002–08) ; le Serpentine Pavilion (Londres, 2008). Gehry travaille actuelle-ment aux projets du Guggenheim Abu Dhabi (E. A. U.) ; de la tour Beekman (New York, New York) ; au musée de la Tolérance (Jérusalem) ; des musées Ohr-O'Keefe (Biloxi, Mississippi), de la salle de concerts New World Symphony (Miami, Floride) et du Lou Ruvo/Cleveland Clinic Brain Institute (Las Vegas, Nevada).

ART GALLERY OF ONTARIO EXPANSION

Toronto, Ontario, Canada, 2005–08

317 Dundas Street West, Toronto, ON M5T 1G4, Canada, +1 416 976 6648, www.ago.net
Area: 9011 m². Client: Art Gallery of Ontario. Cost: $276 million

Called "Transformation AGO", this project was funded in large part by a donation from Ken Thomson. Frank O. Gehry met with the donor for the first time in 2000, and the project was officially launched in 2002. Gehry's schematic design for AGO was revealed in 2004, and construction began in 2005. The new architecture includes a 183-meter-long glass-and-wood façade along Dundas Street West from McCaul Street to Beverely Street, a 137-meter-long sculpture gallery, a social gathering space with a two-level gift and bookshop, a restaurant, café, lecture hall, and contemporary art space. The titanium-and-glass four-story south wing houses a center for contemporary art. The museum increased its gallery space by 47 percent with the new extension. The Art Gallery of Ontario was founded in 1900, and expanded in several phases, most recently in 1993 by Barton Myers. The current project included the renovation of 16 908 square meters in addition to the new construction. Signage for the museum was done by Bruce Mau Design.

Dieses „Transformation AGO" benannte Projekt wurde zum großen Teil durch eine Spende von Ken Thomson finanziert. Frank O. Gehry traf den Spender erstmals im Jahr 2000, das Projekt wurde 2002 offiziell gestartet. Gehrys schematischer Entwurf für die AGO wurde 2004 vorgelegt, Baubeginn war 2005. Die neue Architektur besteht aus einer 183 m langen Fassade aus Glas und Holz an der Dundas Street West von der McCaul Street bis zur Beverely Street, einer 137 m langen Skulpturengalerie, einem Platz für Begegnungen mit einer zweigeschossigen Geschenk- und Buchhandlung, einem Restaurant, einem Café, einem Vortragssaal und, im viergeschossigen Südtrakt aus Titan und Glas, einem Zentrum für zeitgenössische Kunst. Durch diese Erweiterung erhielt das Museum eine um 47 % größere Ausstellungsfläche. Die Art Gallery of Ontario wurde im Jahr 1900 gegründet und in mehreren Phasen erweitert, zuletzt 1993 von Barton Myers. Zu der neuen Baumaßnahme gehörte neben dem Neubau auch die Sanierung von 16 908 m² Ausstellungsbereichen. Das Leitsystem des Museums stammt von Bruce Mau Design.

Intitulé « Transformation AGO », ce projet a été financé en grande partie par une donation de Ken Thomson. Frank O. Gehry a rencontré ce donateur pour la première fois en 2000 et le projet a été officiellement lancé en 2002. Les premiers plans ont été annoncés en 2004 et le chantier a débuté en 2005. Le nouveau bâtiment comprend une façade en bois et verre de 183 mètres de long sur Dundas Street West, entre McCaul Street et Beverly Street, une galerie de sculptures de 137 mètres de long, un atrium, une librairie et une boutique sur deux niveaux, un restaurant, un café, une salle de conférences et un espace pour l'art contemporain. L'aile sud de quatre niveaux à façade de verre et de titane abrite un centre pour l'art contemporain. La nouvelle extension a permis d'agrandir l'espace galerie du musée de 47 %. L'Art Gallery of Ontario a été fondée en 1900 et s'est agrandie en plusieurs phases, dont l'une confiée à Barton Myers en 1993. En plus de la construction nouvelle, le projet actuel comprend la rénovation de 16 908 mètres carrés. La signalétique du musée est due à Bruce Mau Design.

The Art Gallery of Ontario (overall view above) was expanded on several occasions prior to the recent work by Frank O. Gehry—most recently by Barton Myers / KPMB Architects (1993).

Die Art Gallery of Ontario (Gesamtansicht oben) wurde auch vor dem jüngsten Bau von Frank O. Gehry mehrmals erweitert – zuletzt von Barton Myers / KPMB Architects (1993).

L'Art Gallery of Ontario (vue d'ensemble ci-dessus) avait déjà été agrandie à plusieurs reprises en particulier par Barton Myers / KPMB Architects (1993) avant l'intervention toute récente de Frank O. Gehry.

Despite its often sinuous appearance,
the addition to the AGO assumes a
relatively straightforward floor plan,
as seen to the right.

Malgré son aspect souvent sinueux,
l'extension de Gehry suit un plan
relativement orthogonal (à droite).

Trotz seines mehrfach gekrümmten
Erscheinungsbilds hat der Erweiterungsbau des AGO einen relativ
geradlinigen Grundriss, wie auf dem
Plan rechts zu sehen ist.

Gehry's spiraling, flowing additions seem to penetrate the existing spaces in an almost organic way, making older structures seem contemporary.

Gehrys gewundene, fließende Erweiterung scheint die bestehenden Bereiche fast organisch zu durchdringen und lässt die Altbauten dadurch zeitgenössischer erscheinen.

Les interventions de forme spiralée de Gehry semblent pénétrer les espaces existants de manière presque organique, conférant du même coup un aspect contemporain aux structures anciennes.

TEODORO GONZÁLEZ DE LEÓN

Teodoro González de León Arquitectos, S.C.
Amsterdam 63, Col. Hipódromo Condesa
06100 Mexico City
Mexico

Tel: +52 55 5286 5578/5460
Fax: +52 55 5211 3706
E-mail: teodoro@tglarquitectos.com

TEODORO GONZÁLEZ DE LEÓN was born in Mexico City in 1926. From 1942 to 1947, he studied architecture at the old Academia de San Carlos (UNAM, the National Autonomous University of Mexico). In 1947, the French government granted him a scholarship and he worked in Le Corbusier's studio for 18 months. During that time, he was part of the teams in charge of the "Unité d'Habitation Marseille," and the "L'Usine Duval" at Saint Dié. He has been continuously active since the late 1940s, when he returned to Mexico, first in the urban development and public housing fields, and then in the design of large public and private buildings. In 2008, he received the UIA Gold Medal. He paints and sculpts in his leisure time. In collaboration with Abraham Zabludovsky and Francisco Serrano, he designed the Mexican Embassy in Brazil (1972–76). His projects with Abraham Zabludovsky also include the Rufino Tamayo Museum (Mexico City, 1981), and the National Pedagogical University (Mexico City, 1979–82). Some of his individual works are the new headquarters of the publishing house Fondo de Cultura Económica (Mexico City, 1990–92); the Site Museum in El Tajín (El Tajín, Veracruz, 1991–92); the renovation of the Colegio Nacional (National College, Mexico City, 1993–94); the Mexican Gallery at the British Museum in London (UK, 1993–94); the Higher School of Music at the National Center for the Arts (Mexico City, 1993–94); the National Folk Arts Museum (Mexico City, 2001–06); and the "Bella Epoca" Cultural Center (Mexico City, 2004–06). Recently, he built the "Reforma 222" urban complex (Mexico City, 2001–08) and the University Museum of Contemporary Art (UNAM) in Mexico City, (2006–08, published here), all in Mexico unless stated otherwise.

TEODORO GONZÁLEZ DE LEÓN wurde 1926 in Mexiko-Stadt geboren und studierte von 1942 bis 1947 Architektur an der alten Academia de San Carlos (UNAM, Universidad Nacional Autónoma de México). 1947 erhielt er von der französischen Regierung ein Stipendium und arbeitete 18 Monate im Büro von Le Corbusier in den Teams, die für den Bau der Unité d'Habitation Marseille und der Fabrik Duval in Saint Dié verantwortlich waren. Seit seiner Rückkehr nach Mexiko Ende der 1940er-Jahre ist er ohne Unterbrechung aktiv gewesen, zuerst in der Stadtplanung und im Wohnungsbau der öffentlichen Hand, dann in der Planung großer öffentlicher und privater Bauten. 2008 wurde ihm die Goldmedaille der International Union of Architects (UIA) verliehen. In seiner Freizeit beschäftigt er sich mit Malerei und Bildhauerei. In Zusammenarbeit mit Abraham Zabludovsky und Francisco Serrano plante er die mexikanische Botschaft in Brasilien (1972–76). Mit Zabludovsky baute er auch das Museum Rufino Tamayo (Mexiko-Stadt, 1981) und die Universidad Pedagogica Nacional (Mexiko-Stadt, 1979–82). Zu den von ihm allein geplanten Bauten gehören der Neubau des Verlags Fondo de Cultura Económica (Mexiko-Stadt, 1990–92), das Museum in El Tajín (El Tajín, Veracruz, 1991–92), die Sanierung des Colegio Nacional (Mexiko-Stadt, 1993–94), die Mexican Gallery im British Museum (London, 1993–94), die Musikhochschule des Centro Nacional de las Artes (Mexiko-Stadt, 1993–94), das Museo de Arte Popular (Mexiko-Stadt, 2001–06) und das Kulturzentrum „Bella Epoca" (Mexiko-Stadt, 2004–06). Neueste Realisierungen sind der städtebauliche Komplex „Reforma 222" (Mexiko-Stadt, 2001–08) und das Museo Universitario de Arte Contemporaneo (UNAM) in Mexiko-Stadt (2006–08, hier veröffentlicht).

TEODORO GONZÁLEZ DE LEÓN est né à Mexico en 1926. De 1942 à 1947 il étudie l'architecture à l'ancienne Academia de San Carlos (UNAM, Université nationale autonome du Mexique). En 1947, il reçoit une bourse du gouvernement français et part travailler chez Le Corbusier pendant dix-huit mois. Il fait partie des équipes en charge des projets « Unité d'Habitation Marseille », et « Usine Duval » à Saint-Dié. Il rentre au Mexique à la fin des années 1940 et est resté très actif jusqu'à ce jour, tout d'abord dans les domaines de l'urbanisme et du logement social, puis dans la construction de vastes bâtiments publics ou privés. En 2008, il reçoit la médaille d'or de l'UIA. Il peint et sculpte à ses moments de loisir. En collaboration avec Abraham Zabludovsky et Francisco Serrano, il a conçu l'ambassade du Mexique au Brésil (1972–76). Ses projets avec Abraham Zabludovsky comprennent également le musée Rufino Tamayo (Mexico, 1981) et l'Université nationale de pédagogie (Mexico, 1979–82). Parmi ses réalisations personnelles : le nouveau siège de l'éditeur Fondo de Cultura Económica (Mexico, 1990–92) ; le musée à El Tajín (El Tajín, Veracruz, 1991–92) ; la rénovation du Colegio Nacional (Mexico, 1993–94) ; la galerie mexicaine du British Museum à Londres (Royaume-Uni, 1993–94) ; l'École supérieure de musique au Centre national des arts (Mexico, 1993–94) ; le musée national des Arts populaires (Mexico, 2001–06) et le centre culturel « Bella Epoca » (Mexico, 2004–06). Récemment, il a construit le complexe urbain « Reforma 222 » (Mexico, 2001–08) et le musée universitaire d'Art contemporain UNAM à Mexico (2006–08), publié ici.

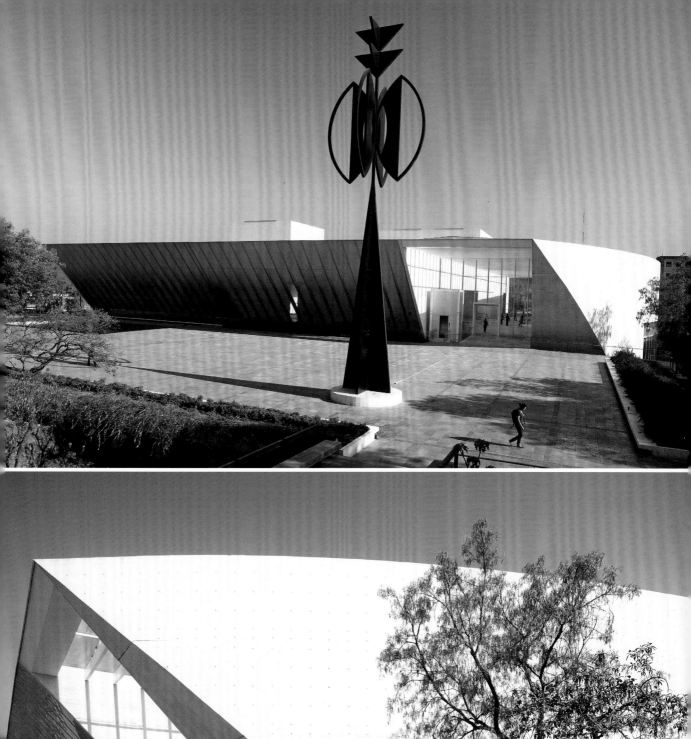

UNIVERSITY MUSEUM
OF CONTEMPORARY ART

National Autonomous University of Mexico (UNAM), Mexico City, Mexico, 2006–08

Address: Insurgentes Sur 3000, Centro Cultural Universitario, Mexico City, CP 04510, Mexico, +52 56 22 69 72, www.muac.unam.mx
Area: 18 000 m². Client: UNAM. Cost: not disclosed. Collaborator: Antonio Rodríguez

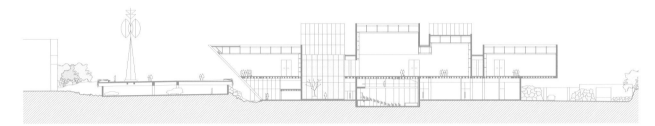

The museum is located at the side of a new plaza that serves as an entrance to the Cultural Center of the University. Slanted at an angle of 45°, the façade of the museum forms a portico leading to the Concert Hall and theaters of the Cultural Center. A double-height lobby cuts through the building, connecting the plaza with the National Library, on the northern side of the complex. Thus, the plaza and the museum "structure the relationships between the different Cultural Center buildings." The museum is laid out on two levels—the plaza level including exhibition galleries, reception, store, and bookshop, as well as educational areas, and a lower level, partially excavated from volcanic rock, where the 300-seat auditorium, offices, storerooms, a cafeteria, restaurant, and mediatheque are located. There are 14 exhibition rooms of various sizes and heights, distributed in four sections, each of which functions as a small museum. Three indoor paths, illuminated by natural light coming from three patios and terraces, interconnect the galleries, which are all designed on a 12-meter module, with heights of 6, 9, or 12 meters. All rooms feature natural overhead lighting. The architect states: "These dimensions were carefully chosen after visiting 35 contemporary art museums and galleries around the world." The architect concludes: "The architectural volumes interact with the surroundings: toward the plaza, the slanted great glass portico; toward the east, a curved frontage dialogs with the Concert Hall's jagged angularity, and toward the west, overlooking the entrance avenue, a cluster of square and rectangular prisms reaching to different heights herald the all-white concrete museum."

Das Museum liegt an einem neuen Platz, der als Zugang zum Kulturzentrum der Universität dient. Die im Winkel von 45 Grad geneigte Fassade des Museums bildet einen Portikus, der zur Konzerthalle und den Theatern des Kulturzentrums führt. Eine doppelgeschosshohe Lobby durchschneidet das Gebäude und verbindet den Platz mit der Staatsbibliothek an der Nordseite der Anlage. Dadurch „strukturieren der Platz und das Museum die Beziehungen der verschiedenen Bauten des Kulturzentrums zueinander". Das Museum ist zweigeschossig – die Ebene auf Höhe des Platzes enthält Ausstellungsräume, Empfang, Lager und Buchhandlung sowie Unterrichtsräume, ein darunter liegendes, teilweise in den vulkanischen Fels geschlagenes Geschoss das Auditorium mit 300 Plätzen, Büroräume, Lagerräume, eine Cafeteria, ein Restaurant und eine Mediathek. Es gibt insgesamt 14 Ausstellungsräume unterschiedlicher Größe und Höhe, die auf vier Abteilungen verteilt sind, von denen jeder für sich als kleines Museum funktioniert. Drei innenliegende Verkehrswege, die durch drei Innenhöfe und Terrassen natürlich belichtet werden, verbinden die Ausstellungsbereiche miteinander. Diese wurden auf einem Raster von 12 m mit Höhen von 6, 9 oder 12 m geplant. Alle Räume erhalten natürliches Licht von oben. Der Architekt erklärt: „Diese Abmessungen wurden sorgfältig erwogen nach dem Besuch von 35 Museen und Galerien für zeitgenössische Kunst in aller Welt." Und er schließt mit folgenden Worten: „Die architektonischen Volumen stehen in Wechselwirkung mit der Umgebung: zum Platz hin mit dem großen, schrägen gläsernen Portikus. In östlicher Richtung nimmt eine gekrümmte Fassade den Dialog mit den scharfkantigen Formen der Konzerthalle auf, nach Westen, zur Erschließungsstraße hin, kündigt eine Gruppe quadratischer und rechteckiger Prismen in unterschiedlicher Höhe das ganz aus weißem Beton bestehende Museum an."

Le musée se trouve sur un côté de la place par laquelle on accède au centre culturel de l'université. Inclinée à quarante-cinq degrés, la façade forme un portique qui conduit à la salle de concerts et aux salles de spectacles du centre culturel. Un atrium double hauteur découpé dans le bâtiment connecte la place à la Bibliothèque nationale au nord. Ainsi, la place et le musée « structurent » les relations entre les différentes constructions du centre culturel. Le musée s'étend sur deux niveaux. Le rez-de-chaussée sur la place comprend les galeries d'exposition, une réception, une boutique, une librairie ainsi que des installations éducatives tandis que le niveau inférieur, en partie creusé dans la roche volcanique, est occupé par un auditorium de trois cents places, des bureaux, des réserves, une cafétéria, un restaurant et une médiathèque. Quatorze salles d'exposition de diverses surfaces et hauteurs sont distribuées en quatre sections, chacune fonctionnant comme un petit musée en soi. Trois cheminements intérieurs, éclairés par la lumière naturelle venant de trois patios et terrasses, réunissent ces galeries qui sont toutes dessinées selon un module de 12 mètres avec des hauteurs variables de 6, 9 ou 12 mètres. Toutes les salles bénéficient d'un éclairage zénithal. « Ces dimensions ont été soigneusement déterminées après la visite de trente-cinq musées et galeries d'art contemporain dans le monde », explique l'architecte qui poursuit : « Les volumes architecturaux sont en interaction avec leur environnement : le portique incliné vers la place, la façade incurvée qui dialogue à l'est avec le profil anguleux déchiqueté de la salle de concerts et à l'ouest, le regroupement de prismes carrés et rectangulaires de différentes hauteurs vers l'avenue de l'entrée signalent la présence de ce musée en béton d'un blanc immaculé. »

A strong cantilever and a raking, glazed façade, seen in the section drawing above, characterize the building and give it its dynamic appearance.

Die oben im Schnitt sichtbare starke Auskragung und die geneigte, verglaste Fassade sind charakteristische Elemente des Gebäudes und verleihen ihm seine dynamische Wirkung.

Un puissant porte-à-faux et une façade vitrée en forme de râteau – visible sur la coupe ci-dessus – caractérisent le musée et lui confèrent son aspect dynamique.

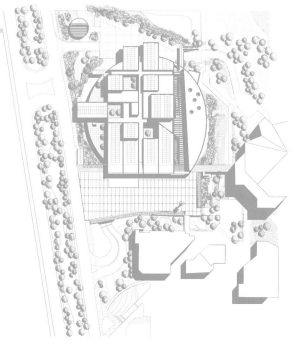

The strong forms of the museum, essentially an accumulation of rectangular volumes, can be seen in the site plan to the left and the overall view (below).

Die eindrucksvollen Formen des Museums, im Wesentlichen eine Anhäufung rechtwinkliger Volumen, sind links im Lageplan und in der Gesamtansicht (unten) zu erkennen.

Les formes puissantes du musée – essentiellement une composition de volumes rectangulaires – sont très présentes sur le plan au sol (à gauche) et dans la vue d'ensemble (ci-dessous).

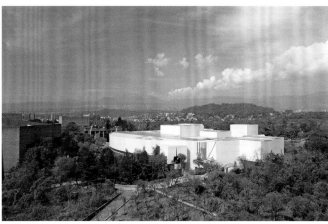

An angled wall and full-height glazing characterize the entrance sequence (above).

Eine schräge Wand und geschosshohe Verglasung charakterisieren den Eingangsbereich (oben).

La séquence de l'entrée se caractérise par son mur incliné et un vitrage toute hauteur (ci-dessus).

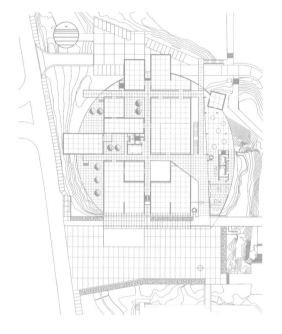

Again, rectangular volumes dominate the design, but the architect's willful cantilevers, as seen in the image below, render the complex quite dynamic and strong.

Aus rechtwinkligen Volumen besteht auch ein Großteil des Entwurfs, aber die von den Architekten bewusst gewählte Auskragung (siehe Abbildung unten) verleiht der Gesamtplanung eine dynamische und starke Wirkung.

Si la rectangularité des volumes fonde l'essentiel du projet, les porte-à-faux (ci-dessous) confèrent une force et un certain dynamisme à l'ensemble.

Generous glazing brings ample natural light into the building, with long vistas being another characteristic of the architecture, as can be seen in these images.

Die großzügige Verglasung lässt reichlich natürliches Licht in das Gebäude einfallen, und weite Ausblicke (wie auf diesen Abbildungen zu sehen) sind ein weiteres Charakteristikum der Architektur.

D'amples parois vitrées laissent pénétrer un généreux éclairage naturel dans le bâtiment qui se caractérise également par de longues perspectives intérieures, comme le montrent ces images.

GRAFT

Graft Gesellschaft von Architekten mbH
Heidestr. 50 / 10557 Berlin / Germany

Tel: +49 30 24 04 79 85 / Fax: +49 30 24 04 79 87
E-mail: berlin@graftlab.com / Web: www.graftlab.com

GRAFT was created in Los Angeles in 1998 "as a label for architecture, art, music, and the pursuit of happiness." Lars Krückeberg, Wolfram Putz, Thomas Willemeit, Gregor Hoheisel, and Alejandra Lillo are the partners of Graft, which today has about 100 employees worldwide. Graft maintains offices in Los Angeles, Berlin, and Beijing. Lars Krückeberg was educated at the Technical University, Braunschweig, as an engineer (1989–96) and at SCI-Arc in Los Angeles (1997–98). Wolfram Putz attended the Technical University, Braunschweig (1988–95), the University of Utah, Salt Lake City (1992–93), and SCI-Arc (1996–98). Thomas Willemeit was also educated in Braunschweig (1988–97), and at the Bauhaus Dessau (1991–92), before working in the office of Daniel Libeskind (1998–2001). Two other partners have since joined the firm, Gregor Hoheisel (founding partner Graft Beijing, 2004) and Alejandra Lillo (Graft Los Angeles, 2004). Taking advantage of their German background combined with US training, Graft declares: "We can see an architecture of new combinations, the grafting of different cultures and styles." They have built a studio and house for the actor Brad Pitt in Los Angeles (2000–03) and, working with Brad Pitt and William McDonough + Partners, Graft are the lead architects for the Pink Project and Make it Right initiative in New Orleans (Louisiana, 2007–). They designed the Hotel Q! in Berlin (Germany, 2002–04), as well as restaurants in the Bellagio and Mirage casinos in Las Vegas (Nevada, 2004 and 2006) and worked on several luxury Resort Hotels in the Caribbean. Their most recent work includes the Gingko Restaurant (Chengdu, China, 2008); the Gong Ti Club (Beijing, China, completion due 2009); Sichuan Airlines VIP Lounge at Terminal 3 (Beijing, China, completion due 2009); and the Russian Jewish Museum of Tolerance (Moscow, Russia, 2007–12, published here).

GRAFT wurde 1998 in Los Angeles „als Label für Architektur, Kunst, Musik und das Streben nach Glück" gegründet. Lars Krückeberg, Wolfram Putz, Thomas Willemeit, Gregor Hoheisel und Alejandra Lillo sind die Partner von Graft, mit heute weltweit etwa 100 Beschäftigten. Graft unterhält Büros in Los Angeles, Berlin und Peking. Lars Krückeberg studierte Ingenieurwesen an der Technischen Universität Braunschweig (1989–96) und am SCI-Arc in Los Angeles (1997–98). Wolfram Putz studierte an der Technischen Universität Braunschweig (1988–95), der University of Utah in Salt Lake City (1992–93) und am SCI-Arc (1996–98), Thomas Willemeit ebenfalls in Braunschweig (1988–97) sowie am Bauhaus in Dessau (1991–92), danach arbeitete er bei Daniel Libeskind (1998–2001). Inzwischen sind zwei weitere Partner in die Firma eingetreten: Gregor Hoheisel (Gründungspartner von Graft Peking, 2004) und Alejandra Lillo (Graft Los Angeles, 2004). Die Architekten nutzen die Verbindung ihrer deutschen Herkunft mit ihrer Ausbildung in den USA und erklären: „Wir erkennen neue Kombinationsmöglichkeiten in der Architektur, die Kreuzung – grafting – unterschiedlicher Kulturen und Stile." Sie haben ein Atelier und Wohnhaus für den Schauspieler Brad Pitt in Los Angeles gebaut (2000–03) und sind, in Zusammenarbeit mit Brad Pitt und William McDonough + Partners, die leitenden Architekten für das Pink Project und die Initiative Make it Right in New Orleans (Louisiana, 2007–). Sie planten das Hotel Q! in Berlin (2002–04) und die Restaurants in den Kasinos Bellagio und Mirage in Las Vegas (Nevada, 2004 bzw. 2006) sowie mehrere Luxusferienhotels in der Karibik. Ihre neuesten Projekte sind das Restaurant Gingko (Chengdu, China, 2008), der Klub Gong Ti (Peking, Fertigstellung für 2009 vorgesehen), die VIP-Lounge der Sichuan Airlines am Terminal 3 (Peking, geplante Fertigstellung 2009) und das Russisch-jüdische Museum der Toleranz (Moskau, 2007–12, hier veröffentlicht).

GRAFT, « label pour l'architecture, l'art, la musique et la recherche du bonheur », a été créé à Los Angeles en 1998. Lars Krückeberg, Wolfram Putz et Thomas Willemeit, Gregor Hoheisel et Alejandra Lillo sont les associés de cette agence qui compte aujourd'hui environ cent employés dans le monde entier. Graft possède des bureaux à Los Angeles, Berlin et Pékin. Lars Krückeberg a fait ses études d'ingénierie à la Technische Universität de Brunswick (Allemagne, 1989–96) et à SCI-Arc à Los Angeles (1997–98). Wolfram Putz a étudié à la même université (1988–95), à celle de l'Utah à Salt Lake City (1992–93) et à SCI-Arc à Los Angeles (1996–98). Thomas Willemeit a aussi étudié à Brunswick (1988–97) et au Bauhaus Dessau (1991–92) avant de travailler auprès de Daniel Libeskind (1998–2001). Deux autres associés ont rejoint l'agence : Gregor Hoheisel (associé fondateur de Graft Pékin, 2004) et Alejandra Lillo (Graft Los Angeles, 2004). À partir de cette formation allemande-américaine, Graft se propose « d'envisager une architecture de combinaisons nouvelles, la greffe de différents styles et cultures ». Ils ont construit un atelier et une maison pour Brad Pitt à Los Angeles (2000–03) et collaboré avec lui et William McDonough + Partners sur les projets Pink et Make it Right à la Nouvelle-Orléans (Louisiana, 2007–), dont ils sont les architectes en chef. Ils ont conçu l'Hotel Q ! à Berlin (2002–04), des restaurants pour les casinos Mirage et Bellagio à Las Vegas (2004 et 2006) et travaillé sur plusieurs complexes hôteliers dans les Caraïbes. Parmi leurs plus récents projets : le Restaurant Gingko (Chengdu, Chine, 2008) ; le Gong Ti Club (Pékin, achèvement prévu en 2009) ; le salon VIP des Sichuan Airlines au terminal 3 (Pékin, achèvement prévu en 2009) et le musée juif russe de la Tolérance (Moscou, Russie, 2007–12), publié ici.

RUSSIAN JEWISH MUSEUM
OF TOLERANCE
Moscow, Russia, 2007–12

Address: Obraztsova Street 12a, 127055 Moscow, Russia
Area: 16 500 m². Client: Federation of the Jewish Communities of Russia. Cost: not disclosed

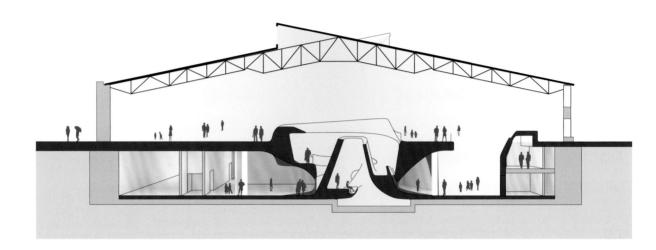

This project is to be located in the Bakhmetevsky Bus Garage, designed by Konstantin Melnikov. The 154-meter-long, 54-meter-wide structure will serve as the shell within which the museum will be built. The new institution will include a series of "studios, a children's museum, a learning center, large areas for multipurpose and changing exhibitions, an 800-seat auditorium and smaller lecture halls, a restaurant and bar, a museum shop, and space for administration and museum staff." The architects approach the museum as a new type of institution, which is intended to relate historical fact to the current activity of a community. Graft's scheme leaves the Melnikov building untouched, "as a monument of Russian heritage," and makes use only of the space originally intended for buses. The historical elements of the museum will be shown in the underground studios—so that "the past seems to be buried in the ground," with current activities coming together at ground level. The architects state: "The artificial topography of this new intervention forms the parametric counterpart to the regular structure of the shell. While the rationale of modernity and the emotional strength of both Russian and Jewish culture have often been seen as antipodes in the history of the 20th century, this museum design ventures to show both in a defined relation of balance." In a symbolic gesture, the original doors of the building are to be left closed, inviting visitors to take a more circuitous route, just as Jews have been obliged to do throughout history.

Dieses Projekt soll in dem von Konstantin Melnikow entworfenen Bachmetiew-Busdepot realisiert werden. Das 154 m lange und 54 m breite Gebäude wird als Hülle dienen, in die das neue Museum gebaut wird. Es soll mehrere „Ateliers, ein Kindermuseum, ein Studienzentrum, große Bereiche für Mehrzwecknutzung und Wechselausstellungen, ein Auditorium mit 800 Plätzen und kleinere Vortragssäle, ein Restaurant mit Bar, einen Museumsshop sowie Verwaltungs- und Personalräume enthalten". Die Architekten sehen das Museum als eine neue Institution, die historische Gegebenheiten mit den gegenwärtigen Aktivitäten einer Gemeinschaft verbindet. Grafts Entwurf lässt das Melnikow-Gebäude „als Monument des russischen Erbes" unangetastet und nutzt nur den ursprünglich für Omnibusse vorgesehenen Raum. Die historischen Elemente des Museums werden in den Ateliers im Untergeschoss gezeigt – sodass „die Vergangenheit scheinbar im Untergrund begraben liegt"; die gegenwärtigen Aktivitäten sind im Erdgeschoss zusammengefasst. Die Architekten erklären: „Die künstliche Topografie dieses neuen Eingriffs bildet das parametrische Gegenstück zur regelmäßigen Struktur der Hülle. Während die Grundlagen der Moderne und die emotionale Kraft der russischen wie auch der jüdischen Kultur in der Geschichte des 20. Jahrhunderts oft als Antipoden betrachtet wurden, versucht dieses Museumsprojekt, beide in einem bestimmten Gleichgewicht zu sehen." Als symbolische Geste bleiben die Originaltüren des Gebäudes geschlossen; die Besucher werden aufgefordert, einen gewundeneren Weg zu wählen – wie man auch die Juden im Verlauf der Geschichte auf einen solchen gezwungen hat.

Ce projet s'insère dans le garage pour autobus Bakhmetevsky, conçu par Konstantin Melnikov. La structure de 154 mètres de long par 54 de large a été traitée comme une coquille à l'intérieur de laquelle le musée sera édifié. La nouvelle institution comprendra une série « d'ateliers, un musée pour les enfants, un centre d'enseignement, de vastes espaces pour des expositions diverses et temporaires, un auditorium de huit cents places, de petites salles de conférence, un bar-restaurant, une boutique et des bureaux pour l'administration et le personnel ». Les architectes ont conçu un nouveau type d'institution chargé de montrer des faits historiques en relation avec l'actualité. Le projet de Graft ne touche pas au bâtiment de Melnikov, « monument du patrimoine russe », et n'utilise que l'espace qui avait été prévu pour les autobus. Les éléments historiques du musée seront exposés dans des ateliers souterrains pour que « le passé semble enterré », les activités du présent étant traitées au rez-de-chaussée. « La topographie artificielle de cette intervention nouvelle forme la contrepartie paramétrique de la structure régulière de la coquille. Si la rationalité de la modernité et la puissance émotionnelle des cultures à la fois juive et russe ont souvent été considérées aux antipodes l'une de l'autre dans l'histoire du XXe siècle, ce projet de musée veut les présenter toutes les deux dans une relation définie d'équilibre », précisent les architectes. Dans un geste symbolique, les portes d'origine du bâtiment sont laissées closes, ce qui invite les visiteurs à emprunter une voie moins directe, comme les Juifs ont été obligés de le faire au cours de leur histoire.

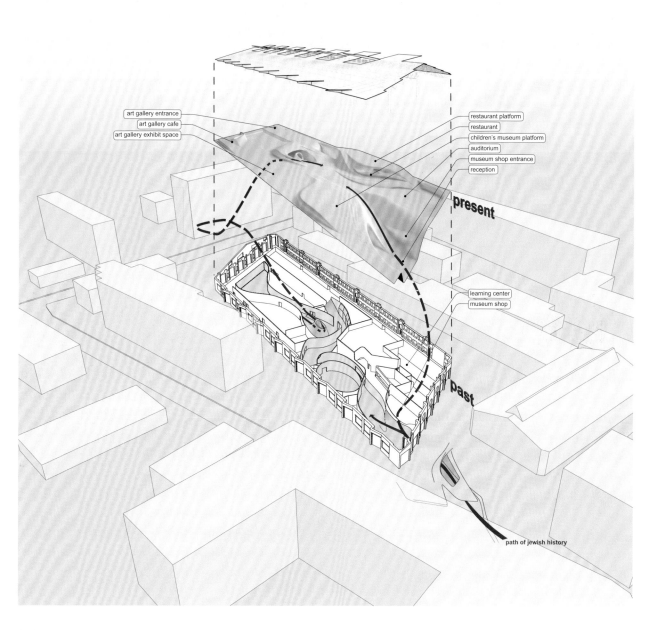

art gallery entrance
art gallery cafe
art gallery exhibit space

restaurant platform
restaurant
children's museum platform
auditorium
museum shop entrance
reception

present

learning center
museum shop

past

path of jewish history

As these drawings show, the architects insert the new volume into the ample spaces of the older bus garage, preserving the original structure while adding a thoroughly new, contemporary element to the composition.

Wie diese Darstellungen zeigen, fügen die Architekten ein neues Volumen in die weiten Räume der alten Omnibushalle ein. Sie erhalten die originale Konstruktion, setzen jedoch ein durchaus aktuelles, neues Element in die Komposition ein.

Comme le montrent ces dessins, les architectes ont inséré le nouveau volume dans celui du vaste garage de bus. Ils ont préservé la structure d'origine tout en installant dans la composition un élément totalement contemporain.

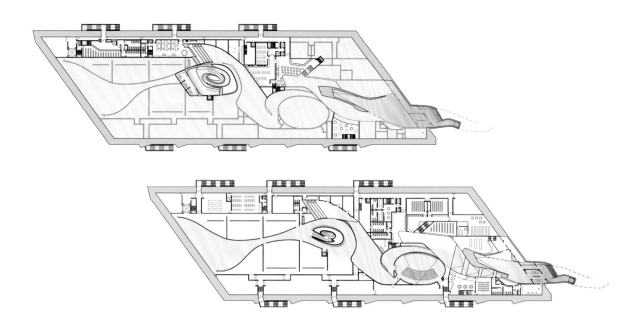

Sinuous curves and flowing spaces offer occasional views of the overarching older structure.

Schwungvolle Kurven und fließende Räume öffnen sich an manchen Stellen zu Ausblicken auf die Überwölbung der alten Konstruktion.

À certains endroits, les courbes sinueuses et le flux des espaces laissent entrapercevoir l'ancienne structure de la toiture.

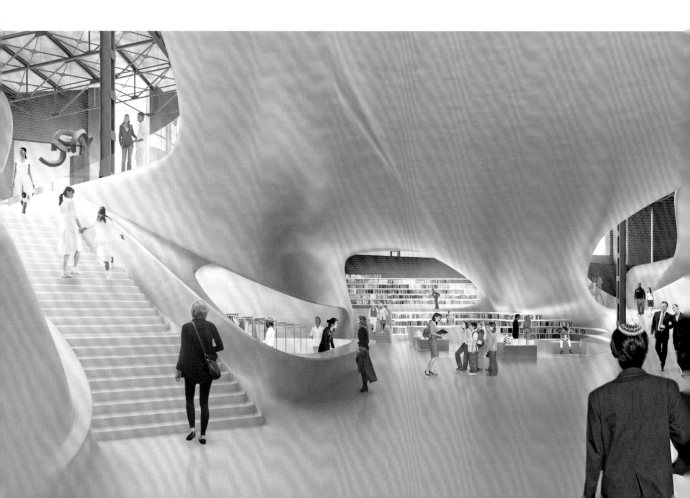

Winding ramps and curved openings contrast with the garage building and make it clear where one piece of architecture ends and the other begins.

Gewundene Rampen und gekrümmte Öffnungen bilden einen Kontrast zum Altbau und machen deutlich, wo eine Architektur endet und die andere beginnt.

Des rampes et des ouvertures incurvées viennent contraster avec les bâtiments de l'ancien garage et marquent clairement les limites entre l'ancienne et la nouvelle architecture.

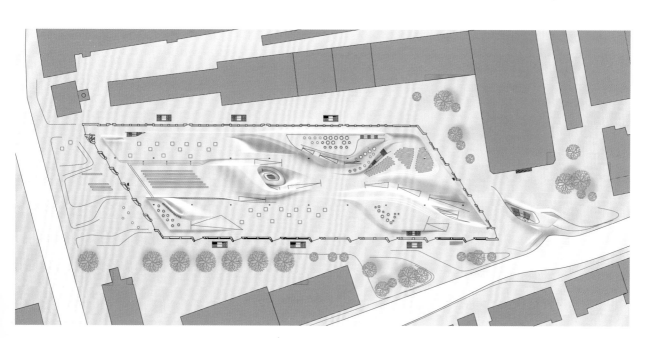

NICHOLAS GRIMSHAW

Grimshaw
57 Clerkenwell Road
London EC1M 5NG
UK

Tel: +44 207 291 41 41
Fax: +44 207 291 41 94
E-mail: communications@grimshaw-architects.com
Web: www.grimshaw-architects.com

A 1965 graduate of the Architectural Association (AA) in London, **NICHOLAS GRIMSHAW** was born in 1939 in that city. He created the firm Nicholas Grimshaw and Partners Ltd. in 1980, now known as Grimshaw. His numerous industrial structures include those built for Herman Miller in Bath (1976); BMW at Bracknell (1980); the furniture maker Vitra (Weil am Rhein, Germany, 1981); and the *Financial Times* in London (1988), all in the UK unless stated otherwise. He also built the British Pavilion at the 1992 Universal Exhibition in Seville. One of his most visible works is the former International Terminal of Waterloo Station (London, 1988–93). Grimshaw currently employs a staff of 200 with offices in London, New York, and Melbourne. Andrew Whalley, a partner in the firm, was educated at the Mackintosh School of Architecture (B.Arch, 1984) and at the AA in London (1986). Vincent Chang, also a partner, received his degrees at the Cambridge University School of Architecture (1988, 1991). Buildings include the Rolls-Royce Manufacturing Plant and Head Office (West Sussex, UK, 2003); Zurich Airport (Zurich, Switzerland, 2003 and 2004); the Sankei Nishi-Umeda Building (Osaka, Japan, 2004); University College London New Engineering Building (London, UK, 2005); Fundacion Caixa Galicia Arts and Cultural Center (A Coruña, Spain, 2006); the UCL Cancer Institute (London, UK, 2007); the Dubai Tower (design 2007); and Horno 3, Museo del Acero (Monterrey, Mexico, 2006–07, published here).

NICHOLAS GRIMSHAW, geboren 1939 in London, beendete 1965 sein Studium an der Architectural Association (AA). 1980 gründete er das Büro Nicholas Grimshaw and Partners Ltd., heute als Grimshaw bekannt. Er baute zahlreiche Industriegebäude, z. B. für die Firmen Herman Miller in Bath (1976), BMW in Bracknell (1980), den Möbelhersteller Vitra in Weil am Rhein (Deutschland, 1981) und das Gebäude der *Financial Times* in London (1988). Grimshaw plante 1992 auch den britischen Pavillon auf der Weltausstellung in Sevilla. Zu seinen spektakulärsten Werken gehört der frühere internationale Terminal der Waterloo Station (London, 1988–93). Grimshaw beschäftigt heute 200 Mitarbeiter und unterhält Büros in London, New York und Melbourne. Andrew Whalley, Partner im Büro Grimshaw, studierte an der Mackintosh School of Architecture (B. Arch. 1984) und an der Architectural Association in London (1986). Ein weiterer Partner, Vincent Chang, erhielt seine akademischen Grade an der Cambridge University School of Architecture (1988, 1991). Zu den Bauten des Büros zählen die Produktionsstätten und die Hauptverwaltung der Firma Rolls-Royce (West Sussex, Großbritannien, 2003), der Flughafen von Zürich (2003 bzw. 2004), das Sankei Nishi-Umeda Building (Osaka, 2004), das New Engineering Building des University College London (2005), das Kultur- und Kunstzentrum der Fundacion Caixa Galicia (A Coruña, Spanien, 2006), das UCL Cancer Institute (London, 2007), der Dubai Tower (Entwurf 2007) und Horno 3, Museo del Acero (Monterrey, Mexiko, 2006–07, hier veröffentlicht).

Diplômé en 1965 de l'Architectural Association (AA) à Londres, **NICHOLAS GRIMSHAW** y est né en 1939. Après avoir fondé l'agence Nicholas Grimshaw and Partners Ltd., actuelle agence Grimshaw, en 1980, il a réalisé de nombreuses structures industrielles, dont celle de Herman Miller à Bath (1976); de BMW à Bracknell (1980); du fabricant de mobilier Vitra (Weil am Rhein, Allemagne, 1981); et de l'imprimerie du *Financial Times* à Londres en 1988. Il a également réalisé le Pavillon britannique de l'Exposition universelle de Séville (1992). L'une de ses réalisations les plus connues est l'ancien terminal international de la gare de Waterloo (Londres, 1988–93). Son agence compte deux cents collaborateurs dans ses bureaux de Londres, New York et Melbourne. Andrew Whalley, partenaire, a étudié à la Mackintosh School of Architecture (B.Arch. 1984) et à l'AA à Londres (1986). Vincent Chang, également partenaire, est diplômé de la Cambridge University School of Architecture (1988 et 1991). Parmi leurs réalisations : l'usine et siège de Rolls-Royce (West Sussex, Royaume-Uni, 2003); l'aéroport de Zurich (Zurich, Suisse, 2003 et 2004); l'immeuble Sankei Nishi-Umeda (Osaka, Japon, 2004); le nouveau bâtiment de l'ingénierie au University College de Londres (Londres, Royaume-Uni, 2005); le centre des Arts et de la Culture de la Fundacion Caixa Galicia (La Corogne, Espagne, 2006); l'UCL Cancer Institute (Londres, Royaume-Uni, 2007); la Dubai Tower (conçue en 2007) et Horno 3, Museo del Acero (Monterrey, Mexique, 2006–07), publié ici.

HORNO 3

Museo del Acero, Monterrey, Mexico, 2006–07

Address: Avenida Fundidora y Adolfo Prieto S/N, Int. Parque Fundidora, Colonia Obrera, Monterrey, CP 64010, Mexico
+52 81 8126 1100, www.horno3.org
Area: 7150 m². Client: Museo del Acero AC. Cost: $17.6 million
Collaboration: Oficina de Arquitectura, Monterrey; Werner Sobek NY (Specialist Structural Engineer)

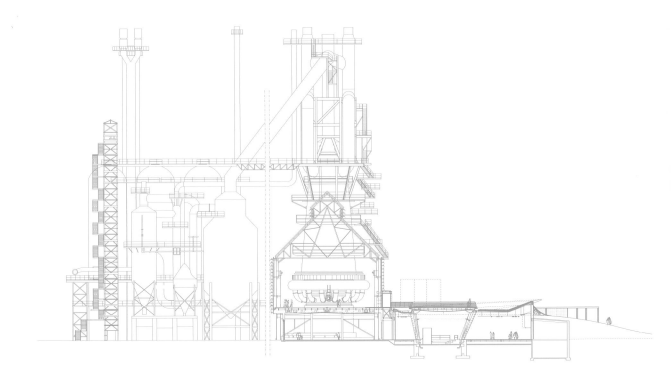

This Museum of Steel was built around one of the three original blast furnaces in the Parque Fundidora. A total of 9000 square meters of indoor and outdoor museum space was created in and around the 70-meter-high 1960s furnace structure. The project was completed for the International Forum of Cultures, hosted by Monterrey in September 2007, and was meant in part to display the qualities of local craftsmanship. A funicular, whose path was once used by an iron-ore elevator, carries visitors 43 meters up the tower for a tour of the furnace structure and a view of the city. The original patina of the industrial facilities has been stabilized and maintained. An entry wing and largely underground Steel Gallery with a tessellated steel roof were added to the existing structure. Here, new green roofs planted with native grasses provide passive cooling in summer and harvest rainwater for use inside the building, one of several sustainable design features implemented by the architects. The facility received 145 000 visitors in its first six months of operation.

Dieses Museum des Stahls wurde um einen von drei originalen Hochöfen im Parque Fundidora errichtet. Die 9000 m² innen- und außenliegende Ausstellungsfläche wurden im und um den 70 m hohen Hochofen aus den 1960er-Jahren geschaffen. Das Projekt wurde zum Internationalen Kulturforum fertiggestellt, das im September 2007 in Monterrey stattfand, und sollte u. a. die Leistungen des örtlichen Handwerks zur Schau stellen. Eine Seilbahn an der Stelle des früheren Eisenerzaufzugs bringt die Besucher den 43 m hohen Turm hinauf zu einem Gang durch den Hochofen und zum Ausblick auf die Stadt. Die originale Patina der Industriebauten wurde dauerhaft erhalten. Ein Eingangstrakt und das überwiegend unter Bodenniveau verlegte Stahlmuseum mit schachbrettartigem Stahldach wurden der bestehenden Bebauung hinzugefügt. Mit einheimischen Gräsern begrünte Dächer sorgen für Kühlung im Sommer und speichern Regenwasser für die Nutzung im Gebäude – eines von mehreren Elementen einer nachhaltigen Planung der Architekten. Die Anlage wurde in den ersten sechs Monaten nach der Eröffnung von 145 000 Personen besucht.

Ce musée de l'Acier a été construit autour de l'un des trois hauts fourneaux originels du Parque Fundidora. Neuf mille mètres carrés d'espaces d'expositions aussi bien intérieurs qu'extérieurs ont été créés dans et autour de la structure du haut-fourneau de 70 mètres datant des années 1960. Le projet, achevé à l'occasion du Forum des cultures accueilli par Monterey en septembre 2007, avait pour objectif d'afficher les qualités de l'industrie locale. Un funiculaire, utilisé naguère pour un élévateur de minerai de fer, monte les visiteurs vers la tour, à 43 mètres de haut, et les conduits à la découverte du haut-fourneau, puis vers une vue panoramique sur la ville. La patine de la vieille installation industrielle a été stabilisée et conservée. Une aile d'entrée, et une galerie de l'Acier en grande partie souterraine, dotée d'un toit carrelé d'acier, ont été ajoutées aux constructions existantes. Les toits recouverts de végétation locale, qui assurent un rafraîchissement passif en été et récupèrent les eaux pluviales utilisées dans le bâtiment, ne sont qu'un exemple des dispositifs de développement durable mis en œuvre par les architectes. Le musée a reçu cent quarante-cinq mille visiteurs au cours de ses six premiers mois de fonctionnement.

The architect has very clearly retained the powerful industrial forms of the original building, while at the same time inserting the new museum.

Der Architekt hat die kraftvollen Industrieformen des Originalbaus sehr klar bewahrt, zugleich aber das neue Museum eingefügt.

L'architecte a conservé les puissantes formes architecturales industrielles du bâtiment d'origine, dans lesquelles il a inséré le nouveau musée.

A spiral staircase and glass-enclosed
elevator shaft symbolize the clarity
and modernity that Grimshaw has
brought to the industrial facility,
whose beams and columns are
everywhere in sight.

Eine Wendeltreppe und ein gläserner
Aufzugsschacht sind Symbole für die
Klarheit und Modernität, die Grimshaw diesem Industriebau hinzugefügt hat, dessen Balken und Stützen
überall sichtbar geblieben sind.

Un escalier en spirale et une cage
d'ascenseur vitrée symbolisent
l'esprit de modernité et de clarté
introduit par Grimshaw dans ces
anciennes installations industrielles
dont les poutres et les piliers restent
omniprésents.

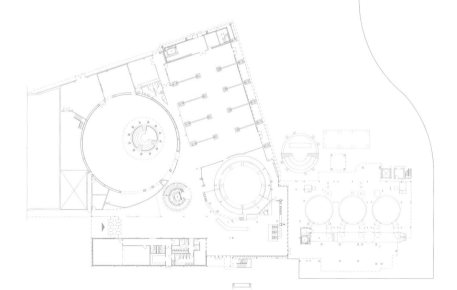

ZAHA HADID

Zaha Hadid
Studio 9 / 10 Bowling Green Lane / London EC1R OBQ / UK
Tel: +44 207 253 51 47 / Fax: +44 207 251 83 22
E-mail: mail@zaha-hadid.com
Web: www.zaha-hadid.com

ZAHA HADID studied architecture at the Architectural Association (AA), London, beginning in 1972 and was awarded the Diploma Prize in 1977. She then became a partner of Rem Koolhaas in the Office for Metropolitan Architecture (OMA) and taught at the AA. She has also taught at Harvard, the University of Chicago, in Hamburg and at Columbia University in New York. In 2004, Zaha Hadid became the first woman to win the coveted Pritzker Prize. Well-known for her paintings and drawings, she has had a substantial influence, despite having built relatively few buildings. She completed the Vitra Fire Station (Weil am Rhein, Germany, 1990–94); and exhibition designs such as that for *The Great Utopia* (Solomon R. Guggenheim Museum, New York, 1992). Significant competition entries include her design for the Cardiff Bay Opera House (1994–96); the Habitable Bridge (London, 1996); and the Luxembourg Philharmonic Hall (1997). More recently, Hadid has entered a phase of active construction with such projects as the Bergisel Ski Jump (Innsbruck, Austria, 2001–02); the Lois & Richard Rosenthal Center for Contemporary Art (Cincinnati, Ohio, 1999–2003); the Phæno Science Center (Wolfsburg, Germany, 2001–05); the Central Building of the new BMW Assembly Plant in Leipzig (Germany, 2005); the Ordrupgaard Museum Extension (Copenhagen, Denmark, 2001–05, published here); and Mobile Art, Chanel Contemporary Art Container (various locations, 2007–, published here). She is working on MAXXI, the National Museum of 21st-Century Arts (Rome, Italy, 1998–2009, also published here); the Guangzhou Opera House (Guangzhou, China, 2006–09); and the Sheik Zayed Bridge (Abu Dhabi, UAE, 2005–10).

ZAHA HADID studierte ab 1972 Architektur an der Architectural Association (AA) in London und erhielt 1977 den Diploma Prize. Dann wurde sie Partnerin von Rem Koolhaas im Office for Metropolitan Architecture (OMA) und lehrte an der AA, außerdem in Harvard, an der University of Chicago, in Hamburg und an der Columbia University in New York. 2004 wurde Zaha Hadid als erster Frau der Pritzker-Preis verliehen. Sie ist durch ihre Gemälde und Zeichnungen bekannt geworden und übt großen Einfluss aus, obgleich sie nur verhältnismäßig wenige Bauten ausgeführt hat. Realisiert hat sie die Feuerwehrstation der Firma Vitra (Weil am Rhein, Deutschland, 1990–94) und mehrere Ausstellungskonzepte, z. B. *The Great Utopia* (Solomon R. Guggenheim Museum, New York, 1992). Bedeutende Wettbewerbsbeiträge waren ihr Entwurf für das Cardiff Bay Opera House (1994–96), die Habitable Bridge (London, 1996) und die Philharmonie in Luxemburg (1997). In letzter Zeit hat für Zaha Hadid eine aktive Bauphase begonnen mit Projekten wie der Skisprungschanze Bergisel (Innsbruck, 2001–02), dem Lois & Richard Rosenthal Center for Contemporary Art (Cincinnati, Ohio, 1999–2003), dem Wissenschaftszentrum Phæno (Wolfsburg, 2001–05), dem Zentralgebäude des neuen BMW-Werks in Leipzig (2005), dem Erweiterungsbau des Ordrupgaard Museums (Kopenhagen, 2001–05, hier veröffentlicht) und Mobile Art, dem Chanel Contemporary Art Container (verschiedene Standorte, 2007–, hier veröffentlicht). Sie arbeitet gegenwärtig am MAXXI, dem Nationalmuseum für Kunst des 21. Jahrhunderts (Rom, 1998–2009, ebenfalls hier veröffentlicht), dem Opernhaus in Guangzhou (China, 2006–09) und der Scheich-Zayed-Brücke (Abu Dhabi, Vereinigte Arabische Emirate, 2005–10).

ZAHA HADID a étudié à l'Architectural Association (AA) de Londres de 1972 à 1977, date à laquelle elle a reçu le prix du Diplôme. Elle est ensuite partenaire de Rem Koolhaas, à l'Office for Metropolitan Architecture (OMA), et enseigne à l'AA ainsi qu'à Harvard, à l'université de Chicago, à Hambourg et à la Columbia University à New York. En 2004, elle a été la première femme a remporter le très convoité prix Pritzker. Célèbre pour ses peintures et dessins, elle a exercé une réelle influence, même si elle n'a que relativement peu construit pendant longtemps. Parmi ses premières réalisations figurent un poste d'incendie pour Vitra (Weil am Rhein, Allemagne, 1990–94) et des projets pour des expositions comme *La Grande Utopie* au Solomon R. Guggenheim Museum à New York (1992). Elle a participé à de nombreux concours dont les plus importants sont le projet pour l'Opéra de la baie de Cardiff (Pays de Galles, 1994–96) ; un pont habitable (Londres, 1996) et la salle de concerts philharmoniques de Luxembourg (1997). Plus récemment, elle est entrée dans une phase active de grands chantiers avec des réalisations comme le tremplin de ski de Bergisel (Innsbruck, Autriche, 2001–02) ; le Lois & Richard Rosenthal Center for Contemporary Art (Cincinnati, Ohio, 1999–2003) ; le musée des Sciences Phæno (Wolfsburg, Allemagne, 2001–05) ; le bâtiment central de la nouvelle usine BMW de Leipzig (Allemagne, 2005) ; l'extension du musée Ordrupgaard (Copenhague, 2001–05, publiée ici) et Mobile Art, Chanel Contemporary Art Container (divers lieux, 2007–), publié ici. Elle met la dernière main au Centre national d'art du XXᵉ siècle MAXXI (Rome, Italie, 1998–2009, également publié ici) ; à l'Opéra de Guangzhou (Guangzhou, Chine, 2006–09) et au chantier du pont Cheikh Sayed (Abou Dhabi, EAU, 2005–10).

ORDRUPGAARD MUSEUM EXTENSION

Copenhagen, Denmark, 2001–05

Address: Vilvordevej 110, 2920 Charlottenlund, Denmark, +45 39 64 11 83, www.ordrupgaard.dk
Area: 11 150 m². Client: Danish Ministry of Culture, Fonden Fealdania, Augusten Fonden. Cost: € 6.6 million

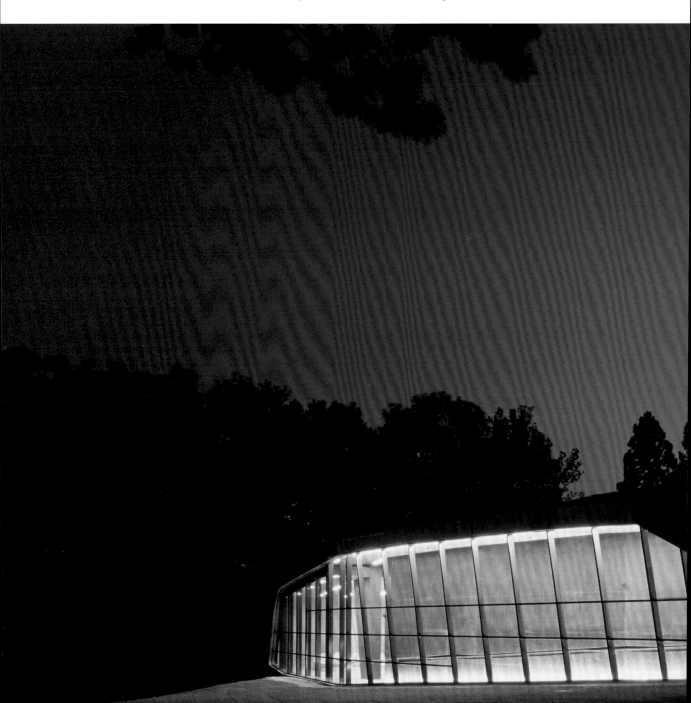

A façade of the extension leans and curves as it is transformed from an opaque surface into one that is glazed from floor to ceiling.

Eine Fassade des Erweiterungsbaus ist geneigt und gekrümmt; sie verändert sich von einer undurchsichtigen Fläche zu einer geschosshoch verglasten.

Une façade de l'extension se penche et s'incurve et passe d'un plan opaque à une surface vitrée toute hauteur.

For this extension of the existing Ordrupgaard Museum, a Danish state museum for 19th-century French and Danish art lodged in the former mansion of the collector Wilhelm Hansen, Zaha Hadid calls on the idea of a distinct relationship between the landscape setting and the new building. According to her project description: "The new extension seeks to establish a new landscape within the territory of its architecture, at the same time allowing new relations with the existing conditions. The logic of the existing landscape is abstracted in the geometry; new contours extend into the collection developing an alternate ground where occupancy and use are extended." The new structure is 87 meters long and 20 meters wide and includes a five-meter-long passage to the old structure. Made of cast black lava concrete, the structure's complex curving geometry suggested an on-site molding process with the self-consolidating concrete pressed into forms from below or pumped into an outer shell through holes. With walls curving into ceilings or floors, the Ordrupgaard extension experiments successfully with the creation of a continuous space where the straight lines that characterize the original museum are the exception rather than the rule. The architect states: "The critique of the edge is thus replaced by a notion of fluid interaction between the garden and the interior program," she says, "and it acts as a constant instrument of gradation that allows for different conditions to appear without necessarily breaking the volume up."

Für diese Erweiterung des Ordrupgaard Museums, eines staatlichen dänischen Museums für französische und dänische Kunst des 19. Jahrhunderts im früheren Herrenhaus des Sammlers Wilhelm Hansen, stellt Zaha Hadid eine eindeutige Beziehung zwischen der landschaftlichen Umgebung und dem neuen Gebäude her. Laut ihrer Projektbeschreibung „versucht der Neubau, eine neue Landschaft im Bereich seiner Architektur zu errichten und zugleich neue Beziehungen zu den bestehenden Verhältnissen einzugehen. Die Logik der vorhandenen Landschaft wird in der Geometrie abstrahiert; neue Konturen erstrecken sich bis in die Sammlung und entwickeln einen sich wechselseitig befruchtenden Bereich, auf dem Besitz und Nutzung erweitert werden." Der Neubau ist 87 m lang und 20 m breit zuzüglich eines 5 m langen Übergangs zum Altbau. Die komplexen, gekrümmten Formen des neuen Gebäudes aus schwarzem Lava-Gussbeton legten ein Verfahren nahe, bei dem der selbstverdichtende Beton vor Ort von unten in Schalungen gepresst oder durch Löcher in eine Außenschale gepumpt wurde. Mit Wänden, die sich zu Decken oder Fußböden krümmen, experimentiert der Neubau des Ordrupgaard Museums erfolgreich mit der Bildung eines durchgehenden Raums, in dem die geraden Linien, die das alte Museum charakterisieren, eher die Ausnahme als die Regel darstellen. Die Architektin erklärt: „Die kritische Kante wird so ersetzt durch eine fließende Interaktion zwischen dem Garten und der Funktion der Innenräume; das wirkt wie ein Instrument des ständigen Übergangs, wodurch verschiedene Bedingungen entstehen können, ohne dass das Volumen aufgebrochen werden muss."

Pour cette extension d'un musée existant, l'Ordrupgaard Museum, musée d'État consacré à l'art danois et français du XIXᵉ siècle, logé dans l'ancienne résidence du collectionneur Wilhelm Hansen, Zaha Hadid a mis en œuvre un concept de relations distinctes entre le cadre du paysage et le nouveau bâtiment : « Cette extension cherche à établir un nouveau paysage à l'intérieur du territoire même de son architecture, tout en permettant des relations nouvelles avec les conditions existantes. La logique du paysage est résumée par la géométrie. Ses nouveaux contours s'étendent à travers les collections et génèrent un sol alternatif où se développent l'occupation et l'usage ». La nouvelle construction de 87 mètres de long par 20 de large est reliée par un passage de 5 mètres de long avec l'ancien bâtiment. Coulée en béton de lave noir, sa forme curviligne complexe suggère un processus de moulage *in situ* dont le béton aurait été compressé par le bas ou pompé dans la coque extérieure par des orifices. L'extension du musée aux murs se transformant en sols ou plafonds réussissent à créer un espace continu dans lequel les lignes droites caractéristiques du musée ancien deviennent l'exception plutôt que la règle. « La limite critique est donc remplacée par une notion d'interaction fluide entre le jardin et le programme intérieur », précise Zaha Hadid, « qui agit comme un instrument permanent de gradation permettant de faire apparaître des conditions différentes, sans nécessairement rompre le volume ».

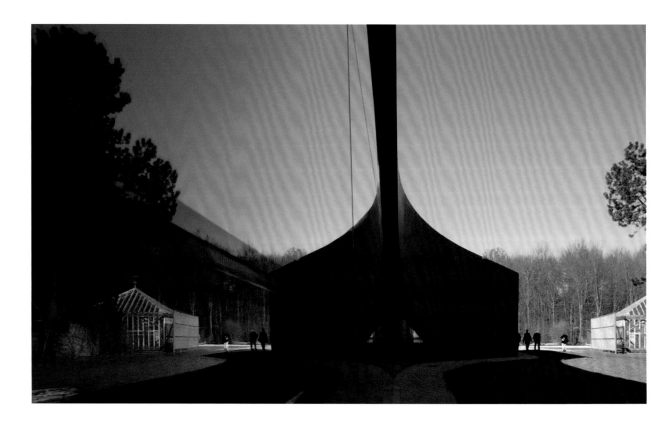

The undulating, dynamic forms conceived by Hadid seem to flow from the original rectilinear structure, offering contrast, but not contradiction.

Die von Zaha Hadid konzipierten gebogenen, dynamischen Formen scheinen aus dem geradlinigen Originalgebäude zu fließen und bilden einen Gegensatz, aber keinen Widerspruch zu ihm.

Les formes dynamiques et ondulées conçues par Hadid semblent littéralement s'écouler de la construction orthogonale d'origine. Elles sont en contraste et non en contradiction avec elle.

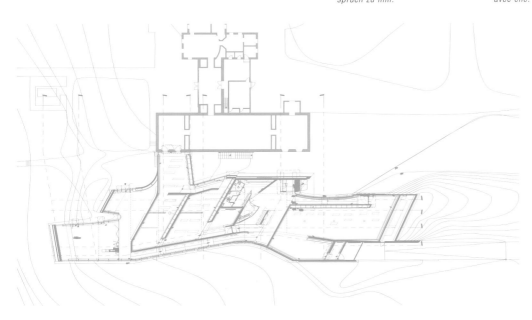

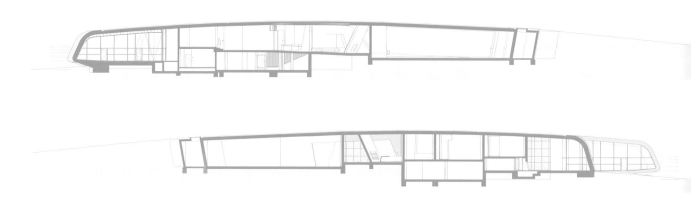

As is often the case, Hadid's walls curve up to become a ceiling, while glazed surfaces also appear and disappear in the rhythm of the structure.

Wie häufig bei Hadid, biegen sich die Wände zu einer Decke, während verglaste Flächen im Rhythmus der Konstruktion auftreten und verschwinden.

Comme souvent chez Hadid, les murs s'incurvent vers le haut pour se transformer en plafond, et des surfaces vitrées apparaissent et disparaissent au rythme de la structure.

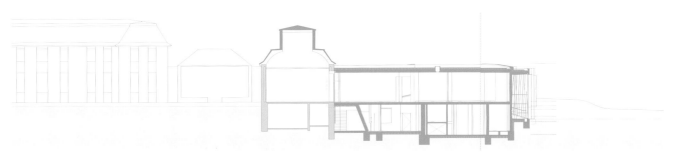

MOBILE ART

Chanel Contemporary Art Container, various locations, 2007–

Chanel Mobile Art – Hong Kong, Tokyo, New York
Area: 700 m². Client: Chanel, Karl Lagerfeld. Cost: not disclosed

Commissioned by Chanel designer Karl Lagerfeld, this traveling exhibition pavilion "is a celebration of the iconic work of Chanel, unmistakable for its smooth layering of exquisite details that together create an elegant, cohesive whole." Made of a series of continuous arch-shaped elements with a 65-square-meter central courtyard and a partially glazed adjustable ceiling, the pavilion is described as a "new artificial landscape for art installations." Twenty-nine meters long and 45 meters wide, the structure is six meters high with a floor raised one meter above ground level. Conceived for easy dismounting and shipment, the Chanel pavilion has structural segments with a maximum width of 2.25 meters. Inspired to some extent by Chanel's famous quilted 2.55 handbag, the pavilion was erected in Hong Kong in March 2008, when Hadid commented: "The complexity and technological advances in digital imaging software and construction techniques have made the architecture of the Mobile Art Pavilion possible. It is an architectural language of fluidity and nature, driven by new digital design, and manufacturing processes have enabled us to create the pavilion's totally organic forms—instead of the serial order of repetition that marks the architecture of the industrial 20th century." When the project was first shown at the 2007 Venice art Biennale, Karl Lagerfeld said of Hadid: "She is the first architect to find a way to part with the all-dominating post-Bauhaus aesthetic. The value of her designs is similar to that of great poetry. The potential of her imagination is enormous." The pavilion has been seen in Tokyo, Hong Kong, and in Central Park, New York.

Dieser vom Chanel-Designer Karl Lagerfeld in Auftrag gegebene mobile Ausstellungspavillon „ist eine Hommage an die zur Ikone gewordene Coco Chanel, deren unverwechselbares Werk durch gelungene Zusammenstellung exquisiter Details ein elegantes, einheitliches Ganzes bildet". Der Pavillon besteht aus einer Verbindung bogenförmiger Elemente mit einem 65 m² großen, zentralen Innenhof und einer teilverglasten, verstellbaren Decke und wird als „neue künstliche Landschaft für Kunstinstallationen" beschrieben. Die 29 m lange und 45 m breite Konstruktion ist 6 m hoch, der Boden liegt 1 m über Geländehöhe. Die konstruktiven Elemente des für leichte Demontage und zum Transport vorgesehenen Pavillons haben eine maximale Spannweite von 2,25 m. Das in gewisser Weise von Chanels berühmter gesteppter Handtasche 2.55 inspirierte Bauwerk wurde im März 2008 in Hongkong errichtet. Hadid kommentierte es wie folgt: „Die Komplexität und die technologischen Fortschritte der Software für die digitale Darstellung und die Bautechnik haben die Architektur des Mobile Art Pavilion ermöglicht. Es handelt sich um eine fließende und natürliche Architektursprache, ermöglicht durch neuartiges digitales Entwerfen und neue Produktionsverfahren für vollkommen organische Formen – statt der seriellen Wiederholung von Bauteilen, die die Architektur des industriellen 20. Jahrhunderts charakterisierte." Als das Projekt erstmals 2007 auf der Kunstbiennale in Venedig vorgestellt wurde, sagte Lagerfeld über Hadid: „Sie ist die erste Architektin, die einen Weg findet, sich von der alles beherrschenden Post-Bauhaus-Ästhetik zu verabschieden. Die Bedeutung ihrer Entwürfe gleicht derjenigen großer Poesie. Das Potenzial ihrer Fantasie ist gewaltig." Der Pavillon war bisher in Tokio, Hongkong und im Central Park in New York zu sehen.

Commande du styliste de Chanel Karl Lagerfeld, ce pavillon pour expositions itinérantes « est la célébration d'une œuvre iconique de Chanel, par sa délicate accumulation de détails sophistiqués qui, tous ensemble, contribuent à créer un tout élégant et cohérent ». Composé d'une succession d'éléments en forme d'arc, d'une cour centrale de 65 mètres carrés et d'un plafond amovible partiellement vitré, ce pavillon est décrit comme « un nouveau paysage artificiel pour installations artistiques ». De 29 mètres de long sur 45 de large, la structure mesure 6 mètres de haut, et son plancher est surélevé d'un mètre par rapport au terrain. Prévu pour être facilement démonté et transporté, le pavillon est constitué de segments structurels de 2,25 mètres maximum de large. Inspiré dans une certaine mesure du fameux sac matelassé de Chanel – le 2.55 – le pavillon a été érigé à Hongkong en mars 2008. À cette occasion, Zaha Hadid a déclaré : « La complexité et les avancées techniques des logiciels d'images numériques et de techniques de construction ont rendu la construction de ce pavillon possible. C'est un langage architectural de fluidité et de naturel, animé par des technologies de conception et de fabrication par ordinateur, qui nous ont permis de créer ces formes totalement organiques, à la place de l'ordre répétitif qui a marqué l'architecture du XXᵉ siècle industriel. » Lorsque le projet a été présenté pour la première fois à la Biennale de Venise en 2007, Karl Lagerfeld a déclaré sur Zaha Hadid : « Elle est le premier architecte à avoir trouvé une voie qui s'écarte de l'esthétique dominante post-Bauhaus. La valeur de ses projets est similaire à celle de la grande poésie. Son potentiel d'imagination est énorme. Le pavillon a été vu à Tokyo, Hongkong et au Central Park, New York.

The interior spaces of the Mobile
Art pavilion are almost organic in
appearance, flowing into one another,
or offering unexpected glimpses
through the enclosed volume.

Die Innenräume des Pavillons Mobile
Art haben ein nahezu organisches
Erscheinungsbild; sie fließen ineinander oder bieten unerwartete Einblicke
durch die geschlossenen Volumen.

Les espaces intérieurs du pavillon
Mobile Art, d'aspect pratiquement
organique, s'interpénètrent ou offrent
des perspectives inattendues à travers leurs volumes.

There is an almost perfect symbiosis between the external curves and design of the building with its equally sensual, curvilinear interior.

Es besteht eine nahezu perfekte Symbiose der Außenkurven und der Gestaltung des Gebäudes mit seinen die Sinne gleichermaßen ansprechenden, gekrümmten Innenräumen.

La symbiose est presque parfaite entre les courbes extérieures du bâtiment et une architecture intérieure curviligne tout aussi sensuelle.

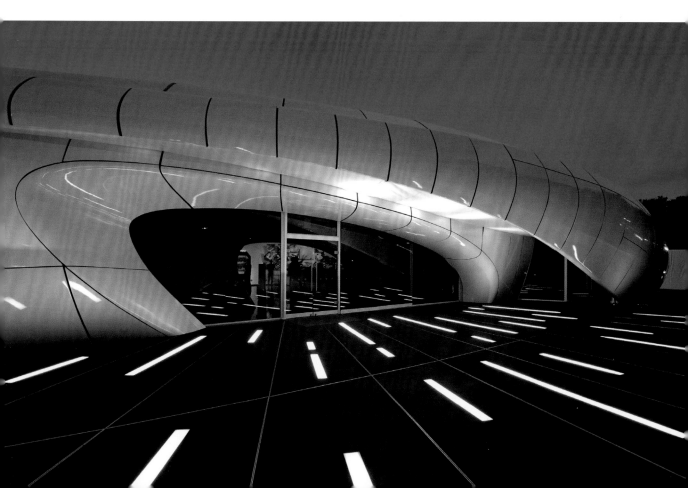

MAXXI

National Museum of 21st-Century Arts, Rome, Italy, 1998–2009

Address: Via Guido Reni 4A, 00196 Roma, Italy, +39 6 3210 1829, www.maxxi.beniculturali.it
Area: 30 000 m². Client: Italian Ministry of Culture. Cost: not disclosed

The client for this project is the Italian Ministry of Culture. Given the date of its conception, its forms may be more related to earlier work of Zaha Hadid, such as her Landscape Formation One (LF one, Weil am Rhein, Germany, 1998–99) than to her most recent designs. The difference here is, of course, the location, no longer related to a natural setting, but rather to the city. Hadid's description of the project explains: "By intertwining the circulation with the urban context, the building shares a public dimension with the city, overlapping tendril-like paths and open space. In addition to the circulatory relationship, the architectural elements are also geometrically aligned with the urban grids that join at the site." Allowing both visitors and curators a good deal of freedom for their movement through the space, or interpretation of its potential, Hadid further explains: "The drift through the Centre is a trajectory through varied ambiences, filtered spectacles and differentiated luminosity. Whilst offering a new freedom in the curators' palette, this in turn digests and recomposes the experience of art spectatorship as liberated dialogue with artifact and environment." The idea of drifting through the space is essential to the concept of the building, as opposed to a predetermined set of "key points." The dissolution of such typical museum elements as the vertical wall intended to hang paintings here allows for walls that turn into ceilings or are transformed into windows. Surely related to the later work that provides for flowing spatial continuity, the MAXXI might be considered a transition toward that increasingly marked theme in Zaha Hadid's work.

Bauherr dieses Projekts ist das italienische Kulturministerium. Da das Konzept bereits vor Jahren entstand, gehören seine Formen eher in den Bereich früherer Werke von Zaha Hadid, wie z. B. dem Gartenschaupavillon Landscape Formation One (LF one, Weil am Rhein, Deutschland, 1998–99), als zu ihren neueren Entwürfen. Den Unterschied stellt hier natürlich der Standort dar: nicht mehr eine natürliche Umgebung, sondern die Stadt. Hadid liefert dazu folgende Erläuterung: „Durch die Verflechtung des Rundgangs mit dem städtischen Kontext erhält das Gebäude eine öffentliche Dimension in der Stadt, indem es rankenartige Wege und offene Bereiche überlappen lässt. Neben dieser Beziehung sind die architektonischen Elemente auch geometrisch auf die städtischen Raster ausgerichtet, die sich an diesem Standort begegnen." Besuchern und Kuratoren wird ausreichend Freiheit zur Bewegung im Raum oder zur Intepretation seines Potenzials geboten. Hadid erklärt weiterhin: „Der ungezwungene Gang durch das Museum ist ein Weg durch verschiedene Stimmungen, gefilterte Anblicke und unterschiedliche Lichtverhältnisse. Diese den Kuratoren gebotene neue Freiheit erweitert und verändert ihrerseits das Erlebnis des Kunstbetrachters als befreienden Dialog mit dem Kunstwerk und seiner Umgebung." Die Vorstellung vom ungezwungenen Gang durch den Raum im Gegensatz zu vorgegebenen „Schwerpunkten" ist wichtig für das Konzept des Gebäudes. Die Auflösung solch typischer Museumselemente wie der vertikalen Wand zum Aufhängen von Gemälden ermöglicht hier die Gestaltung von Wänden, die zu Decken oder in Fenster verwandelt werden. So lässt sich das MAXXI, das durch fließende, ineinander übergehende Räume gekennzeichnet ist, auch als Übergang zu diesem in Zaha Hadids späterem Werk zunehmend stärker betonten Thema betrachten.

Le client de ce projet est le ministère italien de la Culture. Étant donné sa date de conception, ses formes peuvent paraître davantage liées à des œuvres antérieures de Zaha Hadid, comme sa Landscape Formation One (LF one, Weil am Rhein, Allemagne, 1998–99), qu'à ses projets plus récents. La différence tient ici, bien sûr, au site qui n'est pas un cadre naturel mais celui d'une ville. La description du projet par l'architecte est éclairante : « En entrelaçant circulations et contexte urbain, le bâtiment partage avec la ville sa dimension publique, superposant des cheminements qui évoquent des tiges végétales ou forment des espaces ouverts. » En offrant aux visiteurs comme aux conservateurs une grande liberté de déplacement dans le volume, ou dans l'interprétation de son potentiel, « le déplacement à travers le musée devient une trajectoire à travers des ambiances diversifiées, des vues filtrées et des atmosphères lumineuses différenciées. Tout en offrant une liberté nouvelle à la palette de possibilités du conservateur, ce phénomène absorbe et recompose successivement l'expérience du spectateur dans un dialogue libéré avec les artefacts et l'environnement ». L'idée de mouvement à travers l'espace est essentielle dans le concept de cette réalisation, par opposition à un ensemble prédéterminé de « points clés ». La dissolution des éléments constitutifs typiques du musée, comme le plan vertical destiné à suspendre des tableaux, permet aux murs de se transformer en plafonds ou en fenêtres. Dans l'esprit de son travail ultérieur axé sur la continuité spatiale fluide, le MAXXI peut être considéré comme une transition vers cette thématique de plus en plus marquée dans l'œuvre de Zaha Hadid.

While other architects still conceive buildings as an accumulation of geometric volumes, Zaha Hadid here employs flowing volumes that intersect and overlap, creating a multitude of possible paths through the museum.

Während andere Architekten Bauten immer noch als Anhäufung geometrischer Volumen konzipieren, verwendet Zaha Hadid hier fließende Räume, die sich überschneiden und ineinander übergehen und eine Vielzahl möglicher Wege durch das Museum bieten.

Tandis que d'autres architectes conçoivent encore leurs projets comme une accumulation de volumes géométriques, Zaha Hadid emploie des volumes en flux qui s'entrecoupent et s'imbriquent pour créer une multitude de possibilités de cheminements à travers le musée.

HERZOG & DE MEURON

Herzog & de Meuron
Rheinschanze 6 / 4056 Basel / Switzerland

Tel: +41 61 385 57 57
Fax: +41 61 385 57 58
E-mail: info@herzogdemeuron.com

JACQUES HERZOG and **PIERRE DE MEURON** were both born in Basel in 1950. They received degrees in architecture from the ETH, Zurich, in 1975, after studying with Aldo Rossi, and founded their partnership in Basel in 1978. Harry Gugger and Christine Binswanger joined the firm in 1991 and 1994, respectively, while Robert Hösl and Ascan Mergenthaler became partners in 2004. Stefan Marbach became a partner in 2006, followed by Wolfgang Hardt, David Koch, and Markus Widmer in 2009. Jacques Herzog and Pierre de Meuron won the 2001 Pritzker Prize, and both the RIBA Gold Medal and Praemium Imperiale in 2007. They were chosen in early 1995 to design Tate Modern in London, the addition to the Tate Gallery for contemporary art, situated in the Bankside Power Station, on the Thames opposite Saint Paul's Cathedral, which opened in May 2000. In 2005, Herzog & de Meuron were commissioned by the Tate to develop a scheme for the extension of the gallery and its surrounding areas (expected completion 2012). More recently, they have built the Forum 2004 Building and Plaza (Barcelona, Spain, 2001–04); Allianz Arena (Munich, Germany, 2002–05); the de Young Museum (San Francisco, California, 2002–05); the Walker Art Center, Expansion of the Museum and Cultural Center (Minneapolis, Minnesota, 2003–05); the National Stadium, the main stadium for the 2008 Olympic Games in Beijing (China, 2003–08); the CaixaForum (Madrid, Spain, 2001–08); and TEA, Tenerife Espacio de las Artes (Santa Cruz de Tenerife, Canary Islands, Spain, 2003–08, published here). Current work includes VitraHaus, a new building to present Vitra's "Home Collection" on the Vitra campus in Weil am Rhein (Germany, completion 2010); the Elbe Philharmonic Hall in Hamburg (Germany, projected completion 2011); and the new Miami Art Museum (Florida, USA, projected completion 2012).

JACQUES HERZOG und **PIERRE DE MEURON** wurden beide 1950 in Basel geboren. Sie studierten bis 1975 bei Aldo Rossi an der ETH in Zürich und gründeten 1978 ihre Partnerschaft in Basel. Harry Gugger und Christine Binswanger traten 1991 bzw. 1994 in die Firma ein, Robert Hösl und Ascan Mergenthaler wurden 2004 Partner des Büros, Stefan Marbach 2006. Drei Jahre später folgten Wolfgang Hardt, David Koch und Markus Widmer. 2001 erhielten Jacques Herzog und Pierre de Meuron den Pritzker-Preis und 2007 die RIBA Gold Medal sowie den Praemium Imperiale. Das Büro erhielt 1995 den bedeutenden Auftrag zur Planung der im Mai 2000 eröffneten Tate Modern, der Ergänzung der Tate Gallery für zeitgenössische Kunst im Bankside-Kraftwerk an der Themse in London gegenüber der St. Paul's Cathedral. 2005 wurden sie mit dem Entwurf einer Erweiterung der Tate Modern und der Planung der Umgegend beauftragt (geplante Fertigstellung 2012). In letzter Zeit haben Herzog & de Meuron u. a. folgende Projekte realisiert: das Gebäude und die Plaza des Forum 2004 (Barcelona, 2001–04), die Allianz-Arena (München, 2002–05), das Museum De Young (San Francisco, Kalifornien, 2002–05), das Walker Art Center, Museumserweiterung und Kulturzentrum (Minneapolis, Minnesota, 2003–05), das Nationalstadion (Peking 2003–08), das CaixaForum (Madrid, 2001–08) und das TEA, Tenerife Espacio de las Artes (Santa Cruz de Tenerife, Kanarische Inseln, 2003–08, hier veröffentlicht). Gegenwärtig arbeiten sie am VitraHaus, einem Neubau zur Ausstellung der Vitra Home Collection auf dem Vitra-Gelände in Weil am Rhein (Fertigstellung 2010), an der Elbphilharmonie in Hamburg (Fertigstellung für 2011 vorgesehen) und dem neuen Miami Art Museum (Florida, geplante Fertigstellung 2012).

JACQUES HERZOG et **PIERRE DE MEURON**, tous deux nés à Bâle en 1950, sont diplômés en architecture de l'ETH de Zurich (1975) où ils ont étudié auprès d'Aldo Rossi. En 1978, ils s'associent à Bâle. Harry Gugger et Christine Binswanger les rejoignent respectivement en 1991 et 1994, ainsi que Robert Hösl et Ascan Mergenthaler qui deviennent partenaires en 2004, puis Stefan Marbach en 2006, suivi par Wolfgang Hardt, David Koch et Markus Widmer en 2009. Ils ont remporté le prix Pritzker en 2001 et tous deux la médaille d'or du RIBA, ainsi que le Praemium Imperiale en 2007. Ils ont été sélectionnés en 1995 pour l'aménagement de la Tate Modern, consacrée aux collections d'art moderne et contemporain de la Tate Gallery de Londres, dans une ancienne centrale électrique – Bankside Power Station – au bord de la Tamise face à la cathédrale Saint-Paul, réalisation qui fut inaugurée en mai 2000. En 2005, Herzog & de Meuron se sont vu confier par la Tate un projet d'extension de ses nouvelles installations et de l'aménagement de la zone environnante (fin des travaux prévue en 2012). Plus récemment, ils ont construit le bâtiment et la place du Forum 2004 à Barcelone (Espagne, 2001–04) ; le stade Allianz Arena (Munich, Allemagne, 2002–05) ; le musée de Young (San Francisco, Californie, 2002–05) et l'extension du musée et centre culturel du Walker Art Center (Minneapolis, Minnesota, 2003–05) ; le Stade national, principal stade des Jeux olympiques de Pékin (Chine, 2003–08) ; le CaixaForum (Madrid, Espagne, 2008) et le TEA, Tenerife Espacio de las Artes (Santa Cruz de Tenerife, Iles Canaries, Espagne, 2003–08), publié ici. Parmi leurs projets actuels figurent la VitraHaus, nouveau bâtiment de présentation de la « Collection maison » sur le campus Vitra à Weil am Rhein (Allemagne, prévu pour 2010) ; la salle philharmonique de l'Elbe à Hambourg (Allemagne, prévue pour 2011) et le nouveau Miami Art Museum (Floride, États-Unis, achèvement prévu en 2012).

TEA

Tenerife Espacio de las Artes, Santa Cruz de Tenerife, Canary Islands, Spain, 2003–08

Address: Avenida de San Sebastián 8, 38003 Santa Cruz de Tenerife, Islas Canarias, Spain,
+34 922 84 90 57, www.teatenerife.com
Gross floor area: 20 600 m². Client: Cabildo Insular de Tenerife, Santa Cruz de Tenerife, Spain. Cost: not disclosed
Partner Architect: Virgilio Gutiérrez Herreros Arquitecto, Santa Cruz de Tenerife, Spain

The TEA opened on October 31, 2008, on a site that measures 8800 square meters. The four-level structure is 160 meters long, 65 meters wide and 18 meters high. It has three exhibition zones, for temporary exhibitions, photography, and the permanent Oscar Dominguez collection. A 194-seat auditorium, library, café/restaurant, museum shop, and open-air event space and plaza are also part of the program. Two permanent art installations are located in the library: *El Patio* (Mural on Patio Wall) by Juan Gopar and *te01-te09 y 10 h 38m / -25°*, a wall installation of 10 large-scale photographs by Thomas Ruff. From the plaza, visitors enter the building through a lobby that contains the café, shop, and ticket counters. A spiral staircase leads to the upper skylit and lower museum levels, where the galleries have six-meter ceiling heights or more. The Center of Photography is set on the lower level and is more intimate in scale. The plaza cuts through the reading areas of the library. The architects state: "The building typology of our design for the TEA is based on courtyards. The elongated courtyards are important in many ways, providing daylight, views, and orientation for the visitors and users of the museum spaces and the library. One of them, between the office and museum wings of the building complex, is planted with typical plants of the island."

Das am 31. Oktober 2008 eröffnete Museum steht auf einem 8800 m² großen Gelände. Das viergeschossige Gebäude ist 160 m lang, 65 m breit und 18 m hoch. Es hat drei Ausstellungsbereiche: für Wechselausstellungen, für Fotografie und für die ständig gezeigte Sammlung Oscar Dominguez. Das Programm umfasst außerdem ein Auditorium mit 194 Plätzen, eine Bibliothek, ein Café/Restaurant, einen Museumsshop, einen Außenbereich für Veranstaltungen und eine Plaza. In der Bibliothek befinden sich zwei permanente Kunstwerke: *El Patio* (ein Wandgemälde im Patio) von Juan Gopar und *te01-te09 y 10 h 38 m / -25°*, eine Wandinstallation mit zehn großen Fotografien von Thomas Ruff. Von der Plaza aus betreten Besucher das Gebäude durch eine Lobby, die das Café, den Shop und den Ticketschalter enthält. Eine Wendeltreppe führt zu der durch Oberlichter erhellten oberen und zur unteren Museumsebene mit einer Deckenhöhe von jeweils über 6 m. Das Zentrum für Fotografie liegt auf dem unteren Niveau und ist intimer im Maßstab. Die Plaza schneidet durch den Lesesaal der Bibliothek. Die Architekten erklären: „Die Typologie unseres Entwurfs für das TEA beruht auf Innenhöfen. Diese länglichen Höfe sind in vielerlei Hinsicht von Bedeutung: Sie bieten den Besuchern und Nutzern von Museum und Bibliothek Licht, Ausblicke und Orientierung. Einer der Höfe des Komplexes zwischen dem Büro- und dem Museumstrakt ist mit inseltypischen Gewächsen bepflanzt."

Construit sur un terrain de 8800 mètres carrés, le TEA a ouvert ses portes le 31 octobre 2008. Ce bâtiment de quatre niveaux mesure 160 mètres de long par 65 de large et 18 de haut. Il s'organise en trois zones d'expositions : manifestations temporaires, photographie et collection permanente d'œuvres d'Oscar Dominguez. Un auditorium de 194 places, un café-restaurant, une boutique, une bibliothèque, un espace pour manifestations en plein air et une place complètent le programme. Deux œuvres d'art sont présentées en permanence dans la librairie : *El Patio* (fresque murale sur mur de patio) de Juan Gopar et *te01-te09 y 10 h 38 m / -25°*, une installation murale de dix photographies grand format de Thomas Ruff. Les visiteurs accèdent au bâtiment à partir de la place par un hall qui contient la billetterie, le café et la boutique. Un escalier en spirale mène aux niveaux inférieurs et supérieurs du musée, ces derniers éclairés zénithalement. Les galeries possèdent des plafonds de 6 mètres de haut, voire plus. Le centre de la Photographie est installé au niveau inférieur, d'échelle plus intime. La *plaza* traverse le bâtiment jusqu'aux salles de lecture de la bibliothèque. « La typologie constructive de notre projet pour le TEA repose sur les cours. Ces cours allongées sont importantes de multiples façons. Elles apportent la lumière du jour, des vues, des moyens d'orientation pour les visiteurs et les utilisateurs des espaces muséaux et de la bibliothèque. L'une d'elles, entre les ailes des bureaux et le complexe du musée, est plantée de végétaux typiques de l'île », précisent les architectes.

As always, Herzog & de Meuron create a surprising dialogue of forms and surfaces, not quite like anything ever seen before, and yet fully coherent with their own œuvre.

Wie immer erzeugen Herzog & de Meuron einen überraschenden Dialog der Formen und Flächen, der ohne Beispiel ist und dennoch ganz im Einklang mit ihrem bisherigen Werk steht.

Comme toujours, Herzog & de Meuron organisent un surprenant dialogue entre les formes et les surfaces, qui n'est pas semblable à ce que l'on a pu voir chez eux précédemment mais reste néanmoins parfaitement cohérent avec leur œuvre.

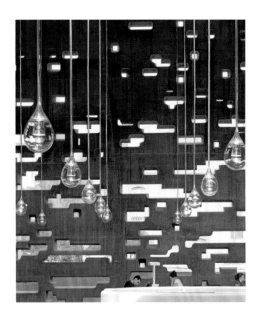

Suspended light fixtures and the
irregular pattern of wall openings
imagined by the architects enliven
this space, creating a rhythm that
is musical in its essence.

Die von den Architekten gestalteten
Hängeleuchten und das unregelmäßige System der Wandöffnungen beleben diesen Raum und erzeugen einen
im Grunde musikalischen Rhythmus.

Les luminaires suspendus et la disposition irrégulière des ouvertures
de formes variées dans les murs
imaginées par les architectes ani-
ment cet espace et créent un rythme
de nature musicale.

High, lightly framed glazing offers
an almost entirely transparent wall
(above), while interior spaces are
open to natural light.

Hohe Verglasung in leichter Rahmung
führt zu einer fast vollständig transparenten Wand (oben), während die
Innenräume zur natürlichen Belichtung geöffnet sind.

De hautes parois vitrées aux enca-
drements discrets ont permis d'obtenir un mur presque entièrement
transparent (ci-dessus). Les espaces
intérieurs s'ouvrent à la lumière
naturelle.

A spiral staircase contrasts in its
lightness with the large, flat surfaces
of the walls and ceiling. Light is
opposed to textured, but otherwise
nearly blank, volumes.

Eine hell belichtete Wendeltreppe
bildet einen Gegensatz zu den ebenso
hellen, großen, ebenen Wandflächen
und der Decke. Das Licht wird in
Kontrast zu den strukturierten, aber
ansonsten fast leeren Räumen
gesetzt.

Un escalier en spirale contraste par
sa légèreté avec les importants plans
rectilignes des murs et des plafonds.
La lumière joue sur des volumes tex-
turés mais presque neutres.

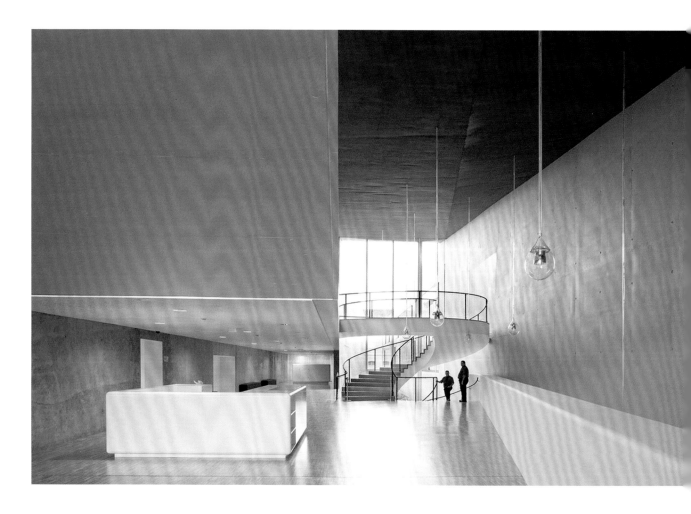

A spiral staircase contrasts with more linear elements, as can be seen in the plan below, where essentially rectangular volumes are the rule.

Die Wendeltreppe steht im Kontrast zu stärker linear betonten Elementen – wie auf dem Grundriss unten zu sehen ist, der hauptsächlich von rechtwinkligen Elementen geprägt ist.

L'escalier contraste avec des éléments plus rectilignes, comme le montre le plan ci-dessous marqué par l'orthogonalité.

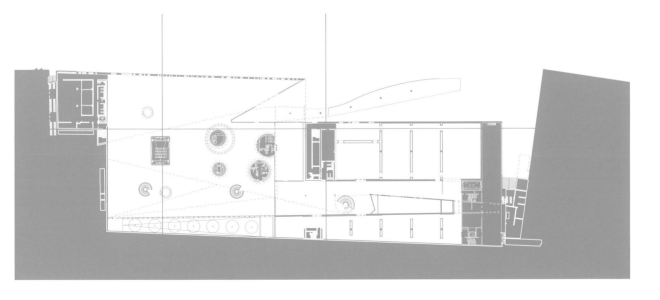

HOK

HOK
One Tampa City Center, Suite 1800
Tampa, FL 33602
USA

Tel: +1 813 229 0300
Fax: +1 813 223 7116
E-mail: HOKContact@hok.com
Web: www.hok.com

Hellmuth, Obata + Kassabaum (**HOK**) is an international architecture, interiors, engineering, planning, and consulting firm created in 1955. The firm is based in Saint Louis, Missouri, and its name is derived from those of its three founding partners—George Hellmuth, Gyo Obata, and George Kassabaum—all graduates of the School of Architecture at Washington University in Saint Louis. After opening a branch office in San Francisco, in 1966, the company turned to international work, winning the commission for the King Saud University in Saudia Arabia in 1975. In 2006, HOK employed approximately 1800 people on four continents. Yann Weymouth was born in 1941. He was educated at Harvard (B. A., 1963) and at MIT (M.Arch, 1966). He was Chief of Design for I. M. Pei on the National Gallery of Art East Building (Washington, D.C., 1966–71), and then Architect in Charge of Design for I. M. Pei on the Louvre Pyramid project in Paris (1983–91). He was an Associate at Ove Arup Partnership (London, 1991–95), and Vice President at Arquitectonica (Miami, 1996–98). He has been a Senior Vice President and Design Director at HOK in Florida since 2001, and was the designer of the Frost Art Museum (Miami, Florida, USA, 2004–08, published here).

Hellmuth, Obata + Kassabaum (**HOK**) ist eine 1955 gegründete internationale Firma für Architektur, Innenarchitektur, Ingenieurbau, Stadtplanung und Consulting. Ihr Sitz ist in St. Louis, Missouri; der Name geht auf die drei Gründungspartner – George Hellmuth, Gyo Obata und George Kassabaum – zurück, die alle an der Washington University School of Architecture in St. Louis studiert haben. Nachdem das Büro 1966 eine Niederlassung in San Francisco eröffnet hatte, begann 1975 die internationale Tätigkeit mit einem Auftrag für die King Saud University in Saudi-Arabien. 2006 arbeiteten etwa 1800 Personen auf vier Kontinenten bei HOK. Yann Weymouth wurde 1941 geboren und studierte in Harvard (B.A., 1963) und am Massachusetts Institute of Technology (M. Arch., 1966). Er war Planungschef bei I.M. Pei für das East Building der National Gallery (Washington, D. C., 1966–71) und dann für die Louvre-Pyramide in Paris (1983–91). Weymouth war Partner bei Ove Arup Partnership (London, 1991–95) und Vizepräsident von Arquitectonica (Miami, 1996–98). Seit 2001 ist er Senior Vice President und Design Director bei HOK in Florida. Von ihm stammt der Entwurf für das Frost Art Museum (Miami, Florida, USA, 2004–08, hier veröffentlicht).

Hellmuth, Obata + Kassabaum (**HOK**) est une agence internationale d'architecture, architecture intérieure, ingénierie, urbanisme et consultance, créée en 1955. Elle est basée à Saint-Louis dans le Missouri. Son nom correspond à l'acronyme de celui de ses trois associés fondateurs : George Hellmuth, Gyo Obata et George Kassabaum, tous diplômés de l'École d'architecture de la Washington University à Saint-Louis. Après avoir ouvert un bureau à San Francisco en 1966, l'agence s'est tournée vers l'international, et a remporté le concours pour l'Université Roi Saoud en Arabie saoudite en 1975. En 2006, HOK comptait environ mille huit cents collaborateurs sur quatre continents. Yann Weymouth est né en 1941. Il a étudié à Harvard (B.A., 1963) et au MIT (M.Arch, 1966). Il a été chef de projet pour I. M. Pei sur le bâtiment est de la National Gallery of Art (Washington, D. C., 1966–71), puis architecte en charge du projet, toujours pour I. M. Pei, de la Pyramide du Louvre à Paris (1983–91). Il a été associé chez Ove Arup Partnership (Londres, 1991–95), et vice-président d'Arquitectonica (Miami, 1996–98). Il est vice-président senior et directeur des projets de HOK en Floride depuis 2001 et a conçu le Frost Art Museum (Miami, Floride, 2004–08), publié ici.

FROST ART MUSEUM

Miami, Florida, USA, 2004–08

Address: Florida International University, University Park, 10975 SW 17th Street, Miami, FL 33199, United States
+1 305 348 2890, http://thefrost.fiu.edu
Area: 3946 m² (929 m² of gallery space). Client: Florida International University. Cost: $18 million
Collaborators: Tim Blair (Project Manager), Marie Mihalik (Construction Administrator),
Skanska Inc. (Construction Management)

Originally created over 30 years ago as the Art Museum at Florida International University, the Patricia and Phillip Frost Art Museum was inaugurated in late 2008. The building was designed by Yann Weymouth, of HOK. A three-story glass atrium and "knife edge" exterior angle certainly bring to mind I. M. Pei's East Building of the National Gallery of Art (Washington, D.C., 1974–78), for which Weymouth was the lead designer. A Discovery Gallery and museum terrace, together with a multipurpose room or lecture hall, members' lounge, café, and museum shop are located on the ground floor. A suspended staircase serves the second and third floors, where the main exhibition spaces are located. An innovative lighting system, developed in collaboration with Arup Lighting, carefully controls such factors as ultraviolet rays. There are nine galleries, of which three are intended for the permanent collection, and six are for temporary shows. The museum benefits from a sharing agreement with Washington's Smithsonian Institution.

Das vor über 30 Jahren als Kunstmuseum der Florida International University gegründete Patricia and Phillip Frost Art Museum wurde von Yann Weymouth vom Büro HOK geplant und Ende 2008 eröffnet. Das dreigeschossige, gläserne Atrium und die „messerscharfen" Außenkanten erinnern natürlich an I. M. Peis East Building der National Gallery of Art (Washington, D. C., 1974–78), für dessen Planung Weymouth verantwortlich war. Eine Galerie der Entdeckung und eine Museumsterrasse sowie ein Mehrzweckraum oder Vortragssaal, eine Mitgliederlounge, ein Café und ein Museumsshop befinden sich im Erdgeschoss. Eine hängende Treppe führt auf die zweite und dritte Ebene, wo die Hauptausstellungsräume liegen. Ein innovatives Beleuchtungssytem, das mit Arup Lighting entwickelt wurde, dient der genauen Kontrolle der Lichtverhältnisse, z. B. der ultravioletten Strahlung. Es gibt insgesamt neun Galerieräume, von denen drei für die ständige Sammlung und sechs für Wechselausstellungen vorgesehen sind. Das Museum profitiert von einer Vereinbarung zur Zusammenarbeit mit Washingtons Smithsonian Institution.

Créé à l'origine il y a plus de trente ans sous le nom de Art Museum à la Florida International University, le Patricia and Phillip Frost Art Museum a été inauguré fin 2008. Le bâtiment a été conçu par Yann Weymouth de l'agence HOK. L'atrium de verre sur trois niveaux et l'angle de la façade en « lame de couteau » rappellent un peu le bâtiment est de la National Gallery of Art d'I. M. Pei à Washington D. C. (1974–78), dont Weymouth avait été chef de projet. Le rez-de-chaussée est consacré à une galerie de découverte, à la terrasse du musée, à une salle polyvalente et de conférences, au salon des membres de l'association du musée, à un café et une boutique. Un escalier suspendu conduit aux second et troisième niveaux où se trouvent les principales salles d'exposition. Un système d'éclairage innovant, développé en collaboration avec Arup Lighting, contrôle divers paramètres, dont la pénétration des rayons ultraviolets. De ces neuf galeries, trois sont consacrées à la collection permanente, et six aux expositions temporaires. Le musée bénéficie d'une convention d'échanges avec la Smithsonian Institution de Washington.

Yann Weymouth's design shows relatively few openings in these images, aside from the high glazing under a triangular canopy.

Yann Weymouths Entwurf zeigt auf diesen Bildern nur verhältnismäßig wenige Öffnungen, abgesehen von der hohen Verglasung unter einem dreieckigen Vordach.

Dans ces images, le projet de Yann Weymouth ne laisse apparaître que peu d'ouvertures, en dehors du haut mur de verre dressé sous l'auvent triangulaire.

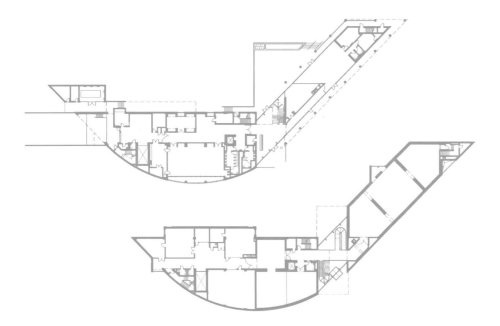

Unlike his mentor I. M. Pei, who
employed almost only triangles in
his East Building of the National
Gallery of Art in Washington, D.C.,
Weymouth combines a long curve
with rectilinear volumes, as seen
in the plans to the left.

Im Gegensatz zu seinem Mentor I. M.
Pei, der sein East Building der National Gallery of Art in Washington D. C.,
fast nur aus Dreiecken gestaltete,
verbindet Weymouth eine lange Kurve
mit geradlinigen Volumen, wie aus
den Grundrissen links ersichtlich ist.

À la différence de son mentor, I. M.
Pei, qui n'avait pratiquement utilisé
que des formes triangulaires pour
le bâtiment est de la National Gallery
of Art à Washington, D. C., Weymouth
a associé une longue courbe à des
volumes rectilignes, comme le montrent ses plans (à gauche).

An innovative lighting system filters natural light entering the galleries at the same time as it adds a modern yet decorative note to the spaces.

Ein innovatives Belichtungssystem filtert das natürliche Licht beim Einfall in die Ausstellungsbereiche und bildet zugleich ein modernes und trotzdem dekoratives Element in den Räumen.

Un système d'éclairage innovant filtre la lumière naturelle qui pénètre dans les galeries tout en apportant un élément moderne et décoratif.

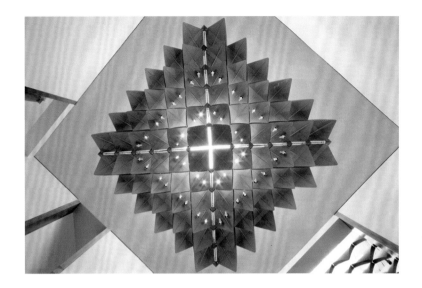

ARATA ISOZAKI

Arata Isozaki & Associates
Nogizaka Atelier
9–6–17 Akasaka, Minato-ku
Tokyo 107–0052
Japan

Tel: +81 3 3405 1526
Fax: +81 3 3475 5265
E-mail: info@isozaki@co.jp
Web: www.isozaki.co.jp

Born in Oita City on the Island of Kyushu in 1931, **ARATA ISOZAKI** graduated from the Architectural Faculty of the University of Tokyo in 1954 and established Arata Isozaki & Associates in 1963, having worked in the office of Kenzo Tange. Winner of the 1986 Royal Institute of British Architects Gold Medal, he has been a juror of major competitions such as that held in 1988 for the new Kansai International Airport. Notable buildings include: The Museum of Modern Art, Gunma (Gunma,1971–74); the Tsukuba Center Building (Tsukuba, 1978–83); The Museum of Contemporary Art (Los Angeles, California, 1981–86); the Art Tower Mito, Mito (1986–90); the Team Disney Building, Florida (1990–94); the Center for Japanese Art and Technology, Cracow, Poland (1991–94); the B-con Plaza, Oita (1991–95); the Higashi Shizuoka Convention and Arts Center (Shizuoka, 1993–98); and Ohio's Center of Science and Industry (COSI, Columbus, Ohio, 1994–99). More recently, aside from the Shenzhen Cultural Center (Shenzhen, China, 1997–2008) and the Art Museum of the Central Academy of Fine Arts in Beijing (China, 2003–08, published here), he has taken on a number of projects in Qatar, including the National Convention Center (Doha, 2004–, under construction). Isozaki has also received a commission from the Aga Khan to develop the three new campuses of the University of Central Asia to be located in Tekeli, Kazakhstan; Naryn, Kyrgyz Republic; and Khorog, Tajikistan.

Der 1931 in der Stadt Oita auf der japanischen Insel Kyushu geborene **ARATA ISOZAKI** beendete 1954 sein Architekturstudium an der Universität Tokio und gründete – nachdem er bei Kenzo Tange gearbeitet hatte – 1963 das Büro Arata Isozaki & Associates. 1986 gewann er die RIBA Gold Medal. Er war Preisrichter bei vielen großen Wettbewerben, z. B. dem von 1988 für den internationalen Flughafen Kansai. Zu seinen wichtigen Bauten zählen das Museum für moderne Kunst (Gunma, 1971–74), das Tsukuba Center Building (Tsukuba, 1978–83), das Museum of Contemporary Art (Los Angeles, Kalifornien, 1981–86), der Mito Art Tower (Mito, 1986–90), das Team Disney Building (Florida, 1990–94), das Zentrum für japanische Kunst und Technologie (Krakau, Polen, 1991–94), B-con Plaza Oita (1991–95), das Kulturzentrum Higashi Shizuoka (Shizuoka, 1989–98) und Ohio's Center of Science and Industry (COSI, Columbus, Ohio, 1994–99). In neuerer Zeit plante er neben dem Kulturzentrum in Shenzhen (China, 1997–2008) und dem Kunstmuseum der Zentralakademie der schönen Künste (Peking, 2003–08, hier veröffentlicht) mehrere Projekte in Katar, darunter das National Convention Center (Doha, 2004–, in Bau). Außerdem erhielt er einen Auftrag vom Aga Khan für die Planung dreier neuer Standorte der Universität von Zentralasien in Tekeli (Kasachstan), Naryn (Kirgisistan) und Khorog (Tadschikistan).

Né à Oita sur l'île de Kyushu au Japon en 1931, **ARATA ISOZAKI** est diplômé de la Faculté d'architecture de l'université de Tokyo (1954) et a créé son agence, Arata Isozaki & Associates, en 1963, après avoir travaillé auprès de Kenzo Tange. Récipiendaire de la médaille d'or du RIBA en 1986, il a été juré pour de grands concours comme celui de l'aéroport international du Kansai en 1988. Parmi ses réalisations les plus connues, essentiellement au Japon : le musée d'Art moderne de Gunma (Gunma, 1971–74) ; l'immeuble du Tsukuba Center (Tsukuba, 1978–83) ; le Museum of Contemporary Art (Los Angeles, Californie, 1981–86) ; l'Art Tower Mito (Mito, 1986–90) ; le Team Disney Building (Floride, 1990–94) ; le Centre de l'art et des technologies du Japon (Cracovie, Pologne, 1991–94) ; la B-con Plaza (Oita, 1991–95) ; le Centre de congrès et des arts Higashi Shizuoka (Shizuoka, 1993–98) et le Center of Science and Industry COSI (Columbus, Ohio, 1994–99). Plus récemment, en dehors du centre culturel de Shenzhen (Shenzhen, Chine, 1997–2008) et le musée d'Art de l'Académie centrale des beaux-arts à Pékin (Chine, 2003–08), publié ici, il a entrepris un certain nombre de projets au Qatar, incluant le centre national de Congrès (Doha, 2004–, en construction). Isozaki a aussi reçu une commande de l'Aga Khan pour développer les plans de trois nouveaux campus pour l'université d'Asie centrale dont la construction est prévue à Tekeli (Kazakhstan), Naryn (République Kirghize) et Khorog (Tadjikistan).

ART MUSEUM

Central Academy of Fine Arts, Beijing, China, 2003–08

*Address: CAFA Art Museum, No. 8, Hua Jia Di Nan Street, Chaoyang District, 100102 Beijing, China,
+86 10 64 77 15 75, www.cafamuseum.org
Area: 14 777 m². Client: Central Academy of Fine Arts. Cost: not disclosed*

Located in the Chaoyang District of Beijing, this structure is 24 meters high and occupies an L-shaped, curvilinear 8,641m² site. The CAFA has departments that teach design, architecture, fashion, and other disciplines. The institution was relocated from the city center to a suburban area beginning in 2001. Arata Isozaki was commissioned to design the Art Museum, which is the last phase of the relocation. The architect took his cue from the unusual shape of the site. The building is entered via a bridge that crosses a sunken garden. The ground floor is linked to this garden via a grand staircase. The generous entrance hall is intended for exhibitions of large installations, paintings, or sculptures. Permanent exhibition spaces are located one floor up in this structure that includes two basement levels and four floors above grade. The largest exhibition spaces, meant for contemporary art, are located on the third and fourth floors. The architect states, "The edgeless, surrounding curved walls can function as background screens for the artwork or can be utilized as the canvas itself on which artists can execute their art and design." The curved building is clad in slate, like earlier buildings by Isozaki in Nara, Shizuoka, or A Coruña, Spain. The complex geometry of the curves in Beijing required manual adjustment of the slate.

Dieses im Pekinger Bezirk Chaoyang gelegene Gebäude ist 24 m hoch und steht auf einem L-förmigen, gekrümmten, 8641 m² großen Gelände. Die Zentralakademie hat Abteilungen für Design, Architektur, Mode und weitere Disziplinen. Ab 2001 verlegte man die Akademie vom Stadtzentrum in einen vorstädtischen Bezirk. Arata Isozaki wurde mit der Planung des Kunstmuseums beauftragt, das als letzte Einrichtung umgesiedelt wurde. Der Entwurf des Architekten ist durch die ungewöhnliche Form des Bauplatzes bestimmt. Das Gebäude wird über eine Brücke erschlossen, die über einen tiefer gelegenen Garten führt. Das Erdgeschoss ist durch eine eindrucksvolle Treppe mit diesem Garten verbunden. Die großzügige Eingangshalle ist zur Präsentation großer Installationen, Gemälde oder Skulpturen vorgesehen. Räume für die ständige Sammlung liegen im ersten Obergeschoss des Gebäudes, das insgesamt zwei Untergeschosse und vier Ebenen über Geländehöhe besitzt. Die größten Ausstellungsräume sind für zeitgenössische Kunst bestimmt und liegen auf der dritten und vierten Ebene. Der Architekt erklärt: „Die kantenlosen, gekrümmten Umfassungsmauern können als Hintergrund für Kunstwerke oder sogar als Leinwand dienen, auf der Künstler ihre Kunst und ihr Design ausführen können." Das gekrümmte Bauwerk ist, wie frühere Bauten Isozakis in Nara, Shizuoka und A Coruña, mit Schiefer verkleidet. Die komplizierten, gebogenen Formen in Peking erforderten die handwerkliche Bearbeitung des Schiefers.

Situé dans le quartier de Chaoyang à Pékin, ce bâtiment de 24 mètres de haut occupe un terrain curviligne en forme de « L » de 8,641 mètres carrés. L'Académie centrale des beaux-arts (CAFA) enseigne, parmi d'autres disciplines, l'architecture, le design et la mode. L'installation a été relocalisée du centre dans ce quartier de banlieue depuis 2001. Le musée d'art, confié à Arata Isozaki, est la dernière phase de ce transfert. Arata Isozaki a tiré parti de la forme inhabituelle du terrain. On pénètre dans le bâtiment par une passerelle qui franchit un jardin en creux relié au rez-de-chaussée par un escalier monumental. Le généreux hall d'entrée peut servir à exposer des installations, peintures ou sculptures de grandes dimensions. Les espaces d'exposition permanente sont situés au premier étage qui comprend six niveaux dont deux en sous-sol. Les espaces les plus vastes, destinés à l'art contemporain, sont situés au troisième et quatrième niveaux. « Les murs incurvés, sans limites apparentes peuvent servir d'écrans de fond pour les œuvres d'art ou même de toile sur lesquelles les artistes viendront travailler », explique l'architecte. Le bâtiment en courbe est habillé d'ardoise à la manière des constructions antérieures de l'architecte à Nara (Shizuoka, Japon) ou à La Corogne (Espagne). La géométrie complexe des courbes de la Central Academy of Fine Arts à Pékin a nécessité l'ajustement à la main de chaque dalle d'ardoise.

In a device he has used in other buildings, Isozaki here makes a single continuum of the roof and exterior walls of the building, privileging curves over harsher straight lines.

Mit einer Geste, die er bereits bei anderen Gebäuden angewendet hat, bildet Isozaki hier ein einziges Kontinuum aus Dach und Außenwänden des Gebäudes, bei dem Kurven Vorzug vor strengen, geraden Linien haben.

Selon un procédé qu'il a déjà utilisé ailleurs, Isozaki crée une continuité entre la couverture et les murs extérieurs du bâtiment, en privilégiant la courbe par rapport à de sèches lignes droites.

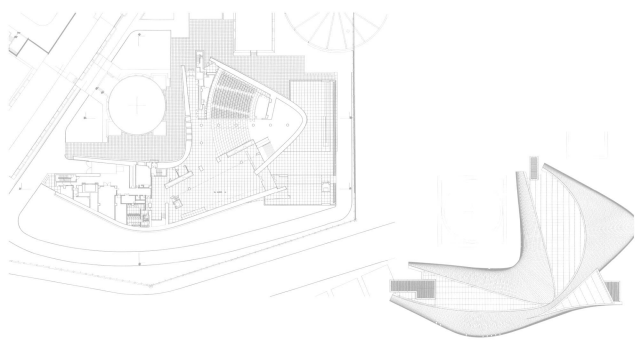

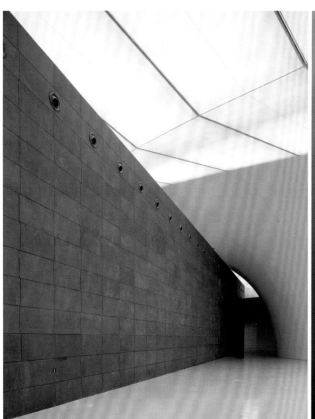

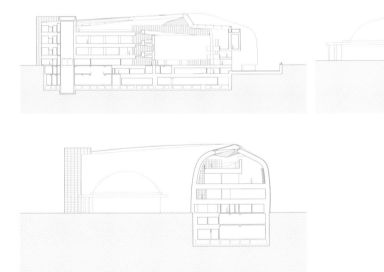

Auf subtile Weise verweisen die Formen der Innenräume auf die äußere
Linienführung des Gebäudes und
erlauben sanfte Übergänge sowie
eine einheitliche Gesamtgestaltung.

Interior volumes evoke the exterior
curves of the building in a subtle
way, giving rise to smooth transitions
and an overall unity of design.

Les volumes intérieurs évoquent de
manière subtile les courbes de l'extérieur du bâtiment, assurant une transition en douceur et l'unité du projet.

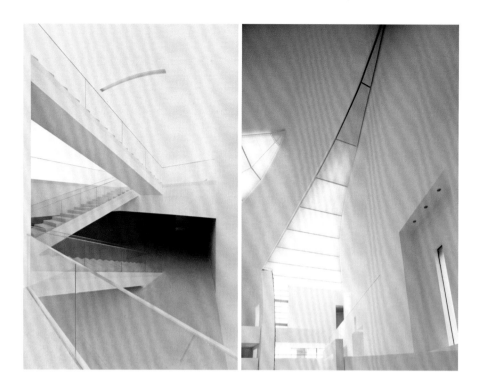

Isozaki's obvious mastery of space and light, as visible in these images, shows that, in his mid-70s, the architect continues to evolve and to imagine space in new ways.

Isozakis offenkundige Meisterschaft im Umgang mit Raum und Licht zeigt, wie auf diesen Abbildungen erkennbar, dass dieser Architekt in seinen Mittsiebzigern nach wie vor Räume auf neuartige Weise entwickelt und gestaltet.

La maîtrise évidente de l'espace et de la lumière chez Isozaki – visible dans ces images – montre que cet architecte de plus de 70 ans continue à évoluer et à imaginer de nouvelles solutions architecturales.

KSV
KRÜGER SCHUBERTH VANDREIKE

KSV Krüger Schuberth Vandreike
Brunnenstr. 196
10119 Berlin
Germany

Tel: +49 30 28 30 31 0
Fax: +49 30 28 30 31 10
E-mail: ksv@ksv-network.de
Web: www.ksv-network.de

Torsten Krüger was born in 1963 in Berlin, and studied architecture at the Bauhaus University (Weimar, 1983–88). Christiane Schuberth was born in 1962 in Thale, Germany, and also studied at the Bauhaus University (1982–87). She worked on the preservation of historic buildings in Quedlinburg and Halle the year of her graduation. Bertram Vandreike was born in Eisenach, Germany, and graduated from the Bauhaus University in 1987. The trio formed **KSV KRÜGER SCHUBERTH VANDREIKE** in Berlin in 1990. Their work includes the Wasserstadt residential building, Schultheiss site (Berlin, Germany 1999); the Maininsel Hotel and Conference Center (Schweinfurt, Germany, 2002); a design for the BMW 1 series promotion tour (Paris, France, 2004); the Museion, Museum of Modern and Contemporary Art in Bolzano (Italy, 2004–08, published here); the Baltic Sea Research Institute (Warnemünde, Rostock, Germany, 2008); and a design for the BMW motor show (Shanghai, China, 2009).

Torsten Krüger wurde 1963 in Berlin geboren und studierte Architektur an der Bauhaus-Universität (Weimar, 1983–88). Christiane Schuberth wurde 1962 in Thale geboren und studierte ebenfalls an der Bauhaus-Universität (1982–87). In ihrem Abschlussjahr arbeitete sie in der Denkmalpflege in Quedlinburg und Halle. Bertram Vandreike stammt aus Eisenach und beendete 1987 sein Studium an der Bauhaus-Universität. Das Trio gründete 1990 das Büro **KSV KRÜGER SCHUBERTH VANDREIKE** in Berlin. Zu ihren Projekten zählen der Wohnungsbau Wasserstadt auf dem Schultheiß-Gelände (Berlin, 1999), das Hotel und Konferenzzentrum Maininsel (Schweinfurt, 2002), die Gestaltung der Werbekampagne für die 1er-Serie von BMW (Paris, 2004), das Museion – Museum für moderne und zeitgenössische Kunst in Bozen (Italien, 2004–08, hier veröffentlicht), das Leibniz-Institut für Ostseeforschung (Warnemünde, Rostock, 2008) und die Gestaltung der BMW-Motorshow (Shanghai, China, 2009).

Torsten Krüger, né en 1963 à Berlin, a étudié l'architecture à l'université du Bauhaus (Weimar, 1983–88). Christiane Schuberth, née en 1962 à Thale (Allemagne), a accompli les mêmes études (1982–87). Elle a travaillé sur des projets de conservation de bâtiments historiques à Quedlinburg et Halle l'année de son diplôme. Bertram Vandreike, né à Eisenach (Allemagne), a obtenu son diplôme d'architecte de l'université du Bauhaus en 1987. Tous trois ont créé l'agence **KSV KRÜGER SCHUBERTH VANDREIKE** à Berlin en 1990. Parmi leurs réalisations : l'immeuble résidentiel Wasserstadt sur le site de Schultheiss (Berlin, 1999) ; l'hôtel et centre de conférences Maininsel (Schweinfurt, Allemagne, 2002) ; la conception d'une tournée promotionnelle pour la BMW série 1 (Paris, 2004) ; le Museion – musée d'Art moderne et contemporain de Bolzano (Italie, 2004–08), publié ici ; l'Institut de recherches sur la mer Baltique (Warnemünde, Rostock, Allemagne, 2008) et la conception d'une exposition des modèles BMW (Shanghaï, Chine, 2009).

MUSEION

Museum of Modern and Contemporary Art, Bolzano, Italy, 2004–08

Address: Via Dante 6, 39100 Bolzano, Italy, +39 0471 223411, www.museion.it
Area: 8370 m². Client: Province of Bolzano, Alto Adige. Cost: €31.8 million
Concept: Bertram Vandreike. Collaborators: Markus Reinhardt, Annemike Banniza

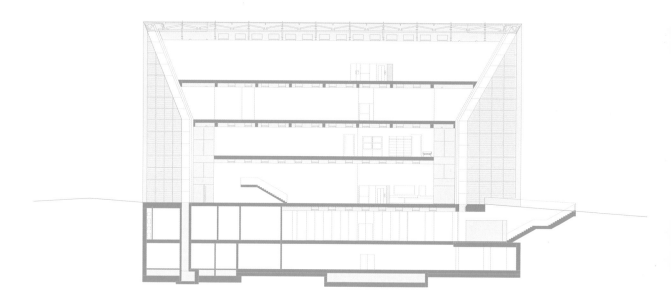

The Museion began its existence in 1985 as the Bolzano Museum of Modern Art, housed in a former hospital facility. The institution took the name Museion in 1991, "intending to reflect the essentially interdisciplinary character of contemporary art." The architects state that the new museum building "reanimates the classic Modernist box style by means of the façades. It is decorated not only in line with its function, but, as an open edifice, such that it becomes an unmistakable symbol, which, being open on two sides, forms a link between the town and the countryside. The communicating façade channels visitors' expectations on the one hand, while on the other ensuring that the projection itself becomes part of the architecture. In this way, the borderlines between the building and the exhibit blur, without the two competing with each other." The façades of the museum are used for nighttime projection of commissioned artworks. The interior spaces of the structure are intended to allow exhibition and performance areas, workshops, a library, a cafeteria, and a shop to flow into each other without any specific limits. A nearby atelier serves an artist-in-residence program.

Das Museion entstand 1985 als Bozener Museum für moderne Kunst in einem früheren Krankenhaus. 1991 erhielt es den Namen Museion „mit dem Ziel, den im Wesentlichen interdisziplinären Charakter der zeitgenössischen Kunst wiederzugeben". Die Architekten erklären, dass der Museumsneubau „den Kistenstil der klassischen Moderne durch seine Fassaden wiederbelebt. Das Museum ist nicht nur in Übereinstimmung mit seiner Funktion gestaltet, sondern als offenes Bauwerk mit zwei geöffneten Seiten das unverkennbare Symbol einer Verbindung zwischen Stadt und Landschaft. Die auf die Fassade projizierten Informationen kanalisieren einerseits die Erwartungen der Besucher und sind zugleich so gestaltet, dass die Projektionen zum Bestandteil der Architektur werden. Auf diese Weise verschwimmen die Grenzen zwischen Gebäude und Ausstellung, ohne dass sie miteinander konkurrieren." Die Fassaden des Museums werden nachts zur Projektion von in Auftrag gegebenen Kunstwerken genutzt. Die Innenräume werden für Ausstellungen und Aufführungen sowie als Werkstätten genutzt; eine Bibliothek, eine Cafeteria und ein Shop gehen nahtlos ineinander über. Ein benachbarter Atelierbau wird für ein Artist-in-Residence-Programm genutzt.

L'histoire du Museion débute en 1985, alors qu'il était logé dans le cadre du musée d'Art moderne de Bolzano, un ancien hôpital. L'institution a pris le nom de « Museion » en 1991 « pour refléter le caractère essentiellement interdisciplinaire de l'art contemporain ». L'architecture précise que la nouvelle construction « revivifie le style de la boîte moderniste classique dans ses façades. Non seulement son décor est en accord avec sa fonction, mais, par son ouverture, le bâtiment devient un symbole original, qui, ouvert sur deux côtés, fait le lien entre la ville et la campagne. Cette façade communicante oriente les attentes des visiteurs, d'une part, et fait de ses projections lumineuses une partie intégrante de l'architecture d'autre part. Ainsi, les frontières entre le bâtiment et ce qu'il expose s'estompent sans créer de concurrence ». Les façades du musée servent donc à des projections nocturnes d'œuvres d'art spécialement commandées. Les volumes intérieurs permettent aussi bien des expositions que des performances et accueillent des ateliers, une bibliothèque, une cafétéria et une boutique qui s'interpénètrent, sans que des limites précises ne soient jamais marquées. À proximité, un atelier est réservé aux programmes d'artistes en résidence.

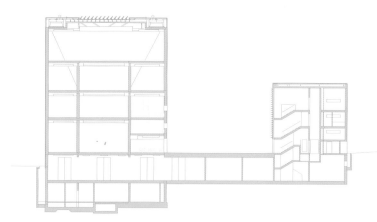

Though section drawings demonstrate
the essentially rectilinear or rectangular design of the building, its fully
glazed façade (above) adds an element of surprise.

Obgleich die Schnitte von der überwiegend geradlinigen oder rechtwinkligen Gestaltung des Gebäudes
zeugen, bildet seine voll verglaste
Fassade (oben) ein zusätzliches,
überraschendes Element.

Si les plans de coupe montrent une
conception essentiellement composée
de formes orthogonales ou rectangulaires, la façade entièrement vitrée
ajoute un élément de surprise.

Interior views show a generous use of natural light that also permits visitors to survey the exterior environment of the structure (above).

Die Innenansichten zeigen den großzügigen Einsatz von natürlichem Licht, wodurch den Besuchern auch Ausblicke auf das äußere Umfeld des Gebäudes geboten werden (oben).

Les vues de l'intérieur témoignent d'un recours généreux à la lumière naturelle qui permet par ailleurs aux visiteurs de percevoir l'environnement du bâtiment (ci-dessus).

BRUNO MADER

Bruno Mader
29 rue Miguel Hidalgo
75019 Paris
France

Tel: +33 1 43 48 78 86
Fax: +33 1 42 38 35 80
E-mail: contact@brunomader.fr

BRUNO MADER was born in 1956 in La Rochelle, France, and graduated in 1983 from the Paris Belleville School of Architecture. He worked in the offices of Roland Simounet, Jean Nouvel, and Reichen + Robert in Paris before opening his own office in 1989. He has worked on a number of highway rest points, such as the Aire de la Baie de Somme (A16, 1998); Aire Jardin des Causses du Lot (A20, 2002); and the Aire de la Corrèze (A89, 2003), all in France. As well as the Museum of the Landes de Gascogne (Sabres, 2006–08, published here), he is completing a tennis complex in Paris (2010); the headquarters of the Regional Council of the Auvergne Region (Clermont-Ferrand, 2010); and is working on the Museum of the War of 1870 (Gravelotte, 2011); and an orientation building for the Mont-Saint-Michel (Normandy, 2002–), all in France.

BRUNO MADER wurde 1956 in La Rochelle geboren und beendete 1983 sein Studium an der Pariser Ecole d'Architecture Belleville. Er arbeitete in den Büros von Roland Simounet, Jean Nouvel und Reichen + Robert in Paris, bevor er 1989 sein eigenes Büro eröffnete. Mader hat verschiedene Autobahnraststätten gebaut: Aire de la Baie de Somme (A 16, 1998), Aire Jardin des Causses du Lot (A 20, 2002) und Aire de la Corrèze (A 89, 2003), alle in Frankreich. Er hat das Musée des Landes de Gascogne (Sabres, 2006–08, hier veröffentlicht) fertiggestellt und arbeitet gegenwärtig an einer Tennisanlage in Paris (2010), am Sitz des Regionalparlaments der Region Auvergne (Clermont-Ferrand, 2010), am Museum für den Krieg von 1870 (Gravelotte, 2011) und einem Informationsgebäude für den Mont Saint-Michel (Normandie, 2002–), alle in Frankreich.

BRUNO MADER, né en 1956 à La Rochelle (France), est diplômé de l'École d'architecture de Paris-Belleville (1983). Il a travaillé dans les agences de Roland Simounet, Jean Nouvel, et Reichen + Robert à Paris avant d'ouvrir sa propre structure en 1989. Il a réalisé un certain nombre d'aires d'autoroute en France, comme celle de la Baie de Somme (A16, 1998); l'aire Jardin des Causses du Lot (A20, 2002), l'aire de la Corrèze (A89, 2003), ainsi que le musée des Landes de Gascogne (Sabres, 2006–08), publié ici. Il achève actuellement un complexe de tennis à Paris (2010); le musée de la Guerre de 1870 (Gravelotte, 2011) et un bâtiment d'orientation du public au Mont-Saint-Michel (Normandie, 2002–).

MUSEUM OF THE LANDES DE GASCOGNE

Sabres, France, 2006–08

Address: Route de Solférino, 40630 Sabres, France, +33 5 58 08 31 31, www.parc-landes-de-gascogne.fr
Area: 2860 m². Client: Parc Naturel Régional des Landes de Gascogne. Cost: € 3.3 million

Bruno Mader won the 2004 competition to restructure and extend the Ecomusée des Landes with a program comprising exhibition galleries, space for conferences, research, and a documentation center. The two existing buildings of the museum, originally opened in 1969, were also part of the program. Using local maritime pine wood for both structure and cladding, the architect created volumes five to six meters high, meeting the rigorous standards of the French Museums Authority (DMF). A generous shuttered wood structure envelops the volumes of the museum's pavilions, forcibly echoing the theme of the institution itself that is sustainability in its various forms. A permanent exhibition retraces the history of the Landes area, while a large room with overhead lighting for temporary exhibitions opens out onto the landscape, thus respecting the emphasis of the Ecomuseum on "ecology and territorial development."

Bruno Mader gewann 2004 den Wettbewerb für den Umbau und die Erweiterung des Ecomusée des Landes mit einem Programm, das Ausstellungsbereiche, Räume für Kongresse und Forschung sowie ein Dokumentationszentrum umfasst. Die beiden bestehenden Gebäude des Museums aus dem Jahr 1969 sollten in die Planung einbezogen werden. Der Architekt verwendete örtlich verfügbares Holz der Strandkiefer für Tragwerk und Verkleidung und schuf 5 bis 6 m hohe Räume, die den strengen Vorschriften der französischen Museumsaufsicht (DMF) genügen. Eine großzügig verschalte Holzkonstruktion umgibt die Volumen der Museumspavillons und entspricht damit ganz dem Thema der Einrichtung, den verschiedenen Formen der Nachhaltigkeit. Eine Dauerausstellung behandelt die Geschichte der Region Landes, während ein großer Raum mit Oberlicht für Wechselausstellungen sich zur Landschaft öffnet und das Thema des Ökomuseums, „Ökologie und territoriale Entwicklung", betont.

C'est en 2004 que Bruno Mader a remporté le concours pour la restructuration et l'extension de l'écomusée des Landes sur un programme comprenant des galeries d'exposition, des salles de conférence, de recherche et un centre de documentation. Les deux bâtiments existants, ouverts en 1969, faisaient également partie de la programmation. Utilisant le pin maritime local pour la structure et l'habillage, l'architecte a créé des volumes de cinq à six mètres de haut qui répondent aux critères rigoureux de la Direction des musées de France. Une généreuse structure en persiennes de bois enveloppe les pavillons du musée, en écho à la thématique de l'institution, axée sur le développement durable sous toutes ses formes. Une exposition permanente retrace l'histoire de la région des Landes et une vaste salle à éclairage zénithal, pour expositions temporaires, ouvre sur le paysage, mettant ainsi l'accent sur « l'écologie et le développement territorial ».

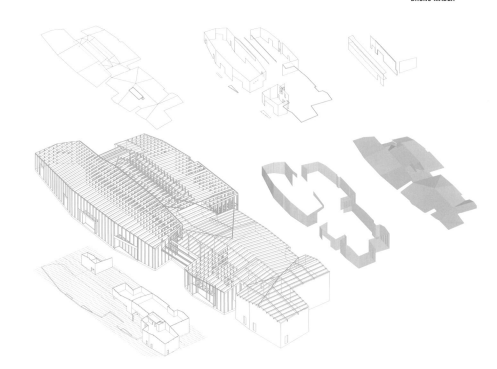

Though barn structures are clearly a source of inspiration, the angled, flowing forms of the museum do set it apart as a work of contemporary architecture that goes beyond traditional shapes.

Obgleich ländliche Scheunen offenbar als Inspirationsquelle dienten, heben die schrägen, fließenden Formen des Museums es als Werk der zeitgenössischen Architektur hervor, das über die traditionellen Formen hinausgeht.

Même si la typologie de la grange a servi de source d'inspiration, les formes inclinées et fuyantes du musée en font une œuvre d'architecture contemporaine qui dépasse les formes traditionnelles.

The "Ecomuseum" function certainly requires the architect to respect the environment as much as possible—the use of wood here is an element in that strategy.

Die Funktion als „Ökomuseum" fordert natürlich auch vom Architekten, die Umwelt soweit wie möglich zu respektieren – die Verwendung von Holz ist ein Element dieser Strategie.

La fonction d'écomusée implique la nécessité pour l'architecte de respecter autant que possible l'environnement. L'utilisation du bois dans ce cadre est un élément de cette stratégie.

Movable wall panels, above, reveal a bit of the auditorium space beyond, also visible in the plan (below).

Verschiebbare Wandtafeln (oben) gewähren einen Blick in den Auditoriumsbereich, wie auch am Grundriss (unten) ablesbar.

Des panneaux muraux mobiles (ci-dessus) ouverts révèlent une partie de l'auditorium, par ailleurs visible dans le plan ci-dessous.

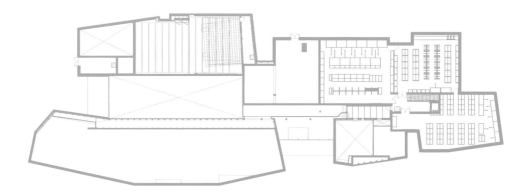

FUMIHIKO MAKI

Maki and Associates
Hillside West Building C / 13–4 Hachiyama-cho
Shibuya-ku / Tokyo 150–0035 / Japan

Tel: +81 3 3780 3880 / Fax: +81 3 3780 3881
Web: www.maki-and-associates.co.jp

Born in Tokyo in 1928, **FUMIHIKO MAKI** received his B.Arch degree from the University of Tokyo in 1952, and M.Arch degrees from the Cranbrook Academy of Art (1953) and the Harvard GSD (1954). He worked for Skidmore, Owings & Merrill in New York (1954–55) and Sert Jackson and Associates in Cambridge, Massachusetts (1955–58), before creating his own firm, Maki and Associates, in Tokyo in 1965. Notable buildings include the Fujisawa Municipal Gymnasium (Fujisawa-shi, Kanagawa, 1984); the Spiral (Minato-ku, Tokyo, 1985); the National Museum of Modern Art (Sakyo-ku, Kyoto, 1986); Tepia (Minato-ku, Tokyo, 1989); the Nippon Convention Center Makuhari Messe (Chiba-shi, Chiba, 1989); the Tokyo Metropolitan Gymnasium (Shibuya-ku, Tokyo, 1990); and the Center for the Arts Yerba Buena Gardens (San Francisco, California, 1993). The Nippon Convention Center Makuhari Messe Phase II (Chiba-shi, Chiba, completed in 1997) and the Hillside West buildings completed in 1998 are examples of his large-scale urban design projects. More recent and current work includes the Shimane Museum of Ancient Izumo (Izumo, Shimane, 2003–06, published here); a new museum of Islamic art for the Aga Khan in Toronto (Canada, 2005–); the Mihara Performing Arts Center (Mihara-shi, Hiroshima, 2007); and the Republic Polytechnic Campus (Woodlands, Singapore, 2007), all in Japan unless stated otherwise. Having recently completed an office building for Novartis Campus in Basel (Switzerland, 2009), Fumihiko Maki is currently working on the MIT Media Arts and Sciences Building in Cambridge (Massachusetts, 2009) and the World Trade Center Tower 4 (New York, 2012).

Der 1928 in Tokio geborene **FUMIHIKO MAKI** erhielt 1952 seinen B. Arch. an der Universität Tokio und den M. Arch. an der Cranbrook Academy of Art (1953) sowie an der Harvard GSD (1954). Bevor er 1965 sein eigenes Büro Maki and Associates in Tokio gründete, arbeitete er bei Skidmore, Owings & Merrill in New York (1954–55) und bei Sert, Jackson and Associates in Cambridge, Massachusetts (1955–58). Zu seinen bekannten Bauwerken zählen die städtische Sporthalle (Fujisawa-shi, Kanagawa, 1984), Spirale (Minato-ku, Tokio, 1985), das Nationalmuseum für moderne Kunst (Sakyo-ku, Kioto, 1986), Tepia (Minato-ku, Tokio, 1989), das Nippon Convention Center Makuhari Messe (Chiba-shi, Chiba, 1989), die städtische Sporthalle Tokio (Shibuya-ku, Tokio, 1990) und das Center for the Arts Yerba Buena Gardens (San Francisco, Kalifornien, 1993). Das Nippon Convention Center Makuhari Messe, Phase II (Chiba-shi, Chiba, fertiggestellt 1997), und die Hillside West Buildings (fertiggestellt 1998) sind Beispiele für seine großen Städtebauprojekte. Zu den neueren und noch in Arbeit befindlichen Projekten zählen das Shimane Museum des antiken Izumo (Izumo, Shimane, 2003–06, hier veröffentlicht), ein neues Museum für islamische Kunst für den Aga Khan in Toronto (2005–), das Zentrum für darstellende Kunst in Mihara (Mihara-shi, Hiroshima, 2007) und der Republic Polytechnic Campus (Woodlands, Singapur, 2007). Kürzlich fertiggestellt wurde ein Bürogebäude für Novartis in Basel (2009). Maki arbeitet derzeit am MIT Media Arts and Sciences Building in Cambridge (Massachusetts, 2009) und am World Trade Center Tower 4 (New York, 2012).

Né à Tokyo en 1928, **FUMIHIKO MAKI** est B.Arch de l'université de Tokyo (1952), et M.Arch de la Cranbrook Academy of Art (1953) et de l'Harvard GSD (1954). Il a travaillé pour Skidmore, Owings & Merrill à New York (1954–55) et Sert Jackson and Associates à Cambridge, Massachusetts (1955–58), avant de fonder sa propre agence, Maki and Associates, à Tokyo en 1965. Parmi ses réalisations notables : le gymnase municipal de Fujisawa (Fujisawa-shi, Kanagawa, 1984) ; le Spiral (Minato-ku, Tokyo, 1985) ; le Musée national d'art moderne (Sakyo-ku, Kyoto, 1986) ; l'immeuble Tepia (Minato-ku, Tokyo, 1989) ; le centre nippon de congrès de Makuhari Messe (Chiba-shi, Chiba, 1989) ; le gymnase métropolitain de Tokyo (Shibuya-ku, Tokyo, 1990) et le Center for the Arts Yerba Buena Gardens (San Francisco, Californie, 1993). Le centre nippon de congrès de Makuhari Messe Phase II (Chiba-shi, Chiba, achevé en 1997) et les immeubles Hillside West achevés en 1998 sont des exemples de projets de grande envergure. Plus récemment ont été réalisés le musée Shimane de l'ancien Izumo (Izumo, Shimane, 2003–06), publié ici ; un nouveau musée d'Art islamique pour l'Aga Khan à Toronto (Canada, 2005–) ; le Mihara Performing Arts Center (Mihara-shi, Hiroshima, 2007) et le Republic Polytechnic Campus (Woodlands, Singapour, 2007). Après avoir récemment achevé un immeuble destiné à des bureaux pour Novartis Campus à Bâle (Suisse, 2009), Fumihiko Maki travaille actuellement sur le MIT Media Arts and Sciences Building à Cambridge (Massachusetts, 2009) et la tour du World Trade Center 4 (New York, 2012).

SHIMANE MUSEUM OF ANCIENT IZUMO

Izumo, Shimane, Japan, 2003–06

Address: 99–4 Kitsuki-Higashi, Taisha, Izumo City, Shimane Prefecture, 699–0701, Japan,
Tel: +81 853 53 8600, www.izm.ed.jp
Area: 9446 m². Client: Shimane Prefecture. Cost: not disclosed
Collaboration: Hanawa Structural Engineers, Sogo Consultants

Fumihiko Maki states: "The landscaping strategy for the Shimane Museum has two fundamental concepts—to appear as an extension of the forested terrain of the Kitayama mountain range and to be implicitly connected to the adjacent Grand Izumo Shrine. The Shrine is not directly visible from within the landscape of the Shimane Museum; however, a series of landscaping strategies were utilized to imply the presence of the neighboring shrine. For example, a grid of Katsura trees planted along the entrance path to the museum suggests the presence of a spiritual location, given the religious connotation of the tree and its customary placement at shrines throughout Japan." Visitors enter through a glazed hall and pass through a Cor-ten steel wall into the exhibition lobby followed by four galleries. Around this exhibition, there are support facilities (storage, research, offices, etc.). The collection includes timber columns from the original Grand Izumo Shrine, said to have been 48 meters tall. Other works in the collection include 358 bronze swords from the Yayoi Period (400 BC–AD 300) and 39 bronze bells discovered in 1996. The Shimane Museum received 300 000 visitors in its first six months of operation.

Fumihiko Maki erläutert: „Die Strategie der Landschaftsgestaltung für das Shimane Museum folgt zwei grundlegenden Zielsetzungen – es soll als Erweiterung des bewaldeten Terrains der Kitayama-Berge erscheinen und eine deutliche Verbindung mit dem benachbarten Großen Izumo-Schrein eingehen. Dieser ist vom Gelände des Shimane Museums aus nicht direkt sichtbar, doch wurden einige landschaftsgestalterische Maßnahmen durchgeführt, um die Präsenz des benachbarten Schreins anzudeuten. So wurden z. B. Katsura-Bäume in regelmäßiger Anordnung am Zugangsweg zum Museum gepflanzt, um die Gegenwart eines sakralen Orts anzudeuten, weil dieser Baum eine religiöse Bedeutung hat und gewöhnlich bei Schreinen in ganz Japan anzutreffen ist." Die Besucher betreten das Museum durch eine verglaste Eingangshalle und gehen durch eine Wand aus Cor-Ten-Stahl in die Ausstellungslobby und die vier darauffolgenden Säle. Um diese Ausstellungsräume herum sind zugehörige Einrichtungen (wie Magazin, Forschung, Büros etc.) angeordnet. Zu den Exponaten gehören Holzsäulen vom originalen Großen Izumo-Schrein, der 48 m hoch gewesen sein soll. Außerdem enthält die Sammlung 358 Bronzeschwerter aus der Yayoi-Periode (400 v. Chr.–300 n. Chr.) und 39 Bronzeglocken, die 1996 entdeckt wurden. Das Shimane Museum hatte in den ersten sechs Monaten nach der Eröffnung 300 000 Besucher.

Pour Fumihiko Maki : « La stratégie paysagère du Shimane Museum repose sur deux concepts fondamentaux : apparaître comme une extension des forêts de la chaîne des montagnes de Kitayama et se connecter implicitement au très proche Grand mausolée Izumo. Le mausolée n'est pas directement visible de l'environnement paysager créé pour le musée, cependant une série de stratégies paysagères ont été mises en œuvre pour impliquer sa proche présence. Par exemple, une trame d'arbres de Katsura le long du chemin d'accès suggère la spiritualité du lieu, car cet arbre aux connotations religieuses est souvent planté auprès des mausolées japonais. » Les visiteurs pénètrent dans le musée par un hall vitré et traversent un mur en acier Corten pour accéder au hall des expositions que suivent quatre galeries. Les installations techniques (réserves, recherche, bureaux, etc.) s'articulent tout autour. La collection contient des colonnes de bois ayant appartenu au mausolée originel qui aurait mesuré 48 mètres de haut, 358 épées de bronze de la période Yayoi (400 av. J.-C.–300 ap. J.-C.) et 39 cloches de bronze découvertes en 1996. Le musée a reçu trois cent mille visiteurs au cours de ses six premiers mois d'existence.

Part of the concept of the museum is that its landscaping should appear "as an extension of the forested terrain of the Kitayama mountain range."

Zum Konzept dieses Museums gehört, dass die Landschaftsgestaltung wie eine „Erweiterung des bewaldeten Terrains der Kitayama-Berge" wirken soll.

Une partie du concept du musée tient à son aménagement paysager censé apparaître comme « une extension du terrain boisé de la chaine des montagnes de Kitayama. »

The landscaping strategy for the Shimane Museum is implicitly connected to the adjacent Grand Izumo Shrine.

Die Strategie der Landschaftsgestaltung des Shimane Museums bezieht auch den benachbarten Großen Izumo-Schrein ein.

La stratégie paysagère du musée Shimane est implicitement connectée à la présence toute proche du Grand mausolée Izumo.

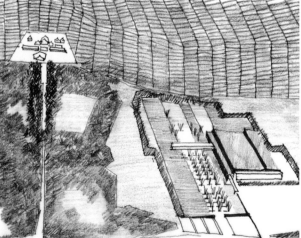

Fumihiko Maki is a master of subtle, understated modern design, as these images clearly demonstrate. The objects are placed in a position to be admired, without undue interference from the architecture.

Fumihiko Maki ist ein Meister der subtilen, zurückhaltenden modernen Gestaltung, wie diese Bilder deutlich zeigen. Die Objekte sind so positioniert, dass man sie bewundern kann, ohne durch die Architektur beeinträchtigt zu werden.

Fumihiko Maki est un des maîtres d'un modernisme subtil et retenu comme le montrent clairement ces images. Les objets sont disposés pour être admirés, sans interférence injustifiée de l'architecture.

FRANCISCO MANGADO

Francisco Mangado
Vuelta del Castillo, 5 Ático
31007 Pamplona, Navarra
Spain

Tel: +34 948 27 62 02
Fax: +34 948 17 65 05
E-mail: mangado@fmangado.com
Web: www.fmangado.com

FRANCISCO MANGADO was born in Estella, Navarra (Spain), in 1957 and obtained his architectural degree in 1981 from the School of Architecture of the University of Navarra. From the beginning of his career, Mangado combined academic duties with the professional activity at his Pamplona studio. He has taught at the University of Navarra, University of Texas (Arlington), Harvard GSD, and at the International University of Catalunya. His most significant projects include the Marco Real Wineries (Olite, Navarra, 1989–91); the Mikaela House (Gorraiz, Navarra, 1997); Pools in A Coruña (1998); urban planning and housing in Mendillorri (Pamplona, 1989–98); Plaza de Dalí (Madrid, 1999); the Golf Club (Zuasti, Navarra, 1992–2000); the Baluarte Auditorium and Convention Center (Pamplona, Navarra, 2000); Offices for the University of Navarra (2000); the Guipúzcoa Center for Technical Studies and Research (San Sebastián, 2001); and the Manduca Restaurant (Madrid, 2003). Other recently completed works include the Teulada Municipal Auditorium (Alicante, 2004); the Ávila Exhibition and Convention Center (Ávila, 2005); the Center for the Development of New Technologies in Galicia (Santiago de Compostela, 2005); the Palma Convention Center and Hotel (2005); the Football Stadium (Palencia, 2007); the Spanish Pavilion for the International Expo in Zaragoza (2008); and the Archeology Museum of Álava (Vitoria, 2004–09, published here), all in Spain.

FRANCISCO MANGADO wurde 1957 in Estella, Navarra (Spanien), geboren und erwarb sein Diplom 1981 an der Architekturabteilung der Universidad de Navarra. Schon zu Beginn seiner Laufbahn verband Mangado seine akademische Lehrtätigkeit mit praktischer Arbeit in seinem Büro in Pamplona. Er hat an der Universität von Navarra, der University of Texas (Arlington), in Harvard (Graduate School of Design) und an der Universitat Internacional de Catalunya gelehrt. Zu seinen wichtigsten Projekten gehören die Weinkellerei Marco Real (Olite, Navarra, 1989–91), das Haus Mikaela (Gorraiz, Navarra, 1997), ein Schwimmbad in A Coruña (1998), städtebauliche Planung und Wohnungsbau in Mendillorri (Pamplona, 1989–98), die Plaza de Dalí (Madrid, 1999), ein Golfklub (Zuasti, Navarra, 1992–2000), das Auditorium und Kongresszentrum Baluarte (Pamplona, Navarra, 2000), ein Bürogebäude für die Universidad de Navarra (2000), das Guipúzcoa-Zentrum für technische Studien und Forschung (San Sebastián, 2001) und das Restaurant Manduca (Madrid, 2003). Zu seinen neueren ausgeführten Bauten zählen das städtische Auditorium Teulada (Alicante, 2004), das Ausstellungs- und Kongresszentrum von Ávila (2005), ein Zentrum für neue Technologien in Santiago de Compostela (Galicien, 2005), ein Kongresszentrum und Hotel in Palma de Mallorca (2005), das Fußballstadion in Palencia (2007), der spanische Pavillon auf der Internationalen Expo in Saragossa (2008) und das Museo de Arqueología de Álava (Vitoria, 2004–09, hier veröffentlicht), alle in Spanien.

FRANCISCO MANGADO, né à Estella (Navarre, Espagne) en 1957, est diplômé de l'École d'architecture de l'université de Navarre (1981). Dès le début de sa carrière, il a associé responsabilités académiques et pratique professionnelle à partir de son studio de Pampelune. Il a enseigné à l'université de Navarre, à l'université du Texas (Arlington), à l'Harvard GSD, et à l'Université internationale de Catalogne. Parmi ses projets les plus significatifs : le chais Marco Real (Olite, Navarra, 1989–91) ; la maison Mikaela (Gorraiz, Navarre, 1997) ; des piscines à La Corogne (1998) ; des plans d'urbanisme et des logements pour Mendillorri (Pampelune, 1989–98) ; la place Dalí (Madrid, 1999) ; un club de golf (Zuasti, Navarra, 1992–2000) ; le Centre de congrès et auditorium Baluarte (Pampelune, Navarra, 2000) ; des bureaux pour l'université de Navarre (2000) ; le Centre d'études et de recherches techniques de Guipúzcoa (San Sebastián, 2001) ; le restaurant Manduca (Madrid, 2003). Plus récemment, il a achevé, toujours en Espagne : l'auditorium municipal de Teulada (Alicante, 2004) ; le Centre d'expositions et de congrès d'Ávila (Ávila, 2005) ; le Centre des technologies nouvelles (Santiago de Compostela, 2005) ; un centre de congrès et hôtel à Palma (2005) ; le stade de football de Palencia (2007) ; le Pavillon espagnol pour l'Exposition internationale de Saragosse (2008) et le musée d'Archéologie de Álava (Vitoria, 2004–09), publié ici.

ARCHEOLOGY MUSEUM OF ÁLAVA
Vitoria, Spain, 2004–09

Address: Calle Cuchillería 54, 01001 Vitoria-Gasteiz, Spain, +34 945 20 37 00
Area: 6000 m². Client: Government of Álava. Cost: €9 million

Inserted into the environment of the city, the museum stands out because of its dark, fairly closed appearance. Light boxes on the roof, seen above, bring daylight into the galleries.

Das in die Stadtstruktur integrierte Museum sticht durch sein dunkles, geschlossenes Erscheinungsbild hervor. Durch die oben sichtbaren Licht-kästen auf dem Dach fällt natürliches Licht in die Ausstellungsbereiche ein.

Inséré dans un environnement ur-bain, le musée s'en détache par son aspect sombre et assez fermé. Les boîtes de verre surmontant la toiture (ci-dessus) orientent la lumière naturelle vers les galeries.

"We like to think of an archeology museum as a compact jewel box concealing the treasure that history has entrusted to us piece by piece," says the architect. The dark-wood floors and ceilings, crossed by "white glazed prisms" in the permanent exhibition spaces, "evoke the passage of time." The site is near the Palace of Ben-daña, currently the Naipes Fournier Museum. The library, work areas, and workshops are located on the ground level, with a separate entrance. Temporary exhibition spaces and an assembly hall are at the public entry level, which is shared with the Naipes Fournier Museum. The permanent exhibition spaces are on the upper levels. Mangado explains: "The façade defining the access courtyard is a grille of cast bronze pieces, a material with clear archeological references; and in the middle, a dou-ble-layered wall of silkscreen printed glass contains the stairs, which offer views of the courtyards as one steps up. In contrast, the façade fronting the lower street is more hermetic, and is made of an outer layer of opaque prefab pieces of cast bronze, with openings where needed, and an inner layer formed by a thick wall containing the display stands and systems."

„Wir stellen uns ein archäologisches Museum als kompakte Schmuckschatulle vor, die den Schatz bewahrt, den die Geschichte uns Stück für Stück anvertraut hat", sagt der Architekt. Die dunklen Holzböden und -decken in den Räumen der ständigen Ausstellung, die von „weißen Glasprismen" durchschnitten werden, „deuten den Ablauf der Zeit" an. Das Grundstück liegt nahe dem Bendaña-Palast, in dem gegenwärtig das Museum Naipes Fournier untergebracht ist. Die Bibliothek, die Arbeits-räume und die Werkstätten befinden sich im Erdgeschoss und haben einen separaten Eingang. Die Räume für Wechselausstellungen und ein Vortragssaal liegen auf dem Niveau des öffentlichen Zugangs, wo auch das Museum Naipes Fournier untergebracht sein wird. Die Räume der Dauerausstellung sind in den oberen Geschossen ange-ordnet. Mangado erläutert: „Die den Eingangshof begrenzende Fassade besteht aus einem Gitter aus gegossenen Bronzeelementen, einem Material mit eindeutigem Bezug zur Archäologie; in der Mitte umschließt eine aus zwei Schichten bestehende, im Siebdruckverfahren bearbeitete Glaswand das Treppenhaus, aus dem man beim Hinaufsteigen in den Hof blickt. Im Gegensatz dazu ist die Fassade an der unteren Straße geschlossener und hat eine undurchsichtige Außenschicht aus vorfabrizierten, gegossenen Bronzeelementen mit gelegentlichen Öffnungen sowie eine aus einer starken Mauer bestehende Innenschicht, in die Ausstellungsständer und -systeme ein-gelassen sind."

« J'aime l'idée de penser un musée d'archéologie comme une boîte à bijoux compacte contenant pièce par pièce les trésors que l'Histoire nous a confiés », explique l'architecte. Les sols et les plafonds en bois sombre piquetés de « prismes de verre blanc » dans les salles d'exposition permanente « évoquent le passage du temps ». Le musée se trouve près du palais de Bendaña, actuellement musée Naipes Fournier. La bibliothèque, les salles de travail et les ateliers situés au rez-de-chaus-sée disposent d'une entrée séparée. Les espaces pour expositions temporaires et un hall de réunions sont implantés au niveau de l'entrée principale partagée avec le Musée Naipes Fournier. « La façade, qui définit une cour d'accès, est une trame faite de pièces en fonte de bronze, matériau aux références archéologiques évidentes. Au centre, un mur creux en verre imprimé contient l'escalier qui offre des vues sur la cour au fur et à mesure que l'on monte. Par contraste, la façade sur la rue infé-rieure est plus hermétique. Elle se compose d'une strate extérieure de panneaux opaques préfabriqués en fonte de bronze percée d'ouvertures par endroits, et d'une strate intérieure constituée d'un mur de forte épaisseur contenant des vitrines et divers systèmes techniques », explique Francisco Mangado.

The architects evoke the idea of a "jewel box" containing archeological treasures in explaining their design strategy. The strong, dark outline of the building confirms this imagery.

Ihre Entwurfsstrategie erläutern die Architekten mit der Vorstellung eines „Schmuckkästchens", das archäologische Schätze enthält. Die strenge, dunkle Außenform des Gebäudes bestätigt diese Metaphorik.

Les architectes ont évoqué l'idée d'une « boîte à bijoux » emplie de trésors archéologiques pour expliquer leur stratégie de conception. Les formes sombres et puissantes du bâtiment confirment cette image.

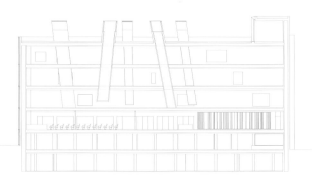
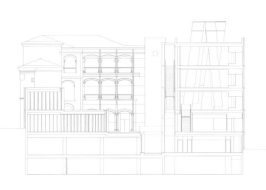

Though it is in good part rectangular, as the section drawings above reveal, the museum's cladding and glazing seem to evoke the older, neighboring buildings more than seek to differentiate the building from its environment.

Obgleich das Museum, wie die Schnitte oben zeigen, überwiegend rechtwinklig geplant ist, erinnern seine Verkleidung und Verglasung offenbar eher an die älteren Bauten der Nachbarschaft, anstatt sich von ihnen abheben zu wollen.

Bien que sa forme soit en grande partie rectangulaire, comme le montrent les dessins de coupe ci-dessus, le musée semble davantage évoquer les constructions voisines anciennes par son habillage et ses vitrages que chercher à s'en différencier.

The light shafts that cut through the building in a slightly diagonal alignment are original and sculptural in their presence. Above, stairway views, with the light shafts visible to the right.

Die Lichtschächte, die in leicht schräger Ausrichtung durch das Gebäude schneiden, haben eine originelle und skulpturale Präsenz. Oben Blicke in das Treppenhaus, rechts auf die Lichtschächte.

Les puits de lumière qui transpercent le bâtiment selon un alignement légèrement en diagonale prennent une présence sculpturale originale. Ci-dessus, vues de l'escalier, et des puits de lumière, page de droite.

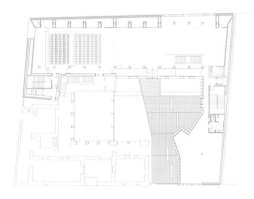
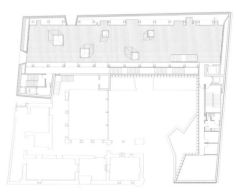

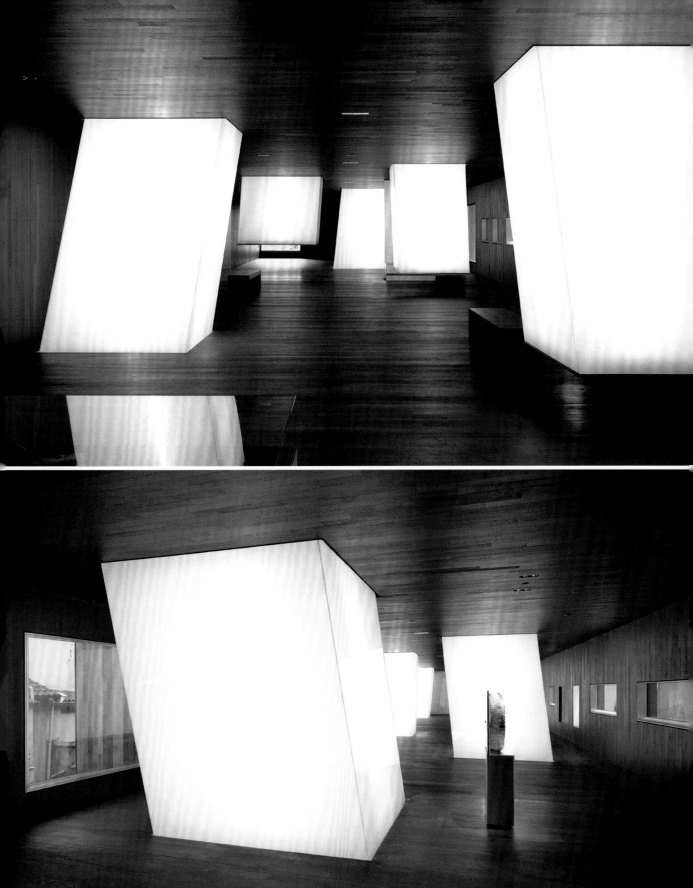

RICHARD MEIER

Richard Meier & Partners
475 Tenth Avenue
New York, NY 10018
USA

Tel: +1 212 967 6060
Fax: +1 212 967 3207
E-mail: mail@richardmeier.com
Web: www.richardmeier.com

RICHARD MEIER was born in Newark, New Jersey, in 1934. He received his architectural training at Cornell University, and worked in the office of Marcel Breuer (1960–63) before establishing his own practice in 1963. In 1984, he became the youngest winner of the Pritzker Prize, and he received the 1988 RIBA Gold Medal. His notable buildings include The Atheneum (New Harmony, Indiana, 1975–79); the High Museum of Art (Atlanta, Georgia, 1980–83); the Museum of Decorative Arts (Frankfurt, Germany, 1979–84); the Canal Plus Headquarters (Paris, France, 1988–91); the City Hall and Library (The Hague, the Netherlands, 1990–95); the Barcelona Museum of Contemporary Art (Barcelona, Spain, 1988–95); and the Getty Center (Los Angeles, California, 1984–97). Recent work includes the US Courthouse and Federal Building (Phoenix, Arizona, 1995–2000); the Yale University History of Art and Arts Library (New Haven, Connecticut, 2001); a 16-story residential building located in Manhattan near the architect's Perry Street apartments (New York, New York, 1999–2002); the 66 Restaurant in New York (New York, 2001–02); the Jubilee Church (Rome, Italy, 2003); the Crystal Cathedral International Center for Possibility Thinking (Garden Grove, California, 2003); 165 Charles Street (New York, New York, 2003–05); and the Ara Pacis Museum (Rome, Italy, 1995–2006). Recent work includes the Arp Museum (Rolandseck, Germany, 1978–2007, published here); the Beach House, a 12-story glass enclosed condominium located on Collins Avenue in Miami (Florida, 2004–07); and the ECM City Tower (Pankrac City, Prague, Czech Republic, 2004–07).

RICHARD MEIER wurde 1934 in Newark, New Jersey, geboren. Er studierte Architektur an der Cornell University und arbeitete im Büro von Marcel Breuer (1960–63), bis er 1963 sein eigenes Büro eröffnete. 1984 wurde ihm als jüngstem Gewinner der Pritzker-Preis verliehen; 1988 erhielt er die RIBA Gold Medal. Zu seinen bekannten Bauten zählen das Atheneum (New Harmony, Indiana, 1975–79), das High Museum of Art (Atlanta, Georgia, 1980–83), das Museum für Angewandte Kunst (Frankfurt am Main, 1979–84), der Hauptsitz von Canal Plus (Paris, 1988–91), Rathaus und Bibliothek in Den Haag (1990–95), das Museo de Arte Contemporaneo (Barcelona, 1988–95) und das Getty Center (Los Angeles, Kalifornien, 1984–97). Neuere Bauten sind das US Courthouse and Federal Building (Phoenix, Arizona, 1995–2000), die History of Art and Arts Library der Yale University (New Haven, Connecticut, 2001), ein 16-geschossiges Wohnhaus in Manhattan nahe von Meiers Apartments in der Perry Street (New York, 1999–2002), das Restaurant 66 in New York (2001–02), die Jubiläumskirche (Rom, 2003), das Crystal Cathedral International Center for Possibility Thinking (Garden Grove, Kalifornien, 2003), das Gebäude 165 Charles Street (New York, 2003–05) und das Museum Ara Pacis (Rom, 1995–2006). Zu den neuesten Arbeiten gehören das Arp Museum (Rolandseck, Deutschland, 1978–2007, hier veröffentlicht), das Beach House, eine zwölfgeschossige, verglaste Wohnanlage an der Collins Avenue in Miami (Florida, 2004–07), und der ECM City Tower (Prag-Pancraz, 2004–07).

RICHARD MEIER, né à Newark (New Jersey) en 1934, a fait ses études d'architecture à la Cornell University et travaillé chez Marcel Breuer (1960–63) avant de créer sa propre agence en 1963. En 1984, il a été le plus jeune architecte à avoir été distingué par le prix Pritzker et a reçu la médaille d'or du RIBA en 1988. Parmi ses réalisations les plus connues : The Atheneum (New Harmony, Indiana 1975–79) ; le High Museum of Art (Atlanta, Georgie, 1980–83) ; le musée des Arts décoratifs (Francfort, Allemagne, 1979–84) ; le siège de Canal Plus (Paris, 1988–91) ; l'hôtel de ville et une bibliothèque (La Haye, Pays-Bas, 1990–95) ; Le musée d'Art contemporain de Barcelone (Barcelone, 1988–95) ; et le Getty Center (Los Angeles, Californie, 1984–97). Plus récemment, il a construit : le Tribunal et immeuble de l'administration fédérale (Phoenix, Arizona, 1995–2000) ; la bibliothèque d'histoire de l'art et des arts à la Yale University (New Haven, Connecticut, 2001) ; un immeuble résidentiel de seize étages à Manhattan près de son immeuble de Perry Street (New York, New York, 1999–2002) ; le restaurant 66 à New York (2001–02) ; l'église du Jubilé (Rome, 2003) ; le Crystal Cathedral, International Center for Possibility Thinking (Garden Grove, Californie, 2003) ; l'immeuble 165 Charles Street (New York, New York, 2003–05) et le Musée de l'Ara Pacis (Rome, 1995–2006). Parmi ses réalisations récentes: le Arp Museum (Rolandseck, Allemagne, 1978–2007), publié ici ; la Beach House, un immeuble d'appartements de douze étages à façade de verre sur Collins Avenue à Miami (Floride, 2004–07) et la tour ECM (Pankrac, Prague, République tchèque, 2004–07).

ARP MUSEUM

Rolandseck, Germany, 1978–2007

Address: Hans-Arp-Allee 1, 53424 Remagen, Germany, +49 22 28 94 25 12, www.arpmuseum.org
Area: 4500 m². Clients: German Ministry of Finance, Rheinland-Pfalz, Arp Museum, Bahnhof Rolandseck.
Cost: not disclosed. Collaboration: Bernhard Karpf (Design Partner), Stefan Scheiber-Loeis (Project Architect),
Ehrensberger & Oertz Architekten (Associate Architects)

Hans Arp (1886–1966) was a German-French sculptor, painter, and poet. He was one of the founding members of the Dada movement in Zurich in 1916. He married Sophie Taeuber, an equally well-known Swiss artist, in 1922. Rolandseck is in the Rhineland-Palatinate region of Germany and is located close to Bonn. The site for the new museum is set on a wooded escarpment above the Rhine. Access to the museum is through the "Künstlerbahnhof," the former railway station of the town. The entrance lobby contains the museum shop. A subterranean passage including exhibition space leads to an elevator that takes visitors up 40 meters to the new building. The Arp Museum displays a collection of works by Hans Arp and Sophie Taeuber-Arp and their circle, including sculpture, drawings, paintings, and textiles. Occupying three levels and a total of 3400 square meters, it includes an outdoor terrace on the western side with a sculpture garden. The upper gallery is designed to permit overhead lighting. Typically clad in white enamel metal panels, the building is divided into a set of layered planes facing east, punctuated by glazed and louvered openings and cantilevered balconies affording panoramic views over the Rhine Valley.

Hans Arp (1886–1966) war ein deutsch-französischer Bildhauer, Maler und Dichter und gehörte zu den Gründungsmitgliedern der Dada-Bewegung 1916 in Zürich. Er heiratete 1922 die ebenso bekannte Schweizer Künstlerin Sophie Taeuber. Rolandseck liegt in Rheinland-Pfalz nicht weit von Bonn. Der Standort des neuen Museums ist ein bewaldeter Steilhang über dem Rhein. Der Zugang zum Museum erfolgt durch den „Künstlerbahnhof", das frühere Stationsgebäude der Stadt. Die Eingangshalle enthält den Museumsshop. Eine unterirdische Passage, die auch Ausstellungsfläche bietet, führt zum Fahrstuhl, der die Besucher 40 m hinauf in den Neubau befördert. Das Arp Museum enthält eine Sammlung von Werken Hans Arps, Sophie Taeuber-Arps und ihres Künstlerkreises, die sich aus Skulpturen, Zeichnungen, Gemälden und textilen Arbeiten zusammensetzt. Das Gebäude besteht aus drei Geschossen mit einer Gesamtfläche von 3400 m² und einer Außenterrasse mit Skulpturengarten an der Westseite. Der obere Ausstellungsbereich wird von oben belichtet. Der mit den für Meier typischen weiß emaillierten Metallplatten verkleidete Bau ist in mehrere geschichtete, nach Osten orientierte Ebenen aufgeteilt und von verglasten, mit Lamellenjalousien versehenen Öffnungen und auskragenden Balkons durchbrochen, die Panoramaausblicke auf das Rheintal bieten.

Hans Arp (1886–1966) est un sculpteur, peintre et poète germano-français, marié en 1922 à Sophie Taeuber, artiste suisse tout aussi renommée. Il fut l'un des membres fondateurs du mouvement Dada à Zurich, en 1916. Rolandseck se trouve dans le Land de Rhénanie-Palatinat, près de Bonn. Le site du nouveau musée est un terrain escarpé et boisé en bordure du Rhin. L'accès se fait par la « Gare de l'artiste », ancienne gare de chemin de fer de la ville. Le hall d'entrée contient la boutique du musée. Un passage souterrain servant aussi d'espace d'exposition conduit à un ascenseur qui mène les visiteurs 40 mètres plus haut vers le nouveau bâtiment. Le Musée présente une collection de sculptures, dessins, peintures et textiles de Hans Arp, Sophie Taeuber-Arp et de leur cercle. Ses trois niveaux de 3400 mètres carrés comprennent également une terrasse côté occidental, avec un jardin de sculptures. La galerie supérieure est éclairée zénithalement. Habillée à la manière typique de Meier de panneaux de métal émaillé blanc, la construction se divise en strates planes côté est, ponctuées d'ouvertures vitrées et protégées par des systèmes de persiennes et des balcons en porte-à-faux qui offrent des vues panoramiques sur la vallée du Rhin.

Richard Meier's layered, varied forms stand out above the old railway station next to the Rhine that serves as the entrance point for the new Arp Museum.

Richard Meiers geschichtete, vielfältige Formen ragen über den alten Bahnhof am Rhein hinaus, der als Eingangsbereich zum neuen Arp Museum dient.

Les formes stratifiées et variées de Richard Meier se détachent sur le paysage de l'ancienne gare en bordure du Rhin, qui sert d'entrée au nouveau musée Arp.

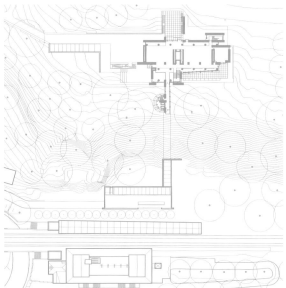

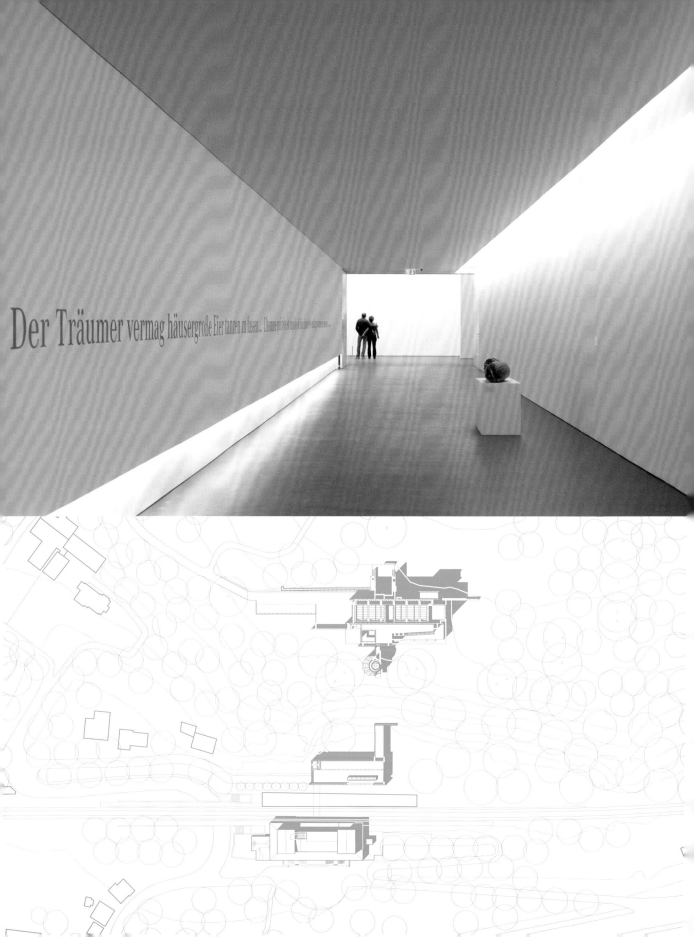

Der Träumer vermag häusergroße Eier tanzen zu lassen... Ut omnino opi tint iti magnis dolupta quae nistum rem...

The white, luminous spaces of the
museum are typical of the work of
Richard Meier, and yet here glazing
and the situation of the building take
on a special importance.

Die weißen, lichtdurchfluteten Räume
des Museums sind typisch für die
Bauten Meiers. Dennoch sind hier die
Verglasung und die Lage des Gebäudes von besonderer Bedeutung.

Les volumes blancs et lumineux
sont caractéristiques de l'œuvre
de Richard Meier. Ce vitrage et la
situation du bâtiment prennent toute-
fois ici une importance particulière.

PAULO MENDES DA ROCHA

Paulo Mendes da Rocha
Rua Bento Freitas 306 – 5º/51
01220–000 São Paulo, SP
Brazil

Tel: +55 11 3259 3175
E-mail: pmr@sti.com.br

PAULO ARCHIAS MENDES DA ROCHA was born in 1928 in the city of Vitória, capital of the state of Espirito Santo in Brazil. He completed his studies at the Mackenzie Architecture School in 1954. Paulo Mendes da Rocha was the 2006 winner of the Pritzker Prize. His first project outside Brazil was the Brazilian Pavilion for the International Expo in Osaka (Japan, 1970). Other significant works include the Paulistano Club Gymnasium (São Paulo, 1957–61); the Clubhouse of the Jockey Club of Goiás (Goiás, 1963); the Beach Club in Guarujá (São Paulo, 1963); a House in Butantã (São Paulo, 1964); a Hotel in Poxoréu (Mato Grosso, 1971); the Jardim Calux School (São Bernardo do Campo, São Paulo, 1972); the Keiralla Sarhan Office Building (São Paulo, 1984–88); the Jaraguá Apartment Building (São Paulo, 1984–88); and the Masetti Residence (Cabreuva, São Paulo, 1995). One of his best-known projects is the Brazilian Museum of Sculpture (São Paulo, 1987–92). His Patriarch Plaza and Viaduct do Cha (São Paulo, 1992), with its great curving wing canopy, is one of the more visible architectural monuments of Brazil's largest city. He has also done interesting renovation work, as was the case in the State Museum of São Paulo (1993). His more recent work includes the Portuguese Language Museum (São Paulo, 2003–06, published here); the Sesc 24 de Maio Building in the center of São Paulo (2001); a master plan for Vigo University in Spain (2004); the Leme Gallery (São Paulo, 2004); the Museum and Theater at the Enseada do Suá (Vitória, Espírito Santo, 2007); and Central Mill Park (Piracicaba, São Paulo, 2007).

PAULO ARCHIAS MENDES DA ROCHA wurde 1928 in Vitória, der Hauptstadt des brasilianischen Bundesstaats Espírito Santo, geboren. 1954 beendete er sein Studium an der Architekturabteilung der Universidade Presbiteriana Mackenzie. 2006 erhielt Paulo Mendes da Rocha den Pritzker-Preis. Sein erstes Projekt außerhalb Brasiliens war der brasilianische Pavillon für die Weltausstellung in Osaka (Japan, 1970). Zu weiteren bedeutenden Bauten von ihm zählen die Sporthalle des Klubs Paulistano (São Paulo, 1957–61), das Klubhaus des Jockeyklubs von Goiás (Goiás, 1963), der Beach Club in Guarujá (São Paulo, 1963), ein Haus in Butantã (São Paulo, 1964), ein Hotel in Poxoréu (Mato Grosso, 1971), die Schule Jardim Calux (São Bernardo do Campo, São Paulo, 1972), das Bürogebäude Keiralla Sarhan (São Paulo, 1984–88), das Apartmenthaus Jaraguá (São Paulo, 1984–88) und das Wohnhaus Masetti (Cabreuva, São Paulo, 1995). Eines seiner bekanntesten Bauwerke ist das Brasilianische Skulpturenmuseum (São Paulo, 1987–92). Seine Praça do Patriarca und das Viaduto do Chá (São Paulo, 1992) mit dem großen, geschwungenen Baldachin gehören zu den auffallendsten Architekturdenkmälern der größten Stadt Brasiliens. Mendes da Rocha hat auch interessante Sanierungsprojekte durchgeführt, z. B. beim Staatlichen Museum von São Paulo (1993). Zu seinen neueren Bauten zählen das Museu da Lingua Portuguesa (São Paulo, 2003–06, hier veröffentlicht), das Gebäude Sesc 24 de Maio im Zentrum von São Paulo (2001), ein Masterplan für die Universität Vigo in Spanien (2004), die Galerie Leme (São Paulo, 2004), das Museum und Theater an der Enseada do Suá (Vitória, Espírito Santo, 2007) und der Parque do Engenho Central (Piracicaba, São Paulo, 2007).

PAULO ARCHIAS MENDES DA ROCHA est né en 1928 à Vitória, capitale de l'État de l'Espírito Santo, au Brésil. Il a achevé ses études à la Mackenzie Architecture School en 1954. En 2006, il a remporté le prix Pritzker. Son premier projet en dehors du Brésil a été le Pavillon brésilien pour l'Exposition internationale d'Osaka au Japon (1970). Parmi ses autres réalisations importantes : le gymnase du club Paulistano (São Paulo, 1957–61) ; le clubhouse du Jockey Club de Goiás (Goiás, 1963) ; un club de plage à Guarujá (São Paulo, 1963) ; une maison à Butantã (São Paulo, 1964) ; un hôtel à Poxoréu (Mato Grosso, 1971) ; l'école Jardim Calux (São Bernardo do Campo, São Paulo, 1972) ; l'immeuble de bureaux Keiralla Sarhan (São Paulo, 1984–88) ; l'immeuble de logements Jaraguá (São Paulo, 1984–88) et la résidence Masetti (Cabreuva, São Paulo, 1995). L'une de ses œuvres les plus connues est le musée brésilien de la Sculpture (São Paulo, 1987–92). Sa place du Patriarche et le viaduc do Cha (São Paulo, 1992), au grand auvent en aile incurvée, constituent l'un des plus remarquables monuments de la plus grande ville du Brésil. Il a également réalisé d'intéressantes interventions en rénovation comme le musée d'État de São Paulo (1993). Parmi ses œuvres plus récentes : le musée de la Langue portugaise (São Paulo, 2003–06), publié ici ; l'immeuble Sesc 24 de Maio au centre de São Paulo (2001) ; un plan directeur pour l'unversité de Vigo en Espagne (2004) ; la galerie Leme (São Paulo, 2004) ; le musée et théâtre à l'Enseada do Suá (Vitória, Espírito Santo, 2007) et le Parque de Engenho central (Piracicaba, São Paulo, 2007).

PORTUGUESE LANGUAGE MUSEUM

São Paulo, São Paulo, Brazil, 2003–06

Praça da Luz, s/n, São Paulo SP, Brazil, +55 11 3362 0775, www.poiesis.org.br/mlp
Area: 3600 m². Client: Fundação Roberto Marinho. Cost: $12 million
Collaboration: Heloisa Maringoni (Structural Engineer), Ralph Appelbaum Associates (Exhibition Design)

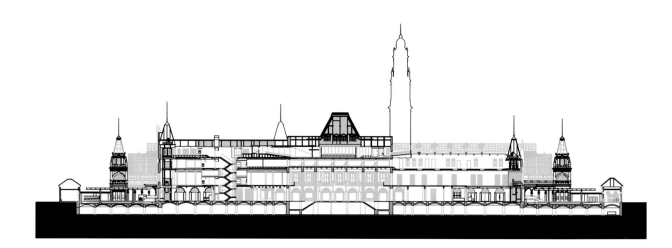

Inserted into the existing railway station, which continues to function as such, the Portuguese Language Museum is signaled by this modern canopy designed by the architect.

Das in den Bahnhof – der noch immer in Betrieb ist – integrierte Museum der portugiesischen Sprache wird durch dieses moderne, vom Architekten gestaltete Vordach angekündigt.

Inséré dans l'ancienne gare qui a conservé sa fonction, le musée de la Langue portugaise se signale par un auvent moderne dessiné par l'architecte.

The Luz Railway Station was designed and built from 1895 to 1901 by the English architect Charles Henry Driver in a Neoclassical style to serve the main coffee supply routes from the countryside of the state of São Paulo to the port of Santos. Recently, the Metropolitan Train Company conceded a little over half of the station's total area of 7500 square meters to the São Paulo State Secretariat of Culture to house the Portuguese Language Museum. Since the station is still in operation, it was important to reconcile the two functions of the building. The allotted area, a long, narrow space 120 meters long and 14 meters wide, had been used to house the railway company headquarters. Skylit entrances with panoramic elevators leading visitors to the third floor were installed at the eastern and western ends of the building. A 160-seat auditorium has been installed on the third floor. The exhibition space is located on the second floor and runs the entire length of the station. Temporary exhibitions are located on the eastern end of the first floor. The architect states: "The proposal harks back to the idea of the machine and the bridge, as it seeks to reaffirm the city's transformation in its mechanical dimension. While mainline and subway trains transit on the horizontal, elevators shuttle up and down the vertical. For this reason the plan required unconventional elevators, understood as vertical urban transport, much like the Lacerda elevator in Salvador or the Chiado lift in Lisbon."

Der Bahnhof Luz wurde von 1895 bis 1901 von dem englischen Architekten Charles Henry Driver in neoklassizistischem Stil geplant und für den Kaffeetransport aus dem ländlichen Bereich des Staats São Paulo zum Hafen Santos gebaut. Vor einiger Zeit überließ die Eisenbahngesellschaft dem Kulturministerium des Staats São Paulo etwas über die Hälfte des insgesamt 7500 m² großen Geländes zur Unterbringung des Museums der portugiesischen Sprache. Da der Bahnhof noch in Betrieb ist, war es wichtig, die beiden Funktionen des Gebäudes zu vereinen. Das vorgesehene Gelände, ein langes, schmales Grundstück von 120 m Länge und 14 m Breite, war von der Verwaltung der Eisenbahnlinie genutzt worden. Aus dem von oben belichteten Eingangsbereich führen Panoramaaufzüge, die an der Ost- und der Westseite des Gebäudes installiert wurden, die Besucher in das dritte Obergeschoss. Dort befindet sich ein Auditorium mit 160 Sitzplätzen. Die Ausstellungsräume liegen im zweiten Obergeschoss und erstrecken sich über die ganze Länge des Bahnhofsgebäudes. Wechselausstellungen finden auf der Ostseite des ersten Obergeschosses statt. Der Architekt erklärt: „Die Lösung geht auf die Idee der Maschine und der Brücke zurück und sucht die Veränderung der Stadt in ihrer technischen Dimension wiederzugeben. Während Fernzüge und U-Bahn horizontal verkehren, verlaufen die Aufzüge vertikal. Aus diesem Grund mussten unkonventionelle Fahrstühle eingeplant werden, die als vertikaler Stadtverkehr aufgefasst werden, etwa so wie der Lacerda-Aufzug in Salvador oder der Chiado-Lift in Lissabon."

La gare Luz a été conçue et construite de 1895 à 1901 par l'architecte britannique Charles Henry Driver dans un style éclectique pour desservir les plantations de café de l'État de Sao Paulo et les relier au port de Santos. Récemment, la Compagnie du train métropolitain a concédé un peu plus de la moitié de 7500 mètres carrés de bureaux au secrétariat à la culture de l'État de Sao Paulo pour accueillir le musée de la Langue portugaise. Comme les trains desservent encore la gare, il était important de concilier les deux fonctions. La surface allouée, un étroit espace de 120 mètres de long par 14 de large, était jadis le siège de la compagnie de chemin de fer. Des entrées éclairées par des verrières et desservies par des ascenseurs panoramiques conduisent les visiteurs aux extrémités est et ouest du troisième niveau, où a également été aménagé un auditorium de cent soixante places. L'espace d'exposition se trouve au second niveau et court sur la totalité du bâtiment. Les expositions temporaires se déroulent à l'extrémité est du premier niveau. « La proposition renvoie à l'idée de machine et de pont, et cherche à réaffirmer la transformation de la ville dans sa dimension mécanique. Pendant que les trains et le métro filent à l'horizontale, les ascenseurs s'élèvent à la verticale. C'est pour cette raison que le plan nécessitait des ascenseurs non conventionnels, conçus comme un mode de transport vertical un peu comme l'ascenseur de Lacerda à Salvador ou celui du Chiado à Lisbonne. »

Within the structure, Paulo Mendes da Rocha has carved out a modern museum dedicated to the language of his country.

Im Gebäude hat Paulo Mendes da Rocha ein modernes Museum eingerichtet, das der Sprache seines Landes gewidmet ist.

Paulo Mendes da Rocha a inséré un musée moderne consacré à la langue de son pays à l'intérieur de la structure existante.

RAFAEL MONEO

Rafael Moneo
Cinca 5
28002 Madrid
Spain

Tel: +34 91 564 22 57 / Fax: +34 91 563 52 17
E-mail: r.moneo@rafaelmoneo.com

RAFAEL MONEO was born in Tudela, Navarra (Spain), in 1937. He graduated from the ETSA in Madrid in 1961. The following year, he went to work with Jørn Utzon in Denmark. Rafael Moneo has taught extensively at the ETSA in Madrid and Barcelona. He was chairman of the Department of Architecture at Harvard GSD from 1985 to 1990. He won the 1995 Pritzker Prize, and the 2003 RIBA Gold Medal. His work includes the National Museum of Roman Art (Mérida, 1980–86); the San Pablo Airport Terminal in Seville (1989–91) built for Expo '92; the Atocha railway station in Madrid (1991); the Miró Foundation in Palma (1992); the interior architecture of the Thyssen-Bornemisza Collection in Madrid (1992); the Davis Museum at Wellesley College (Wellesley, Massachusetts, 1993); Potsdamer Platz Hotel and Office Building (Berlin, Germany, 1993–98); the Murcia Town Hall (Murcia, 1995–98); the Kursaal Auditorium and Congress Center (San Sebastián, Guipúzcoa, 1990–99); the Cathedral of Our Lady of the Angels (Los Angeles, California, 2000–02); and an extension of the Prado Museum (Madrid, 2001–07), all in Spain unless stated otherwise. He has also worked on the Souks in Beirut; the Laboratory for Interface and Engineering at Harvard; the Chace Student Center for the Rhode Island School of Design (Providence, Rhode Island, 2008); and the Museum of the Roman Theater (Cartagena, 2002–08, published here). He completed a laboratory for the Novartis Campus (Basel, Switzerland, 2009); and is presently working on the Northwest Science Building for Columbia University (New York); and the Princeton University Neuroscience and Psychology Building (New Jersey).

RAFAEL MONEO wurde 1937 in Tudela, Navarra (Spanien), geboren und studierte bis 1961 an der Escuela Técnica Superior de Arquitectura (ETSA) in Madrid. Im folgenden Jahr ging er nach Dänemark, um bei Jørn Utzon zu arbeiten. Rafael Moneo hat lange Zeit an der ETSA in Madrid und Barcelona gelehrt. Er war von 1985 bis 1990 Vorsitzender der Architekturabteilung an der Harvard Graduate School of Design. 1995 wurde ihm der Pritzker-Preis und 2003 die RIBA Gold Medal verliehen. Zu seinen Werken zählen das Museo de Arte Romana (Mérida, 1980–86), der für die Expo '92 errichtete Terminal des Flughafens San Pablo in Sevilla (1989–91), der neue Atocha-Bahnhof in Madrid (1991), die Stiftung Miró in Palma de Mallorca (1992), die Innenarchitektur des Museums für die Sammlung Thyssen-Bornemisza in Madrid (1992), das Davis Museum am Wellesley College (Wellesley, Massachusetts, 1993), ein Hotel und Bürogebäude am Potsdamer Platz (Berlin, 1993–98), das Rathaus von Murcia (1995–98), das Auditorium und Kongresszentrum Kursaal (San Sebastián, Guipúzcoa, 1990–99), die Kathedrale Our Lady of the Angels (Los Angeles, Kalifornien, 2000–02) sowie die Erweiterung des Prado (Madrid, 2001–07), alle in Spanien, sofern nicht anders angegeben. Er hat auch an den Souks von Beirut mitgearbeitet sowie das Laboratory for Interface and Engineering an der Harvard University, das Chace Student Center für die Rhode Island School of Design (Providence, Rhode Island, 2008) und das Museo del Teatro Romano in Cartagena (Spanien, 2002–08, hier veröffentlicht) geplant. Ferner hat er einen Laboratoriumsbau auf dem Gelände der Pharmafirma Novartis (Basel, Schweiz, 2009) errichtet und arbeitet gegenwärtig am Northwest Science Building für die Columbia University (New York) und am Princeton University Neuroscience and Psychology Building (New Jersey).

RAFAEL MONEO est né à Tudela, Navarre (Espagne), en 1937. Il est diplômé de l'ETSA à Madrid en 1961. En 1962, il part travailler chez Jørn Utzon au Danemark. Il a beaucoup enseigné à l'ETSA à Madrid et Barcelone, a présidé le Département d'architecture de la GSD à Harvard de 1985 à 1990 et a remporté le prix Pritzker en 1995, ainsi que la médaille d'or du RIBA en 2003. Parmi ses réalisations : le musée national d'Art roman de Mérida (1980–86) ; le terminal de l'aéroport San Pablo à Séville (1989–91) pour Expo '92 ; la gare d'Atocha à Madrid (1991) ; la Fondation Miró à Palma (1992) ; l'architecture intérieure de la Collection Thyssen-Bornemisza à Madrid (1992) ; le Davis Museum du Wellesley College (Wellesley, Massachusetts, 1993) ; un hôtel et un immeuble de bureaux au Potsdamer Platz (Berlin, 1993–98) ; l'hôtel de ville de Murcie (1995–98) ; l'auditorium et centre de congrès du Kursaal (San Sebastián, Guipúzcoa, 1990–99) ; la cathédrale Our Lady of the Angels (Los Angeles, Californie, 2000–02) et l'extension du Musée du Prado (Madrid, 2001–07). Il a également travaillé sur le projet de nouveaux *souks* à Beyrouth ; réalisé le Laboratory for Interface and Engineering d'Harvard ; le Chace Student Center de la Rhode Island School of Design (Providence, Rhode Island, 2008) et le musée du Théâtre romain (Cartagena, 2002–08), publié ici. Il a récemment achevé un laboratoire pour le campus Novartis (Bâle, Suisse, 2009) et travaille actuellement au projet du Northwest Science Building de la Columbia University (New York) et sur celui du bâtiment des neurosciences et de la psychologie de la Princeton University (New Jersey).

MUSEUM OF THE ROMAN THEATER

Cartagena, Spain, 2002–08

Address: Plaza del Ayuntamiento 9, 30201 Cartagena, Spain, +34 968 52 51 49, www.teatroromanocartagena.org
Area: 20 542 m². Clients: Casa Murcia Foundation, Regional Government of Murcia. Cost: not disclosed
Team: Juan Manuel Nicàs (Project Architect), Carla Bovio, Angel Huertas Suanzes

The construction of the Roman theater of Carthago Nova began in the 1st century BC. The development of the city hid its ruins until it was rediscovered only in 1987. The objects discovered during the archeological digs fully justify the creation of a Museum of the Roman Theater. The museum involves two structures—one including sections of the Riquelme Palace, and the other where exhibition rooms, escalators, and lifts are located. The two are connected by an underground corridor. Moneo's project has sought to tie together the disparate elements of a city that is rich in history. Rafael Moneo's sensitive style takes the urban situation into account, as he did with his expansion of the Prado in Madrid. Mixing elements in ruins with architecture of other periods and finally with contemporary buildings is by no means a task that is without risk. Here, the modern elements are clearly visible, and the project unites pieces that could not have formed a whole without such a thoughtful intervention.

Der Bau des römischen Theaters von Carthago Nova begann im 1. Jahrhundert v. Chr. Die Ruinen verschwanden unter der Bebauung der Stadt und wurden erst 1987 wiederentdeckt. Die während der Ausgrabungen gefundenen archäologischen Exponate rechtfertigen zweifellos die Gründung dieses Museums. Das Gebäude besteht aus zwei Trakten – einer enthält Bestandteile des Palasts Riquelme, der andere die Ausstellungsräume, Rolltreppen und Aufzüge. Beide sind durch einen unterirdischen Korridor miteinander verbunden. Moneo hat bei diesem Projekt versucht, zwei disparate Elemente einer an historischen Denkmälern reichen Stadt zusammenzuführen. Rafael Moneos sensibler Baustil nimmt – ebenso wie bei seinem Museumsneubau für den Prado in Madrid – Rücksicht auf die städtebauliche Situation. Die Mischung von Elementen aus einem Ruinenbestand mit Architektur aus anderen Perioden und aktuellen Neubauten ist eine höchst riskante Angelegenheit. Hier sind die modernen Elemente deutlich ablesbar, und der Entwurf führt Teile zusammen, die nur durch derart rücksichtsvolles Eingreifen ein einheitliches Ganzes bilden können.

La construction du Théâre romain de Carthago Nova avait débuté au premier siècle av. J.-C. Le développement de la cité recouvrit peu à peu ses ruines et il ne fut remis au jour qu'en 1987. Les objets trouvés pendant les fouilles archéologiques justifiaient la création de ce musée du Théâtre romain. Il comprend deux constructions, l'une intégrant des parties du palais Riquelme, l'autre qui regroupe les salles d'exposition, les escaliers mécaniques et les ascenseurs. Toutes deux sont connectées par un corridor souterrain. Le projet de Moneo cherche à relier les composantes disparates d'une ville riche d'histoire. Le style sensible de l'architecte a pris la situation urbaine en compte, comme lors de l'extension du Prado à Madrid. Mêler des éléments en ruine à l'architecture d'autres périodes et finalement des constructions contemporaines n'est pas une tâche sans risque. Ici, les composantes modernes sont clairement visibles et le projet regroupe et connecte des éléments qui n'auraient pu former un tel ensemble sans une intervention aussi bien pensée.

The challenge of creating a museum in and around the ruins of a Roman amphitheater suits the talents of Rafael Moneo who creates a skillful blend of old and new.

Die Herausforderung, ein Museum in und um die Ruinen eines römischen Amphitheaters zu planen, entspricht der Begabung von Rafael Moneo – er hat eine geschickte Mischung aus Alt und Neu geschaffen.

Le défi de créer un musée dans et autour des ruines d'un amphithéâtre romain convenait au talent de Rafael Moneo qui a su habilement fusionner l'ancien et le nouveau.

Sketches by Rafael Moneo show the amphitheater itself and the design of the new spaces. What remains of the theater is skillfully highlighted against the background of the existing city.

Moneos Skizzen zeigen das Amphitheater und den Entwurf der neuen Bereiche. Die Ruinen des Theaters werden geschickt gegen den Hintergrund der bestehenden Stadtstruktur hervorgehoben.

Les croquis de Rafael Moneo montrent l'amphithéâtre et les nouveaux espaces aménagés. Les vestiges du théâtre ont été mis en valeur avec art devant la toile de fond que leur offre la ville.

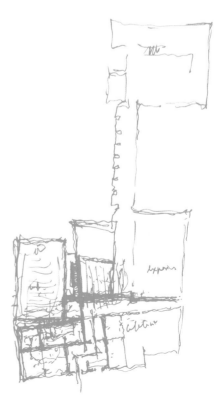

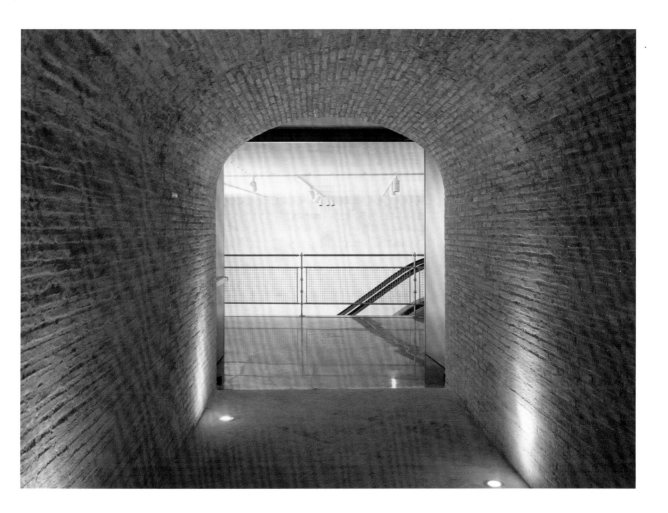

Moneo's work here recalls the success he had in the 1980s with his
National Museum of Roman Art in
Mérida, or even the delicate work of
juxtaposition with historic buildings
accomplished in his more recent
expansion of the Prado Museum in
Madrid.

Dieses Gebäude Moneos erinnert an
seinen Erfolg der 1980er-Jahre mit
seinem Museum für römische Kunst
in Mérida oder auch, in neuerer Zeit,
an seine sensible Gegenüberstellung
mit historischen Bauten bei seinem
Erweiterungsbau für den Prado in
Madrid.

Ce travail de Moneo rappelle la
réussite de son musée national de
l'Art roman à Mérida dans les années
1980, ou sa juxtaposition pleine
de délicatesse d'une architecture
moderne avec des bâtiments historiques lors de l'extension du musée
du Prado à Madrid.

TOSHIKO MORI

Toshiko Mori Architect
199 Lafayette Street
Suite 5A
New York, NY 10012
USA

Tel: +1 212 337 9644
Fax: +1 212 337 9647
E-mail: info@tmarch.com
Web: www.tmarch.com

TOSHIKO MORI attended the Cooper Union School of Art, and School of Architecture (1970–76), and received an Honorary M.Arch degree from the Harvard GSD in 1996. From 2002 to 2008, she was Chair of the Department of Architecture at the Harvard GSD, where she has taught since 1995. Prior to joining the faculty at Harvard, Toshiko Mori taught for more than a decade at Cooper Union. She has served as a visiting faculty member at Columbia University and Yale University, where she was the Eero Saarinen Visiting Professor in 1992. Toshiko Mori has worked on numerous institutional projects, such as the addition to Syracuse University's Link Hall (Syracuse, New York, 2008); the renovation of Brown University's Pembroke Hall (Providence, Rhode Island, 2008); the Syracuse Center of Excellence in Environmental and Energy Systems Headquarter Building (Syracuse, New York, 2009); and a master plan for New York University. She has built houses in Maine (2001, 2004); Florida (2005); Connecticut (1994, 2009); New York (2008, 2009); and designed the Visitor Center for Frank Lloyd Wright's Darwin D. Martin House (Buffalo, New York, 2008–09, published here). The firm created the design for the Cooper-Hewitt National Design Museum's exhibition *Fashioning Felt* (New York, March 6 to September 7, 2009). In March 2009, Toshiko Mori won the competition to design a pavilion for the Penobscot Marine Museum in Searsport (Maine), all in the USA.

TOSHIKO MORI studierte an der Cooper Union School of Art und School of Architecture (1970–76) und erhielt 1996 einen Honorary M. Arch. an der Harvard Graduate School of Design. Von 2002 bis 2008 hatte sie den Vorsitz der Architekturabteilung an der Harvard School of Design inne, wo sie seit 1995 lehrt. Davor lehrte sie über ein Jahrzehnt an der Cooper Union. Sie war Gastfakultätsmitglied an den Universitäten Columbia und Yale, an letzterer hatte sie 1992 die Eero-Saarinen-Gastprofessur inne. Toshiko Mori hat an zahlreichen öffentlichen Projekten gearbeitet, wie dem Anbau der Link Hall an der Syracuse University (Syracuse, New York, 2008), der Sanierung der Pembroke Hall der Brown University (Providence, Rhode Island, 2008), dem Hauptgebäude des Syracuse Center of Excellence in Environmental and Energy Systems (Syracuse, New York, 2009) und einem Generalbebauungsplan für die New York University. Sie hat Häuser in Maine (2001, 2004), Florida (2005), Connecticut (1994, 2009) und New York (2008, 2009) gebaut und das Besucherzentrum für Frank Lloyd Wrights Haus Darwin D. Martin (Buffalo, New York, 2008–09, hier veröffentlicht) geplant. Ihr Büro gestaltete auch die Ausstellung *Fashioning Felt* im Cooper-Hewitt National Design Museum (New York, 6.3.–7.9.2009). Im März 2009 gewann Toshiko Mori den Wettbewerb für eine Erweiterung des Penobscot Marine Museum in Searsport (Maine), alle in den USA.

TOSHIKO MORI a étudié à la Cooper Union School of Art and School of Architecture (1970–76). Elle est M.Arch honoraire de l'Harvard University Graduate School of Design (1996). De 2002 à 2008, elle a présidé le Département d'architecture de l'Harvard School of Design, où elle enseigne depuis 1995. Auparavant, elle avait déjà enseigné pendant plus de dix ans à la Cooper Union. Elle a aussi été professeur invité à la Columbia University et à la Yale University (Eero Saarinen Visiting Professor en 1992). Elle a travaillé à de nombreux projets institutionnels, comme l'ajout au Syracuse University's Link Hall, (Syracuse, New York, 2008); la rénovation du Pembroke Hall de Brown University (Providence, Rhode Island, 2008); l'immeuble du siège du Syracruse Center of Excellence in Environmental and Energy Systems (Syracuse, New York, 2009) et un plan directeur pour la New York University. Elle a construit des maisons dans le Maine (2001, 2004); en Floride (2005); dans la Connecticut (1994, 2009); dans l'État de New York (2008, 2009) et a conçu le centre d'accueil des visiteurs de la maison Darwin D. Martin de Frank Lloyd Wright (Buffalo, New York, 2008–09), publié ici. Son agence a créé la mise en scène de l'exposition *Fashioning Felt* du Cooper Hewitt National Design Museum (New York, 6 mars–7 septembre 2009). En mars 2009, Toshiko Mori a remporté le concours pour l'extension du Penobscot Marine Museum à Searsport (Maine).

VISITOR CENTER FOR FRANK LLOYD WRIGHT'S DARWIN D. MARTIN HOUSE

Buffalo, New York, USA, 2008–09

Address: 125 Jewett Parkway - Buffalo, NY 14214, United States, +1 716 856 3858, www.darwinmartinhouse.org
Area: 530 m². Client: Martin House Restoration Corporation. Cost: $5 million
Team: Sonya Lee (Project Architect), Alexandra Barker (Designer)

Toshiko Mori has created a high, light building with full-height glazing, topped by a thin slab roof. The horizontality of the structure echoes the neighboring Darwin D. Martin House.

Toshiko Mori hat ein helles, leichtes Gebäude mit wandhoher Verglasung geschaffen, das von einer dünnen Dachplatte gekrönt wird. Die Horizontalität des Gebäudes entspricht der des Nachbarhauses Darwin D. Martin.

Toshiko Mori a créé ici un bâtiment d'apparence légère, entièrement vitré et protégé par un toit en dalle mince. L'horizontalité du bâtiment fait écho à celle de la maison Darwin D. Martin voisine.

The Darwin D. Martin House complex was built from 1903 to 1905 and is considered to be one of the most significant early houses of Frank Lloyd Wright. The Visitor Center designed by Toshiko Mori includes a permanent gallery, orientation, and gathering spaces. The architect states: "Our design strategy creates a dialogue with the Martin House through contrast rather than imitation. The Visitor Center reinterprets Wright's lifelong interest in innovation through the exploration of materials, technologies, and techniques, reflecting the structural, infrastructural, and programmatic relationships of the Martin House in a contemporary and abstract design." Specifically, Mori has sought to contrast with the "introverted" nature of Wright's house by using a glass façade and open plan for the Visitor Center. Geothermal heating and displacement ventilation are used to reduce energy consumption, a fact that the architect relates naturally to current trends, but also to Wright's interest in techno-logical innovation. The structure of the pavilion is related to that of the pergola that is part of the original Martin House complex. Toshiko Mori concludes: "The Visitor Center is a reinterpretation of Wright's organic architecture into a contemporary concept of integration for sustainable principles. The pavilion's simplicity and clarity give the Martin House Visitor Center a monumental quality in contrast to its small size."

Die Wohnanlage Darwin D. Martin wurde zwischen 1903 und 1905 erbaut und gilt als eines der bedeutendsten unter den frühen Häusern von Frank Lloyd Wright. Das von Toshiko Mori geplante Besucherzentrum umfasst eine Dauerausstellung sowie Informations- und Konferenzräume. Die Architektin erklärt: „Unsere Entwurfsstra-tegie bestand darin, einen Dialog mit dem Haus Martin durch Kontrast und nicht durch Imitation herzustellen. Das Besucherzentrum ist eine Neuinterpretation von Wrights lebenslangem Streben nach Innovation durch Erforschung von Materialien, Technologien und Techniken, die die konstruktiven, infrastrukturellen und programmatischen Beziehungen des Hauses Martin in einem zeitgemäßen und abstrakten Entwurf ausdrücken." Mori hat insbesondere versucht, einen Kontrast zu Wrights „introvertiertem" Haus herzustellen, indem sie das Besucherzentrum mit einer Glasfassade und einem offenen Grundriss plante. Erdwärmeheizung und ein Verdrängungsbelüftungssystem dienen zur Reduzierung des Energieverbrauchs – eine Maßnahme, welche die Architektin natürlich mit heutigen Bestrebungen, aber auch mit Wrights Interesse an inno-vativer Technik in Verbindung bringt. Die Struktur dieses Pavillons entspricht der der Pergola, die Bestandteil des originalen Hauses Martin ist. Toshiko Mori bemerkt abschließend: „Das Besucherzentrum ist eine Übertragung von Wrights organischer Architektur in ein zeitgemäßes Konzept für nachhaltiges Bauen. Die Schlichtheit und Klarheit verleihen dem Besucherzentrum des Hauses Martin trotz seiner geringen Größe eine monumentale Qualität."

La maison Darwin D. Martin construite entre 1903 et 1905 est considérée comme l'une des œuvres les plus importantes des débuts de la carrière de Frank Lloyd Wright. Le centre d'accueil des visiteurs, conçu par Toshiko Mori, comprend une galerie permanente, un espace d'orientation et de réunion. « Notre stratégie pour ce pro-jet est de créer un dialogue avec la maison Martin, en contraste plutôt que dans un esprit d'imitation. Le centre des visiteurs réinterprète le goût constant que Wright manifesta tout au long de sa carrière pour l'innovation à travers des explorations de matériaux, de technologies et de techniques qui reflètent les relations structurale, infrastructurelle et programmatique de la maison dans un esprit contemporain et abstrait », explique l'architecte. Spécifiquement, Mori a recherché le contraste avec la nature « introvertie » de la maison de Wright en mettant en place une façade de verre et un plan ouvert. Le chauffage géothermique et la ventilation par mouvement de l'air permettent de réduire la consommation énergétique, ce que les architectes relient aux tendances actuelles, mais aussi à l'intérêt de Wright pour l'innovation tech-nologique. La structure du pavillon est en rapport avec celui de la pergola qui fait partie du complexe original de la maison Martin. « Le centre d'accueil des visiteurs est une réinterprétation de l'architecture organique de Wright en un concept contemporain d'intégration de principes de développement durable. La simplicité et la lisibilité de ce pavillon lui confèrent une qualité monumentale qui contraste avec sa petite taille », conclut Toshiko Mori.

The pure geometry of the pavilion surely contrasts with Wright's fuller volumes, but the sweeping roof nonetheless is an homage to the great 20th-century master.

Die klare Geometrie des Pavillons steht sicher im Gegensatz zu Wrights üppigeren Volumen, aber das ausla-dende Dach ist dennoch eine Hom-mage an den großen Meister des 20. Jahrhunderts.

L'effet de pure composition géomé-trique du pavillon contraste certaine-ment avec les volumes plus pleins de Wright mais son toit débordant n'en est pas moins un hommage au grand maître de l'architecture du XXe siècle.

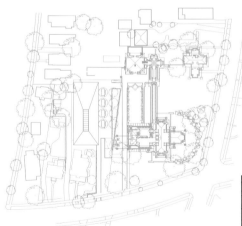

In the image above, the Darwin D. Martin House is visible in the background, highlighting the affinity between the structures and also the view from the visitor's pavilion toward the Wright house.

Die obere Abbildung mit dem Haus Darwin D. Martin im Hintergrund betont den Zusammenhang beider Gebäude und zeigt auch den Blick vom Besucherpavillon zum Bauwerk von Wright.

Image ci-dessus : les visiteurs peuvent apercevoir la maison Darwin D. Martin dans le fond, ce qui souligne les affinités entre les deux constructions.

In these views, the direct relationship between the new and the old is clear—with the exhibition cases of the pavilion in a direct and almost uninterrupted line of sight to the house.

Auf diesen Ansichten wird die enge Beziehung zwischen Neu- und Altbau deutlich – die Ausstellungsvitrinen im Pavillon liegen auf einer direkten und durchgehenden Sichtachse zum Haus.

Dans ces vues, la relation directe entre l'ancien et le nouveau est claire. Les vitrines d'exposition du pavillon s'alignent dans l'axe de vision de la maison.

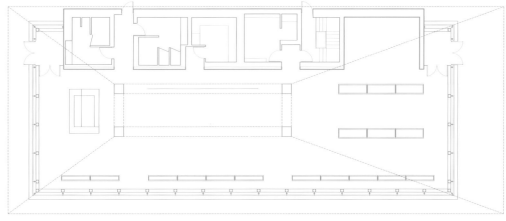

MVRDV

MVRDV
Postbus 63136
3002 JC Rotterdam
The Netherlands

Tel: +31 10 477 28 60
Fax: +31 10 477 36 27
E-mail: office@mvrdv.nl
Web: www.mvrdv.nl

MVRDV was created in 1991 by Winy Maas, Jacob van Rijs, and Nathalie de Vries. The name of the firm is made up of the initials of the surnames of the partners. Born in 1959 in Schijndel, Maas, like his two partners, studied at the Technical University in Delft. Jacob van Rijs was born in Amsterdam in 1964, and Nathalie de Vries in Appingedam in 1964. Both Maas and van Rijs worked for OMA. Maas and de Vries worked in the office of Ben van Berkel before founding MVRDV, and Nathalie de Vries also worked with Mecanoo in Delft. Aside from the Villa VPRO (Hilversum, 1997), their work includes the RVU Building in Hilversum (1994–97); the Double House in Utrecht (1995–97); and WoZoCo, 100 apartments for elderly people (Amsterdam-Osdorp, 1997), all in the Netherlands. The architects designed the spectacular Dutch Pavilion at Expo 2000 in Hanover (Germany); and the Matsudai Cultural Village Center (Matsudai, Niigata, Japan, 2002–03, published here). Their plan for a temporary pavilion that would have completely engulfed the Serpentine Gallery in London was delayed for technical reasons in 2004. MVRDV have also worked on urban development schemes, such as their "Shadow City Bergen Op Zoom" project (1993); the master plan for Parklane Airport, Eindhoven; and the master plan for Subdivision 10 in Ypenburg. Recent work includes the GYRE Building (Shibuya-ku, Tokyo, Japan, 2007); their Celosia housing in Madrid (Spain, 2001–08); Westerdokseiland housing (Amsterdam, under construction); and the Torre Huerta (Valencia, Spain, 2007–10).

MVRDV wurde 1991 von Winy Maas, Jacob van Rijs und Nathalie de Vries gegründet. Der Name des Büros setzt sich aus den Initialen der Nachnamen der Partner zusammen. Der 1959 in Schijndel geborene Maas studierte wie seine beiden anderen Partner an der Technischen Universität Delft. Jacob van Rijs wurde 1964 in Amsterdam geboren und Nathalie de Vries 1964 in Appingedam. Maas und van Rijs arbeiteten im Büro OMA, Maas und de Vries bei Ben van Berkel, bevor sie MVRDV gründeten; Nathalie de Vries war außerdem bei Mecanoo in Delft tätig. Zu ihren realisierten Projekten zählen die Villa VPRO in Hilversum (1997), das RVU-Gebäude in Hilversum (1994–97), das Doppelhaus in Utrecht (1995–97) und die Seniorenwohnanlage WoZoCo mit 100 Wohnungen (Amsterdam-Osdorp, 1997), alle in den Niederlanden. Außerdem planten sie den spektakulären niederländischen Pavillon für die Expo 2000 in Hannover und das Matsudai Cultural Village Center (Matsudai, Niigata, Japan, 2002–03, hier veröffentlicht). Ihr Entwurf für einen temporären Pavillon, der die Serpentine Gallery in London vollkommen umgeben hätte, wurde 2004 aus technischen Gründen nicht realisiert. MVRDV hat auch städtebauliche Entwürfe erarbeitet, z. B. 1993 das Projekt „Shadow City Bergen Op Zoom", einen Masterplan für den Flughafen in Eindhoven und den Masterplan für Subdivision 10 in Ypenburg. Zu den neueren Arbeiten des Büros zählen das GYRE Building (Shibuya-ku, Tokio, 2007), der Wohnkomplex Celosia in Madrid (2001–08), die Wohnanlage Westerdokseiland (Amsterdam, im Bau) und die Torre Huerta (Valencia, 2007–10).

L'agence **MVRDV** a été créée en 1991 par Winy Maas, Jacob van Rijs et Nathalie de Vries. Son sigle reprend les initiales des noms de ses associés. Né en 1959 à Schijndel, Maas, comme ses deux partenaires, a étudié à l'Université technique de Delft. Jacob van Rijs est né à Amsterdam en 1964, et Nathalie de Vries à Appingedam en 1964. Maas et van Rijs ont tous deux travaillé pour OMA, Maas et de Vries dans l'agence de Ben van Berkel, avant de fonder MVRDV. Nathalie de Vries a également travaillé pour Mecanoo à Delft. Parmi leurs réalisations : la villa VPRO (Hilversum, 1997) ; l'immeuble RVU à Hilversum (1994–97) ; la Double House à Utrecht (1995–97) et WoZoCo, cent appartements pour personnes âgées (Amsterdam-Osdorp, 1997), toutes aux Pays-Bas. Ils ont conçu le spectaculaire Pavillon néerlandais à Expo 2000 à Hanovre et le centre du village culturel de Matsudai (Matsudai, Niigata, Japon, 2002–03), publié ici. Leur plan de pavillon temporaire pour la Serpentine Gallery à Londres, qui aurait dû entièrement entourer celle-ci, a été annulé pour des raisons techniques (2004). MVRDV est également intervenu sur des projets d'urbanisme comme leur « Shadow City Bergen Op Zoom » (1993) ; le plan directeur de l'aéroport Parklane (Eindhoven) et le plan directeur de la Subdivision 10 à Ypenburg. Récemment, ils ont réalisé l'immeuble GYRE (Shibuya-ku, Tokyo, Japon, 2006–07) ; les logements Celosia à Madrid (Espagne, 2001–08) ; les logements Westerdokseiland (Amsterdam, Pays-Bas, en construction) et la Torre Huerta (Valence, Espagne, 2007–10).

MATSUDAI CULTURAL VILLAGE CENTER

Matsudai, Niigata, Japan, 2002–03

Address: Matsudai Ooaza 3743-1, Matsudai-Cho, Japan
Area: 1500 m². Client: Municipality of Matsudai. Cost: not disclosed
Collaboration: Super-OS, Tokyo

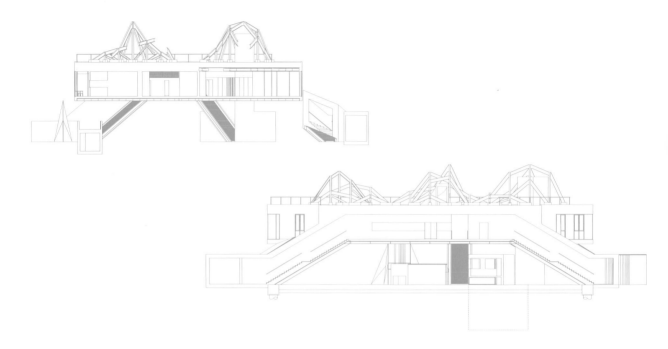

This structure is located in a mountainous area of Japan, subject to significant snowfalls. It was conceived in part to hold events related to the Niigata Art Triennial. The structure is lifted off the ground, to provide an area that is free of snow in winter, and to create space for performances. The structure of the building is designed around "legs" that cut through it and provide functional spaces within, compared by the architects to a "Kasbah" or internal streets. The architects also placed an emphasis on the roof: "On the rooftop, a landscape is formed as a 'force-scape', shaped by the dynamic demands of the leg-shaped bridges. It echoes the surrounding hills. This artificial 'icy' roofscape, covered with white carpet, provides an attractive playground and viewing platform for the mountains and art. It might also remind summer visitors of wintertime, when Matsudai will be hidden under a massive layer of snow."

Dieses Gebäude liegt in einer gebirgigen Region Japans mit starken Schneefällen. Es wurde u. a. geplant, um dort Veranstaltungen im Zusammenhang mit der Kunsttriennale Niigata durchzuführen. Der Bau ist vom Boden angehoben, um im Winter einen schneefreien Bereich und Platz für Vorführungen zu gewinnen. Das Gebäude ist um „Beine" herum entworfen, die das Gebäude durchschneiden und innen funktionale Bereiche bilden, welche die Architekten mit einer „Kasbah" oder innenliegenden Straßen vergleichen. Besondere Beachtung wurde auch dem Dach zuteil: „Oben auf dem Dach ist eine ‚Landschaft der Kräfte' entstanden, gebildet durch den Verlauf der dynamischen Kräfte der beinförmigen Brücken. Sie nimmt Bezug auf die Berge der Umgebung. Diese künstliche, ‚eisige' Dachlandschaft ist mit weißem Teppichboden ausgelegt und bildet einen attraktiven Spielbereich sowie eine Plattform mit Aussicht auf die Berge und für die Kunst. Im Sommer kann sie die Besucher auch an die Winterzeit erinnern, wenn Matsudai unter einer dicken Schneedecke versinkt."

Ce bâtiment se trouve dans une région montagneuse du Japon soumise à des chutes de neige importantes. Elle a en partie été conçue pour accueillir des manifestations liées à la Triennale artistique de Niigata. Le bâtiment est donc surélevé par rapport au sol pour créer une zone dégagée de neige en hiver, et créer un espace d'accueil pour certains spectacles. La structure du bâtiment s'organise autour de « jambes » qui la pénètrent et déterminent des espaces fonctionnels comparés par l'architecte à une casbah ou à des rues intérieures. Les architectes ont également traité le toit avec originalité : « Pour la toiture, le paysage se forme à partir des forces issues des contraintes dynamiques des passages des jambes. Il fait écho aux collines avoisinantes. Cette toiture *gelée*, recouverte d'un revêtement blanc, est un terrain de jeu sympathique et offre un point de vue sur les montagnes et les œuvres exposées. Aux visiteurs estivaux, elle peut également rappeler la saison d'hiver lorsque Matsudai est enfouie sous une épaisse couche de neige. »

The main level of the Center is lifted off the ground, providing covered spaces for performances and setting the main body of the building above potentially high winter snow levels.

Die Hauptebene des Zentrums ist vom Boden abgehoben, um einen überdachten Bereich für Veranstaltungen zu gewinnen und den Baukörper über das im Winter gelegentlich hohe Schneeniveau zu erheben.

Le niveau principal du Centre est surélevé par rapport au sol afin d'offrir un espace pour divers spectacles et protéger le corps principal du bâtiment des importantes chutes de neige.

Above, the open space beneath the center with the angled stairways leading upward. To the right, a glass box volume is cantilevered over the ground level.

Oben der Freiraum unter dem Zentrum mit den schräg aufwärts führenden Treppen. Rechts ein kistenförmiges, gläsernes Volumen, das über Bodenniveau auskragt.

Ci-dessus, l'espace ouvert sous le Centre dont les escaliers conduisent au niveau supérieur. À droite, un volume en forme de boîte de verre est déporté en porte-à-faux au-dessus du sol.

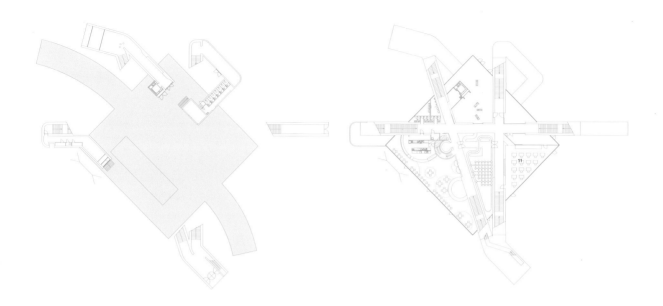

NIETO SOBEJANO

Nieto Sobejano Arquitectos S. L.
Talavera, 4 L–5 / 28016 Madrid / Spain
Tel: +34 91 564 38 30 / Fax: +34 91 564 38 36
E-mail: nietosobejano@nietosobejano.com / Web: www.nietosobejano.com

Schlesische Str. 26 / 2. OG Aufgang B / 10997 Berlin / Germany
Tel: +49 30 69 53 86 811 / Fax: +49 30 69 53 86 899

FUENSANTA NIETO and **ENRIQUE SOBEJANO** graduated as architects from the ETSA Madrid (ETSAM) and the Graduate School of Architecture at Columbia University in New York. They are currently teaching at the Universidad Europea de Madrid (UEM) and at the University of the Arts (UdK) in Berlin, and are the managing partners of Nieto Sobejano Arquitectos S. L. Both have been visiting critics and/or teachers at various Spanish and international universities and institutions, such as the GSD at Harvard University, University of Arizona, Technical University Munich, ETSA Barcelona, University of Torino, University of Stuttgart, University of the Arts (UdK) in Berlin, Germany, University of Cottbus, Germany, Columbia University, and the University of Texas, Austin. From 1986 to 1991, they were the editors of the architectural journal *Arquitectura* issued by the Architectural Association of Madrid (Colegio Oficial de Arquitectos de Madrid). Their work has been exhibited, amongst other locations, at the Venice Biennale (2000 and 2002), Bienal Española de Arquitectura 2003, Extreme Eurasia (Tokyo, 2005), and *On Site: New Architecture in Spain* (MoMA, New York, 2006). They also participated in *Arquitectura Contemporánea en Galicia* (Centro Gallego de Arte Contemporáneo, Santiago de Compostela, Spain, 2007); in exhibitions held at the Aedes Gallery (Berlin, Germany, 2008); and the Kunsthaus in Graz (Austria, 2008). They won the National Prize for Conservation and Restoration of Cultural Patrimony for their extension of the National Sculpture Museum (Valladolid, Spain, 2007); and have recently completed the Moritzburg Museum Extension (Halle, Saale, Germany, 2006–08, published here); and the Madinat al-Zahra Museum and Research Center (Córdoba, Spain, 2005–08, also published here).

FUENSANTA NIETO und **ENRIQUE SOBEJANO** studierten Architektur an der ETSA Madrid (ETSAM) und der Graduate School of Architecture an der Columbia University in New York. Gegenwärtig lehren sie an der Universidad Europea de Madrid (UEM) sowie an der Universität der Künste (UdK) in Berlin und sind die leitenden Partner des Büros Nieto Sobejano Arquitectos S. L. Beide waren Gastkritiker und/oder -lehrer an verschiedenen spanischen und internationalen Universitäten und Institutionen, z. B. an der Graduate School of Design der Harvard University, der University of Arizona, der Technischen Universität München, der ETSA Barcelona, der Università di Torino, der Universität Stuttgart, der UdK in Berlin, der Universität Cottbus, der Columbia University und der University of Texas in Austin. Von 1986 bis 1991 waren sie Redakteure der Architekturzeitschrift *Arquitectura*, die von der Architektenvereinigung Madrid herausgegeben wird. Ihre Bauten wurden u. a. auf den Biennalen in Venedig (2000 und 2002), der Bienal Española de Arquitectura 2003, der Extreme Eurasia (Tokio, 2005) und in der Ausstellung *On Site: New Architecture in Spain* (MoMA, New York, 2006) vorgestellt. Sie waren zudem an der *Arquitectura Contemporánea en Galicia* (Centro Gallego de Arte Contemporáneo, Santiago de Compostela, 2007) beteiligt sowie an Ausstellungen in der Galerie Aedes (Berlin, 2008) und im Kunsthaus Graz (Österreich, 2008). Für ihren Neubau des Staatlichen Skulpturenmuseums (Valladolid, 2007) erhielten sie den Premio Nacional de Restauración. Vor kurzem haben sie die Erweiterung der Staatlichen Galerie Moritzburg Halle (Halle an der Saale, 2006–08, hier veröffentlicht) sowie das Museum und Forschungszentrum Madinat al-Zahra (Córdoba, 2005–08, ebenfalls hier veröffentlicht) fertiggestellt.

FUENSANTA NIETO et **ENRIQUE SOBEJANO** sont architectes diplômés de l'ETSA Madrid (ETSAM) et de la Graduate School of Architecture de la Columbia University à New York. Ils enseignent actuellement à la Universidad Europea de Madrid (UEM) et à l'UdK Berlin, tout en dirigeant Nieto Sobejano Arquitectos S. L. Tous deux ont été critiques invités et/ou enseignants dans diverses universités et institutions espagnoles et internationales, dont la Harvard University GSD, University of Arizona, Technische Universität (Munich), ETSA Barcelone (Espagne), l'université de Turin (Italie), l'université de Stuttgart (Allemagne), l'université des Arts (UdK) Berlin, l'université de Cottbus (Allemagne), la Columbia University (New York, NY) et la University of Texas (Austin). De 1986 à 1991, ils ont été rédacteurs en chef du magazine spécialisé *Arquitectura* publié par le Colegio Oficial de Arquitectos de Madrid. Leurs travaux ont été exposés, entre autres, à la Biennale de Venise (2000 et 2002), la Bienal Española de Arquitectura 2003, Extreme Eurasia (Tokyo, 2005) et lors de l'exposition *On Site : New Architecture in Spain* (MoMA, New York, 2006). Ils ont aussi participé à l'exposition *Arquitectura Contemporánea en Galici*a (Centro Gallego de Arte Contemporáneo, Santiago de Compostela, Espagne, 2007) ; exposé à la galerie Aedes (Berlin, Allemagne, 2008) et à la Kunsthaus de Graz (Autriche, 2008). Ils ont remporté le Prix national pour la Conservation et la Restauration du patrimoine culturel pour l'extension du musée national de Sculpture (Valladolid, Espagne, 2007) et ont récemment achevé l'extension du Moritzburg Museum (Halle, Saale, Allemagne, 2006–08), publiée ici, ainsi que le musée et centre de recherches de Madinat al-Zahra (Cordoue, Espagne, 2005–08), également publié dans ces pages.

MORITZBURG MUSEUM EXTENSION
Halle, Saale, Germany, 2006–08

Address: Friedemann-Bach-Platz 5, 06108 Halle (Saale), Germany, +49 345 21 25 90, www.stiftung-moritzburg.de
Area: 4500 m². Client: Stiftung Moritzburg, State of Sachsen-Anhalt. Cost: €18 million
Team: Sebastian Sasse, Nina Nolting, Udo Brunner

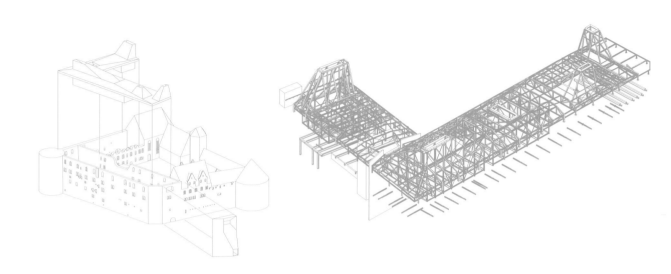

Built in the late 15th century, the castle of Moritzburg was partially destroyed in the 17th century during the Thirty Years' War. Though Karl Friedrich Schinkel proposed work on the building in 1828, nothing substantial has been done to engage this building and its partial ruins since that time. An art museum was installed in the castle in 1904. The museum now houses a fine collection of German Expressionist paintings, including important works by Lyonel Feininger. The Gerlinger donation provided the museum with a new group of works from the artist's association Die Brücke, and encouraged expansion. Nieto and Sobejano chose to add roofs and a metal tower that contrast with the existing structures, in the spirit of the uneasy and expressive forms painted by Feininger. The architects state: "Our proposal for enlargement is based on a single and clear architectural idea. It involves a new roof, conceived as a large folded platform, which rises and breaks to allow natural light to enter, and from which the new exhibition areas hang. The result of this operation is to free completely the floor of the ancient ruin, providing a unique space that allows a range of exhibition possibilities. This design is complemented with the building of two new vertical communication cores. The first is located in the north wing to connect the levels that must be intercommunicated. The second is a new, contemporary tower, 25 meters high, in the place once occupied by the bastion, which provides access to the new exhibition areas with their distant views over the city."

Die Ende des 15. Jahrhunderts erbaute Moritzburg wurde im 17. Jahrhundert während des Dreißigjährigen Kriegs teilweise zerstört. Obgleich Karl Friedrich Schinkel 1828 eine Restaurierung vorschlug, ist seit dieser Zeit nichts Entscheidendes unternommen worden, um das in diesem Zustand erhaltene Gebäude zu nutzen. 1904 wurde ein Kunstmuseum in der Burg eingerichtet. Es besitzt heute eine gute Sammlung deutscher Expressionisten und auch bedeutende Werke von Lyonel Feininger. Durch die Schenkung Gerlinger erhielt das Museum einige Werke der Künstlervereinigung Die Brücke, wodurch eine Erweiterung angeregt wurde. Nieto und Sobejano entschieden sich für neue Dächer und einen Metallturm im Geist der unruhigen, expressiven Formen der Feininger-Gemälde als Kontrast zum alten Baubestand. Die Architekten erläutern: „Unser Vorschlag für die Erweiterung beruht auf einer eindeutigen architektonischen Idee. Er besteht in einem neuen Dach in Form einer großen, gefalteten Plattform, die aufsteigt und abbricht, um natürliches Licht einzulassen, und an der die neuen Ausstellungsbereiche aufgehängt sind. Dadurch wurde die Geschossfläche der Ruine vollkommen frei und bildet so einen einzigartigen Raum, der alle Möglichkeiten für Ausstellungen bietet. Ergänzt wird diese Planung durch die Errichtung zweier neuer, vertikaler Verkehrskerne. Der erste liegt im Nordflügel und bildet die notwendige Verbindung zu den verschiedenen Ebenen. Der zweite ist ein neuer, moderner, 25 m hoher Turm an der früher von der Bastion eingenommenen Stelle, der die neuen Ausstellungsräume mit weitem Ausblick über die Stadt erschließt."

Édifié à la fin du XVᵉ siècle, le château du Moritzburg fut en partie démoli au XVIIᵉ siècle pendant la guerre de Trente Ans. Depuis cette époque, malgré des propositions de Karl Friedrich Schinkel en 1828, rien d'important ne fut entrepris pour le restaurer. Un musée d'art s'y installa en 1904. Le musée actuel abrite une collection de qualité de peintures de l'expressionisme allemand, dont des œuvres importantes de Lyonel Feininger. La donation Gerlinger a apporté un nouvel ensemble d'œuvres du groupe d'artistes Die Brücke et rendu possible cette extension. Nieto et Sobejano ont décidé de créer une toiture et une tour métalliques qui contrastent avec l'existant, dans l'esprit des formes expressives de Feininger. «Notre proposition d'agrandissement repose sur un concept architectural original et clair. Il implique une nouvelle toiture, conçue comme une vaste plate-forme pliée qui s'élève et se rompt pour laisser pénétrer l'éclairage naturel, et à laquelle sont suspendues les nouvelles salles d'exposition. Le résultat de cette opération est de libérer entièrement le sol de l'ancien bâtiment en ruine et d'offrir un espace unique qui autorise une vaste gamme de possibilités d'expositions. Ce projet se complète par la mise en œuvre de deux nouveaux noyaux de communication verticale. Le premier, dans l'aile nord, connecte les niveaux qui doivent rester en communication. Le second est une toute nouvelle tour de 25 mètres de haut occupant la place de l'ancien bastion, qui offre accès aux nouvelles salles d'exposition et des perspectives sur la ville dans le lointain», expliquent les architectes.

Drawings on the left page show how the new volume was dropped onto the existing structure. Its white, modern presence can be seen in the images on this page.

Die Zeichnungen auf der linken Seite zeigen, wie der neue Trakt dem Altbau aufgesetzt wurde. Seine weiße, moderne Gestalt ist auf den Abbildungen dieser Seite sichtbar.

Les dessins de la page de gauche montrent la façon dont le nouveau volume repose sur la construction existante. Sa modernité et sa couleur blanche immaculée apparaissent nettement sur ces photos.

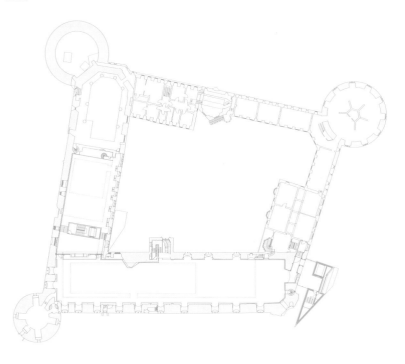

Though added to an ancient structure, the extension is entirely
modern, even when such elements
as the arched openings, below,
recall the historic context.

Obgleich der Erweiterungsbau dem
Altbau hinzugefügt wurde, ist er
ganz modern, auch wenn gewisse
Elemente, wie zum Beispiel die gebogenen Öffnungen (unten), auf den
historischen Kontext Bezug nehmen.

Bien qu'ajoutée à une construction
ancienne, l'extension est totalement
moderne, même si des éléments
comme les ouvertures cintrées ci-
dessous rappellent son contexte
historique.

The architects have left old stones visible where the extension meets the original building, emphasizing the symbiotic nature of their work in this instance.

An der Stelle, wo die Erweiterung auf den Altbau trifft, haben die Architekten alte Steine sichtbar gelassen, um den symbiotischen Aspekt ihrer Planung zu betonen.

Les architectes ont laissé visibles des pierres anciennes à la jonction de l'extension et du bâtiment d'origine, ce qui met en valeur la nature symbiotique de leur travail.

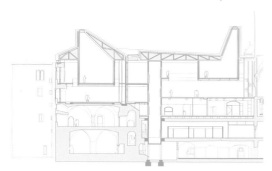

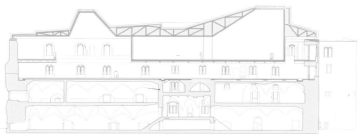

MADINAT AL-ZAHRA MUSEUM AND RESEARCH CENTER

Córdoba, Spain, 2005–08

Address: Carretera de Palma del Río, km. 5.5., 14071 Córdoba, Spain, +34 957 35 28 74, www.juntadeandalucia.es/cultura/museos/CAMA
Area: 5800 m². Client: Junta de Andalucía, Consejería de Cultura. Cost: €12.5 million

The architects came into the project determined not to "build on the landscape" of the archeological site of this old Arab city. They conceived three structures to house the museum, auditorium, and workshop-warehouse. A certain number of archeological remains were discovered during the work and integrated into the structures. They explain: "The building articulates its new uses around a sequence of full and empty spaces; covered spaces and open patios that guide travelers on their visit. From the main vestibule, a broad patio spreads out on a square plan, blue from the reflection of the pond presiding over it. Like a cloister, the main public spaces are organized around it: model exhibits, book and catalogue sales, coffee shop, auditorium, and exhibition hall." Two other patios provide a private area for the administration and museum functions, and for the outdoor display of some archeological finds. Materials that contrast with old ones have been selected, such as fair face concrete, and limestone patios. The architects planned the design to allow for future expansions, advancing a bit along the lines of an archeological dig. They state: "The new Madinat al-Zahra Museum will be an introverted building with no outward disclosure of the sequence of its spaces: it will have appeared silently in the landscape, unearthed over the coming years like the remains of the ancient city of Abd al-Rahman III."

Die Architekten begannen dieses Projekt in der festen Absicht, nicht „auf der Landschaft" des archäologischen Geländes dieser alten arabischen Stadt zu bauen. Sie planten drei Strukturen zur Unterbringung des Museums, des Auditoriums sowie für Werkstätten und Lager. Viele archäologische Relikte wurden während der Bauarbeiten entdeckt und in die Neubauten integriert. Die Architekten erklären: „Das Gebäude drückt seine neuen Nutzungen in einer Abfolge geschlossener Räume und Freiräume, überdachter Bereiche und offener Patios aus, welche die Besucher durch das Gebäude leiten. Von der großen Eingangshalle aus öffnet sich ein geräumiger Innenhof mit quadratischem Grundriss; das darüberliegende Wasserbecken färbt ihn blau. Die großen öffentlichen Bereiche – Modellausstellungen, Buch- und Katalogverkauf, Café, Auditorium und Ausstellungssaal – sind wie bei einem Kreuzgang angeordnet." Zwei weitere Innenhöfe bilden einen nichtöffentlichen Bereich für die Verwaltung und sonstige Museumsfunktionen sowie zur Ausstellung archäologischer Funde im Freien. Als Materialien wurden solche gewählt, die einen Kontrast zu den alten Baustoffen bilden: glatter Beton und Kalkstein. Der Entwurf sieht auch künftige Erweiterungen vor, die sich z. T. entlang der archäologischen Ausgrabungen erstrecken. Dazu geben die Architekten folgende Erläuterung: „Das neue Museum Madinat al-Zahra wird ein introvertiertes Gebäude werden, die Raumfolge von außen nicht ablesbar sein. Es wird still in der Landschaft stehen und in den kommenden Jahren nicht ausgegraben werden, wie die Ruinen der antiken Stadt Abd al-Rahmans III."

Les architectes sont intervenus avec la détermination de ne pas « construire sur le paysage » du site archéologique de cette ancienne cité arabe. Ils ont conçu trois structures pour le musée, l'auditorium et des ateliers-réserves. Un certain nombre de vestiges archéologiques ont été découverts au cours des travaux et intégrés aux constructions nouvelles. « Le bâtiment articule ses nouveaux usages autour d'une séquence d'espaces vides et pleins, couverts et ouverts, qui guident les visiteurs pendant leur visite. À partir du vestibule principal, s'ouvre un grand patio carré, teinté de bleu par les reflets d'un bassin. Comme dans un cloître, les principaux espaces publics s'organisent autour ce lieu : exposition de maquettes, vente de livres et de catalogues, cafétéria, auditorium et salle d'exposition », expliquent les architectes. Deux autres patios sont réservés à l'administration et aux fonctions muséales techniques, et à la présentation en extérieur de certaines découvertes archéologiques. Certains matériaux neufs contrastent avec les anciens comme le béton surfacé et la pierre calcaire des patios. Les architectes ont prévu de futures extensions le long des axes de fouilles archéologiques : « Le nouveau musée est un bâtiment introverti qui ne révèle pas de l'extérieur la séquence de ses espaces : il apparaîtra silencieusement dans le paysage, comme s'il avait été mis à jour au fil des ans tel un vestige de l'ancienne cité d'Abd al-Rahman III. »

The stunning horizontality and simplicity of the museum and research center make it fit into the surrounding countryside as though it were part of the topography.

Die beeindruckende Horizontalität und Schlichtheit des Museums und Forschungszentrums lassen es in der umgebenden Landschaft erscheinen, als wäre es Teil der Topografie.

La simplicité et l'horizontalité étonnantes du complexe l'aident à s'intégrer à la campagne environnante, comme si les bâtiments faisaient partie de la topographie.

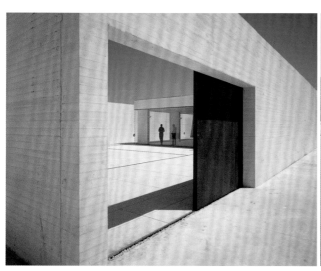

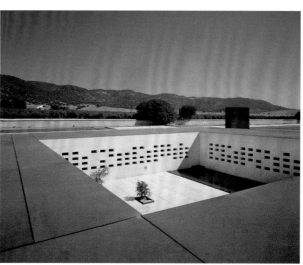

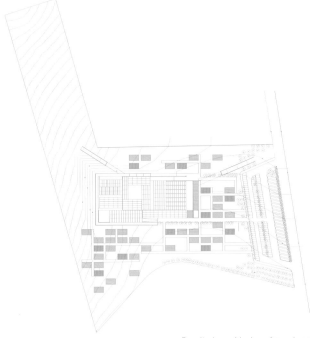

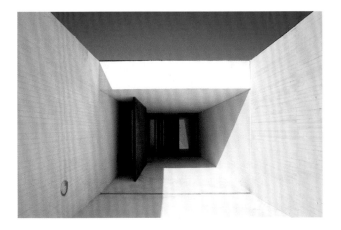

Despite large blank surfaces in some locations, the building is punctuated by irregular openings and changes in cladding that continue to emphasize the overall horizontality of the composition.

Trotz teilweise großer, leerer Flächen beleben an anderen Stellen unterschiedliche Öffnungen und wechselnde Verkleidungen das Gebäude und tragen zur Betonung seiner Horizontalität bei.

En dehors d'importants plans aveugles, le bâtiment est ponctué d'ouvertures de disposition irrégulière et de changements de parement qui mettent en valeur l'horizontalité d'ensemble de sa composition.

An orchestrated alternation of opaque and light spaces characterizes the image on the left page. In these drawings and the photo below, the building's low-lying sweep is the most obvious design element.

Une alternance orchestrée d'espaces opaques et lumineux caractérise l'intérieur (à gauche). Ces plans et la photographie ci-dessous expriment l'élément le plus évident du projet : le parti pris de surbaissement.

Ein inszenierter Wechsel von hellen und dunkleren Räumen kennzeichnet die Abbildung auf der linken Seite. Auf den Abbildungen auf dieser Seite ist die tiefliegende, horizontale Auslegung des Gebäudes das auffälligste Gestaltungselement.

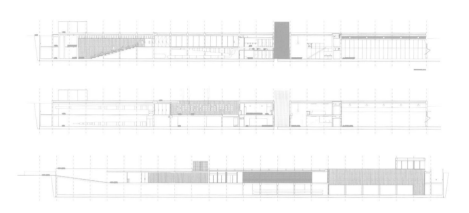

RYUE NISHIZAWA

Office of Ryue Nishizawa
1–5–27 Tatsumi
Koto-ku
Tokyo 135–0053
Japan

Tel: +81 3 5534 0117
Fax: +81 3 5534 1757
E-mail: office@ryuenishizawa.com
Web: www.ryuenishizawa.com

RYUE NISHIZAWA was born in Tokyo in 1966. He graduated from Yokohama National University with an M.Arch in 1990, and joined the office of Kazuyo Sejima & Associates in Tokyo the same year. In 1995, he established SANAA with Kazuyo Sejima, and two years later his own practice, the Office of Ryue Nishizawa. He has worked on all the significant projects of SANAA and has been a visiting professor at Yokohama National University (2001–), the University of Singapore (2003), Princeton (2006), and the Harvard GSD (2007). His work outside of SANAA includes a Weekend House (Gunma, 1998); the N Museum (Kagawa, 2005); the Moriyama House (Tokyo, 2006); House A (East Japan, 2006); and the Towada Art Center (Aomori, 2006–08, published here), all in Japan.

RYUE NISHIZAWA wurde 1966 in Tokio geboren und erhielt seinen M. Arch. 1990 an der Staatlichen Universität von Yokohama. Im gleichen Jahr trat er in das Büro Kazuyo Sejima & Associates, Tokio, ein. 1995 gründete er zusammen mit Kazuyo Sejima die Firma SANAA und zwei Jahre später ein eigenes Büro, das Office of Ryue Nishizawa. Er hat an allen bedeutenden Projekten von SANAA mitgearbeitet und war Gastprofessor an der Staatlichen Universität Yokohama (seit 2001), den Universitäten Singapur (2003), Princeton (2006) und der Harvard Graduate School of Design (2007). Von seinen Arbeiten bei SANAA abgesehen, zählen zu seinen Bauten ein Wochenendhaus (Gunma, 1998), das Museum N (Kagawa, 2005), das Haus Moriyama (Tokio, 2006), das Haus A (Ostjapan, 2006) und das Kunstzentrum Towada (Aomori, 2006–08, hier veröffentlicht), alle in Japan.

RYUE NISHIZAWA, né à Tokyo en 1966, obtient son M.Arch de l'Université nationale de Yokohama en 1990 et rejoint l'agence de Kazuyo Sejima & Associates à Tokyo la même année. En 1995, il fonde SANAA avec Kazuyo Sejima, et deux ans plus tard sa propre agence, l'office of Ryue Nishizawa. Il a travaillé sur tous les projets importants de SANAA et a été professeur invité de l'Université nationale de Yokohama (2001–), de l'université de Singapour (2003), de Princeton (2006), et de l'Harvard GSD (2007). Son œuvre, en dehors de SANAA, est entièrement réalisée au Japon et comprend une maison de week-end (Gunma, 1998) ; le N Museum (Kagawa, 2005) ; la maison Moriyama (Tokyo, 2006) ; la maison A (Japon oriental, 2006) et le Centre artistique Towada (Aomori, 2006–08), publié ici.

TOWADA ART CENTER

Towada City, Aomori, Japan, 2006–08

Address: Nishi Nibancho 10–9, Towada, Aomori 034–0082, Japan, +81 176 20 1127, www.city.towada.lg.jp/artstowada
Area: 2078 m². Client: Towada City. Cost: not disclosed

This municipal museum in the north of Japan includes space for contemporary art and for community activities. The program of the building includes spaces for lectures, workshops, a café, library, community activity rooms, and exhibitions rooms. It is set on an oblong site along the street where government offices are located, and was intended to revitalize this street, and, if possible, the city beyond. Most of the artworks were commissioned specifically for the museum and are intended for permanent display. Individual artists are given individual exhibition rooms connected by glass corridors. These exhibition spaces are clustered together "like a colony" while making up "a continuous landscape." The architect placed an emphasis on the ability of the museum to open itself to its environment, thus fulfilling the brief concerning the relation to the street and the city. Ryue Nishizawa states: "We assumed that different structural systems, lighting conditions, and proportions for each commission would allow for a closer relationship between the architecture and the artwork. The dispersed arrangement of boxes and corridors also creates semiprivate outdoor spaces that can be used as exhibition space and for other activities. The building should be experienced like a small town: as if visitors travel from independent house to independent house while experiencing the urban environment between art pieces."

Dieses städtische Museum im Norden Japans enthält Bereiche zur Ausstellung von zeitgenössischer Kunst sowie für Aktivitäten der Gemeinde. Das Bauprogramm forderte Räume für Vorträge, Gemeindeveranstaltungen, Werkstätten, ein Café, eine Bibliothek sowie Ausstellungsräume. Der Bau steht auf einem länglichen Gelände entlang einer Straße, an der sich auch die Büros der Stadtverwaltung befinden, und sollte diese Straße und, soweit möglich, die umliegende Stadt beleben. Die meisten der Kunstwerke wurden speziell für dieses Museum in Auftrag gegeben und sollen Bestandteil der ständigen Ausstellung sein. Einzelnen Künstlern wurden eigene, durch verglaste Korridore miteinander verbundene Ausstellungsräume gewidmet. Diese Räume sind „wie eine Kolonie" zusammengefasst und bilden eine „zusammenhängende Landschaft". Der Architekt legte Wert darauf, dass das Museum sich zu seiner Umgebung öffnet und damit die Forderung nach dem Bezug zur Straße und zur Stadt erfüllt. Ryue Nishizawa erklärt: „Wir meinten, dass durch die unterschiedlichen konstruktiven Systeme, die Lichtverhältnisse und die Proportionen jedes Bereichs eine engere Beziehung zwischen der Architektur und dem Kunstwerk hergestellt würde. Die verteilte Anordnung der kistenförmigen Räume und Korridore schafft zudem halböffentliche Außenbereiche, die für Ausstellungen und andere Aktivitäten genutzt werden können. Das Gebäude sollte wie eine kleine Stadt empfunden werden, als ob die Besucher von einem Haus zu einem anderen gehen und dabei die städtische Umgebung zwischen Kunstwerken erleben."

Ce musée municipal d'une ville du nord du Japon regroupe des installations destinées à l'exposition d'œuvres d'art contemporain et à des activités communales. Son programme comprend des salles de conférences, des ateliers, un café, une bibliothèque, des salles pour activités communales, et des salles d'exposition. Le bâtiment est implanté sur un terrain en longueur en bordure d'une rue longée de constructions administratives. L'objectif était de revitaliser ce quartier et, si possible, la ville même. La plupart des œuvres d'art ont été spécialement commanditées pour le musée et devraient être exposées en permanence. Chaque artiste s'est vu attribuer une salle, reliée aux autres par des corridors vitrés. Ces espaces d'exposition sont regroupés comme « une colonie » qui constitue un « paysage continu ». L'architecte a mis l'accent sur la possibilité du bâtiment de s'ouvrir sur son environnement, répondant ainsi à la demande précise du client d'un lien avec la rue et la ville. Ryue Nishizawa précise : « Nous avons présumé que les différents systèmes structurels, conditions d'éclairage et proportions de chaque commande permettraient une relation plus étroite entre l'architecture et les œuvres d'art. L'implantation dispersée des boîtes et des corridors génère également des espaces extérieurs semi-privés qui peuvent servir d'espace d'exposition ou à d'autres activités. Le bâtiment doit se voir comme une petite ville, comme si les visiteurs allaient d'une maison indépendante à une autre en découvrant un environnement urbain entre les œuvres d'art. »

Nishizawa employs a varied juxtaposition of essentially geometric elements to obtain an overall impression of modernity and lightness.

Nishizawa bedient sich einer vielschichtigen Gegenüberstellung vorwiegend geometrischer Elemente, um eine Gesamtwirkung von Modernität und Leichtigkeit zu erreichen.

Nishizawa juxtapose des éléments variés, essentiellement géométriques, pour aboutir à une impression générale de modernité et de légèreté.

The blank forms of the center give
it an enigmatic aspect that sits well
with its refined simplicity.

Die klaren Formen des Zentrums
erzeugen einen geheimnisvollen
Eindruck, der seiner eleganten
Schlichtheit durchaus entspricht.

Les formes aveugles du Centre lui
confèrent un aspect énigmatique dans
l'esprit d'une simplicité raffinée.

Works of art are exhibited in ways
that imply a collaboration between
architect and curator, and a community of spirit that is evident in these
images.

Wie diese Bilder zeigen, wurden die
Kunstwerke so platziert, dass sie von
der Zusammenarbeit und Geistesver-
wandtschaft von Architekt und Kura-
tor zeugen.

La mise en place des œuvres d'art
a impliqué une collaboration étroite
entre l'architecte et le conservateur
dans une communauté d'esprit qui
se révèle dans ces images.

A plan shows how the partly irregular placement of geometric elements generates a highly unusual complexity of space. Views through the architecture are accompanied by the deliberate placement of artworks.

Der Grundriss zeigt, dass die zum Teil unregelmäßige Anordnung der geometrischen Elemente eine ungewöhnliche räumliche Vielfalt erzeugt. Blicke durch das Gebäude werden begleitet von der gezielten Platzierung von Kunstwerken.

Ce plan montre comment la disposition en partie irrégulière d'éléments géométriques a généré une complexité spatiale assez rare. Les axes des perspectives s'accompagnent d'indications sur le placement des œuvres.

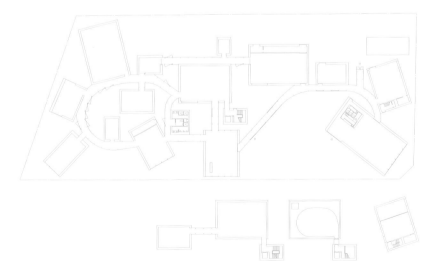

VALERIO OLGIATI

Valerio Olgiati
Senda Stretga 1
7017 Flims
Switzerland

Tel: +41 81 650 33 11
Fax: +41 81 650 33 12
E-mail: mail@olgiati.net
Web: www.olgiati.net

VALERIO OLGIATI was born in Chur in 1958. He studied architecture at the ETH in Zurich and in 1986, he created his own architectural office in that city. From 1993 to 1995, he collaborated with Frank Escher in Los Angeles. Escher is a specialist in the work of the architect John Lautner (1911–94). Since 1998, he has been teaching at the ETH Zurich and has served as Guest Lecturer at the Architectural Association (AA) in London and Cornell University (Ithaca, New York, USA). Since 2001, he has been a full Professor at the Accademia di Architettura at the Università della Svizzera Italiana in Mendrisio (Switzerland). He currently holds the Kenzo Tange Chair at Harvard University (Cambridge, Massachusetts, USA). He has built a number of private homes and participated in competitions such as that for the National Palace Museum (Taiwan, 2004, finalist); and the Learning Center of the EPFL, in Lausanne. Two of his recent projects, the Peak Gornergrat and the University of Lucerne—both in Switzerland—were 2003 competition-winning entries. Valerio Olgiati opened a new office in Flims in 2008 and completed the Swiss National Park Visitor Center that same year (Zernez, Switzerland, 2006–08, published here).

VALERIO OLGIATI wurde 1958 in Chur geboren. Er studierte Architektur an der Eidgenössischen Technischen Hochschule in Zürich und gründete dort 1986 sein eigenes Büro. Von 1993 bis 1995 arbeitete er zusammen mit Frank Escher in Los Angeles. Escher ist Spezialist für die Bauten des Architekten John Lautner (1911–94). Seit 1998 lehrt Olgiati an der ETH Zürich und hält Gastvorlesungen an der Architectural Association in London und der Cornell University in Ithaca (New York). Seit 2001 ist er ordentlicher Professor an der Accademia di Architettura der Università della Svizzera Italiana in Mendrisio (Schweiz). Derzeit hat er den Kenzo-Tange-Lehrstuhl in Harvard (Cambridge, Massachusetts) inne. Er hat viele Einfamilienhäuser gebaut und an Wettbewerben teilgenommen, z. B. für das National Palace Museum (Taiwan, 2004, Finalist) und das Lernzentrum der École Polytechnique Fédérale (EPFL) in Lausanne. Zwei seiner neuesten Projekte, der Peak Gornergrat, Zermatt, und die Universität Luzern (beide in der Schweiz), sind preisgekrönte Wettbewerbsentwürfe. Valerio Olgiati eröffnete 2008 ein neues Büro in Flims und brachte das Besucherzentrum des Schweizer Nationalparks (Zernez, Schweiz, 2006–08, hier veröffentlicht) zum Abschluss.

VALERIO OLGIATI, né à Chur en 1958, a étudié l'architecture à l'ETH de Zurich. En 1986, il ouvre son agence à Zurich puis, de 1993 à 1995, collabore à Los Angeles avec Frank Escher, spécialiste de l'œuvre de l'architecte John Lautner (1911–94). Depuis 1998, il enseigne à l'ETH et est conférencier invité à l'Architectural Association de Londres et à la Cornell University (Ithaca, New York, États-Unis). Depuis 2001, il est professeur titulaire à l'Accademia di Architettura de l'Università della Svizzera Italiana à Mendrisio (Suisse). Actuellement il occupe la Kenzo Tange Chair à Harvard (Cambridge, Massachusetts, États-Unis). Il a réalisé un certain nombre de résidences privées et participé à des concours comme celui du musée national du Palais (Taiwan, 2004, finaliste) et du centre de formation de l'EPFL à Lausanne. Deux de ses projets récents, le Pic Gornergrat et l'université de Lucerne – tous deux en Suisse – ont été remportés en 2003 à l'issue de concours. En 2008, Olgiati a ouvert une nouvelle agence à Flims et achevé le Centre d'information des visiteurs du Parc national suisse de Zernez (2006–08), publié ici.

SWISS NATIONAL PARK VISITOR CENTER

Zernez, Switzerland, 2006–08

Address: Visitor Centre, Swiss National Park, 7530 Zernez, Switzerland, +41 81 851 41 41, www.nationalpark.ch
Area: 1780 m². Client: Swiss National Park, Zernez. Cost: €6.228 million
Team: Aldo Duelli (Project Manager)

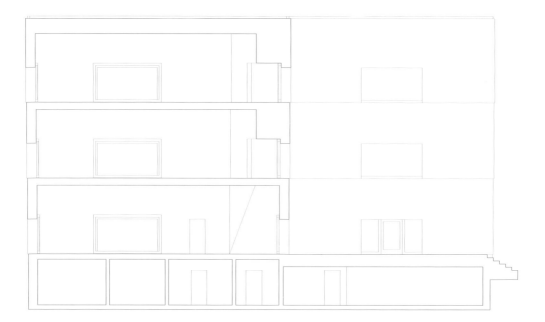

The Lower Engadine village of Zernez is the entrance point of the Swiss National Park, Switzerland's biggest nature preserve with an area of 172 square kilometers. Created in 1914, this is the only Swiss National Park. The three-story Visitor Center contains exhibitions, an ecology platform comprising five partner organizations, an information center, a shop, and Zernez tourist information. The building was made of light concrete, which, as well as gravel, water, and cement, contains clay (Liapor or expanded clay) pellets. As a result of the use of these Liapor pellets, the building needs no further insulation. The walls thus serve both as supporting elements and as the insulation layer. The building is heated by a communal wood chip-fired furnace. It was decided to do without air-conditioning. A geothermal heat pump that controls the ventilation system regulates the supply of warm or cold air as needed.

Das Dorf Zernez im Unterengadin ist der Eingangsort zum Schweizer Nationalpark, der mit 172 km² das größte Naturschutzgebiet der Schweiz ist. Er wurde 1914 gegründet und ist auch der einzige Schweizer Nationalpark. Das dreigeschossige Besucherzentrum enthält Ausstellungen, eine von fünf Partnerorganisationen unterhaltene Ökostation, ein Informationszentrum, einen Laden und die Touristeninformation von Zernez. Der Bau besteht aus Leichtbeton, der außer Kies, Wasser und Zement auch Tonpellets (Liapor oder Blähton) enthält. Letztere sind der Grund dafür, dass keine weitere Isolierung erforderlich war. Die Wand dient daher sowohl als tragendes Element wie auch als Isolierungsschicht. Das Gebäude hat eine kommunale Holzhackschnitzelheizung. Auf eine Klimaanlage wurde verzichtet. Eine Erdwärmepumpe, die das Lüftungssystem kontrolliert, reguliert je nach Bedarf die Versorgung mit Kalt- und Warmluft.

Le village de Zernez en Basse-Engadine est le point d'entrée du Parc national suisse, créé en 1914, premier et seul parc national et plus grande zone naturelle protégée du pays avec ses 172 kilomètres carrés. Sur trois niveaux, le centre d'accueil des visiteurs contient des salles d'exposition, une « plate-forme écologique » pour cinq organismes partenaires, un centre d'information, une boutique et l'office de tourisme de Zernez. Le bâtiment est en béton léger, un matériau fait de gravier, de ciment, d'eau et de billes d'argile (Liapor ou argile expansée). Le bâtiment ne nécessite ainsi aucune isolation supplémentaire. Les murs sont en même temps éléments de soutien et d'isolation. Le bâtiment est chauffé au bois communal et il a été décidé de se passer du conditionnement de l'air. Une pompe à chaleur géothermique, qui contrôle le système de ventilation, régule l'arrivée d'air chaud ou froid selon les besoins.

Valerio Olgiati rejects the branding of his work as minimalism and, indeed, the apparent simplicity of this structure is deceptive—what looks like a simple, weighty cube divides itself into two adjoined blocks.

Valerio Olgiati lehnt die Klassifizierung seiner Bauten als minimalistisch ab, und in der Tat ist die scheinbare Schlichtheit dieses Gebäudes täuschend. Was wie ein einfacher, gewichtiger Kubus aussieht, teilt sich in zwei aneinander angrenzende Blöcke.

Valerio Olgiati rejette l'étiquette de minimalisme. En fait, la simplicité apparente de ce bâtiment est trompeuse. Ce qui fait penser à un simple cube massif se divise en deux blocs adjacents.

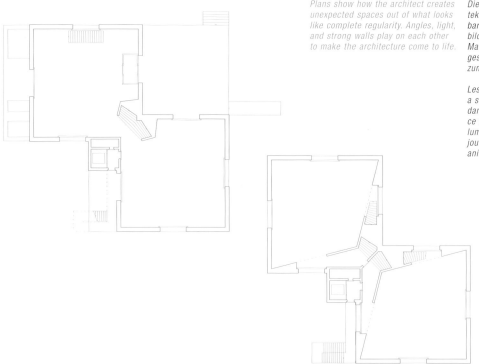

Plans show how the architect creates unexpected spaces out of what looks like complete regularity. Angles, light, and strong walls play on each other to make the architecture come to life.

Die Grundrisse zeigen, wie der Architekt unerwartete Räume aus scheinbar vollständiger Regelmäßigkeit bildet. Schrägen, Licht und starke Mauern werden gegeneinander ausgespielt und erwecken die Architektur zum Leben.

Les plans montrent que l'architecte a su créer des volumes inattendus dans un ordonnancement d'apparence régulière. Des pans inclinés, la lumière et la forte présence des murs jouent les uns avec les autres pour animer cette architecture.

These images further emphasize the duality of the structure, contrasting well-anchored solidity with volumes that lift and split between light and shadow.

Diese Abbildungen betonen weiterhin die Dualität des Gebäudes, in dem fest verankerte Solidität mit Volumen abwechseln, die sich zwischen Licht und Schatten erheben und aufteilen.

Ces images confirment la dualité de la structure qui met en contraste une massivité bien ancrée et des volumes suspendus et fragmentés par le jeu de l'ombre et de la lumière.

I. M. PEI

I. M. Pei Architect
88 Pine Street
New York, NY 10005
USA

Tel: +1 212 8 72 4010
Fax: +1 212 872 4222

Born in 1917 in Canton (now Guangzhou), China, **I. M. PEI** came to the United States in 1935. He received his B.Arch degree from MIT (1940); and his M.Arch from Harvard (1942). He formed I. M. Pei & Associates in 1955. He won the AIA Gold Medal (1979); the Pritzker Prize (1983); and the Praemium Imperiale in Japan (1989). His notable buildings include the National Center for Atmospheric Research (Boulder, Colorado, 1961–67); the Federal Aviation Agency Air Traffic Control Towers, 50 buildings, various locations (1962–72); the National Gallery of Art, East Building (Washington, D. C., 1968–78); the John F. Kennedy Library (Boston, Massachusetts, 1965–79); the Bank of China Tower (Hong Kong, 1982–89); the Grand Louvre (Paris, France, 1983–93); the Rock and Roll Hall of Fame and Museum (Cleveland, Ohio, 1987–95); and the Miho Museum (Shigaraki, Shiga, Japan, 1991–97). He collaborated with his sons (Pei Partnership Architects) on the recent Bank of China Headquarters (Beijing, China, 1994–2001). His most recent projects include the German Historical Museum (Extension/Temporary Exhibition Building, Berlin, 2003); Mudam, Musée d'Art Moderne Grand-Duc Jean (Luxembourg, 2006); and the Suzhou Art Museum (Suzhou, China), inaugurated in 2006. His Museum of Islamic Art (Doha, Qatar, published here), was opened in November 2008.

Der 1917 im chinesischen Kanton (heute Guangzhou) geborene **I. M. PEI** kam 1935 in die Vereinigten Staaten. Er erhielt seinen B. Arch. am Massachusetts Institute of Technology (1940) und seinen M. Arch. an der Harvard University (1942). 1955 gründete er das Büro I. M. Pei Associates. Ihm wurden die AIA Gold Medal (1979), der Pritzker-Preis (1979) und der Praemium Imperiale in Japan (1989) verliehen. Zu seinen bemerkenswerten Bauten zählen das National Center for Atmospheric Research (Boulder, Colorado, 1961–67), die Federal Aviation Agency Air Traffic Control Towers (50 Bauten an verschiedenen Standorten, 1962–72), das East Building der National Gallery of Art (Washington, D. C., 1968–78), die John F. Kennedy Library (Boston, Massachusetts, 1965–79), das Hochhaus der Bank of China (Hongkong, 1982–89), der Grand Louvre (Paris, 1983–93), die Rock and Roll Hall of Fame mit Museum (Cleveland, Ohio, 1987–95) und das Miho Museum (Shigaraki, Shiga, Japan, 1991–97). Mit seinen Söhnen (Pei Partnership Architects) plante er vor kurzem die Hauptverwaltung der Bank of China (Peking, 1994–2001). Zu seinen neuesten Projekten gehören die Erweiterung/das Wechselausstellungsgebäude des Deutschen Historischen Museums (Berlin, 2003), das Musée d'Art Moderne Grand-Duc Jean (Mudam) in Luxemburg (2006) und das 2006 eröffnete Kunstmuseum Suzhou (China). Sein Museum für islamische Kunst (Doha, Katar, hier veröffentlicht) wurde im November 2008 eingeweiht.

Né en 1917 à Canton (aujourd'hui Guangzhou, Chine), **I. M. PEI** arrive aux États-Unis en 1935. Il est B.Arch du MIT (1940), et M.Arch en architecture d'Harvard (1942). Il a créé son agence I. M. Pei & Associates (1955), a remporté la médaille d'or de l'AIA (1979), le prix Pritzker (1983) et le Praemium Imperiale du Japon (1989). Parmi ses réalisations les plus connues : The National Center for Atmospheric Research (Boulder, Colorado,1961–67) ; cinquante tours de contrôle aérien pour la Federal Aviation Agency (1962–72) ; le bâtiment est de la National Gallery of Art (Washington D. C., 1968–78) ; la bibliothèque John F. Kennedy (Boston, Massachusetts, 1965–79) ; la tour de la Banque de Chine (Hongkong, 1982–89) ; le Grand Louvre (Paris, 1983–93) ; le Rock and Roll Hall of Fame et musée (Cleveland, Ohio, 1993–95) et le musée Miho (Shigaraki, Shiga, Japon, 1991–97). Il a collaboré avec ses fils (Pei Partnership Architects) au projet de nouveau siège de la banque de Chine à Pékin (1994–2001). Ses plus récents projets comprennent le musée de l'Histoire allemande (extension/bâtiment des expositions temporaires, Berlin, 2003) ; le Mudam, Musée d'Art moderne Grand-Duc Jean (Luxembourg, 2006) et le musée d'Art de Suzhou (Suzhou, Chine) inauguré en 2006. Son musée de l'Art islamique à Doha (Qatar), publié ici, a ouvert ses portes en novembre 2008.

MUSEUM OF ISLAMIC ART

Doha, Qatar, 2003–08

Address: Corniche Doha Harbour, Doha, Ad Dawhah, Qatar, +974 422 4444 www.mia.org.qa
Area: 35 000 m². Client: Qatar Museums Authority. Cost: not disclosed
Project Team: Perry Y. Chin (Project Manager), Hiroshi Okamoto (Design, Site Representative),
Toh Tsun Lim (Design, Job Captain, Site Representative), Fatma Aslihan Demirtas (Lead Designer). Interior Design: Jean-Michel Wilmotte

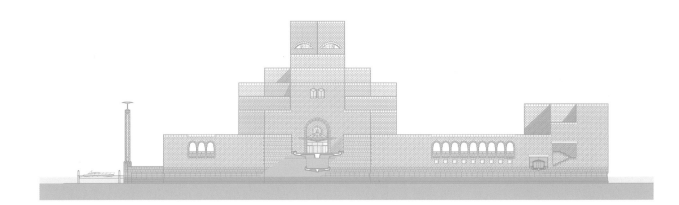

Located on an artificial island set 60 meters from the southern end of the prestigious Corniche in Doha, the new Museum of Islamic Art is an ambitious project, the design of which is the result of I. M. Pei's search for the "essence" of Islamic architecture. Working on this design initially at the invitation of Luis Monreal, General Manager of the Aga Khan Trust for Culture, Pei found that the purest expression of Islamic architecture is the mosque of Ibn Tulun (876–79), one of the oldest of Cairo's monuments. Pei has developed a geometric progression "from the circle to the square and from the square to the octagon" based on his study of Islamic design. The spectacular entrance area of the museum with its sweeping double staircase and 65-meter-high dome with a central oculus is one of his finest and most sophisticated spaces. The actual exhibition spaces were designed by Jean-Michel Wilmotte of Paris, who had worked extensively with Pei in the past on such projects as the temporary exhibition areas under the Louvre Pyramid (1989) and the later Decorative Arts galleries in the same museum. With minimal visible glazing on the land side, the museum features an enormous opening on the side of the sea. A very large area of the new structure is devoted to teaching spaces, a library, and other facilities destined to bring Qatar up to international standards in the area of the study and appreciation of art. Pei's successful attempt to assimilate the lessons of his own know-ledge of Western, modern architecture with those of the geometric Islamic traditions marks one of his most significant buildings outside Western Europe and the United States.

Das neue, auf einer künstlichen Insel 60 m vom Südende der berühmten Corniche in Doha entfernt gelegene Museum für islamische Kunst ist ein ehrgeiziges Projekt, dessen Erscheinungsbild auch auf I. M. Peis Suche nach dem „Wesen" der islamischen Architektur beruht. Während seiner ursprünglich auf Einladung von Luis Monreal, dem Generaldirektor des Aga Khan Trust for Culture, begonnenen Arbeit kam Pei zu dem Schluss, dass die Moschee Ibn Tulun (876–879), eines der ältesten und am wenigsten veränderten Baudenkmäler Kairos, den reinsten Ausdruck islamischer Architektur darstelle. Pei hat eine geometrische Progression „vom Kreis zum Quadrat und vom Quadrat zum Oktogon" entwickelt, die auf seinem Studium der islamischen Architektur basiert. Der spektakuläre Eingangsbereich des Museums mit seiner schwungvollen Doppeltreppe und der 65 m hohen Kuppel mit einem zentralen Okulus gehört zu Peis schönsten und raffiniertesten Räumen. Die eigentlichen Ausstellungsräume wurden von Jean-Michel Wilmotte aus Paris gestaltet, der schon in der Vergangenheit viel mit Pei zusammengearbeitet hat, z. B. an den Wechselausstellungsräumen unter der Pyramide des Louvre (1989) und den späteren Galeries des Arts Décoratifs im gleichen Museum. Während das Museum in Doha auf der Landseite kaum verglast ist, hat es eine gewaltige Öffnung zur Seeseite. Ein großer Teil des neuen Gebäudes ist Lehrzwecken gewidmet; eine Bibliothek und andere Einrichtungen sollen Katar auf internationalen Standard in Bezug auf die Erforschung und das Verständnis von Kunst bringen. Peis erfolgreicher Versuch, sein eigenes Verständnis von der abendländischen modernen Baukunst der traditionellen geometrischen islamischen Architektur anzupassen, kennzeichnet dieses Bauwerk, das zu seinen bedeutendsten außerhalb Westeuropas und der Vereinigten Staaten gehört.

Implanté sur une île artificielle créée à 60 mètres de l'extrémité sud de la prestigieuse corniche de Doha, le musée d'Art islamique est un ambitieux projet qui repose en partie sur la recherche par I. M. Pei de « l'essence » de l'architecture islamique. Travaillant initialement sur ce projet à l'invitation de Luis Monreal, directeur général de la fondation Aga Khan pour la Culture, Pei juge que la plus pure expression de l'architecture islamique s'exprime dans la mosquée d'Ibn Touloun (876–879), l'un des plus anciens monuments du Caire. Il a mis au point une progression géométrique « du cercle au carré et du carré à l'octogone » à partir de son étude de plans historiques. La spectaculaire entrée du musée à double grand escalier et coupole de 65 mètres de haut à oculus central est l'un des espaces les plus raffinés qu'il ait jamais réalisés. Les salles d'exposition ont été aménagées par Jean-Michel Wilmotte (Paris) qui avait déjà beaucoup travaillé avec Pei dans le passé sur des opérations comme les salles d'expositions temporaires sous la Pyramide du Louvre (1989) ou les salles des arts décoratifs pour la même institution, quelques années plus tard. En grande partie fermé du côté des terres, le musée présente une énorme ouverture du côté de la mer. Une très grande partie du nouveau bâtiment est consacrée à des espaces pour l'enseignement, à une bibliothèque et à d'autres installations destinées à élever le Qatar au niveau des standards internationaux dans les domaines de l'étude et de la connaissance de l'art. La tentative réussie de Pei d'assimiler les leçons de sa connaissance de l'architecture occidentale moderne avec celle des traditions islamiques d'inspiration géométrique font de ce musée l'une de ses réalisations les plus importantes en dehors de l'Europe occidentale et des États-Unis.

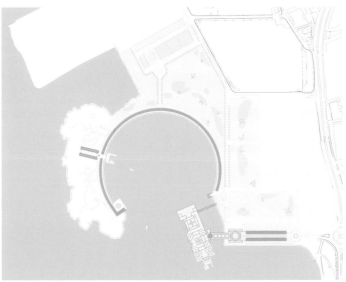

The Museum of Islamic Art is set on an artificial island at the end of Doha's Corniche drive. The museum and the circular basin behind it are visible on the site drawing to the left.

Das Museum für islamische Kunst steht auf einer künstlichen Insel am Ende des Corniche Drive in Doha. Das Gebäude und das kreisförmige Wasserbecken dahinter sind auf dem Lageplan links zu sehen.

Le musée de l'Art islamique est implanté sur une île artificielle à l'extrémité de la route de la Corniche de Doha. Sur le plan du site, à gauche, le musée et son bassin circulaire.

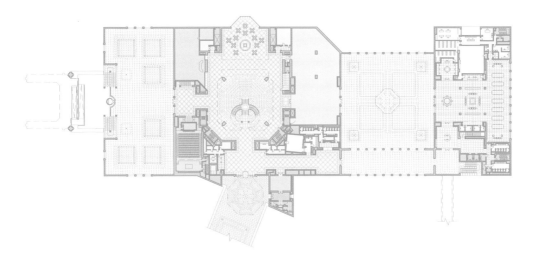

A floor plan shows the museum (left of center) and the education wing to the right. Below, the main atrium of the museum with its window looking out onto the bay. Right, looking up to the cupola of the atrium.

Der Grundriss zeigt das Museum (Mitte links) und rechts den Bildungstrakt. Unten ist das große Atrium des Museums zu sehen, dessen Fenster zur Bucht orientiert sind. Rechts ein Blick in die Kuppel des Atriums.

Plan au sol montrant le musée (à gauche du centre) et l'aile consacrée à l'éducation (à droite). Ci-dessous, l'atrium principal du musée dont l'énorme baie donne sur la mer. À droite, la coupole de l'atrium en contre-plongée.

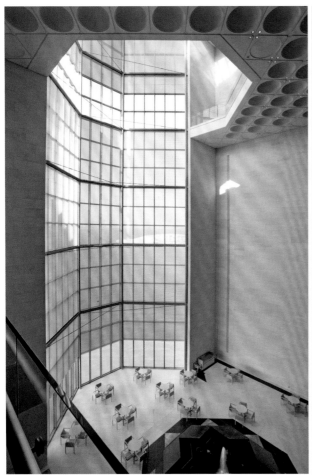

RENZO PIANO

Renzo Piano Building Workshop
34 rue des Archives / 75004 Paris / France
Tel: +33 1 42 78 00 82 / Fax: +33 1 42 78 01 98
Via Rubens 29 / 16158 Genoa / Italy

Tel: +39 010 61 711 / Fax: +39 010 61 71 350
E-mail: info@rpbw.com / Web: www.rpbw.com

RENZO PIANO was born in 1937 in Genoa, Italy. He studied at the University of Florence and at the Polytechnic Institute of Milan (1964). He formed his own practice (Studio Piano) in 1965, then associated with Richard Rogers (Piano & Rogers, 1971–78). Piano completed the Centre Pompidou in Paris in 1977. From 1978 to 1980, he worked with Peter Rice (Piano & Rice Associates). He created the Renzo Piano Building Workshop in 1981 in Genoa and Paris. Piano received the RIBA Gold Medal in 1989. His built work includes the Menil Collection Museum (Houston, Texas, 1981–86); the San Nicola Stadium (Bari, Italy, 1987–90); the 1988–90 extension of the IRCAM (Paris, France); the Kansai International Airport Terminal (Osaka, Japan, 1988–94); Cité Internationale de Lyon (Lyon, France, 1985–96); the Beyeler Foundation Museum (Riehen, Basel, Switzerland, 1991–97); the Jean-Marie Tjibaou Cultural Center (New Caledonia, South Pacific, 1991–98); the Mercedes-Benz Center (Stuttgart, Germany, 1993–98); the reconstruction of a section of Potsdamer Platz (Berlin, Germany, 1992–2000); the Parma Auditorium (Italy, 1997–2001); Maison Hermès (Tokyo, Japan, 1998–2001); the Rome Auditorium (Italy, 1994–2002); the conversion of the Lingotto Factory Complex (Turin, Italy, 1983–2003); the Padre Pio Pilgrimage Church (San Giovanni Rotondo, Foggia, Italy, 1991–2004); the renovation and expansion of the Morgan Library (New York, New York, 2000–06); the New York Times Building (New York, New York, 2005–07); and the California Academy of Sciences (San Francisco, California, 2005–08). Current work includes the Woodruff Arts Center Expansion (Atlanta, Georgia); the London Bridge Tower (London, UK); and the Modern Wing of the Art Institute of Chicago (Illinois, 2005–09, published here).

RENZO PIANO wurde 1937 in Genua geboren und studierte an der Universität Florenz sowie am Politecnico di Milano (1964). Er gründete 1965 sein eigenes Büro (Studio Piano) und schloss sich dann mit Richard Rogers zusammen (Piano & Rogers, 1971–78). Piano vollendete 1977 das Centre Pompidou in Paris. Von 1978 bis 1980 arbeitete er mit Peter Rice zusammen (Piano & Rice Associates). 1981 gründete er Renzo Piano Building Workshop in Genua und Paris. Piano wurde 1989 mit der RIBA Gold Medal ausgezeichnet. Zu seinen ausgeführten Werken zählen das Museum der Menil Collection (Houston, Texas, 1981–86), das Stadion San Nicola (Bari, Italien, 1987–90), der Erweiterungsbau für das IRCAM (Paris, 1988–90), der internationale Flughafen Kansai (Osaka, 1988–94), die Cité Internationale de Lyon (1985–96), das Museum der Fondation Beyeler (Riehen, Basel, Schweiz, 1991–97), das Kulturzentrum Jean-Marie Tjibaou (Neukaledonien, Südpazifik, 1991–98), das Mercedes-Benz Center (Stuttgart, 1993–98), die Rekonstruktion eines Bauabschnitts am Potsdamer Platz (Berlin, 1992–2000), ein Auditorium in Parma (1997–2001), die Maison Hermès (Tokio, 1998–2001), das Auditorium Parco della Musica in Rom (1994–2002), der Umbau der Fabrikanlage Lingotto (Turin, 1983–2003), die Wallfahrtskirche Padre Pio (San Giovanni Rotondo, Foggia, 1991–2004), die Erneuerung und Erweiterung der Morgan Library (New York, 2000–06), das Gebäude der *New York Times* (New York, 2005–07) und die California Academy of Sciences (San Francisco, Kalifornien, 2005–08). In Arbeit befinden sich die Erweiterung des Woodruff Arts Center (Atlanta, Georgia), der London Bridge Tower (London) und der Modern Wing of the Art Institute of Chicago (Illinois, 2005–09, hier veröffentlicht).

RENZO PIANO, né en 1937 à Gênes (Italie), a étudié à l'université de Florence et à l'Institut Polytechnique de Milan (1964). Il crée son agence, Studio Piano, en 1965, puis s'associe à Richard Rogers (Piano & Rogers, 1971–78). Ils achèvent le Centre Pompidou à Paris en 1977. De 1978 à 1980, il collabore avec Peter Rice (Piano & Rice Associates). Il fonde le Renzo Piano Building Workshop en 1981 à Gênes et Paris. Il a reçu la médaille d'or du RIBA en 1989. Parmi ses réalisations : le musée de la Ménil Collection (Houston, Texas, 1981–86) ; le stade San Nicola (Bari, Italie, 1987–90) ; l'extension de l'Ircam, Paris (1988–90) ; le terminal de l'aéroport international de l'aéroport du Kansai (Osaka, Japon, 1988–94) ; la Cité internationale de Lyon (France,1985–96) ; le musée de la Fondation Beyeler (Riehen, Bâle, Suisse, 1991–97) ; le centre culturel Jean-Marie Tjibaou (Nouvelle-Calédonie, Pacifique Sud, 1991–98) ; le centre Mercedes-Benz (Stuttgart, Allemagne, 1993–98) ; la reconstruction d'une partie de la Potsdamer Platz (Berlin, 1992–2000) ; l'auditorium de Parme (1997–2001) ; la Maison Hermès (Tokyo, 1998–2001) ; l'auditorium de Rome (Italie, 1994–2002) ; la reconversion de l'usine du Lingotto (Turin, Italie, 1983–2003) ; l'église de pèlerinage Padre Pio (San Giovanni Rotondo, Foggia, Italie, 1991–2004) ; la rénovation et l'agrandissement de la Morgan Library (New York, 2000–06) ; la tour du *New York Times* (New York, 2005–07) et la California Academy of Sciences (San Francisco, Californie, 2005–08). Parmi ses œuvres récentes : l'extension du Woodruff Arts Center (Atlanta, Georgie) ; la London Bridge Tower (Londres) et le Modern Wing of the Art Institute of Chicago (Illinois, 2005–09) , publié ici.

MODERN WING OF THE ART INSTITUTE OF CHICAGO

Chicago, Illinois, USA, 2005–09

Address: 111 South Michigan Avenue, Chicago, IL 60603-6404, USA, +1 312 443 3600, www.artic.edu
Area: 11 799 m². Client: The Art Institute of Chicago. Cost: $283 million

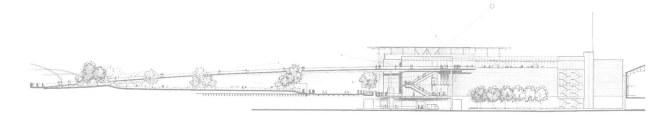

A bridge designed by Piano leads from the Modern Wing to the neighboring Millennium Park. Above, an elevation drawing shows the bridge and the building.

Eine von Piano geplante Brücke führt vom Modern Wing zum benachbarten Millennium Park. Die Ansicht oben zeigt die Brücke und das Gebäude.

Le pont dessiné par Piano conduit du Modern Wing au Millenium Park voisin. Ci-dessus, une élévation du pont et du bâtiment.

Piano's light, airy building with a broad, flat canopy roof stands out from the rest of the Art Institute.

Pianos leichtes, luftiges Gebäude mit breitem, flachem Vordach hebt sich von den übrigen Bauten des Art Institute ab.

Léger et aérien, le bâtiment au vaste auvent de Piano se détache du reste de l'Art Institute.

The City of Chicago has embarked on a large-scale cultural program centered on the Lakefront Millennium Park, a 10-hectare former zone of railway tracks and parking lots. Frank O. Gehry designed a 200-meter-long trellis and a band shell for the park, while Renzo Piano was called on to build a $283-million addition to the Chicago Art Institute. His L-shaped building is replacing the former Goodman Theater at the corner of Columbus and Monroe Streets. Using glass, steel and limestone, Piano carefully thought out the connection between the old and the new—the old being the original 19th-century *beaux-arts* museum building. A "minimalist" pedestrian bridge (the Nichols Bridgeway) across Monroe Street connects the park to the cultural facility. The 11 799-square-meter addition has what has been called a "flying-carpet" roof. Though this design is seen locally as being a complement to Gehry's pavilion in the park, this airy form of roof can also be seen in the Pinacoteca recently added to the Lingotto factory (Turin, Italy, 2002). With the development of the Lakefront Park, the Chicago Art Institute, one of America's richest museums, is located between two green areas, since it is also close to Grant Park. An essential element of the program was that the new structure links the two older existing buildings, straddling a railway line. Piano refers to immense railroad yards as being the starting point of his inspiration for this structure. In an interesting homage to a great Chicago architect, Renzo Piano has proposed to relocate the entrance arch of Louis Sullivan's demolished Chicago Stock Exchange Building (formerly at the southwest corner of Monroe and Columbus) closer to the museum's preserved and renovated "Stock Exchange Trading Room."

Die Stadt Chicago investiert in ein großes Kulturprogramm im Lakefront Millennium Park, einem 10 ha großen, früheren Bahngelände und Parkplatz. Frank O. Gehry plante eine 200 m lange Gitterwand und einen Musikpavillon für den Park, während Renzo Piano mit dem 283 Millionen Dollar teuren Ergänzungsbau des Chicago Art Institute beauftragt wurde. Sein L-förmiger Bau ersetzt das frühere Goodman Theater an der Ecke Columbus und Monroe Street. Piano verwendete dafür Glas, Stahl und Kalkstein und legte besonderen Wert auf die Verbindung von Alt und Neu – der Altbau ist das ursprüngliche Beaux-Art-Museum aus dem 19. Jahrhundert. Eine „minimalistische" Fußgängerbrücke (Nichols Bridgeway) über die Monroe Street verbindet den Park mit der Kultureinrichtung. Der 11 799 m² große Erweiterungsbau hat ein als „fliegender Teppich" bezeichnetes Dach. Obgleich dieses Gebäude vor Ort als Gegenstück zu Gehrys Pavillon im Park betrachtet wird, findet sich die luftige Form des Dachs bereits bei der kürzlich auf dem Gelände der Lingotto-Fabrik errichteten Pinacoteca (Turin, 2002). Durch die Gestaltung des Lakefront Parks liegt das Chicago Art Institute, eines der reichsten Museen Amerikas, jetzt zwischen zwei Grünbereichen, da es auch an den Grant Park grenzt. Ein entscheidender Punkt des Programms war die Forderung, dass der Neubau die beiden bestehenden Altbauten verbinden und eine Bahnlinie überqueren sollte. Piano bezeichnet das riesige Bahngelände als Inspiration für seinen Entwurf. Als interessante Hommage an den großen Chicagoer Architekten Louis Sullivan schlug Renzo Piano vor, den Eingangsbogen von dessen abgerissener Chicagoer Börse (die früher an der Südwestecke von Monroe und Columbus Street stand) näher an den erhaltenen und restaurierten „Stock Exchange Trading Room" des Museums zu versetzen.

La ville de Chicago s'est lancée dans un vaste projet culturel centré sur le Lakefront Millenium Park, constitué de dix hectares d'anciennes voies de chemin de fer et parkings. Frank O. Gehry a conçu un treillis de 200 mètres de long et un auditorium de plein air pour le parc, tandis que Renzo Piano a été appelé pour agrandir le Chicago Art Institute d'une extension de 283 millions de dollars. Son bâtiment en forme de « L » remplace l'ancien Goodman Theater situé à l'angle des rues Columbus et Monroe. Par le choix des matériaux, comme le verre, l'acier et la pierre, Piano a soigneusement traité les connexions entre le nouveau et l'ancien, c'est-à-dire le bâtiment d'origine du musée de style beaux-arts. Une passerelle « minimaliste » (Nichols Bridgeway) au-dessus de la rue Monroe relie le musée au parc. Cette extension de 11 799 mètres carrés est dotée ce que l'on a appelé un toit en « tapis volant ». Si, à Chicago, elle vient accompagner le pavillon de Gehry dans le parc, cette forme aérienne était déjà présente dans la pinacothèque de l'usine du Lingotto (Turin, Italie, 2002). Grâce au développement du Lakefront Park, le Chicago Art Institute, l'un des plus riches musées américains, se trouve maintenant entre deux espaces verts, puisqu'il est également proche du Grant Park. Une des demandes essentielles du programme était que la nouvelle structure relie les deux bâtiments existants, en franchissant une voie de chemin de fer. Piano évoque les immenses gares de dépôt de la ville comme source de son inspiration. Dans un hommage intéressant à un grand architecte de Chicago, il a proposé de transférer l'arche d'entrée de l'immeuble de la Bourse de Chicago de Louis Sullivan (aujourd'hui démolie, mais qui se trouvait jadis à l'angle sud des rues Columbus et Monroe) près de la « Salle des cours de la Bourse » rénovée et conservée dans le musée.

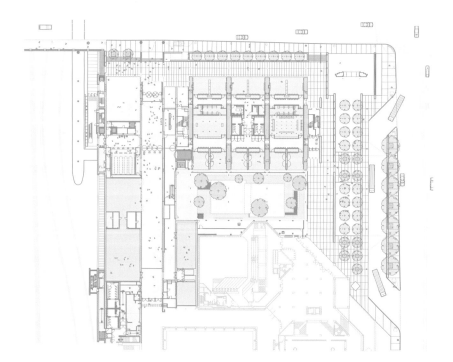

The vertical detailing of the exterior of the building finds a convincing echo in the stairway, seen in the image to the right. Left, a plan of the museum.

Die vertikale Gliederung der Außenfront wird überzeugend auch für das Treppenhaus übernommen, das auf der rechten Abbildung zu sehen ist. Links ein Grundriss des Museums.

La verticalité de la construction de la façade se retrouve en un écho convaincant dans cet escalier (à droite). À gauche, plan du musée.

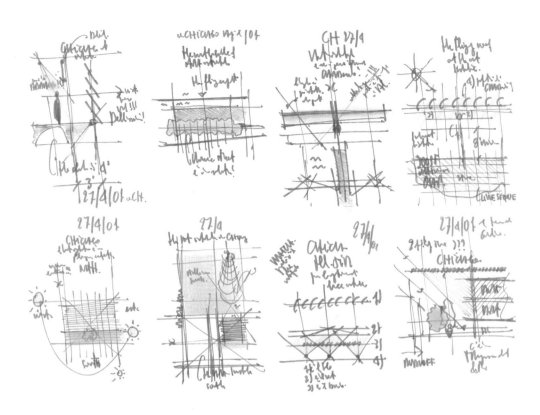

Sketches by Renzo Piano are here juxtaposed with views of the generous spaces inside the museum. Above, a sculpture by Alberto Giacometti (right) looks out to the urban surroundings from within the Modern Wing.

Renzo Pianos Skizzen sind Ansichten der großzügigen Räume im Innern des Museums gegenübergestellt. Oben blickt eine Skulptur von Alberto Giacometti (rechts) aus dem Modern Wing auf das städtische Umfeld.

À gauche, croquis de Renzo Piano juxtaposés à des vues des vastes volumes intérieurs du musée. Ci-dessus, une sculpture d'Alberto Giacometti (à droite) regarde vers l'environnement urbain du Modern Wing.

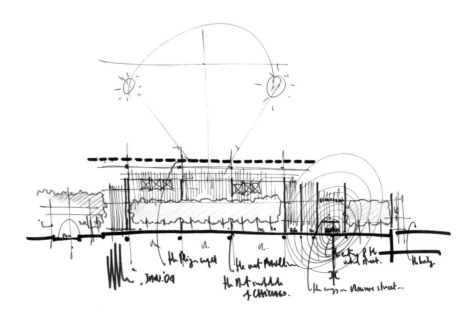

QUERKRAFT

Querkraft Architekten ZT GmbH
Mariahilfer Str. 51
1060 Vienna
Austria

Tel: +43 1 548 77 11
Fax: +43 1 548 77 11 44
E-mail: info@querkraft.at
Web: www.querkraft.at

Jakob Dunkl was born in Frankfurt am Main, Germany, in 1963. He studied at the Technical University in Vienna (1986–90) and worked in 1989 in the office of Behnisch & Partner in Stuttgart. In 1990, he created **QUERKRAFT** Architects with Gerd Erhartt and Peter Sapp—and Michael Zinner in 1998 (until 2004). Dunkl was a Guest Professor at Roger Williams University (Rhode Island, 2001/2004). Gerd Erhartt was born in 1964 in Vienna. He also studied at the Technical University in Vienna (1989–90), receiving his diploma in 1992. He has also taught at Roger Williams University (2001) and at the Technical University in Vienna (2001–04). Peter Sapp was born in Linz, Austria, in 1961. He created his own office (1989–92) before participating in the creation of Querkraft with Dunkl and Erhartt. Their work includes the Römermuseum (Vienna); headquarters for BIG (Vienna, 2006); the Liaunig Museum (Neuhaus/Suha, Carinthia, 2007–08, published here); and a number of private houses, restaurants, shops, and residential buildings, all in Austria.

Jakob Dunkl wude 1963 in Frankfurt am Main geboren und studierte an der Technischen Universität Wien (1986–90). 1989 arbeitete er im Büro Behnisch & Partner in Stuttgart. 1990 gründete Dunkl mit Gerd Erhartt und Peter Sapp das Büro **QUERKRAFT** – dem 1998 bis 2004 auch Michael Zinner angehörte. Dunkl war Gastprofessor an der Roger Wiliams University (Rhode Island, 2001/2004). Gerd Erhartt wurde 1964 in Wien geboren und studierte ebenfalls an der Technischen Universität Wien (1989–90), wo er 1992 sein Diplom machte. Auch er lehrte an der Roger Williams University (2001) sowie an der Technischen Universität Wien (2001–04). Peter Sapp wurde 1961 in Linz geboren und führte ein eigenes Büro (1989–92), bevor er mit Dunkl und Erhartt Querkraft gründete. Zu den ausgeführten Bauten des Büros zählen das Römermuseum (Wien), die Hauptverwaltung von BIG (Wien, 2006), das Museum Liaunig (Neuhaus/Suha, Kärnten, 2007–08, hier veröffentlicht) und eine Reihe von privaten Wohnhäusern, Restaurants, Läden und Wohngebäuden, alle in Österreich.

Jakob Dunkl est né à Francfort (Allemagne) en 1963. Il a fait ses études à l'Université polytechnique de Vienne (1986–90) et a travaillé en 1989 chez Behnisch & Partner à Stuttgart. En 1990, il a créé **QUERKRAFT** avec Gerd Erhartt et Peter Sapp que Michael Zinner est venu rejoindre en 1998 (jusqu'en 2004). Il a été professeur invité à la Roger Williams University (Rhode Island, 2001 et 2004). Gerd Erhartt, né en 1964 à Vienne, a également étudié à l'Université polytechnique de Vienne (1989–90), dont il est diplômé (1992). Il a lui aussi enseigné à la Roger Williams University (2001) et à l'Université polytechnique de Vienne (2001–04). Peter Sapp, né à Linz (Autriche) en 1961, a créé sa propre agence (1989–92) avant de participer à la fondation de Querkraft avec Dunkl et Erhartt. Parmi leurs réalisations : le Römermuseum (Vienne) ; le siège social de BIG (Vienne, 2006) ; le musée Liaunig (Neuhaus/Suha, Carinthie, 2007–08), publié ici, et un certain nombre de résidences privées, restaurants, magasins et immeubles d'appartements, tous en Autriche.

LIAUNIG MUSEUM

Neuhaus/Suha, Carinthia, Austria, 2007–08

Address: Neuhaus 41, 9155 Neuhaus, Austria, +43 4356 211 15, www.museumliaunig.at
Area: 4400 m². Client: Dkfm. Herbert Liaunig. Cost: € 9.5 million
Team: Erwin Sättner (Project Architect)

This unusual structure cantilevers 30 meters over a wooded, steep embankment and is suspended above the Drau River, situated 70 meters below. The architects state: "Planted into the site, the new museum emerges more like a work of Land Art; only a small part of the outstretched museum building is visible." The museum entrance is oriented toward the center of Neuhaus and a nearby castle owned by the museum's patron. A "wine cellar of art," an underground, flexible exhibition space is located along the entrance approach of the museum. The building is 160 meters long, and the main exhibition hall, with its overhead lighting, features protected terraces at each end. The site is 15 000 square meters in area.

Dieses ungewöhnliche Bauwerk kragt 30 m über ein steiles, bewaldetes Ufergelände aus und hängt über dem 70 m tiefer gelegenen Flussbett der Drau. Die Architekten erläutern: „Das neue, in das Gelände eingesetzte Museum wirkt eher wie ein Werk der Land-Art; nur ein kleiner Teil des langgestreckten Gebäudes ist sichtbar." Der Eingang zum Museum ist zum Zentrum von Neuhaus und einer im Besitz des Museumseigners befindlichen Burg orientiert. Ein „Weinkeller der Kunst", ein flexibler, unterirdischer Ausstellungsraum, liegt im Eingangsbereich des Museums. Das Gebäude ist 160 m lang. Der große Ausstellungssaal mit Belichtung von oben ist auf beiden Seiten von geschützten Terrassen eingefasst. Das Grundstück hat eine Fläche von 15 000 m².

Cette curieuse construction en porte-à-faux de 30 mètres est accrochée à la rive boisée et escarpée de la Drau qui s'écoule 70 mètres plus bas. « Littéralement planté dans son site, le nouveau musée en émerge telle une œuvre de *land art*. Seule une faible partie du bâtiment étiré en longueur est visible », explique l'architecte. L'entrée du musée est orientée vers le centre de Neuhaus et un château voisin, propriété du mécène qui a permis ces travaux. Une « cave de l'art », espace d'exposition polyvalent souterrain, a été implantée le long du chemin d'entrée au musée. Le bâtiment mesure 160 mètres de long, et la salle principale d'exposition à éclairage zénithal se termine de chaque côté par une terrasse. Le terrain mesure 15 000 mètres carrés.

As the site drawing above and images to the right show, the Liaunig Museum's most visible element is a long, rectangular, cantilevered tube.

Wie der Lageplan oben und die Abbildungen rechts zeigen, ist das auffälligste Element des Museum Liaunig eine lange, rechteckige, auskragende Röhre.

Comme le montrent le plan du site ci-dessus et les images de droite, la caractéristique principale du Museum Liaunig est un long tube en porte-à-faux de section rectangulaire.

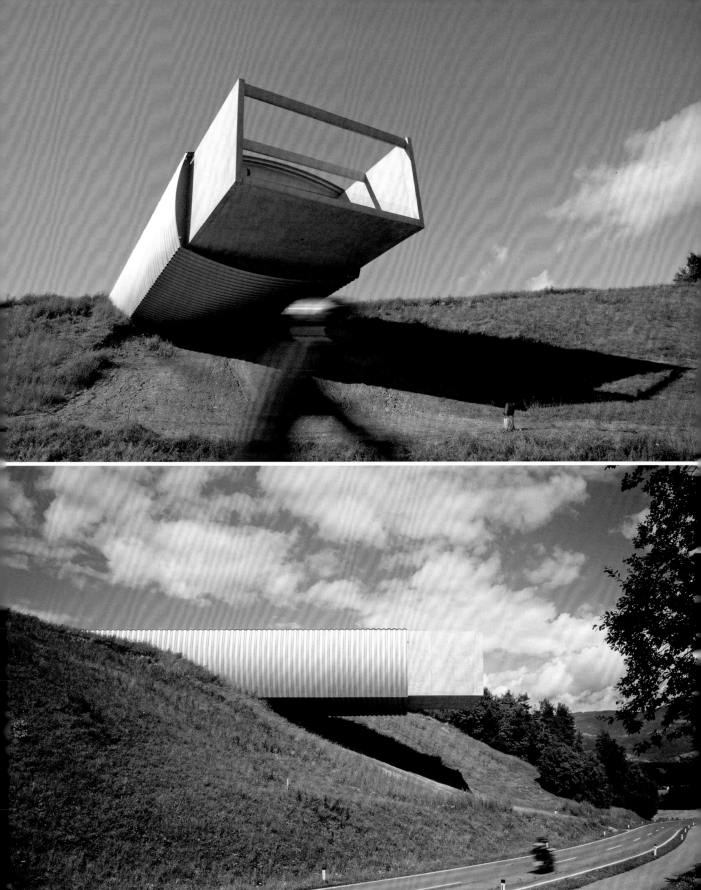

The low-lying form of the structure almost resembles a work of sculpture more than architecture from certain angles.

Aus einigen Blickwinkeln ähnelt die flache Form des Gebäudes eher einer Skulptur als einem Bauwerk.

Vue sous certains angles, la forme surbaissée du bâtiment fait presque davantage penser à une sculpture qu'à une œuvre d'architecture.

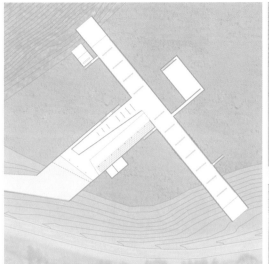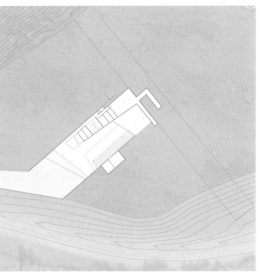

The broad opening at one end of the structure frames the mountainous landscape. Above, plans show the cruciform design.

Die weite Öffnung auf einer Seite des Gebäudes rahmt die Berglandschaft ein. Die Grundrisse darüber zeigen die kreuzförmige Anlage.

La grande ouverture aménagée à une extrémité de la structure cadre le paysage de montagne. Ci-dessus, le plan cruciforme du projet.

Interior spaces are relatively closed
and long, as is implied by the overall
structure of the museum.

Die Innenräume sind relativ geschlossen und lang, wie von der Gesamt-
anlage des Museums vorgegeben.

Les espaces intérieurs sont plutôt
fermés, conséquence de la conception de la structure même du musée.

SANAA
KAZUYO SEJIMA + RYUE NISHIZAWA

Kazuyo Sejima + Ryue Nishizawa / SANAA
1–5–27 Tatsumi
Koto-ku
Tokyo 135–0053
Japan

Tel: +81 3 5534 1780
Fax: +81 3 5534 1757
E-mail: press@sanaa.co.jp

Born in Ibaraki Prefecture in 1956, Kazuyo Sejima studied architecture at the Japan Women's University before joining the practice of architect Toyo Ito. She launched her own practice in 1987 and was named the Japan Institute of Architects' Young Architect of the Year in 1992. Born in Tokyo in 1966, Ryue Nishizawa studied architecture at Yokohama National University, from which he graduated in 1990. He began working with Sejima the same year, and the pair created the new firm **KAZUYO SEJIMA + RYUE NISHIZAWA / SANAA** in 1995. In addition to his work with Sejima, Nishizawa has also maintained an independent practice since 1997. Sejima and Nishizawa were jointly awarded the Golden Lion at the 9th Venice Architecture Biennale in 2004. The work of SANAA includes the 21st-Century Museum of Contemporary Art (Kanazawa, Ishikawa, 2002–04); the Glass Pavilion of the Toledo Museum of Art (Ohio, 2003–06); Dior Omotesando (Tokyo); and a building for the New Museum of Contemporary Art in New York (New York, 2005–07). SANAA won the competitions to design the Learning Center of the EPFL in Lausanne, Switzerland (2007–09); and the new building of the Louvre-Lens, France (2009–12, published here).

Die 1956 in der Präfektur Ibaraki geborene Kazuyo Sejima studierte Architektur an der Frauenuniversität von Japan bevor sie bei Toyo Ito arbeitete. 1987 eröffnete sie ihr eigenes Büro und wurde 1992 als Young Architect of the Year vom Japan Institute of Architects geehrt. Ryue Nishizawa wurde 1966 in Tokio geboren und schloss 1990 sein Studium an der Staatlichen Universität in Yokohama ab. Im gleichen Jahr begann die Zusammenarbeit mit Sejima, und 1995 gründeten sie die neue Firma **KAZUYO SEJIMA + RYUE NISHIZAWA / SANAA**. Daneben hat Nishizawa seit 1997 auch eine eigene Firma. Bei der IX. Architekturbiennale von Venedig wurden Sejima und Nishizawa 2004 mit dem Goldenen Löwen ausgezeichnet. Zu den Arbeiten von SANAA gehören das Museum für die Kunst des 21. Jahrhunderts (Kanazawa, Ishikawa, 2002–04), der Glaspavillon des Toledo Museum of Art (Ohio, 2003–06), Dior Omotesando (Tokio) und ein Gebäude für das New Museum of Contemporary Art in New York (2005–07). SANAA gewannen den Wettbewerb für das Lernzentrum der École Polytechnique Fédérale in Lausanne (Schweiz, 2007–09) und den Neubau des Louvre-Lens (Frankreich, 2009–12, hier veröffentlicht).

Née dans la préfecture d'Ibaraki en 1956, Kazuyo Sejima étudie l'architecture à l'université des Femmes du Japon, avant de s'engager avec Toyo Ito. Elle crée sa propre agence à Tokyo en 1987, et est nommée Jeune architecte de l'année par l'Institut des architectes du Japon en 1992. Né en 1966 à Tokyo, Ryue Nishizawa a étudié l'architecture à l'université nationale de Yokohama, dont il est sorti diplômé en 1990. Il a commencé à travailler avec Sejima la même année, avant qu'ils ne fondent ensemble **KAZUYO SEJIMA + RYUE NISHIZAWA / SANAA** en 1995. En plus de son travail avec Sejima, Nishizawa a maintenu une pratique indépendante depuis 1997. Sejima et Nishizawa ont été conjointement récompensés à la IXᵉ Biennale d'architecture de Venise en 2004, par le prix du Lion d'or. Le travail de SANAA comprend le musée d'Art contemporain du XXIᵉ siècle (Kanazawa, Ishikawa, 2002–04) ; le pavillon de verre du Toledo Museum of Art (Toledo, Ohio, 2003–06) ; Dior Omotesando (Tokyo) et un immeuble pour le New Museum of Contemporary Art à New York (New York, 2005–07). SANAA a remporté les concours pour le Centre de formation de l'EPFL à Lausanne (Suisse, 2007–09) et les nouvelles installations du Louvre-Lens (France, 2009–12), publiées ici.

LOUVRE-LENS

Lens, France, 2009–12

*Address: Rue Hélène Boucher, 62300 Lens, France, www.louvrelens.fr
Area: 23 000 m². Client: Région Nord-Pas de Calais, Musée du Louvre. Cost: €127 million (estimate)
Collaboration: Imery Culbert LLP, Catherine Mosbach*

In an unusual coincidence, the two major Paris museums, the Centre Pompidou and the Louvre, have turned to noted Japanese architects to design their new extensions located in provincial French cities. Shigeru Ban is designing the Centre Pompidou-Metz and SANAA the Louvre-Lens. While the Centre Pompidou had a tradition of reference to contemporary architecture dating from their original Piano & Rogers building, the Louvre, despite its makeover by I. M. Pei, remains more traditional in its image. SANAA's open, bright project calls for an assemblage of slightly skewed rectangular forms, and high, broadly glazed spaces that bring to mind the 21st-Century Museum of Contemporary Art (Kanzawa, Ishikawa, 2002–04). Roughly 5500 square meters of the new building will be used for the presentation of works of art. Six to eight hundred works from the Louvre in Paris will be placed on semipermanent display. Some 1700 square meters will be devoted to temporary exhibitions. The buildings are set in a broad green space, designed by the noted French landscape architect Catherine Mosbach.

Die beiden großen Pariser Museen, das Centre Pompidou und der Louvre, haben in zufälliger Übereinstimmung bekannte japanische Architekten beauftragt, ihre neuen Bauten in französischen Provinzstädten zu entwerfen. Shigeru Ban plant das Centre Pompidou-Metz und SANAA den Louvre-Lens. Während das Centre Pompidou sich – aufgrund seines Originalgebäudes von Piano & Rogers – der modernen Architektur verbunden fühlt, bleibt der Louvre, trotz seiner Umgestaltung durch I. M. Pei, eher im Traditionellen verhaftet. SANAAs offener, heller Entwurf besteht in einer Ansammlung rechtwinkliger, leicht abgeschrägter Formen und hoher, großzügig verglaster Räume, die an das Museum für die Kunst des 21. Jahrhunderts (Kanazawa, Ishikawa, 2002–04) erinnern. Etwa 5500 m² des Neubaus dienen der Ausstellung von Kunstwerken. 600 bis 800 Werke aus dem Pariser Louvre werden als teilpermanente Ausstellung gezeigt. 1700 m² sind für Wechselausstellungen vorgesehen. Die Bauten stehen in einer weitläufigen Grünzone, die von der bekannten französischen Gartenarchitektin Catherine Mosbach gestaltet wurde.

Par une curieuse coïncidence, les deux principaux musées parisiens, le Centre Pompidou et le Louvre, se sont adressés à de célèbres architectes japonais pour créer leurs nouvelles extensions dans des régions françaises. Shigeru Ban travaille sur le projet du Centre Pompidou-Metz, et SANAA sur celui du Louvre-Lens. Si le Centre Pompidou possède une tradition de référence à l'architecture contemporaine, qui remonte à Piano & Rogers, le Louvre, malgré sa rénovation par I. M. Pei, a conservé une image plus traditionnelle. Le projet ouvert et lumineux de SANAA s'appuie sur un assemblage de formes rectangulaires légèrement décalées et de vastes volumes largement vitrés qui ne sont pas sans rappeler leur musée d'Art contemporain du XXIe siècle (Kanzawa, Ishikawa, 2002–04). Quelque 5500 mètres carrés de la nouvelle construction seront réservés à la présentation des œuvres. De six à huit cents pièces des collections du Louvre y seront présentées en dépôt semi-permanent. Mille sept cents mètres carrés seront consacrés à des expositions temporaires. Les bâtiments sont implantés dans un grand espace vert confié à la remarquable paysagiste française Catherine Mosbach.

Renderings of the Louvre-Lens (above) show the kind of geometric simplicity that the architects employed in their 21st-Century Museum of Contemporary Art in Kanazawa. Left, a site plan.

Die Renderings des Louvre-Lens (oben) zeigen die geometrische Schlichtheit, in der die Architekten auch ihr Museum für die Kunst des 21. Jahrhunderts in Kanazawa geplant haben. Links ein Lageplan.

Les perspectives du Louvre-Lens (ci-dessus) rappellent le type de simplicité géométrique déjà mis en œuvre par les architectes dans leur musée d'Art contemporain du XXIe siècle à Kanazawa. À gauche, plan du site.

SAUERBRUCH HUTTON

Sauerbruch Hutton
Lehrter Str. 57
10557 Berlin
Germany

Tel: +49 30 39 78 21 25
Fax: +49 30 39 78 21 30
E-mail: pr@sauerbruchhutton.com
Web: www.sauerbruchhutton.com

Matthias Sauerbruch was born in Constance, Germany, in 1955. After doing an apprenticeship as a draftsman (1975–77), he attended the University of Arts (HdK, Berlin, 1977–84) and then the Architectural Association (AA) in London (1982–84). After having graduated from both schools, he worked as project leader on the Housing at Checkpoint Charlie (Berlin, 1984–88) for OMA. Together with Louisa Hutton, he founded **SAUERBRUCH HUTTON** Architects in London in 1989. He is now director of Sauerbruch Hutton GmbH, based in Berlin since 1993. Louisa Hutton was born in 1957 in Norwich, England. She attended Bristol University (1976–80), and the AA, where she received her degree in 1985. She worked with A & P Smithson Architects (London, 1984–88) before joining Matthias Sauerbruch in founding their firm in 1989. Sauerbruch Hutton currently employs about 100 architects, designers, engineers, model makers, and administrative staff. This team is led by Matthias Sauerbruch, Louisa Hutton, and Juan Lucas Young. Recent and current work includes University Jessop West (Sheffield, UK, 2008); the Maciachini Center (Milan, Italy, 2010); the master plan for the southern entrance of Tilburg (The Netherlands, 2015); and the ADAC headquarters (Munich, Germany, 2012). Among winning competition entries are the Museum of Contemporary Art (Sydney, Australia, 2001), the BMW-Welt (Munich, Germany, 2001); and the Brandhorst Museum (Munich, Germany, competition 2002; 2005–08, published here).

Matthias Sauerbruch wurde 1955 in Konstanz geboren. Nach einer Lehre als Bauzeichner (1975–77) studierte er an der Hochschule der Künste HdK (Berlin, 1977–84) und 1982 bis 1984 an der Architectural Association (AA) in London. Nachdem er an beiden Schulen diplomiert worden war, arbeitete er als Projektleiter an einer Wohnanlage am Checkpoint Charlie (Berlin, 1984–88). 1989 gründete er zusammen mit Louisa Hutton in London **SAUERBRUCH HUTTON** Architects. Außerdem ist er Direktor der Sauerbruch Hutton GmbH, die seit 1993 ihren Sitz in Berlin hat. Louisa Hutton wurde 1957 in Norwich, England, geboren und studierte an der Bristol University (1976–80) und an der Architectural Association (AA), wo sie 1985 ihr Studium abschloss. Bevor sie mit Matthias Sauerbruch 1989 das Büro gründete, arbeitete sie bei A & P Smithson Architects (London, 1984–88). Sauerbruch Hutton beschäftigt zurzeit etwa 100 Architekten, Designer, Ingenieure, Modellbauer und Verwaltungsangestellte. Das Team wird von Matthias Sauerbruch, Louisa Hutton und Juan Lucas Young geleitet. Zu den neueren und aktuellen Werken des Büros zählen die Universität Jessop West (Sheffield, 2008), das Maciachini Center (Mailand, 2010), ein Masterplan für die Süderschließung der niederländischen Stadt Tilburg (2015) und die ADAC-Hauptverwaltung in München (2012). Zu ihren preisgekrönten Wettbewerbsentwürfen gehören das Museum of Contemporary Art (Sydney, Australien, 2001), die BMW-Welt in München (2001) sowie das Museum Brandhorst (München, Wettbewerb 2002, Ausführung 2005–08, hier veröffentlicht).

Matthias Sauerbruch est né en 1955 à Constance (Allemagne). Après un apprentissage de dessinateur (1975–77), il étudie à l'université des Arts HdK (Berlin, 1977–84), puis à l'Architectural Association (AA) de Londres, dont il sort diplômé (1982–84). Il travaille ensuite sur un projet d'immeubles de logements à Checkpoint Charlie (Berlin, 1984–88) pour OMA, avant de cofonder avec Louisa Hutton l'agence **SAUERBRUCH HUTTON** Architects en 1989 à Londres. Il dirige actuellement l'agence Sauerbruch Hutton GmbH, installée à Berlin depuis 1993. Louisa Hutton, née en 1957 à Norwich (Royaume-Uni), a étudié l'architecture à la Bristol University (1976–80) et à l'AA, dont elle est sortie diplômée en 1985. Elle travaille pour A & P Smithson Architects (Londres, 1984–88) avant de rejoindre Matthias Sauerbruch et de fonder ensemble leur agence en 1989. Sauerbruch Hutton emploie actuellement environ cent architectes, designers, ingénieurs, maquettistes et collaborateurs administratifs. Cette équipe est animée par Matthias Sauerbruch, Louisa Hutton et Juan Lucas Young. Parmi leurs réalisations récentes et en cours : l'université de Jessop West (Sheffield, Royaume-Uni, 2008) ; le centre Maciachini (Milan, Italie, 2010) ; un plan directeur pour l'entrée sud de la ville de Tilburg (Pays-Bas, 2015) ; le siège de l'ADAC (Munich, Allemagne, 2012). Ils ont remporté le concours pour le Museum of Contemporary Art (Sydney, Australie, 2001) ; le BMW-Welt (Munich, Allemagne, 2001) et le musée Brandhorst (Munich, concours 2002, 2005–08), publié ici.

BRANDHORST MUSEUM

Munich, Germany, 2005–08

Address: Theresienstr. 35a, 80333 Munich, Germany, +49 89 23805 2286, www.museum-brandhorst.de
Area: 3200 m² (exhibition space). Client: Freistaat Bayern. Cost: €48.15 million

The vertically oriented exterior cladding of the museum differentiates it
from its environment and emphasizes
its height.

Die vertikal ausgerichtete Außenver-
kleidung des Museums unterscheidet
es von seinem Umfeld und betont
seine Höhe.

L'habillage extérieur vertical du
musée le singularise par rapport à
son environnement et fait ressortir
sa hauteur.

The Brandhorst Museum is located on Türkenstraße in Munich, in the museum quarter that includes the Alte Pinakothek and other major cultural institutions. Its entrance is planned in symmetry to the southern entrance of the Pinakothek der Moderne. The project includes a longitudinal structure and main entrance building connected by a continuous strip window. There are three exhibition levels with ceiling heights of nine meters, with top-floor spaces of up to 450 square meters with natural overhead lighting and continuous translucent fabric ceilings. A foyer, café, bookshop, seminar rooms, administrative offices, storage, and workshops are included in the new project. The polygonally shaped gallery situated above the foyer was specially designed for the 12 paintings of Cy Twombly's *Lepanto Cycle*. All galleries on the ground floor have natural overhead lighting, which is projected into the spaces by a complex system of reflectors. A 460-square-meter, 7-meter-high central patio is located below grade with six smaller galleries for photography or works on paper. A black-box media suite of 240 square meters for video and electronic art complements these galleries. Energy-saving strategies have been used to reduce use of thermal energy by up to 50 percent and electricity consumption by 26 percent for an annual savings of EUR 70 000. The multi-layered polychromatic ceramic rod façade is "similar to a large, abstract painting."

Das Museum Brandhorst steht in München in der Türkenstraße, wo sich auch die Alte Pinakothek und andere große Kultureinrichtungen befinden. Sein Zugang liegt auf der Achse des Südeingangs zur Pinakothek der Moderne. Es besteht aus einem langgestreckten Gebäude und einem Haupteingangstrakt, die ein durchgehendes Fensterband miteinander verbindet. Das Museum hat drei Ausstellungsebenen mit einer Deckenhöhe von 9 m, im obersten Geschoss mit Räumen von bis zu 450 m², die von oben natürlich belichtet werden und mit durchgehenden, lichtdurchlässigen Textildecken versehen sind. Der Neubau enthält auch ein Foyer, ein Café, eine Buchhandlung, Seminarräume, Verwaltungsbüros, Lagerraum und Werkstätten. Der polygonale Ausstellungsraum über dem Foyer wurde speziell für die zwölf Gemälde von Cy Twomblys *Lepanto Cycle* geplant. Die Räume im Erdgeschoss haben natürliches Licht von oben, das durch ein kompliziertes System von Reflektoren in die Räume projiziert wird. Unter Geländeniveau liegt ein 460 m² großer, 7 m hoher, zentraler Patio mit sechs kleineren Ausstellungsräumen für Fotos oder Grafiken. Ein 240 m² großer Black-Box-Medienbereich für Video- und elektronische Kunst ergänzt diese Galerieräume. Durch Energiesparmaßnahmen können bis zu 50 % Heizungsenergie und bis zu 26 % Stromverbrauch eingespart werden, was die Kosten um jährlich 70 000 Euro senkt. Die mehrschichtige, vielfarbige Fassade aus Keramikstäben ähnelt „einem großen, abstrakten Gemälde".

Le musée Brandhorst se trouve dans la Türkenstraße à Munich, dans le quartier qui regroupe l'Alte Pinakothek et d'autres grandes institutions culturelles. Son entrée est symétrique à l'entrée sud de la Pinakothek der Moderne. Le projet comprend une construction allongée et un bâtiment servant d'entrée principale réunis par un bandeau vitré continu. Trois niveaux sont consacrés aux salles d'exposition qui peuvent atteindre 9 mètres de haut. Mesurant jusqu'à 450 mètres carrés, les salles du dernier niveau sont éclairées par des verrières zénithales sous lesquelles sont tendues des toiles translucides. Le nouveau projet est également doté d'un hall d'accueil, d'un café, d'une librairie, de salles de séminaires, de bureaux administratifs, de réserves et d'ateliers. La galerie polygonale au-dessus de ce hall a été spécialement dessinée pour accueillir douze toiles de Cy Twombly, le *Lepanto Cycle*. Toutes les salles du rez-de-chaussée reçoivent un éclairage naturel supplémentaire, projeté dans les volumes par un système complexe de réflecteurs. Un patio central de 460 mètres carrés et 7 mètres de haut en sous-sol est entouré de six petites galeries réservées à la photographie ou aux travaux sur papier. Une salle aveugle de 240 mètres carrés est destinée à la vidéo et à l'art électronique. Des mesures d'économie d'énergie ont été mises en œuvre pour réduire les besoins en chaleur de 50 % et en électricité de 26 %, ce qui représente des économies annuelles de 70 000 euros. Une composition en baguettes de céramique polychromes, « semblable à une vaste peinture abstraite », orne la façade.

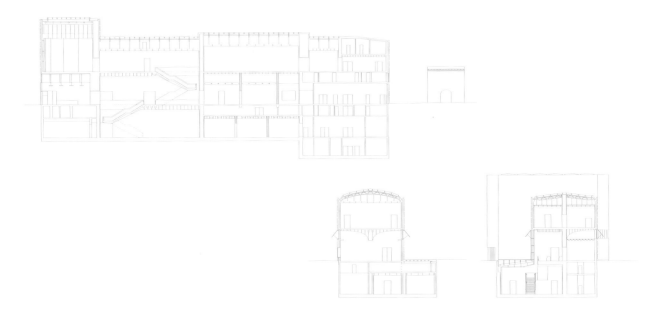

Elevations of the building (above) show its essentially rectangular disposition—with the main stairway visible left of center in the drawings and in the photo top right.

Die Ansichten des Gebäudes (oben) zeigen seine überwiegend rechtwinklige Ausrichtung – die Haupttreppe ist links von der Mitte auf den Zeichnungen und auf dem Foto rechts oben zu erkennen.

Les élévations (ci-dessus) montrent un plan de composition essentiellement rectangulaire. L'escalier principal (photo de droite) figure à gauche de la partie centrale des plans.

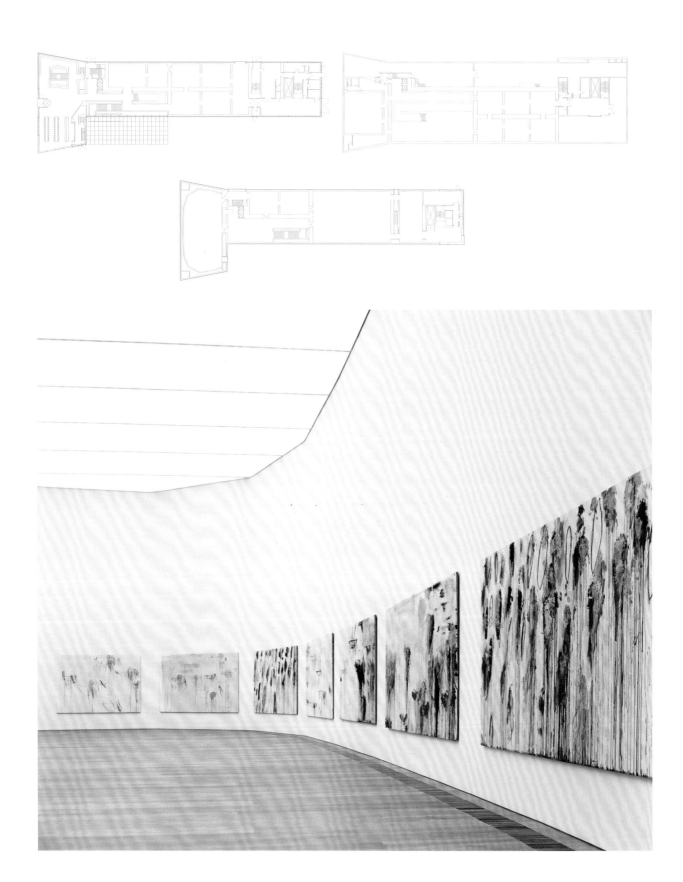

Generous exhibition spaces with overhead lighting are visible in the images on this double page, and in the floor plans above left.

Die großzügigen Ausstellungsräume mit Belichtung von oben sind auf den Abbildungen dieser Doppelseite und den Grundrissen links oben zu sehen.

Sur cette double page et dans les plans ci-dessus à gauche, les amples espaces du musée éclairé zénithalement.

HARTWIG N. SCHNEIDER

Hartwig N. Schneider
Birkenwaldstr. 54
70191 Stuttgart
Germany

Tel: +49 711 901 14 70
Fax: +49 711 90 11 47 11
E-mail: info@hartwigschneider.de
Web: www.hartwigschneider.de

HARTWIG N. SCHNEIDER was born in Stuttgart, Germany, in 1957, and studied architecture at the University of Stuttgart and at the Illinois Institute of Technology in Chicago (1977–84). He worked in the office of Norman Foster in London (1986–88). He created his office in Stuttgart with Gabriele Schneider in 1990. Their work includes the Birkenwaldstraße (Stuttgart, 2000–03); Kunsthalle Ernst-Sachs-Bad (Schweinfurt, 2006–08); Stihl Art Gallery and Art School Waiblingen (2007–08, published here); the Lude-Hopf House (Kornwestheim, 2008–09); and a Café and Gallery (Waiblingen, 2008–09), all in Germany.

HARTWIG N. SCHNEIDER wurde 1957 in Stuttgart geboren und studierte Architektur an der Universität Stuttgart sowie am Illinois Institute of Technology in Chicago (1977–84). Er arbeitete im Büro von Norman Foster in London (1986–88) und gründete 1990 mit Gabriele Schneider ein eigenes Büro in Stuttgart. Zu ihren ausgeführten Bauten zählen ein Haus in der Birkenwaldstraße (Stuttgart, 2000–03), die Kunsthalle Ernst-Sachs-Bad (Schweinfurt, 2006–08), die Kunstgalerie Stihl und Kunstschule (Waiblingen, 2007–08, hier veröffentlicht), das Haus Lude-Hopf (Kornwestheim, 2008–09) und ein Café mit Kunstgalerie (Waiblingen, 2008–09).

HARTWIG N. SCHNEIDER, né à Stuttgart (Allemagne) en 1957, a étudié l'architecture à l'université de cette ville et à l'Illinois Institute of Technology à Chicago (1977–84). Il a travaillé chez Norman Foster à Londres (1986–88) et a créé sa propre agence à Stuttgart avec Gabriele Schneider en 1990. Parmi leurs réalisations : Birkenwaldstraße (Stuttgart, 2000–03) ; la Kunsthalle Ernst-Sachs-Bad (Schweinfurt, 2006–08) ; la galerie d'art Stihl et l'école d'art de Waiblingen (Waiblingen, 2007–08) publiées ici ; la maison Lude-Hopf (Kornwestheim, 2008–09) et un café et une galerie à Waiblingen (Allemagne, 2008–09), le tout en Allemagne.

STIHL ART GALLERY
AND ART SCHOOL WAIBLINGEN

Waiblingen, Germany, 2007–08

Address: Weingärtner Vorstadt 12, 71332 Waiblingen, Germany, +49 7151 5001 666, www.galerie-stihl-waiblingen.de
Area: 1800 m². Client: City of Waiblingen. Cost: €6 million

The curving glass façades of the structure mark its modest height—though decidedly modern, it does not appear to be antithetic with its green surroundings.

Die gekrümmten Glasfassaden des Gebäudes zeigen seine bescheidene Höhe – obgleich entschieden modern, erscheint es dennoch im Einklang mit seiner grünen Umgebung.

Les façades de verre incurvées du bâtiment confirment la modestie de sa hauteur. Bien que résolument moderne, il ne paraît pas en conflit avec son cadre de verdure.

This project involves a new building for the city gallery of the southwestern German town of Waiblingen and the Unteres Remstal school of arts. It is intended as a "workshop for art and culture." It is located between the historical part of the city and the River Rems, outside the city walls. Set in a green area, the structures (gallery and school) had to be of moderate height and to be distinguished from each other while engaging in a mutual dialogue. The architect states: "Our intention was not to create an extravagant form, but to seek the natural integration of the construction in the sensitive area of the 'Remsaue' and the creation of new spatial reference lines and area edges. The free building forms resulting from these urban development vectors guide the movements and views of passersby." The city gallery rooms are at ground level, and participate in the formation of a museum square that relates back to the historical parts of the city.

Dieses Projekt umfasst Neubauten für die städtische Galerie der Stadt Waiblingen und für die Kunstschule Unteres Remstal. Sie sind als „Werkstatt für Kunst und Kultur" geplant und liegen außerhalb der Stadtmauern zwischen der historischen Altstadt und dem Flussbett der Rems. Die auf einer Grünfläche gelegenen Gebäude (Museum und Schule) sollten in der Höhe moderat und unterschiedlich gestaltet sein, doch einen spürbaren Dialog miteinander führen. Der Architekt erklärt dazu: „Wir hatten keine extravagante Form im Sinn, versuchten vielmehr, die Anlage natürlich in den sensiblen Bereich der ‚Remsaue' einzufügen sowie neue räumliche Bezugslinien und Randbereiche zu schaffen. Die freien Architekturformen, die das Ergebnis dieser städtebaulichen Zielsetzung sind, leiten die Bewegung und den Blick der Passanten." Die Ausstellungsräume der städtischen Galerie liegen im Erdgeschoss und folgen der Form eines Quadrats, das auf den historischen Bereich der Stadt Bezug nimmt.

Situé dans un espace vert entre le cœur historique de Waiblingen (Allemagne du Sud) et la rivière Rems, hors des remparts, ce projet regroupe un nouveau bâtiment pour la galerie municipale et la nouvelle école d'art d'Unteres Remstal. Il se veut « un atelier pour l'art et la culture ». Les bâtiments (galerie et école) devaient être de hauteur modérée et se distinguer l'un de l'autre tout en entretenant un dialogue formel. « Notre intention n'était pas de créer une forme extravagante, mais de rechercher l'intégration naturelle de la construction dans cette zone sensible du *Remsaue* et la création de nouveaux axes de références spatiales et de limites. Les formes libres résultant de ces vecteurs de développement urbain orientent les déplacements et la vision des passants », commente l'architecte. Au rez-de-chaussée, les salles de la galerie municipale participent à la mise en forme de la place du musée qui renvoie aux éléments historiques de la ville ancienne.

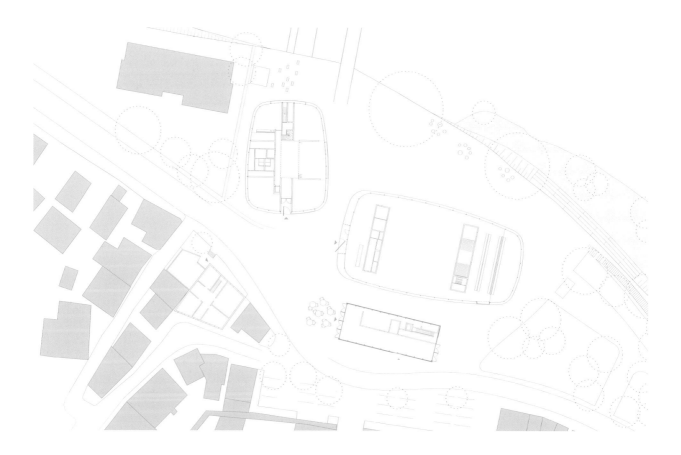

The freestanding structures, one housing a school and the other the museum, can be seen in the site plan above and in the images to the right.

Die freistehenden Bauten, von denen einer eine Kunstschule und der andere das Museum enthält, sind auf dem Lageplan oben und auf den Abbildungen rechts zu sehen.

Les structures indépendantes – l'une abritant une école, l'autre le musée – sont visibles sur le plan ci-dessus et sur les images de droite.

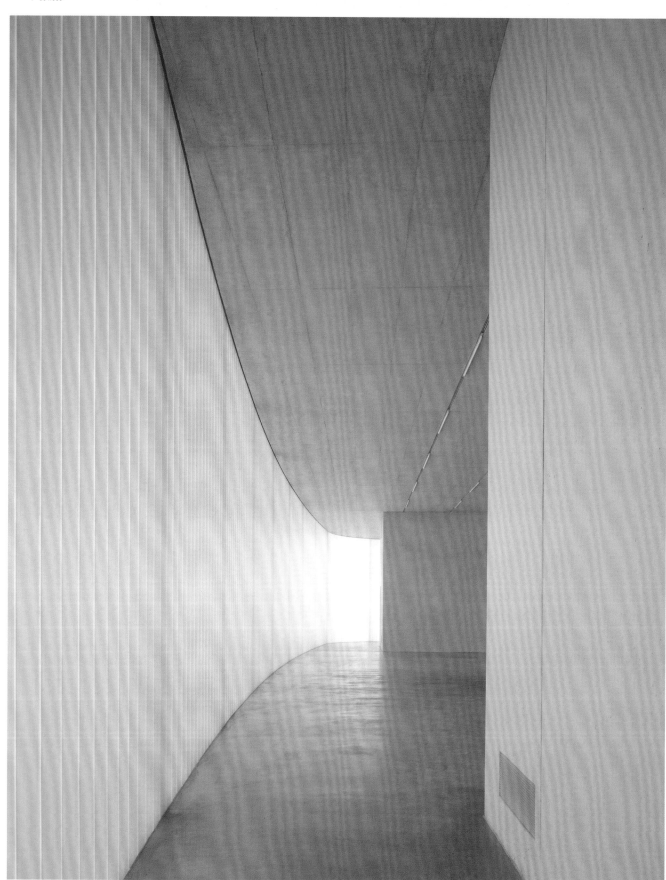

The interior of the museum is marked by the curving wall of light that forms the outside shell. The simplicity of the exterior is echoed in these interior images.

Der Innenraum des Museums wird von der gekrummten Wand aus Licht bestimmt, welche die Außenhülle bildet. Die Schlichtheit des äußeren Erscheinungsbilds kennzeichnet auch diese Innenansichten.

L'intérieur du musée se caractérise par un mur lumincux incurvé qui constitue la coque extérieure. La simplicité de l'extérieur se retrouve dans ces images de l'intérieur.

ÁLVARO SIZA VIEIRA
AND RUDOLF FINSTERWALDER

Álvaro Siza Arquitecto, Lda
Rua do Aleixo 53 2 / 4150–043 Porto / Portugal
Tel: +351 226 16 72 70 / Fax: +351 226 16 72 79
E-mail: siza@mail.telepac.pt

Finsterwalder Architekten
Finsterwalderstr. 5 / 83071 Stephanskirchen / Germany
Tel: +49 8031 900 83 54 / Fax: +49 8031 900 83 55
E-mail: mail@finsterwalderarchitekten.com
Web: www.finsterwalderarchitekten.com

Born in Matosinhos, Portugal, in 1933, **ÁLVARO SIZA** studied at the University of Porto School of Architecture (1949–55). He created his own practice in 1954, and worked with Fernando Tavora from 1955 to 1958. He has been a Professor of Construction at the University of Porto since 1976. He received the European Community's Mies van der Rohe Prize in 1988 and the Pritzker Prize in 1992. He has built many small-scale projects in Portugal, and has worked on the restructuring of the Chiado (Lisbon, Portugal, 1989–); the Meteorology Center (Barcelona, Spain, 1989–92); the Vitra Furniture Factory (Weil am Rhein, Germany, 1991–94); the Porto School of Architecture (Porto University, Portugal, 1986–95); and the University of Aveiro Library (Aveiro, Portugal, 1988–95). More recent projects include the Portuguese Pavilion for the Expo '98 in Lisbon; the Serralves Foundation (Porto, 1998); and the Aldega Mayor Winery, Argamassas Estate, Campo Maior (2005–06), all in Portugal. He designed the 2005 Serpentine Pavilion (London) with Eduardo Souto de Moura. His Museum for the Iberê Camargo Foundation in Porto Alegre, Brazil, opened in 2008. Siza collaborated with **RUDOLF FINSTERWALDER** on the Hombroich Museum (Neuss-Hombroich, Germany, 2006–08, published here). Finsterwalder was born in Rosenheim, Germany, in 1966. He studied architecture at the Technical University in Berlin (1992–96) while working in Siza's office in Porto (1994–96).

Der 1933 im portugiesischen Matosinhos geborene **ÁLVARO SIZA** studierte Architektur an der Universität Porto (1949–55). 1954 gründete er sein eigenes Büro und arbeitete von 1955 bis 1958 zusammen mit Fernando Tavora. Ab 1976 war er Professor für Baukonstruktion an der Universität Porto. Er erhielt 1988 den Mies-van-der-Rohe-Preis der Europäischen Gemeinschaft und 1992 den Pritzker-Preis. Siza hat viele kleinere Projekte in Portugal ausgeführt sowie die Umstrukturierung des Chiado (Lissabon, 1989–), das Centro Meteorológico (Barcelona, 1989–92), die Möbelfabrik Vitra (Weil am Rhein, 1991–94), die Architekturschule Porto (Universität Porto, 1986–95) und die Universitätsbibliothek Aveiro (Portugal,1988–95). Zu seinen neueren Werken zählen der portugiesische Pavillon für die Expo '98 in Lissabon, die Stiftung Serralves (Porto, 1998) und das Weingut Aldega Mayor, Gut Argamassas, Campo Maior (2005–06), alle in Portugal. 2005 plante er mit Eduardo Souto de Moura den Serpentine Pavilion (London). Sein Museum für die Stiftung Iberê Camargo in Porto Alegre, Brasilien, wurde 2008 eröffnet. Das hier veröffentlichte Museum Hombroich (Neuss-Hombroich, 2006–08) ist das Ergebnis einer Zusammenarbeit mit **RUDOLF FINSTERWALDER**. Finsterwalder wurde 1966 in Rosenheim geboren und studierte Architektur an der Technischen Universität Berlin (1992–96). Gleichzeitig arbeitete er im Büro von Álvaro Siza in Porto (1994–96).

Né à Matosinhos (Portugal) en 1933, **ÁLVARO SIZA** a étudié à l'École d'architecture de l'université de Porto (1949–55). Il a créé son agence en 1954 et travaillé avec Fernando Tavora de 1955 à 1958. Il est professeur de construction à l'université de Porto depuis 1976. Il a reçu le prix Mies van der Rohe de la Communauté européenne en 1988 et le prix Pritzker en 1992. Il a réalisé beaucoup de projets de petites dimensions au Portugal et est intervenu sur la restructuration du quartier du Chiado (Lisbonne, 1989–). Il a construit le Centre de météorologie (Barcelone, 1989–92) ; l'usine de meubles Vitra (Weil am Rhein, Allemagne, 1991–94) ; l'École d'architecture de Porto (université de Porto, 1986–95) et la bibliothèque de l'université d'Aveiro (Aveiro, Portugal, 1988–95). Parmi ses projets plus récents : le Pavillon portugais pour l'Expo '98 à Lisbonne ; la Fondation Serralves (Porto, 1998) ; et le chais Aldega Mayor (domaine d'Argamassas, Campo Maior, 2005–06), tous au Portugal. Il a conçu le Serpentine Pavilion 2005 à Londres en collaboration avec Eduardo Souto de Moura, et le musée pour la Fondation Iberê Camargo à Porto Alegre (Brésil, 2008). Le musée Hombroich (Neuss-Hombroich, Allemagne, 2006–08), publié ici, est né d'une collaboration entre Álvaro Siza et **RUDOLF FINSTERWALDER**. Finsterwalder, né à Rosenheim (Allemagne) en 1966, a étudié l'architecture à l'université polytechnique de Berlin (1992–96), tout en travaillant chez Álvaro Siza à Porto (1994–96).

HOMBROICH MUSEUM

Neuss-Hombroich, Germany, 2006–08

Address: Minkel 2, 41472 Neuss-Holzheim, Germany, +49 2182 2094, www.inselhombroich.de
Area: 656 m². Client: Stiftung Insel Hombroich. Cost: €1.161 million
Collaboration: Álvaro Siza with Rudolf Finsterwalder

Located with other exhibition buildings on the grounds of a former rocket base on Hombroich Island, only the roof of this structure is visible from any distance. The exhibition rooms are distributed around a patio, and the building itself has irregular brick façades that recall those of others on the island. Fairly low windows and rooms contribute to the earthy feel of the building, which has oak floors. The facility is to be used as a museum for architectural models and drawings, most of which relate to the other projects on the island. An important photographic archive will also be housed here and displayed. As is often the case in Siza's work, this new museum building is deceptively simple in its design and organization. Everything is in the subtle details and in the ways in which views are framed and simplicity attained.

Dieses Gebäude befindet sich neben anderen auf dem Gelände der Stiftung Insel Hombroich, zu dem auch eine ehemalige Raketenstation gehört. Von dem Museum ist von überallher nur das Dach zu sehen. Die Ausstellungsräume sind um einen Innenhof angeordnet; das Gebäude hat unregelmäßige Backsteinfassaden, die mit der Bauweise auf dem Gelände harmonieren. Relativ niedrige Fenster und Räume betonen die erdgebundene Wirkung des Gebäudes mit Böden aus Eichenholz. Es handelt sich um ein Museum für Architekturmodelle und -zeichnungen, größtenteils von anderen Bauten der Stiftung Insel Hombroich. Auch ein bedeutendes Fotoarchiv wird hier untergebracht und ausgestellt werden. Wie die meisten von Sizas Bauten ist auch dieser täuschend einfach in seiner Form und Organisation. Die Besonderheit liegt in den subtilen Details und in der Art, wie die Ausblicke eingefasst sind und die Schlichtheit erzielt wurde.

Cette structure est située, ainsi que d'autres bâtiments d'exposition, sur le terrain d'une ancienne base de lancement de fusées de l'île d'Hombroich. Vue de loin, elle n'est perceptible que par sa toiture. Les salles d'exposition sont distribuées autour d'un patio et le bâtiment présente des façades en brique de pose irrégulière qui rappellent certaines constructions de l'île. Les salles et baies de hauteur relativement faible contribuent à donner un aspect tellurique à ce bâtiment dont les sols sont en chêne. Le musée est consacré à des dessins et maquettes d'architecture, essentiellement liés aux autres projets réalisés sur l'île. Des archives photographiques importantes seront également exposées et conservées. Comme c'est souvent le cas chez Siza, ce nouveau musée paraît trompeusement simple dans sa conception et son organisation. Tout réside dans les détails subtils et la façon dont les vues sont cadrées dans un esprit de très grande pureté.

The long, low, rectangular volumes of the structure assume a modesty that is uncommon in the area of contemporary art museums, an impression that is heightened by the irregular brick patterning of the façades.

Die langen, niedrigen, rechtwinkligen Volumen des Gebäudes zeugen von einer Bescheidenheit, die im Bereich der Museen für zeitgenössische Kunst ungewöhnlich ist – ein Eindruck, der durch die ungleichmäßige Struktur der Backsteinfassaden verstärkt wird.

Les volumes rectangulaires allongés du bâtiment assument une modestie assez rare dans le domaine de l'architecture contemporaine des musées, impression renforcée par le motif irrégulier des façades en brique.

The museum almost resembles a private residence in its scale and style. This type of modernity is, however, quite typical of the designs of Álvaro Siza—working in this instance with Rudolf Finsterwalder.

Das Museum ähnelt in Maßstab und Stil eher einem privaten Wohnhaus. Diese Form der Modernität ist jedoch typisch für die Architektur von Álvaro Siza – in diesem Fall in Zusammenarbeit mit Rudolf Finsterwalder.

Par son échelle et son style, ce musée ressemble presque à une résidence privée. Ce type de modernité est cependant assez typique des projets d'Álvaro Siza, ici en collaboration avec Rudolf Finsterwalder.

The interior volumes of the museum, announced in some sense by the large, glazed opening seen to the right, are visible in the image below.

Die Innenräume des Museums, gewissermaßen angekündigt durch die große, verglaste Öffnung auf dem Foto rechts, sind auf der Abbildung unten zu sehen.

Ci-dessous, les volumes intérieurs du musée, préfigurés en quelque sorte par les vastes ouvertures vitrées (à droite).

SNØHETTA

Snøhetta AS
Skur 39, Vippetangen / 0150 Oslo / Norway
Tel: +47 24 15 60 60 / Fax: +47 24 15 60 61
E-mail: contact@snohetta.com / Web: www.snohetta.com

SNØHETTA is a mountain in central Norway. It is a key theme in early Viking sagas and is the mythical home of Valhalla. Henrik Ibsen developed the story of *Peer Gynt* around Snøhetta, which gave its name to the architectural practice founded in 1987 in Oslo. Directed by two majority owners, Kjetil Trædal Thorsen and Craig Dykers, and four minority partners, Snøhetta has a staff of 92 employees: 54 architects, 11 interior architects, 15 landscape architects, and administration. Aside from the Alexandria Library completed in 2002 (Alexandria, Egypt), Snøhetta won an anonymous, open international competition for the New National Opera house in Oslo (Norway, 2003–08). Other work of the firm includes the Lillehammer Art Museum, the centerpiece cultural building for the 1994 Winter Olympics in Norway; the Skistua School (Skistua, Narvik, 1998); the Karmøy Fishing Museum (Karmøy, 1999); Hamar Town Hall (Hamar, 2000); and the Petter Dass Museum (Alstahaug, Sandnessjøen, Nordland, 2001–07, published here), all in Norway. Kjetil Thorsen designed the 2007 Serpentine Pavilion in London with Olafur Eliasson. The firm's New York office is working on the National September 11 Memorial Museum Pavilion on Ground Zero (New York, 2012). Snøhetta was selected in 2007 to create an iconic gateway building for the new capital city of Ras Al-Khaimah in the United Arab Emirates. This 300 000-square-meter complex will contain a Congress Center, Exhibition Halls, Shopping Center, and three luxury hotels. The office is also working on the King Abdulaziz Center for Knowledge and Culture in Dhahran, Saudi Arabia. The client is Saudi Aramco Oil Company. The center contains some 45 000 square meters of diverse cultural facilities, including an auditorium, cinema, library, exhibition hall, museum, and archive (2009–11).

SNØHETTA ist ein Berg in der Mitte Norwegens und ein zentrales Thema der frühen Wikingersagen; er gilt als der sagenhafte Ort Walhalla. Henrik Ibsen schrieb die Geschichte von *Peer Gynt* um Snøhetta, der dem 1987 in Oslo gegründeten Architekturbüro seinen Namen gab. Die von den Haupteignern Kjetil Trædal Thorsen und Craig Dykers sowie vier weiteren Partnern geleitete Firma hat 92 Beschäftigte, unter ihnen 54 Architekten, 11 Innenarchitekten, 15 Landschaftsarchitekten sowie Verwaltungsangestellte. Außer dem Wettbewerb für die 2002 fertiggestellte Bibliotheca Alexandrina (Alexandria, Ägypten) hat Snøhetta einen anonymen, offenen internationalen Wettbewerb für die neue Staatsoper in Oslo (Norwegen, 2003–08) gewonnen. Zu weiteren Werken des Büros zählen das Kunstmuseum Lillehammer, das zentrale Kulturgebäude für die Olympischen Winterspiele 1994 in Norwegen, eine Schule in Skistua (Skistua, Narvik, 1998), das Fischereimuseum Karmøy (Karmøy, 1999), die Stadthalle Hamar (Hamar, 2000) und das Museum Petter Dass (Alstahaug, Sandnessjøen, Nordland, 2001–07, hier veröffentlicht), alle in Norwegen. Kjetil Thorsen entwarf 2007 den Serpentine Pavilion in London mit Olafur Eliasson. Das New Yorker Büro der Firma arbeitet derzeit am National September 11 Memorial Museum Pavilion auf dem Ground Zero in New York (2012). 2007 wurde Snøhetta beauftragt, einen eindrucksvollen Torbau für die neue Hauptstadt von Ras Al-Khaimah in den Vereinigten Arabischen Emiraten zu entwerfen. Dieser 300 000 m² große Komplex wird ein Kongresszentrum, Ausstellungshallen und drei Luxushotels enthalten. Daneben arbeitet das Büro am König-Abdulasis-Zentrum für Wissenschaft und Kultur in Dhahran, Saudi-Arabien. Bauherr ist die Saudi Aramco Oil Company. Das Kulturzentrum umfasst etwa 45 000 m² für kulturelle Einrichtungen wie ein Auditorium, Kino, Bibliothek, Ausstellungshalle, Museum und Archiv (2009–11).

SNØHETTA est le nom d'une montagne du centre de la Norvège qui serait le mythique Valhalla des sagas vikings. Henrik Ibsen l'a mise en scène dans *Peer Gynt*. C'est aujourd'hui également le nom d'une agence d'architecture fondée en 1987 à Oslo. Dirigée par deux associés majoritaires, Kjetil Trædal Thorsen et Craig Dykers, et quatre autres associés, Snøhetta emploie 92 employés, soit 54 architectes, 15 architectes paysagistes, 11 architectes d'intérieur et du personnel administratif. En dehors de la Bibliothèque d'Alexandrie (Égypte) achevée en 2002, l'agence a remporté un concours international anonyme ouvert pour le nouvel Opéra d'Oslo (2003–08). Parmi ses autres réalisations, toutes en Norvège : le musée d'Art de Lillehammer, principal équipement culturel des Jeux olympiques d'hiver 1994 ; l'école de Skistua (Skistua, Narvik, 1998) ; le musée de la Pêche de Karmøy (1999) ; l'hôtel de ville de Hamar (2000) et le musée Petter Dass (Alstahaug, Sandnessjøen, Nordland, 2001–07), publié ici. Kjetil Thorsen a conçu en collaboration avec Olafur Eliasson le pavillon Serpentine à Londres en 2007. L'agence de New York travaille sur le projet du pavillon du musée du Mémorial national du 11 Septembre (New York, 2012). Snøhetta a été sélectionnée en 2007 pour concevoir un immeuble qui sera une porte d'entrée monumentale pour la nouvelle capitale de l'émirat de Ras Al-Khaimah (EAU). Ce complexe de 300 000 mètres carrés contiendra un centre de congrès, des halls d'exposition, un centre commercial et trois hôtels de luxe. L'agence travaille également sur le King Abdulaziz Center for Knowledge and Culture à Dhahran (Arabie saoudite). Le commanditaire est la Saudi Aramco Oil Company. Ce centre culturel comprend quelque 45 000 mètres carrés d'espaces culturels équipés diversement, incluant un auditorium, un cinéma, une bibliothèque, un hall d'exposition, un musée, et une salle d'archives (2009–11).

PETTER DASS MUSEUM

Alstahaug, Sandnessjøen, Nordland, Norway, 2001–07

Address: Alstahaug, 8800 Sandnessjøen, Norway, +47 75110150, www.petterdass.no
Area: 1350 m². Client: KF Petter Dass Eindom. Cost: €7.5 million

Alstahaug is a municipality with a population of about 7500 people located in the Nordland county of Norway, on the west coast facing the Norwegian Sea. This project involves a new museum building, landscape plan for the site, parking areas, and a service building. Petter Dass (1637–1707) was one of Norway's best-known poets and also the vicar of Alstahaug Church. Because of the sensitive nature of the site near the church, the architects decided to make a cut in the landscape and into this insert the volume of the museum: 11.5 meters wide, set between two 70-meter rock walls. The roof of the museum is intended to blend in with the terrain, and large glass surfaces at either end allow views of the church on one side and the sky on the other.

Alstahaug ist eine Gemeinde mit etwa 7500 Einwohnern in der norwegischen Provinz Nordland an der Westküste des europäischen Nordmeers. Dieses Projekt umfasst einen Museumsneubau, den Landschaftsplan für das Gelände, einen Autoparkplatz und ein Versorgungsgebäude. Petter Dass (1637–1707) war einer der bekanntesten norwegischen Dichter und Pfarrer an der Kirche von Alstahaug. Wegen der sensiblen Natur des Bauplatzes neben der Kirche beschlossen die Architekten, in die Landschaft einzuschneiden und das Bauvolumen des Museums – mit 11,5 m Breite zwischen zwei 70 m langen Felswänden – in diesen Einschnitt einzusetzen. Das Dach des Gebäudes soll sich in das Gelände einfügen; große Glasflächen an beiden Enden bieten auf einer Seite Ausblick zur Kirche, auf der anderen zum Himmel.

Alstahaug est une ville de 7500 habitants du comté du Nordland, sur la côte ouest de la mer de Norvège. Ce projet comprend un nouveau bâtiment pour le musée, un aménagement paysager pour le site, des parkings et un bâtiment de services. Petter Dass (1637–1707), un des plus célèbres poètes norvégiens, fut l'un des vicaires de la paroisse d'Alstahaug. Du fait de la nature sensible de ce site près de l'église, les architectes ont pratiqué une découpe dans le sol de 11,5 mètres de large, entre deux murs de roche de 70 mètres de long, pour y insérer le volume du musée. La toiture se fond avec le terrain et les vastes plans vitrés des deux extrémités donnent sur l'église d'un côté, et le ciel de l'autre.

The modern form of the building stands out next to the Alstahaug Church seen on the left page.

Die moderne Form des Gebäudes hebt sich von der benachbarten Kirche Alstahaug ab, die auf der linken Seite zu sehen ist.

La forme moderne du bâtiment contraste avec celle de l'église d'Alstahaug, visible sur la page de gauche.

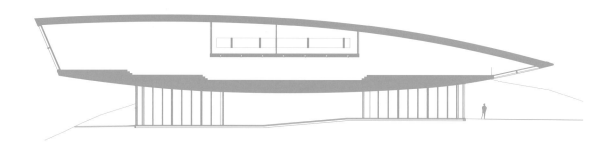

The slightly curving roof of the building finishes in a point at one end and in a large angled window at the other.

Das leicht gekrümmte Dach des Gebäudes endet auf einer Seite in einer Spitze und auf der anderen in einem großen, schrägen Fenster.

La toiture légèrement incurvée du musée se termine en pointe d'un côté et par une vaste baie vitrée de l'autre.

The museum looks out onto the water through its main angled window.

Durch das große, schräge Fenster ist das Museum zum Wasser orientiert.

Le musée s'ouvre sur le panorama de la rivière par une grande baie vitrée.

EDUARDO SOUTO DE MOURA

Souto Moura Arquitectos Lda
R. do Aleixo, 531° A
4150–043 Porto
Portugal

Tel: +351 226 18 75 47
Fax: +351 226 10 80 92
E-mail: souto.moura@mail.telepac.pt

EDUARDO SOUTO DE MOURA was born in Porto, Portugal, in 1952. He graduated from the School of Architecture of Porto (ESBAP) in 1980. He was an Assistant Professor at the Faculty of Architecture in Porto (FAUP) from 1981 to 1991. He worked in the office of Álvaro Siza from 1974 to 1979 and created his own office the following year. His work includes row houses in the Rua Lugarinho (Porto, Portugal, 1996); the renovation of the Municipal Market in Braga (Portugal, 1997); the Silo Norte Shopping Building; a house and wine cellar (Valladolid, Spain, 1999); and the project for the Portuguese Pavilion, Expo Hanover (with Álvaro Siza, 1999). More recent work includes the conversion of the building of the Carvoeira da Foz (Porto); two houses at Ponte de Lima (2002); and the Braga Stadium (2004). He was co-author of the Serpentine Pavilion 2005 in London with Álvaro Siza and completed the Bragança Contemporary Art Museum (Bragança, Portugal, published here) in 2008.

EDUARDO SOUTO DE MOURA wurde 1952 in Porto, Portugal, geboren und beendete 1980 sein Studium an der Architekturabteilung der Universidade do Porto (ESBAP). Von 1981 bis 1991 war er Lehrbeauftragter an der Architekturfakultät von Porto (FAUP). Von 1974 bis 1979 arbeitete er im Büro von Álvaro Siza und gründete im darauffolgenden Jahr seine eigene Firma. Zu seinen ausgeführten Bauten zählen Reihenhäuser in der Rua Lugarinho (Porto, 1996), die Sanierung der städtischen Markthalle in Braga (Portugal, 1997), das Geschäft Silo Norte, ein Wohnhaus mit Weinkellerei (Valladolid, Spanien, 1999) und der portugiesische Pavillon auf der Expo 2000 in Hannover (mit Álvaro Siza, 1999). Zu seinen neueren Werken gehören der Umbau des Gebäudes der Carvoeira da Foz (Porto), zwei Wohnhäuser in Ponte de Lima (2002) und das Stadion von Braga (2004). Mit Álvaro Siza plante er 2005 den Serpentine Pavilion in London, und 2008 baute er das Museu de Arte Contemporanea in Bragança (Portugal, 2002–08, hier veröffentlicht).

EDUARDO SOUTO DE MOURA, né à Porto (Portugal) en 1952, est diplômé de l'École d'architecture de Porto (ESBAP, 1980). Il a été professeur assistant à la Faculté d'architecture de Porto (FAUP) de 1981 à 1991. Il a travaillé dans l'agence d'Álvaro Siza de 1974 à 1979 et a créé sa propre structure l'année suivante. Son œuvre comprend : des maisons en bande dans la Rua Lugarinho (Porto, Portugal,1996) ; la rénovation du marché municipal de Braga (Portugal, 1997) ; le centre commercial Silo Norte ; une maison et un chais (Valladolid, Espagne, 1999) et le Pavillon portugais pour Expo Hanover (avec Álvaro Siza, 1999). Plus récemment, il a construit les immeubles de logements Carvoeira da Foz (Porto) ; deux maisons à Ponte de Lima (2002) et le stade de Braga (2004). Il a été co-auteur du pavillon Serpentine de 2005 à Londres avec Álvaro Siza et a achevé le musée d'Art contemporain de Bragance (Portugal, 2002–08), publié ici.

BRAGANÇA CONTEMPORARY ART MUSEUM

Bragança, Portugal, 2002–08

Rua Abílio Beça 105, 5300 – 011 Bragança, Portugal, +351 273 302 410, http://centroartegracamorais.cm-braganca.pt
Area: 240 m² (temporary exhibitions). Client: Bragança City Hall. Cost: not disclosed
Team: Joaquim Portela, Teresa Fonseca, Tiago Coelho, Jorge Domingues, Maria Vasconcelos,
Diogo Machado Lima, Ana Fortuna, Cândida Corrêa de Sá, Patrícia Diogo, Cátia Bernardo,
Ricardo Prata, Susana Monteiro

The new building designed by Eduardo Souto de Moura has a 240-square-meter temporary exhibition space with ceilings 8.3 meters high, capable of meeting all international standards for art. The project also involved the rehabilitation of the former Banco de Portugal building for a library, reception area, and restaurant on the ground floor, and permanent exhibition space on the upper level. These two buildings are connected by another new volume, where educational service, administrative, and technical spaces are located. Materials were defined to a good extent by local zoning restrictions on urban requalification operations, but the architect has managed to create a strikingly modern volume, faithful to his own style, which often surprises by its audacity.

Dieses neue, von Eduardo Souto de Moura geplante Gebäude hat einen 240 m² großen Raum mit 8,30 m hohen Wänden für Wechselausstellungen, der alle internationalen Standards für Kunst erfüllt. Das Projekt umfasst auch die Umnutzung des früheren Gebäudes der Banco de Portugal zu einer Bibliothek, einem Empfangsbereich und einem Restaurant im Erdgeschoss sowie Raum für eine ständige Ausstellung im Obergeschoss. Diese beide Bauten sind durch einen weiteren neuen Trakt miteinander verbunden, der Räume für Unterricht, Verwaltung und Technik enthält. Die Materialien waren zum Großteil durch die örtlichen Bauvorschriften für städtebauliche Sanierungsmaßnahmen vorgegeben, aber dem Architekten ist dennoch ein eindrucksvolles, modernes Gebäude gelungen, das seinem Stil treu geblieben ist und immer wieder durch seine Kühnheit überrascht.

Cette nouvelle réalisation d'Eduardo Souto de Moura est dotée d'un espace d'exposition de 240 mètres carrés sur 8,3 mètres de haut qui répond à tous les critères internationaux de présentation des œuvres d'art. Le projet couvrait également la restructuration de l'ancien immeuble du Banco de Portugal en bibliothèque, hall de réception et restaurant au rez-de-chaussée, et espace d'expositions permanentes à l'étage. Les deux bâtiments sont reliés par un nouveau volume où sont installés les services éducatifs de l'administration et les départements techniques. Les matériaux ont été déterminés en grande partie par la réglementation locale sur les opérations de requalification urbaine, mais l'architecte a cependant réussi à créer un volume éminemment moderne, fidèle à son style personnel, qui surprend toujours par son audace.

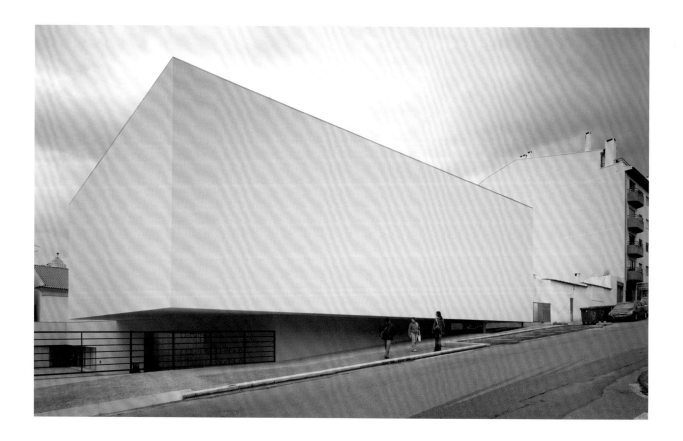

The main volume of the museum appears to hover over its much smaller base, with an overall scale that permits it to be well integrated into its surroundings, as the images and the elevation and section drawings below show.

Die große Masse des Museums scheint über seiner viel kleineren Basis zu schweben. In der Gesamtgröße fügt es sich gut in seine Umgebung ein, wie die Abbildungen sowie die Ansicht und der Schnitt darunter zeigen.

Le volume principal du musée semble suspendu au-dessus d'une base de dimensions beaucoup plus réduites. Son échelle lui permet de bien s'intégrer au quartier, comme le montrent les photographies, l'élévation et la coupe ci-dessous.

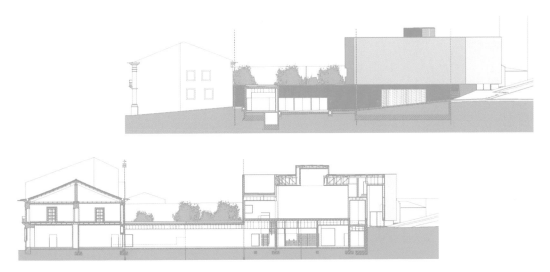

Eduardo Souto de Moura shares the modern sensibilities of his colleague Álvaro Siza. Light enters both from above and below the space visible in the image to the left.

Eduardo Souto de Moura pflegt den gleichen sensiblen Umgang mit der Moderne wie sein Kollege Álvaro Siza. Das Licht fällt von oben und unten in den Raum auf dem Bild links.

Eduardo Souto de Moura partage avec Álvaro Siza la même sensibilité moderniste. Dans ce passage (page de gauche), la lumière pénètre à la fois par le plafond et par le bas des murs.

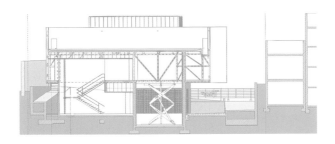

SSM ARCHITEKTEN

SSM Architekten AG
Gibelinstr. 2
4503 Solothurn
Switzerland

Tel: +41 32 625 24 44
Fax: +41 32 625 24 45
E-mail: mail@ssmarchitekten.ch
Web: www.ssmarchitekten.ch

SSM was established by Jürg Stäuble, Theo Schnider, and Reto Mosimann in 2007 in Solothurn, Switzerland. Jürg Stäuble was born in 1957, and graduated from the Biel University of Applied Sciences in architecture (1981). Before the creation of SSM, he founded Jürg Stäuble Architects in 1985. Theo Schnider was born in 1963. He graduated from the Swiss Federal Institute of Technology Lausanne (EPFL) in architecture in 1993, and established Theo Schnider Architect in 1995. Reto Mosimann was born in 1973, and graduated from the Burgdorf University of Applied Sciences in architecture in 1999. Their most recent work includes an apartment building (Solothurn, 2006); single-family houses in Solothurn, Feldbrunnen, and Oberdorf (2008); an old people's home (Biberist, 2008); and the Grenchen Art Museum Extension (Grenchen, 2007–08, published here), all in Switzerland.

Das Büro **SSM** wurde 2007 von Jürg Stäuble, Theo Schnider und Reto Mosimann in Solothurn, Schweiz, gegründet. Jürg Stäuble wurde 1957 geboren und studierte bis 1981 Architektur an der Hochschule für Angewandte Wissenschaften in Biel. Vor der Gründung von SSM betrieb er ab 1985 das Büro Jürg Stäuble Architects. Theo Schnider wurde 1963 geboren, beendete 1993 sein Architekturstudium an der Hochschule für Technik in Lausanne (EPFL) und gründete 1995 das Architekturbüro Theo Schnider. Reto Mosimann wurde 1973 geboren und beendete 1999 sein Architekturstudium an der Hochschule für Angewandte Wissenschaften in Burgdorf. Zu ihren neueren Bauten zählen ein Apartmentgebäude (Solothurn, 2006), Einfamilienhäuser in Solothurn, Feldbrunnen und Oberdorf (2008), ein Altenheim (Biberist, 2008) und die Erweiterung des Kunsthauses Grenchen (Grenchen, 2007–08, hier veröffentlicht), alle in der Schweiz.

L'agence **SSM** a été fondée par Jürg Stäuble, Theo Schnider et Reto Mosimann en 2007 à Solothurn (Suisse). Jürg Stäuble, né en 1957, est diplômé en architecture de l'université des sciences appliquées de Bienne (1981). Avant SSM, il avait créé l'agence Jürg Stäuble Architects en 1985. Theo Schnider, né en 1963, est diplômé en architecture de l'École Polytechnique Fédérale de Lausanne (EPFL) en 1993, et avait créé l'agence Theo Schnider Architect en 1995. Reto Mosimann, né en 1973, est diplômé en architecture de l'université des sciences appliquées de Burgdorf en 1999. Leurs interventions les plus récentes, toutes en Suisse, comprennent : un immeuble d'appartements (Solothurn, 2006) ; des maisons monofamiliales à Solothurn, Feldbrunnen et Oberdorf (2008) ; une maison de retraite (Biberist, 2008) et l'extension du musée d'Art de Grenchen (Grenchen, 2007–08), publié ici.

GRENCHEN ART MUSEUM EXTENSION

Grenchen, Switzerland, 2007–08

Address: Bahnhofstr. 53, vis-à-vis Südbahnhof, 2540 Grenchen, Switzerland, +41 32 652 50 22, www.kunsthausgrenchen.ch
Area: 458 m². Client: Baudirektion Stadt Grenchen, Switzerland. Cost: € 1.9 million

The architects explain: "The project aims at a holistic view of the Kunsthaus entity, but equally taking its near as well as its extended urban architectural surrounding into consideration." A new glass entry creates a relation to the train station. The word "Kunsthaus" is written in large white letters, which are lit at night, above this entrance. Column-free exhibition space with mobile walls at the entrance level is intended for temporary shows. Doors offer a view onto the outdoor sculpture courtyard. Floors are in anthracite-colored cement, while the walls are white. A basement area is used for storage and workspace. Exterior surfaces are treated with braided steel strips intentionally allowed to oxidize. A park area for the potential display of art is covered in gravel alternating with geometrical lawns and fruit trees. Despite the rather local nature of such a project, the architects have received very encouraging reactions from around the world, and from Japan in particular.

Die Architekten erklären: „Der Entwurf geht von einer holistischen Sicht auf das Kunsthaus als Ganzes aus, berücksichtigt aber auch seine nähere und weiter entfernte städtische Umwelt." Ein neuer, gläserner Eingang stellt einen Bezug zum Bahnhof her. Das Wort „Kunsthaus" steht in großen, weißen, bei Nacht beleuchteten Buchstaben über diesem Eingang. Der stützenfreie Ausstellungsraum mit mobilen Wänden auf Eingangsebene ist für Wechselausstellungen bestimmt. Türen bieten Ausblick auf den Skulpturenhof im Freien. Die Fußböden sind aus anthrazitfarbenem Zement, die Wände weiß. Das Untergeschoss wird als Lager und Arbeitsbereich genutzt. Die Außenwände sind mit geflochtenen Stahlbändern überzogen, die mit der Zeit oxidieren werden. Eine Parkfläche, auf der auch Kunst ausgestellt werden kann, ist abwechselnd mit Kies und geometrischen Rasenflächen bedeckt, auf denen Obstbäume stehen. Trotz der vergleichsweise regionalen Bedeutung dieses Projekts haben die Architekten sehr ermutigende Reaktionen aus der ganzen Welt, besonders aus Japan, erfahren.

Pour SSM Architekten : « Le projet tend à une vision holistique de l'entité Kunsthaus, tout en prenant en considération son environnement architectural urbain aussi bien proche que lointain. » La nouvelle entrée en verre fait lien avec la gare. Le mot de « Kunsthaus » est repris en grands caractères blancs, éclairés la nuit, au-dessus de cette entrée. Un espace d'exposition dégagé de toute colonne et à murs déplaçables est prévu pour les expositions temporaires. Les portes laissent voir la cour extérieure consacrée aux sculptures. Les murs sont blancs et les sols en ciment de couleur anthracite. Le sous-sol est destiné aux réserves et aux ateliers. Les façades extérieures sont recouvertes de bandeaux d'acier torsadés qui se patineront avec le temps. Le sol d'un petit parc, qui permettra également l'exposition d'œuvres, est en gravier alternant avec des pelouses de forme géométrique et des arbres fruitiers. Malgré la nature assez locale de ce projet, les architectes ont reçu des réactions encourageantes du monde entier, et du Japon en particulier.

The extension with its large-scale graphic signage makes for a modest, but convincing, addition to the original structure.

Die Erweiterung mit der großen Beschriftung ist ein bescheidener, aber überzeugender Anbau für das bestehende Gebäude.

L'extension annoncée par une signalétique surdimensionnée est un ajout modeste mais convaincant à la structure d'origine.

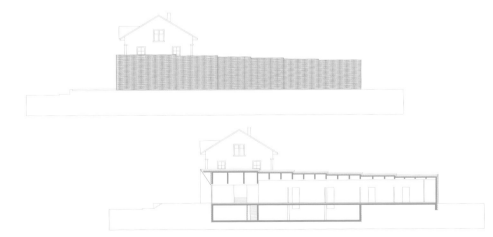

The main gallery space is of varying
width—its substantial length is lit
by an irregular pattern of overhead
lights.

Der Hauptausstellungsbereich ist von
unterschiedlicher Breite – in seiner
beachtlichen Länge wird er durch
unregelmäßig angeordnete Decken-
lampen erhellt.

De longueur substantielle, l'espace
d'exposition principal de largeur
variable a reçu un éclairage artificiel
posé selon un plan irrégulier.

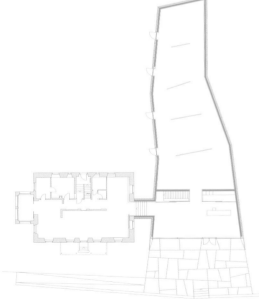

RANDALL STOUT

Randall Stout Architects, Inc.
12964 Washington Boulevard
Los Angeles, CA 90066
USA

Tel: +1 310 827 6876
Fax: +1 310 827 6879
E-mail: info@stoutarc.com
Web: www.stoutarc.com

RANDALL STOUT obtained his B.Arch degree from the University of Tennessee (1981) and his M.Arch from Rice University (1988). He worked as an Intern Architect for the Tennessee Valley Authority (1979–82), and was a project designer and project architect for Skidmore, Owings & Merrill (1984–87) and then a Senior Associate with Frank O. Gehry & Associates, Inc. (1989–96), before creating his own firm in Los Angeles, Randall Stout Architects, Inc., in 1996. He is presently the President and Principal in charge of the firm. His museum projects include an extension of the Hunter Museum of American Art (Chattanooga, Tennessee, 2005); the conceptual design for the new Holocaust Museum Houston (Houston, Texas, 2008); the programming for a renovation and addition to the New Mexico Museum of Art (Santa Fe, New Mexico, 2008); the design of the Taubman Museum of Art (Roanoke, Virginia, 2006–08, published here); and the Art Gallery of Alberta (Edmonton, Alberta, Canada, 2009), all in the USA unless stated otherwise.

RANDALL STOUT erhielt seinen B. Arch. an der University of Tennessee (1981) und seinen M. Arch. an der Rice University (1988). Er machte ein Praktikum bei der Tennessee Valley Authority (1979–82) und war Projektdesigner und Projektarchitekt bei Skidmore, Owings & Merrill (1984–87), danach Teilhaber bei Frank O. Gehry & Associates, Inc. (1989–96), bevor er 1996 sein eigenes Büro, Randall Stout Architects, Inc., in Los Angeles gründete. Gegenwärtig ist er Vorstand und Leiter dieser Firma. Zu seinen Museumsprojekten zählen eine Erweiterung für das Hunter Museum of American Art (Chattanooga, Tennessee, 2005), die Konzeption des neuen Holocaustmuseums in Houston (Houston, Texas, 2008), die Erweiterung und Sanierung des New Mexico Museum of Art (Santa Fe, New Mexico, 2008), das Taubman Museum of Art (Roanoke, Virginia, 2006–08, hier veröffentlicht), alle in den USA, und die Art Gallery of Alberta (Edmonton, Alberta, Kanada, 2009).

RANDALL STOUT est B.Arch de l'université du Tennessee (1981) et M.Arch de la Rice University (1988). Il a travaillé comme architecte stagiaire pour la Tennessee Valley Authority (1979–82) et a été concepteur de projet puis architecte projet chez Skidmore, Owings & Merrill (1984–87) avant de devenir associé senior chez Frank O. Gehry & Associates, Inc. (1989–96) et de créer sa propre agence à Los Angeles, Randall Stout Architects, Inc. en 1996 dont il est président et directeur. Parmi ses projets dans le domaine des musées figurent l'extension du Hunter Museum of American Art (Chattanooga, Tennessee, 2005) ; un projet conceptuel pour le nouveau musée de l'Holocauste à Houston (Houston, Texas, 2008) ; la programmation de la rénovation et d'une addition du New Mexico Museum of Art (Santa Fe, New Mexico, 2008) ; la conception du Taubman Museum of Art (Roanoke, Virginie, 2006–08), publié ici, tous aux États-Unis, et l'Art Gallery of Alberta (Edmonton, Alberta, Canada, 2009).

TAUBMAN MUSEUM OF ART
Roanoke, Virginia, USA, 2006–08

Address: 110 Salem Avenue SE, Roanoke, VA 24011, USA, +1 540 342 5760, www.taubmanmuseum.org
Area: 6500 m². Client: Taubman Museum of Art. Cost: $44.6 million

The overlapping forms of the museum are visible in the aerial view to the right. With its broad, curving shapes, the structure does bring to mind the work of Frank O. Gehry.

Die übergreifenden Formen des Museums sind auf der Luftaufnahme rechts zu erkennen. Mit seinen ausladenden, gekrümmten Gestaltungselementen erinnert das Gebäude an gewisse Bauten von Frank O. Gehry.

Page de droite : vue aérienne du chevauchement de formes du musée. Dans ses amples courbes, le bâtiment rappelle certaines œuvres de Frank O. Gehry.

The Taubman Museum of Art was the first major purpose-built museum in this city of just under 95 000 people. Its forms and materials were "chosen to pay homage to the famed Blue Ridge and Appalachian Mountains" that are nearby. The architect states: "The finish on the undulating, stainless-steel roof forms reflects the rich variety of color found in the sky and the seasonal landscape. Inspired by mountain streams, translucent glass surfaces emerge from the building's mass to create canopies of softly diffused light over the public spaces and gallery level. As it rises to support the stainless-steel roof, a layered pattern of angular exterior walls is surfaced in shingled patinated zinc to give an earthen and aged quality to the façade." The structure includes flexible exhibition galleries for the museum's collection of 19th- and 20th-century American art, contemporary art, and decorative arts. It also has educational facilities, a library, an auditorium, a black box theater, a café, a store, and ample outdoor terraces providing views of the city. The functions of the building are organized around a 23-meter-high atrium on three levels. Administration is located on the upper floor, with permanent and temporary exhibition galleries on the second level.

Das Taubman Museum of Art war das erste große echte Museum in dieser Stadt mit knapp 95 000 Einwohnern. Seine Formen und Materialien „wurden als Hommage an die benachbarten, berühmten Blue Ridge und Appalachian Mountains" ausgewählt. Der Architekt erklärt: „Die gebogenen Dachflächen aus Edelstahl reflektieren die vielfältigen, je nach Jahreszeit unterschiedlichen Färbungen des Himmels und der Landschaft. Von den Gebirgsflüssen inspiriert, erheben sich lichtdurchlässige Glasflächen von der Baumasse und bilden Baldachine aus mildem, diffusem Licht über den öffentlichen Bereichen und der Ausstellungsebene. Das geschichtete System aus schrägen Außenwänden, die das Edelstahldach tragen, ist mit patinierten Zinkschindeln verkleidet, die der Fassade eine erdverbundene und gealterte Wirkung verleihen." Das Gebäude enthält flexible Ausstellungsräume für die Museumssammlung von amerikanischer Kunst, zeitgenössischer Kunst und Kunstgewerbe aus dem 19. und 20. Jahrhundert. Das Museum umfasst auch pädagogische Einrichtungen, eine Bibliothek, ein Auditorium, eine Studiobühne, ein Café, Lagerraum und großzügige Freiterrassen mit Blick auf die Stadt. Die Funktionen des Gebäudes sind auf drei Ebenen um ein 23 m hohes Atrium verteilt. Die Verwaltungsräume liegen im ersten Obergeschoss, die Räume für die ständige Sammlung und Wechselausstellungen im zweiten Obergeschoss.

Le Taubman Museum of Art est le premier vrai musée construit dans cette ville de près de 95 000 habitants. Ses formes et ses matériaux de construction ont été choisis « en hommage aux fameuses montagnes des Blue Ridge et des Appalaches » qui sont voisines. L'architecte explique : « La finition des formes du toit ondulé en acier inoxydable reflète la riche variété des couleurs du ciel et du changement des saisons. Inspirés par les torrents des montagnes, des plans de verre translucide émergent de la masse du bâtiment pour créer des auvents distribuant une lumière légèrement diffuse dans les espaces publics et au niveau des galeries. Les murs extérieurs anguleux qui s'élèvent en une composition stratifiée qui vient soutenir le toit d'acier sont recouverts de bardeaux de zinc patiné qui confèrent un caractère minéral et ancien à la façade. » La structure comprend des galeries d'exposition transformables pour les collections d'art américain des XIXe et XXe siècle, d'art contemporain et d'arts décoratifs. Elle possède également des salles d'enseignement, une bibliothèque, un auditorium, un théâtre sans ouvertures, un café, une boutique et des terrasses donnant sur la ville. Les différentes fonctions s'organisent autour d'un atrium s'élevant sur trois niveaux (23 mètres). L'administration est logée au dernier étage, les galeries permanentes ou d'expositions temporaires au second niveau.

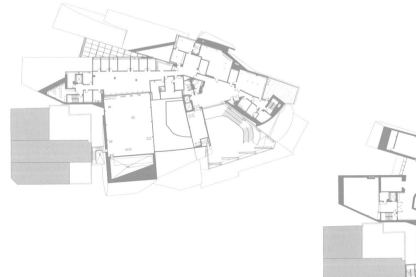

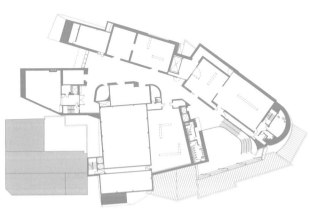

The relatively complex pattern of the plans above is echoed in the angular, irregular shape of the entrance atrium, seen above right.

Das relativ komplexe System der Grundrisse (oben) wird von der schrägen, unregelmäßigen Form des Eingangsbereichs (rechte Seite, oben) aufgenommen.

La complexité relative des plans (ci-dessus) se retrouve dans la forme anguleuse et irrégulière de l'atrium de l'entrée (en haut page de droite).

BERNARD TSCHUMI

Bernard Tschumi Architects
227 West 17th Street
New York, NY 10 011
USA

Tel: +1 212 807 6340
Fax: +1 212 242 3693
E-mail: nyc@tschumi.com
Web: www.tschumi.com

BERNARD TSCHUMI was born in Lausanne, Switzerland, in 1944. He studied in Paris and at the ETH, Zurich. He taught at the Architectural Association (AA), London (1970–79), and at Princeton (1976–80). He was Dean of the Graduate School of Architecture, Planning and Preservation of Columbia University in New York from 1984 to 2003. He opened his own office, Bernard Tschumi Architects (Paris, New York), in 1981. Major projects include the Second Prize in the Kansai International Airport Competition (Japan, 1988); the Video Gallery (Groningen, The Netherlands, 1990); Parc de la Villette (Paris, France, 1982–95); Le Fresnoy National Studio for Contemporary Arts (Tourcoing, France, 1991–97); the Lerner Student Center, Columbia University (New York, New York, 1994–98); the School of Architecture (Marne-la-Vallée, France, 1994–98); the Interface Flon train station in Lausanne (2001); the Vacheron-Constantin Headquarters (Geneva, Switzerland, 2004); the Linder Athletic Center at the University of Cincinnati (Cincinnati, Ohio, 2006); and the Zénith Concert Hall in Limoges (France, 2007). Among the firm's more recent projects are BLUE, a 17-story residential tower on the Lower East Side of New York (completed in 2007); a museum and interpretive center at the Parc Archéologique d'Alésia (France, 2001–08); and the New Acropolis Museum in Athens (Greece, 2004–09, published here). Other recent projects include the West Diaoyutai Hotel and Residence in Beijing (China) and the Grote Markstraat mixed-use center (The Hague, The Netherlands).

BERNARD TSCHUMI wurde 1944 in Lausanne, Schweiz, geboren. Er studierte in Paris und an der Eidgenössischen Technischen Hochschule (ETH) in Zürich. Er hat an der Architectural Association (AA) in London (1970–79) und an der Princeton University (1976–80) gelehrt und war von 1984 bis 2003 Dekan der Graduate School of Architecture, Planning and Preservation der Columbia University in New York. 1981 eröffnete er sein eigenes Büro, Bernard Tschumi Architects (Paris, New York). Zu seinen wichtigsten Projekten zählen der mit dem zweiten Preis ausgezeichnete Wettbewerbsentwurf für den internationalen Flughafen Kansai (Japan, 1988), die Video Gallery (Groningen, Niederlande, 1990), der Parc de la Villette (Paris, 1982–95), das Studio national des arts contemporains, Le Fresnoy (Tourcoing, Frankreich, 1991–97), das Lerner Student Center, Columbia University (New York, 1994–98), die École d'architecture (Marne-la-Vallée, Frankreich, 1994–98), der Bahnhof Interface Flon in Lausanne (2001), die Hauptverwaltung Vacheron-Constantin (Genf, Schweiz, 2004), das Linder Athletic Center der University of Cincinnati (Ohio, 2006) und die Zénith-Konzerthalle in Limoges (2007). Zu Tschumis neueren Projekten gehören BLUE, ein 17-geschossiges Wohnhochhaus in der Lower East Side in New York (2007 fertiggestellt), ein Museum und Informationszentrum im Parc Archéologique d'Alésia (Frankreich, 2001–08) und das Neue Akropolismuseum in Athen (2004–09, hier veröffentlicht). Weitere Projekte aus neuester Zeit sind das West Diaoyutai Hotel und Wohnungen in Peking sowie das Mehrzweckzentrum Grote Markstraat (Den Haag).

BERNARD TSCHUMI, né à Lausanne, Suisse, en 1944, a étudié à Paris et à l'École polytechnique fédérale de Zurich (ETH). Il a enseigné à l'Architectural Association de Londres (1970–79) et à Princeton (1976–80). Il a été doyen de la Graduate School of Architecture, Planning and Preservation de la Columbia University à New York de 1984 à 2003 et a ouvert son agence, Bernard Tschumi Architects (Paris, New York) en 1981. Parmi ses interventions majeures : le second prix au concours pour l'aéroport international du Kansai (Japon, 1988) ; la Video Gallery (Groningen, Pays-Bas, 1990) ; le Parc de la Villette (Paris, 1982–85) ; le Studio national des arts contemporains du Fresnoy (Tourcoing, France, 1991–97) ; le Lerner Student Center, Columbia University (New York, 1994–98) ; l'École d'architecture de Marne-la-Vallée (France, 1994–98) et la plate-forme d'échanges ferroviaires de Lausanne (2001). Plus récemment, il a réalisé le siège de Vacheron-Constantin (Genève, 2004) ; le Linder Athletic Center (University of Cincinnati, Cincinnati, Ohio, 2006) et la salle de concerts du Zénith de Limoges (France, 2007). Parmi ses projets plus récents de l'agence figurent : BLUE, une tour d'appartements de dix-sept niveaux dans le Lower East Side à New York (achevée en 2007) ; un musée et centre d'interprétation pour le Parc archéologique d'Alésia (France, 2001–08) ; et le nouveau musée de l'Acropole d'Athènes (2004–09), publié ici. Autres projets : le West Diaoyutai Hotel and Residence (Pékin, Chine) et le centre mixte de Grote Markstraat (La Haye, Pays-Bas).

NEW ACROPOLIS MUSEUM

Athens, Greece, 2004–09

Address: 15 Dionysiou Areopagitou Street, Athens 11742, Greece, +30 210 9000900, www.theacropolismuseum.gr
Area: 14 000 m² (exhibition space). Client: OANMA (Organization for the Construction of the New Acropolis Museum). Cost: €130 million
Collaborator: Michael Photiadis (Associate Architect)

Located at the foot of the Acropolis in Athens, this project has been subject to a good deal of controversy and delay, as any such visible project might be. "Combined with a hot climate in an earthquake region, these conditions," says Bernard Tschumi, "moved us to design a simple and precise museum with the mathematical and conceptual clarity of ancient Greece." The base of the museum is set on pilotis over an archeological excavation. The base contains the entrance lobby with a glass floor, temporary exhibition space, an auditorium, and support facilities. A glass ramp overlooks the dig and leads to a double-height room with high columns where works from the Archaic Period to the Roman Empire are exhibited. At the top of the museum, the Parthenon Gallery shows marbles from the great monument's frieze as they appeared on the Parthenon. It is hoped, as has been known for years, that other parts of the frieze, such as those in the British Museum in London, may one day return to Greece, and, now, to this room. Natural light is provided in the galleries to allow the appreciation of the art objects in their original light. Tschumi concludes: "Materials have been selected for simplicity and sobriety: glass, concrete, and marble are the materials of choice. Perfectly transparent glass gently filters the light through a silkscreen-shading process. Concrete (both precast and cast-in-place) provides the main building structure and is the background for most of the artwork. Marble marks the floor: black for circulation, light beige for the galleries. Construction has progressed according to exacting standards so that the building will age gracefully, despite the heavy traffic of an international travel destination."

Das am Fuß der Akropolis in Athen gelegene Museum hat – wie wohl viele derartige Projekte – zahlreiche Kontroversen ausgelöst und Verzögerungen erfahren. Bernard Tschumi erläutert: „Die Verhältnisse vor Ort in Verbindung mit dem heißen Klima und der Erdbebengefährdung veranlassten uns zu einem schlichten und exakten Museumsentwurf in der mathematischen und konzeptuellen Klarheit des antiken Griechenland." Über einer archäologischen Ausgrabungsstätte wurde die Basis des Gebäudes auf Pilotis gesetzt. Sie enthält die Eingangshalle mit gläsernem Fußboden, Raum für Wechselausstellungen, ein Auditorium und Versorgungseinrichtungen. Eine gläserne Rampe führt über die Ausgrabungen zu einem doppelgeschosshohen Saal mit hohen Stützen, in dem die Werke von der archaischen Periode bis zur römischen Herrschaft ausgestellt sind. Im oberen Bereich des Museums zeigt die Parthenon-Galerie die Marmorteile des großen Frieses in gleicher Anordnung wie seinerzeit am Parthenontempel. Wie seit Jahren bekannt ist, besteht die Hoffnung, dass andere Teile des Frieses, u. a. die aus dem Britischen Museum in London, eines Tages nach Griechenland in ebendiesen Raum zurückkehren. Die Ausstellungsräume werden natürlich belichtet, um die Exponate in ihrem ursprünglichen Licht betrachten zu können. Tschumi erklärt abschließend: „Wir haben uns für schlichte und nüchterne Materialien entschieden: Glas, Beton und Marmor sind die Baustoffe unserer Wahl. Das durchsichtige Glas filtert das Licht sanft dank eines Aufdrucks im Siebdruckverfahren. Vorgefertigter Beton und Ortbeton bilden das Haupttragwerk und zugleich den Hintergrund für die Mehrzahl der Kunstwerke. Marmor kennzeichnet die Böden: schwarz für Verkehrsflächen, hellbeige für die Ausstellungsräume. Der Bau wurde nach hohen Standards ausgeführt, sodass er ansehnlich altern wird, trotz des starken Verkehrs an diesem internationalen Reiseziel."

Implanté au pied de l'Acropole d'Athènes, ce nouveau musée a été victime de multiples controverses et retards, ce qui est le lot de tout projet aussi visible. « Combinées à un climat chaud et à des risques de tremblements de terre », explique Bernard Tschumi, « les conditions du projet nous ont poussés à concevoir un musée simple et précis reposant sur la clarté conceptuelle et mathématique de la Grèce ancienne. » La base du musée repose sur des pilotis posés au-dessus de fouilles archéologiques. Elle contient un hall d'entrée au sol de verre, des espaces pour expositions temporaires, un auditorium et des installations techniques. Une rampe de verre qui passe au-dessus des fouilles conduit à une salle double hauteur ponctuée de colonnes où sont présentés des vestiges datant de la période archaïque jusqu'à la période de l'empire romain. Au sommet du bâtiment, la galerie du Parthénon expose des marbres faisant partie de la célèbre frise, présentés selon leur emplacement d'origine sur le monument lui-même. On espère, comme on le sait depuis des années, que d'autres parties de cette frise, en particulier celles conservées au British Museum de Londres, rejoindront un jour la Grèce et trouveront leur place dans cette salle. Les galeries bénéficient de la lumière naturelle pour que l'on puisse apprécier les œuvres dans leur intensité originale. Tschumi conclut : « Les matériaux ont été sélectionnés pour leur simplicité et leur sobriété : verre, béton et marbre. Un verre parfaitement transparent filtre délicatement la lumière par un système d'écrans. Le béton (préfabriqué ou coulé en place) constitue la structure du bâtiment principal et le fond de la plupart des œuvres. Le marbre des sols est noir pour les espaces de circulation et beige clair pour les galeries. Le chantier a respecté des critères de qualité extrêmement rigoureux pour que le bâtiment vieillisse avec grâce, malgré l'afflux de visiteurs pour cette destination connue dans le monde entier. »

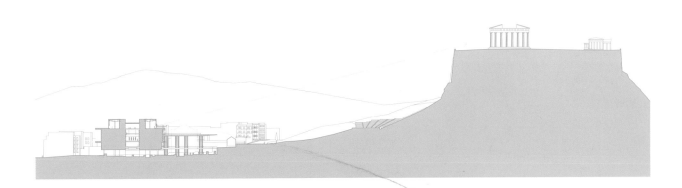

Given its subject, it is appropriate that the museum is placed within site of the Acropolis and its monuments. The classical simplicity of the structure echoes, but does not compete with, the Parthenon.

Angesichts seiner Thematik ist es angemessen, dass das Museum auf dem Gelände der Akropolis und ihrer Baudenkmäler steht. Die klassische Schlichtheit des Gebäudes entspricht, aber konkurriert nicht mit der des Parthenons.

Étant donné son objet, il était naturel que le musée fasse partie du site de l'Acropole. La simplicité classique du nouveau bâtiment n'entre pas en concurrence avec celle du Parthénon mais renvoie d'une certaine façon à celle du monument.

Archeological vestiges are integrated
into the museum itself, whose overall
plan is essentially rectangular, as
seen in the plans below.

Die archäologischen Funde sind in
das Museum integriert, dessen
Gesamtplanung überwiegend rechtwinklig ist, wie die Grundrisse unten
zeigen.

Les fouilles archéologiques ont été
conservées dans le sol du musée,
dont le plan d'ensemble est essentiellement rectangulaire, comme
le montrent les plans ci-dessous.

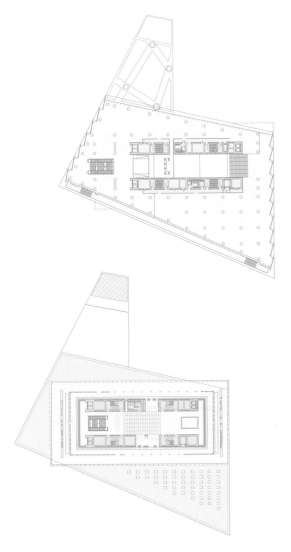

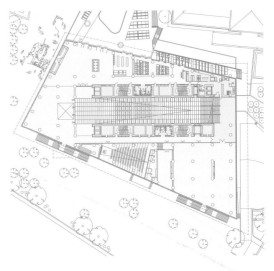

Tschumi's elegant modernity makes for a simple, fitting background for the classical sculptures contained in the collections.

Tschumis elegante, moderne Architektur bildet einen schlichten, passenden Hintergrund für die klassischen Skulpturen der Sammlung.

L'élégante simplicité mise en œuvre par Tschumi offre un cadre adapté aux sculptures antiques des collections.

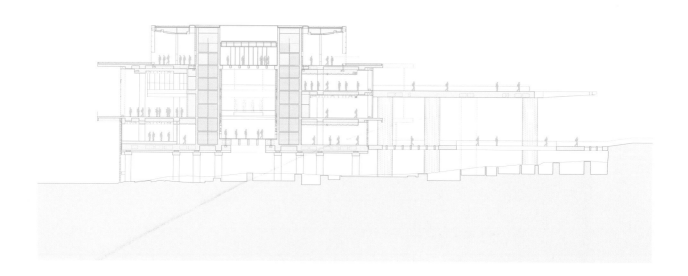

The point of departure of the museum and its eventual destination are summed up in Culture Minister Melina Mercouri's demand that the British Museum return to Greece the so-called Elgin Marbles.

Der Ausgangspunkt für den Bau des Museums und seine eigentliche Zielsetzung basieren auf der Forderung der Kultusministerin Melina Mercouri, dass das Britische Museum die sogenannten Elgin-Marbles an Griechenland zurückgeben sollte.

Le point de départ de la décision de construire ce musée est la demande de la ministre de la Culture Melina Mercouri de restitution des « Marbres d'Elgin » conservés au British Museum de Londres.

UNSTUDIO

UNStudio
Stadhouderskade 113
1070 AJ Amsterdam
The Netherlands

Tel: +31 20 570 20 40
Fax: +31 20 570 20 41
E-mail: info@unstudio.com
Web: www.unstudio.com

Ben van Berkel, born in Utrecht in 1957, studied at the Rietveld Academy in Amsterdam and at the Architectural Association (AA) in London, receiving the AA Diploma with honors in 1987. After working briefly in the office of Santiago Calatrava in 1988, he set up his practice in Amsterdam with Caroline Bos, Van Berkel & Bos Architectural Bureau, **UNSTUDIO** since 1998. He has been a Visiting Professor at Columbia and a visiting critic at Harvard (1994). He was a Diploma Unit Master at the AA (1994–95). As well as the Erasmus Bridge in Rotterdam (inaugurated in 1996), UNStudio has built the Karbouw and ACOM office buildings (1989–93), and the REMU Electricity Station (1989–93), all in Amersfoort; and housing projects and the Aedes East Gallery for Kristin Feireiss in Berlin. More recent projects include an extension for the Rijksmuseum Twente (Enschede, 1992–96); the Möbius House (Naarden, 1993–98); Het Valkhof Museum (Nijmegen, 1998); and the NMR Laboratory (Utrecht, 2000), all in the Netherlands; a Switching Station (Innsbruck, Austria, 1998–2001); an Electricity Station (Innsbruck, 2002); VilLA NM (Upstate New York, 2000–06); the Mercedes-Benz Museum (Stuttgart, Germany, 2003–06); a Music Facility (Graz, Austria, 1998–2007); and the Arnhem Station (The Netherlands, 1986–2007). Recent work includes the IBG and Tax Offices (Groningen, The Netherlands, 2007–); Orchard Road, residential tower (Singapore 2008–); the Hyundai S-Project Master Plan (Seoul, South Korea, 2008–); and MOMEMA, Museum of Middle East Modern Art (Khor Dubai, UAE, published here), due for completion in 2011.

Ben van Berkel, 1957 in Utrecht geboren, studierte an der Rietveld-Academie in Amsterdam und an der Architectural Association (AA) in London, wo er 1987 sein Diplom mit Auszeichnung machte. Nachdem er 1988 kurze Zeit im Büro von Santiago Calatrava gearbeitet hatte, gründete er zusammen mit Caroline Bos Van Berkel & Bos Architectural Bureau in Amsterdam, 1998 umbenannt in **UNSTUDIO**. Er war Gastprofessor an der Columbia University und Gastkritiker in Harvard (1994) sowie Diploma Unit Master an der AA (1994–95). UNStudio hat die Erasmusbrücke in Rotterdam gebaut (1996 eingeweiht) sowie die Bürohäuser Karbouw und ACOM (1989–93) und ein REMU-Umspannwerk (1989–93), alle in Amersfoort, außerdem Wohnbauprojekte und die Galerie Aedes-Ost für Kristin Feireiss in Berlin. Neuere Projekte sind ein Neubau für das Rijksmuseum Twente (Enschede, 1992–96), das Möbius-Haus (Naarden, 1993–98), das Museum Het Valkhof (Nimwegen, 1998) und die NMR Laboratorien (Utrecht, 2000), alle in den Niederlanden, ein Umspannwerk (Innsbruck, 1998–2001), ein Elektrizitätswerk (Innsbruck, 2002), VilLA NM (Upstate New York, 2000–06), das Mercedes-Benz Museum (Stuttgart, 2003–06), eine Musikhalle (Graz, 1998–2007) und der Bahnhof Arnhem (Niederlande, 1986–2007). Zu den neuesten Bauten gehören Büros für die IBG und das Finanzamt (Groningen, 2007–), das Wohnhochhaus Orchard Road (Singapur, 2008–), der Masterplan Hyundai S-Project (Seoul, Südkorea, 2008–) und das MOMEMA, Museum of Middle East Modern Art (Khor Dubai, Vereinigte Arabische Emirate, hier veröffentlicht), das 2011 fertiggestellt werden soll.

Ben van Berkel, né à Utrecht en 1957, a étudié à l'académie Rietveld à Amsterdam et à l'Architectural Association (AA) de Londres, dont il est sorti diplômé avec mention en 1987. Après avoir brièvement travaillé pour Santiago Calatrava en 1988, il a créé, en association avec Caroline Bos, son agence à Amsterdam, Van Berkel & Bos Architectural Bureau, **UNSTUDIO** depuis 1998. Il a été professeur invité à la Columbia University, critique invité à Harvard (1994) et responsable de l'unité du diplôme à l'AA (1994–95). Accédant à la notoriété grâce à son projet pour le pont Erasmus à Rotterdam (inauguré en 1996), UNStudio a réalisé les immeubles de bureaux Karbouw et ACOM (1989–93) et la sous-station électrique REMU (1989–93) à Amersfoort ainsi que des immeubles de logements et la galerie Aedes-Ost de Kristin Feireiss à Berlin. Plus récemment, l'agence a réalisé une extension du Rijksmuseum Twente (Enschede, 1992–96) ; la maison Möbius (Naarden, 1993–98) et le musée Het Valkhof (Nimègue, 1998) ; le laboratoire NMR (Utrecht, 2000) ; un poste d'aiguillage (Innsbruck, Autriche, 1998–2001) ; une station électrique (Innsbruck, 2002) ; la vilLA NM (État de New York, 2000–06) ; le musée Mercedes-Benz (Stuttgart, Allemagne, 2003–06) ; une salle de concert (Graz, Autriche, 1998–2007) et la gare d'Arnhem (Pays-Bas, 1986–2007). Parmi leurs œuvres récentes : l'immeuble d'IBG et de l'administration des impôts (Groningen, Pays-Bas, 2007–) ; la tour résidentielle d'Orchard Road (Singapour, 2008–) ; le plan directeur du S-Project Hyundai (Séoul, Corée du Sud, 2008–) et le MOMEMA, musée d'Art moderne du Moyen-Orient (Khor Dubaï, EAU), publié ici, qui devrait être achevé en 2011.

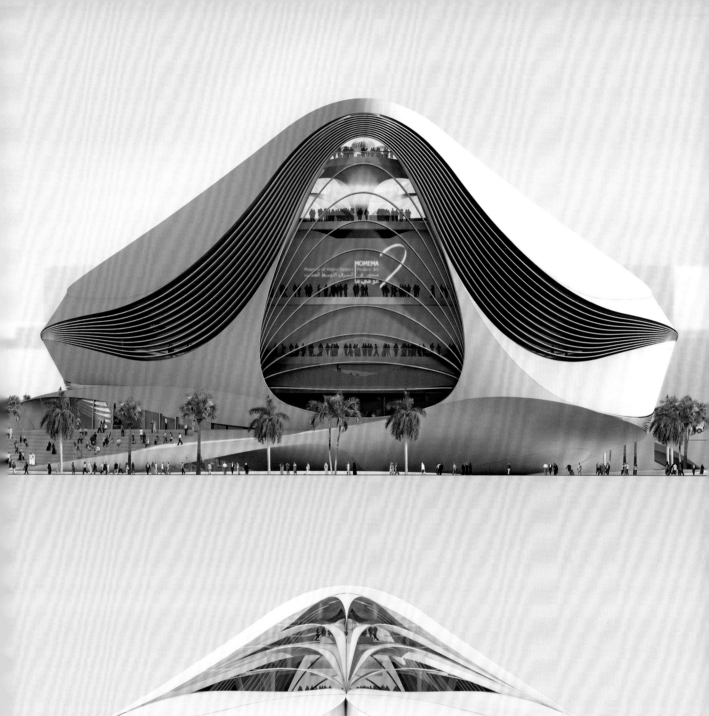

MOMEMA, MUSEUM OF MIDDLE EAST MODERN ART

Khor Dubai, United Arab Emirates, 2008–11

Address: Al Jaddaf, Dubai, United Arab Emirates
Area: 25 000 m². Client: Dubai Properties. Cost: not disclosed

The astonishing, sweeping forms of the museum may sum up the generation of buildings designed for Dubai, the center of a building boom in the Gulf region that has been slowed by recent economic conditions.

Die erstaunlichen, geschwungenen Formen des Museums verweisen möglicherweise auf eine Generation von Bauten für Dubai, Zentrum eines Baubooms in der Golfregion, der sich infolge der jüngsten wirtschaftlichen Bedingungen verlangsamt hat.

Les étonnantes courbes du musée résument en elles-mêmes la nouvelle génération d'immeubles édifiés à Dubaï, centre de l'explosion de chantiers immobiliers dans la région du Golfe, ralentie par la situation économique récente.

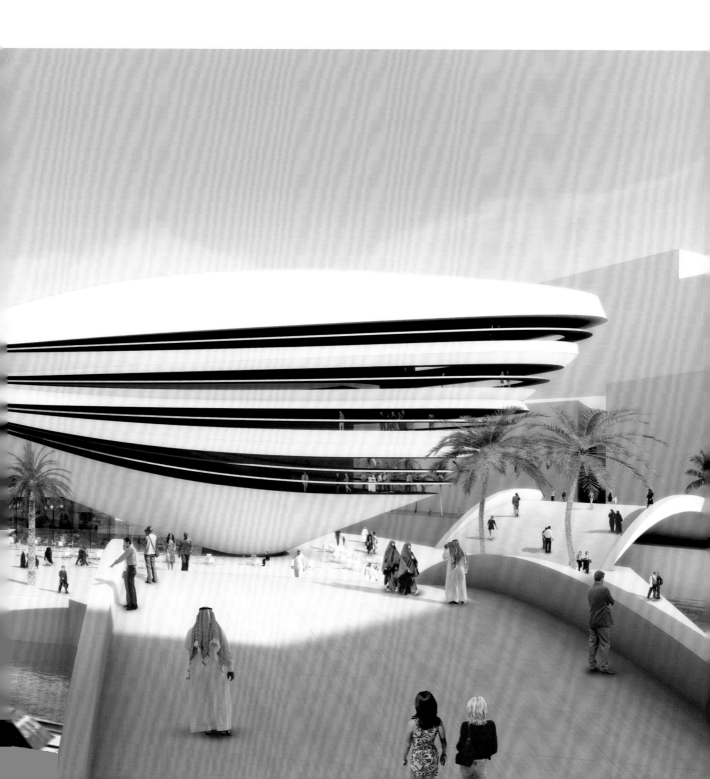

Although economic circumstances may change plans, MOMEMA has been conceived as the basis for the creation of a cultural hub in Dubai, with the goal of making the Emirate a center for "multicultural understanding." Part of a Cultural Village to be created on a 372-hectare site at Dubai Creek, MOMEMA is to include an amphitheater for live performances, an exhibition hall and smaller museums for local and international art, and a shipyard for traditional dhow builders. The overall project includes residential, commercial, and retail areas. A 60-room boutique hotel, retail space, and a top-floor restaurant are part of the plan. Ben van Berkel states: "In MOMEMA Dubai we recognize the opportunity to create an entirely new type of museum, which consists of a vibrant urban centre, where professionals, collectors, and the public meet each other. In this way, MOMEMA will be a community-building institution within the city, and offer both visitors and residents a continuously changing palette of experiences and events."

Obgleich die wirtschaftlichen Verhältnisse die Planung noch verändern können, soll das MOMEMA den Ausgangspunkt für die Entstehung eines Kulturzentrums in Dubai bilden mit dem Ziel, das Emirat zu einem Mittelpunkt „multikulturellen Verständnisses" zu machen. Das MOMEMA als Teil eines Kulturdorfs, das auf einem 372 ha großen Gelände am Fluss Dubai entstehen soll, wird ein Auditorium für Aufführungen, eine Ausstellungshalle und kleinere Museen für lokale und internationale Kunst enthalten sowie eine Werft zum Bau traditioneller Dauen. Das Gesamtprojekt soll auch Wohnungen, Geschäftsbauten und Läden umfassen. Ein Boutique-Hotel mit 60 Zimmern, Einzelhandelsgeschäften und einem Restaurant im obersten Geschoss ist ebenfalls Bestandteil der Planung. Ben van Berkel erklärt: „Im MOMEMA Dubai sehen wir die Chance, einen völlig neuen Museumstyp zu erschaffen, der ein lebendiges, urbanes Zentrum bildet, wo Fachleute, Sammler und das Publikum einander begegnen. Auf diese Weise wird das MOMEMA eine gemeinschaftsfördernde Institution in der Stadt darstellen sowie Besuchern und Bewohnern eine ständig wechselnde Palette von Erlebnissen und Ereignissen bieten."

Le MOMEMA devrait être la base de la plate-forme culturelle prévue à Dubaï pour faire de l'Émirat un centre de « compréhension multiculturelle », si les circonstances économiques ne modifient pas ces plans. Faisant partie d'un village culturel qui doit être créé sur un terrain de 372 hectares dans la crique de Dubaï, le MOMEMA devrait comprendre un amphithéâtre pour spectacles vivants, un hall d'exposition et d'autres musées plus petits destinés à l'art local et international, ainsi qu'un chantier naval de construction de bateaux traditionnels, les *dhows*. Le projet porte également sur des zones résidentielles, commerciales et de bureaux. Une boutique hôtel de soixante chambres, des commerces et un restaurant au dernier étage complètent le projet du musée. « Dans le MOMEMA, nous avons vu l'opportunité de créer un type de musée entièrement nouveau, qui soit un centre urbain actif, où les professionnels, les collectionneurs et le public puissent se rencontrer. Ainsi, le MOMEMA sera une institution communautaire au cœur de la cité, et offrira aux visiteurs comme aux résidants une palette perpétuellement changeante d'expériences et de manifestations », précise Ben van Berkel.

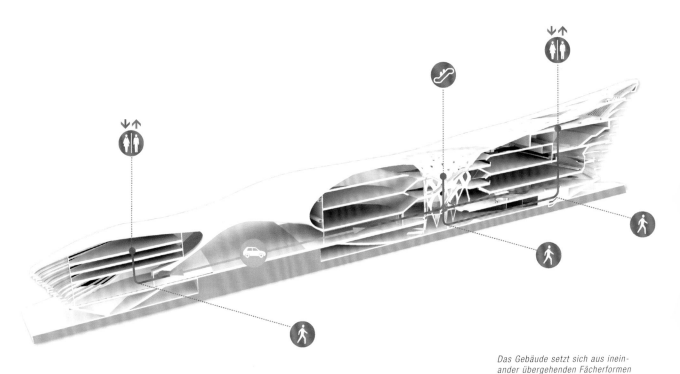

The structure is made up of alveolar forms that flow into one another. The external envelope seen to the right follows the same lines.

Das Gebäude setzt sich aus ineinander übergehenden Fächerformen zusammen. Die rechts abgebildete Außenhülle folgt den gleichen Linien.

La construction se compose d'éléments alvéolaires qui s'interpénètrent comme dans un flux continu. L'enveloppe externe (à droite) suit les mêmes axes.

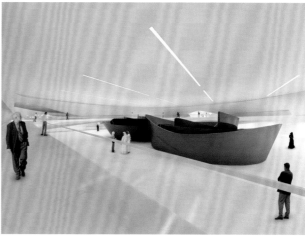

The galleries are seen above in computer renderings.

Die Ausstellungsräume sind auf den Computer-Renderings (oben) zu sehen.

Ci-dessus, les galeries vues en images de synthèse.

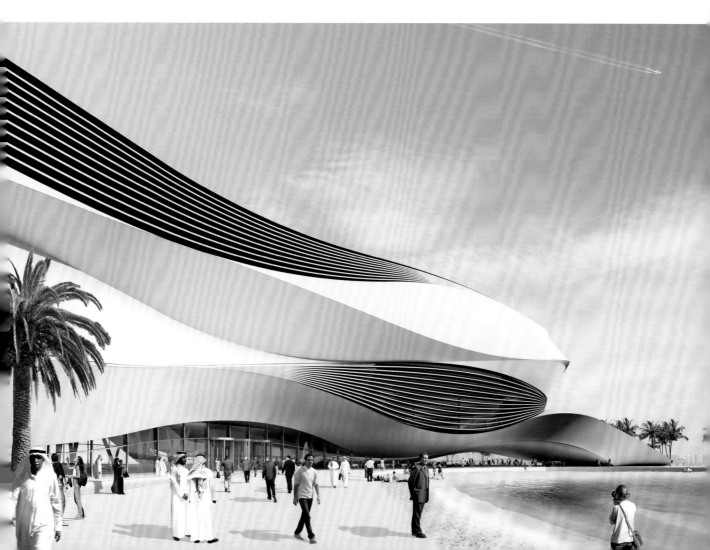

An interior escalator is encased in treelike forms that rise up through the building.

Eine innenliegende Rolltreppe ist in die baumähnlichen Strukturen eingesetzt, die sich im Gebäude erheben.

Un escalier mécanique s'inscrit dans une ossature en forme d'arbre qui s'élève à travers le musée.

The structure is seen in an "exploded" form in the drawing below. The apparently freely flowing forms are in fact assembled in a careful design.

Das Gebäude ist unten in einer „Explosions"-Zeichnung zu sehen. Tatsächlich sind die scheinbar frei fließenden Formen das Ergebnis einer sorgfältigen Planung.

Ci-dessous : la structure présentée sous forme « explosée ». Les formes en flux apparemment libre sont en fait assemblées avec précision.

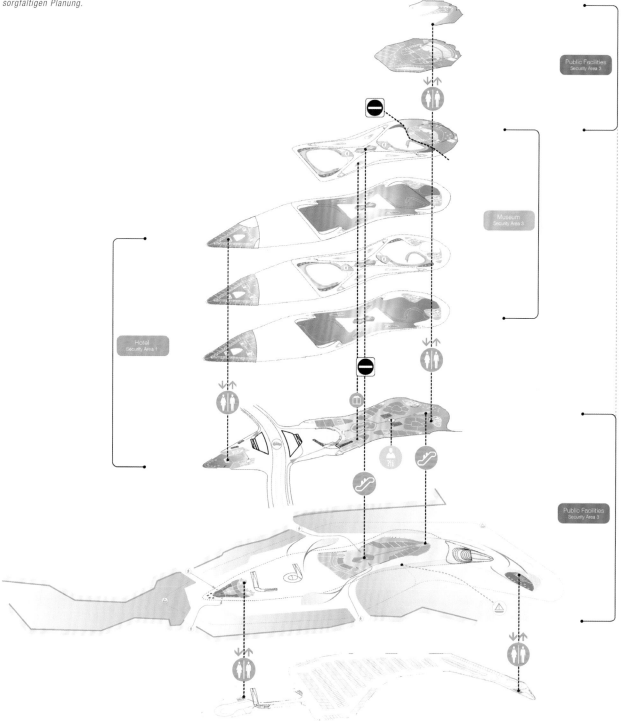

Public Facilities
Security Area 3

Museum
Security Area 3

Hotel
Security Area 1

Public Facilities
Security Area 3

URBANUS ARCHITECTURE & DESIGN

URBANUS Architecture & Design, Inc.
Beijing / Shenzhen, China

Tel: +86 10 840 33 551 (BJ) / +86 755 8609 6345 (SZ)
E-mail: office@urbanus.com.cn
Web: www.urbanus.com.cn

Liu Xiaodu is one of the founding partners of **URBANUS**. Prior to establishing Urbanus, Liu was a project architect and designer at Design Group Inc. (Columbus, Ohio) and Stang & Newdow Inc. in Atlanta, Georgia. He received his B.Arch from Tsinghua University (1985), and M.Arch from Miami University (Oxford, Ohio, 1997). He has six years of teaching experience at Tsinghua University. Prior to cofounding Urbanus, Meng Yan was a project architect and designer at Kohn Pedersen Fox Associates PC; Meltzer Mandl Architects in New York; Brown & Bills Architects in Dayton; and Yongmao Architects and Engineers in Beijing. Wang Hui, another cofounder of the firm, worked with Gruzen Samton Architects, Gensler, and Gary Edward Handel + Associates. Like his two partners, he was educated at Tsinghua University and Miami Univeristy. Their completed works include Diwang Park A (Shenzhen, 2000); the CRL and Constellation Development Sales Office (Beijing, 2003); the OCT Contemporary Art Terminal (Shenzhen, 2004); the Xinhai Garden Residential Development (Shenzhen, 2004); the Metro Office Tower (Shenzhen, 2005); the Teda Vanton U-Club (Tianjin, 2005); and Diwang Park B (Shenzhen, 2005). Current projects include the Shenzhen International Yacht Club (Shenzhen, 2006); the Public Art Plaza (Shenzhen, 2006); the Dafen Art Museum (Shenzhen, 2006); the Shanghai Multimedia Valley Office Park (Shanghai, 2007); Digital Beijing (with Pei Zhu, Beijing, 2007); the Nanyou Shopping Park (Shenzhen, 2007); the OCT Art & Design Gallery (Shenzhen, 2006–08, published here); and the Tangshan Urban Planning Museum (Tangshan, 2008, also published here), all in China.

Liu Xiaodu ist einer der Gründungspartner von **URBANUS**. Davor war er Projektarchitekt und Designer bei Design Group Inc. (Columbus, Ohio) und Stang & Newdow Inc. in Atlanta, Georgia. Er erhielt seinen B. Arch. an der Universität Tsinghua (1985) und den M. Arch. an der Miami University (Oxford, Ohio, 1997). Sechs Jahre lehrte er an der Universität Tsinghua. Meng Yan, Mitbegründer von Urbanus, war vorher Projektarchitekt und Designer bei Kohn Pedersen Fox Associates PC, Meltzer Mandl Architects in New York, Brown & Bills Architects in Dayton und Yongmao Architects and Engineers in Peking. Wang Hui, ein weiterer Mitbegründer der Firma, arbeitete bei Gruzen Samton Architects, Gensler und Gary Edward Handel + Associates. Wie seine beiden Partner studierte auch er an der Universität Tsinghua und der Miami University. Zu ihren ausgeführten Bauten zählen Diwang Park A (Shenzhen, 2000), CRL and Constellation Development Sales Office (Peking, 2003), der OCT Contemporary Art Terminal (Shenzhen, 2004), die Wohnanlage Xinhai-Garten (Shenzhen, 2004), der Metro Office Tower (Shenzhen, 2005), der Teda Vanton U-Club (Tianjin, 2005) und Diwang Park B (Shenzhen, 2005). Neuere Projekte sind der internationale Jachtklub Shenzhen (Shenzhen, 2006), die Public Art Plaza (Shenzhen, 2006), das Kunstmuseum Dafen (Shenzhen, 2006), der Shanghai Multimedia Valley Office Park (Shanghai, 2007), Digital Peking (mit Pei Zhu, Peking, 2007), der Nanyou-Einkaufspark (Shenzhen, 2007), die OCT Art & Design Gallery (Shenzhen, 2006–08, hier vorgestellt) und das Museum für Stadtplanung Tangshan (Tangshan, 2008, ebenfalls hier veröffentlicht), alle in China.

Liu Xiaodu, l'un des associés et fondateurs d'**URBANUS** a été auparavant architecte de projet et concepteur chez Design Group Inc. (Columbus, Ohio) et Stang & Newdow Inc. à Atlanta (Géorgie). Il est B.Arch de l'Université de Tsinghua (Chine, 1985) et M.Arch de la Miami University (Oxford, Ohio, 1997). Il a enseigné pendant six ans à l'université de Tsinghua. Avant de participer à la fondation d'Urbanus, Meng Yan a été architecte de projet et concepteur chez Kohn Pedersen Fox Associates PC, Meltzer Mandl Architects à New York, Brown & Bills Architects à Dayton et Yongmao Architects and Engineers à Pékin. Wang Hui, autre cofondateur de l'agence, a travaillé pour Gruzen Samton Architects, Gensler et Gary Edward Handel + Associates. Comme ses deux associés, il a fait ses études à l'université de Tsinghua et à la Miami University. Parmi leurs réalisations, toutes en Chine : le Diwang Park A (Shenzhen, 2000) ; les bureaux CRL et Constellation Development (Pékin, 2003) ; le terminal d'art contemporain OCT (Shenzhen, 2004) ; la cité jardin de Xinhai (Shenzhen, 2004) ; la tour Metro Office (Shenzhen, 2005) ; le Teda Vanton U-Club (Tianjin, 2005) et le Diwang Park B (Shenzhen, 2005). Parmi leurs projets actuels, également tous en Chine : le Yacht club international de Shenzhen (Shenzhen, 2006) ; une place aménagée pour des présentations d'œuvres artistiques (Shenzhen, 2006) ; le musée d'Art Dafen (Shenzhen, 2006) ; le parc de bureaux de la Multimedia Valley (Shanghaï, 2007) ; le parc commercial Nanyou (Shenzhen, 2007) ; Digital Beijing (avec Studio Pei-Zhu, 2007) ; la OCT Art & Design Gallery (Shenzhen, 2006–08), publiée ici, et le musée de l'Urbanisme de Tangshan (Tangshan, 2008), publié ici.

TANGSHAN URBAN PLANNING MUSEUM

Tangshan, China, 2008

Wenhua St, Tangshan, Hebei, China, www.tsghj.gov.cn
Area: 22 850 m². Client: Tangshan Urban Planning Bureau. Cost: $6 million

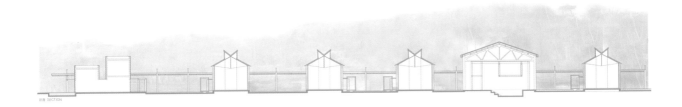

The older warehouse structures are set parallel to the newer building, seen in the foreground in the image below.

Die alten Lagerhäuser stehen parallel zum Neubau, der auf der unteren Abbildung im Vordergrund zu sehen ist.

Le nouveau bâtiment a été implanté parallèlement aux anciens entrepôts, comme le montre le premier plan de la photographie ci-dessous.

The principal architect of this project was Wang Hui. Following a destructive earthquake in 1976, the city of Tangshan has sought to "erase less appealing urban structures," amongst them the former grain depot, seen to block the path from the city to the neighboring Da Cheng Hill. A total of four grain structures built during the Japanese occupation and two warehouses built after the earthquake were selected to serve as museum structures. Within this existing composition of buildings set at right angles to the hill, the architects added VIP reception areas, a museum store, and a café parallel to the older stucco structures, cladding them in metal grating and wood. A patio was added to each of the old structures. The architects state: "The new layout of the whole building group also forms a spatial sequence to introduce the hill to the city through a series of gardens, courtyards, and the park." The museum is devoted to the history and new plan of the city. An antiques market is placed near the entry. The architects take some pride in reusing old buildings, unlike larger cities such as Beijing or Shanghai, given to "crazy designs," according to Urbanus.

Der verantwortliche Architekt für dieses Projekt war Wang Hui. Nach dem katastrophalen Erdbeben von 1976 wollte die Stadt Tangshan die „weniger ansprechenden Stadtstrukturen abreißen", u. a. das frühere Lagerhaus für Getreide, das vermeintlich den Weg von der Stadt zum benachbarten Berg Da Cheng blockierte. Insgesamt vier während der japanischen Besatzung errichtete Getreideschuppen und zwei nach dem Erdbeben gebaute Lagerhäuser wurden für die neuen Museumsbauten ausgewählt. Dieses senkrecht zum Berg gerichtete Gebäudeensemble ergänzten die Architekten durch VIP-Bereiche, einen Museumsshop und ein Café parallel zu den alten Putzbauten, die mit Metallgittern und Holz verkleidet wurden. Alle Altbauten erhielten einen Patio. Die Architekten erläutern: „Die Neuplanung der gesamten Baugruppe bildet auch eine räumliche Sequenz zur Einbeziehung des Bergs in die Stadt durch eine Reihe von Gärten, Innenhöfen und den Park." Das Museum ist der Geschichte und der Neuplanung der Stadt gewidmet. Am Eingang befindet sich ein Antiquitätenmarkt. Die Architekten sind stolz auf die gelungene Umnutzung der Altbauten im Gegensatz zu größeren Städten, z. B. Peking und Shanghai, die, laut Urbanus, sich für „verrückte Neubauten" entschieden.

Wang Hui a été l'architecte en charge de ce projet. À la suite du tremblement de terre destructeur de 1976, la ville de Tangshan a cherché a « effacé les structures urbaines les moins séduisantes », dont l'ancien grenier à grains qui bloquait sa sortie vers la colline voisine de Da Cheng. Quatre silos construits sous l'occupation japonaise et deux entrepôts édifiés après le séisme furent choisis pour constituer la structure du musée. À l'intérieur de cette composition de bâtiments perpendiculaires à la colline, les architectes ont ajouté parallèlement des salles de réception pour VIP, une boutique pour le musée et un café, et les ont habillés d'une trame métallique et de bois. Un patio complète chacune des anciennes constructions. « Le nouveau plan d'ensemble de ces bâtiments forme une séquence spatiale qui relie la colline à la ville par une succession de jardins, de cours et le parc », précisent les architectes. Le musée se consacre à l'histoire et aux projets de la ville. Un marché d'antiquités a été aménagé près de l'entrée. Les architectes sont assez fiers d'avoir réutilisé les bâtiments anciens, à la différence d'autre villes plus importantes comme Pékin et Shanghaï qui préfèrent les « projets fous », selon Urbanus.

Broad open spaces are arranged in the former warehouses, allowing for a modern museum display within the walls of old buildings.

In den früheren Lagerhäusern wurden weite, offene Räume geplant, die sich für moderne Ausstellungsgestaltungen eignen.

De vastes espaces ouverts ont été aménagés dans les anciens entrepôts, permettant des accrochages et des installations muséales modernes.

OCT ART & DESIGN GALLERY

Shenzhen, China, 2006–08

*Address: Shennan Avenue OCT, Nanshan District, Shenzhen 518053, China
Area: 2620 m². Client: Shenzhen OCT Real Estate Co., Ltd. Cost: $3 million*

Although other architects have used patterned facades, the way this building is completely wrapped in a translucent mesh skin with a varied design makes it stand out in an original way.

Obwohl bereits andere Architekten gemusterte Fassaden eingesetzt haben, hebt die durchscheinende, unregelmäßige Gitternetzhaut, welche das gesamte Gebäude umgibt, es auf originelle Weise hervor.

Bien que d'autres architectes aient utilisé ce principe de façade texturée, la manière dont le bâtiment est intégralement enveloppé d'un treillis métallique translucide à trame variable est originale.

The irregular, honeycomb-like façade mesh gives a decidedly modern air to the structure of the actual gallery. This structure is nonetheless interrupted by a rising and irregular internal form.

Die unregelmäßige, wabenartige Fassadenstruktur gibt dem jetzigen Galeriegebäude ein entschieden modernes Erscheinungsbild. Innen wird der Bau jedoch von aufsteigenden, unregelmäßigen Formen bestimmt.

La façade en treillis métallique en forme de nid d'abeille étiré donne un aspect résolument moderne à ce lieu d'exposition. Son rythme est bousculé par un important élément que l'on voit s'élever à l'intérieur de la structure.

The museum was built on the site of the former laundry of the Shenzhen Bay Hotel. Given the rapid development of Shenzhen, the owner decided to redevelop the site. The architects state: "For Urbanus, the remodeling of the site poses difficult questions of how to address the existing urban condition, and how new interventions would relate to it. The main architectural gesture is to wrap the entire warehouse with a hexagonal glass curtain wall. The pattern is created from four different sizes of hexagons. As a result, the new wall becomes a lively theatrical screen." This geometric pattern is imagined as a "three-dimensional matrix of intersecting elements that project into the gallery spaces, structuring the building's interior design. The result is the creation of delightful and unexpected spatial experiences," according to the architects.

Dieses Museum wurde auf dem Grundstück der früheren Wäscherei des Shenzhen Bay Hotel errichtet. Angesichts der rasanten Entwicklung von Shenzhen beschloss der Besitzer, das Gelände der alten Wäscherei und des Lagerhauses umzunutzen. Die Architekten erklären: „Die Umgestaltung des Grundstücks stellte Urbanus vor schwierige Fragen: wie auf die bestehenden städtischen Bedingungen zu reagieren sei, wie neue Eingriffe mit diesen in Einklang zu bringen seien. Die zentrale architektonische Geste besteht in der Umhüllung des ganzen Lagergebäudes mit einer sechseckigen Glasvorhangfassade. Das System der Verkleidung besteht aus Sechsecken in vier verschiedenen Größen. Das Ergebnis ist eine neue Wand, die einem lebendigen Bildschirm ähnelt." Dieses geometrische System stellen sich die Architekten vor als „dreidimensionale Matrix sich überschneidender Elemente, die in den Galeriebereich hineinragen und die Innenarchitektur des Gebäudes strukturieren. Dies führt zu ansprechenden und unerwarteten Raumerlebnissen."

Ce musée a été édifié sur le site d'une ancienne blanchisserie de l'hôtel de la Baie de Shenzhen. Sous la pression du développement rapide de la ville, le propriétaire du terrain a décidé de rénover le site de ces anciens bâtiments industriels. Selon les architectes: «Pour Urbanus, le remodelage du site pose les questions difficiles de comment aborder l'urbain existant et comment faire que les interventions nouvelles puissent y trouver leur place. Le geste architectural principal a été d'envelopper l'ancien entrepôt tout entier d'un mur-rideau de verre dont le motif est créé par des hexagones de quatre tailles différentes. Ce nouveau mur devient ainsi une sorte de rideau de scène animé». Ce motif géométrique a été conçu comme «une matrice tridimensionnelle d'éléments s'entrecoupant qui se projettent dans les volumes des galeries, et structurent l'aménagement intérieur du bâtiment. Ainsi se créent des expériences spatiales raffinées et inattendues», expliquent les architectes.

Angled interior walls echo the exterior honeycomb design, as seen in these images and in the corresponding axonometric drawings.

Die schrägen Innenwände nehmen die äußere Wabenstruktur auf, wie auf diesen Abbildungen und den entsprechenden axonometrischen Zeichnungen zu sehen ist.

À l'intérieur, les murs inclinés rappellent le motif en nid d'abeille de l'extérieur comme le montrent ces images et les dessins axonométriques correspondants.

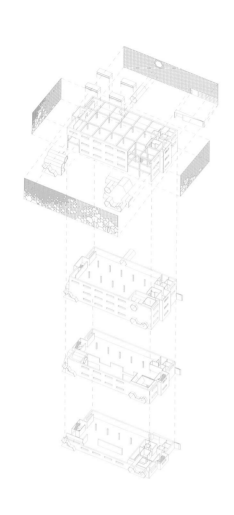

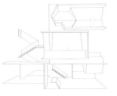
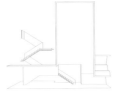

The basic rectangle of the museum is interrupted by this rising, angular well, lifted up off the ground and rising to a ceiling light.

Die rechteckige Grundform des Museums wird durch diesen aufsteigenden, schrägen Lichtschacht unterbrochen, der vom Boden abhebt und bis zu einem Oberlicht reicht.

La forme rectangulaire et simple du musée est interrompue par ce puits anguleux, suspendu et s'élevant vers une verrière zénithale.

WANG SHU

Wang Shu
Amateur Architecture Studio
1B206, 218 Nanshan Road
310002 Hangzhou
China

Tel: +86 571 8720 0602
E-mail: caajzhx@163.com

WANG SHU was born in Wulumuqi, China, in 1963. He founded the Amateur Architecture Studio in Hangzhou, China (1997). Since 2007, he has been the head of the Architecture School at the China Academy of Art in Hangzhou. His major built works include Wenzheng College Library (Suzhou, 1999–2000); the Ningbo Art Museum (Ningbo, 2001–05); the Ceramic House (Jinhua, 2003–06); the Tiles Garden, Chinese Pavilion, 10th International Architecture Exhibition, Venice Biennale (Venice, Italy, 2006); Vertical Housing (Hangzhou, 2002–07); the New Academy Campus of the China Academy of Art (Hangzhou, 2002–07); and the Ningbo History Museum (Ningbo, 2003–08, published here), all in China unless stated otherwise.

WANG SHU wurde 1963 in Wulumuqi, China, geboren und gründete 1997 das Amateur Architecture Studio in Hangzhou. Seit 2007 ist er Leiter der Architekturabteilung der Chinesischen Kunstakademie in Hangzhou. Zu seinen wichtigsten ausgeführten Bauten zählen die Bibliothek des Wenzheng College (Suzhou, 1999–2000), das Kunstmuseum Ningbo (Ningbo, 2001–05), das Keramikhaus (Jinhua, 2003–06), Fliesengarten im chinesischen Pavillon auf der X. Architekturbiennale in Venedig (2006), das Vertikale Wohnhaus (Hangzhou, 2002–07), der neue Campus der Chinesischen Kunstakademie (Hangzhou, 2002–07) und das Historische Museum Ningbo (Ningbo, 2003–08, hier veröffentlicht), alle in China, sofern nicht anders angegeben.

WANG SHU, né à Wulumuqi (Chine) en 1963, a fondé l'Amateur Architecture Studio à Hangzhou en 1997. Depuis 2007, il dirige l'École d'architecture de l'Académie chinoise de l'art à Hangzhou. Parmi ses principales réalisations, la bibliothèque du collège de Wenzheng (Suzhou, 1999–2000) ; le musée d'Art de Ningbo Art (Ningbo, 2001–05) ; la maison Ceramic (Jinhua, 2003–06) ; Tiles Garden au Pavillon chinois de la Xe Exposition internationale d'architecture, Biennale de Venise (2006) ; l'immeuble de logements Vertical (Hangzhou, 2002–07) ; le nouveau campus de l'Académie chinoise des arts (Hangzhou, 2002–07) et le musée d'Histoire de Ningbo (Ningbo, 2003–08), publié ici.

NINGBO HISTORY MUSEUM
Ningbo, China, 2003–08

Address: 1000 Shounan Middle Street, Yinzhou District, Ningbo, China, +86 574 8281 5533, www.nbmuseum.cn
Area: 30 000 m². Client: not disclosed. Cost: €16.649 million

Without a hint of irony, the architect writes: "This building was designed as an artificial mountain. The concept was derived from the location of the site, which was plains surrounded by mountains that was crop-filled not long ago." Urban development has brought government administrative buildings to the area, as well as numerous high-rise buildings being designed by Ma Qing Yun of Mada SPAM. Wang Shu explains: "The lower part of the museum is a simple square, while the upper part is a mountain-like shape. People enter the museum from a 30-meter-long hole in the middle. Viewed from inside, there are three valleys with big stairs—two in the interior, one in the open-door; there are four caves, in the entrance, the hall and the two sides of the steep slope of the exterior valley; there are four tunnel-shaped courtyards, two in the center and two in the quiet and deep location. The interior and exterior of the building were covered with bamboo-plate-modeled concrete and more than 20 kinds of recycled bricks, which is like a magnificent and thrifty substance existing between artificiality and nature." Built on a 45 333-square-meter site, the museum is still relatively isolated, like a solitary mountain. Seeking to preserve local know-how with the stonework, the architect reached a compromise solution between nature and design here, in the process generating a truly original form.

Der Architekt schreibt ohne jegliche Ironie: „Dieses Gebäude wurde als künstlicher Berg gestaltet. Das Konzept geht auf seinen Standort zurück, der aus Grasflächen besteht, die von Bergen umgeben sind und die bis vor kurzem noch bewirtschaftet wurden." Die Stadt bebaute das Gebiet mit Verwaltungsgebäuden sowie zahlreichen Hochhäusern, die von Ma Qing Yun von Mada SPAM geplant wurden. Wang Shu erläutert: „Der untere Teil des Museums ist ein einfaches Quadrat, der obere Teil hat die Form eines Bergs. Die Besucher betreten das Gebäude durch ein 30 m großes Loch in der Mitte. Von innen gesehen gibt es drei Täler mit großen Treppen – zwei innenliegende, eine im Freien –, weiterhin vier Höhlen, im Eingangsbereich, der Halle und zu beiden Seiten der steilen Abhänge des äußeren Tals. Es gibt vier tunnelartige Innenhöfe, zwei davon im Zentrum und zwei an ruhigen und tief gelegenen Standorten. Das Gebäude wurde innen und außen mit Beton verkleidet, der Bambusplatten nachgebildet ist, sowie mit über 20 Arten von recyceltem Backstein überzogen, die ein großartiges und sparsames, zwischen künstlich und natürlich angesiedeltes Volumen bilden." Das Museum, erbaut auf einem 45 333 m² großen Gelände, steht noch relativ isoliert wie ein einzelner Berg. Der Architekt hat sich bemüht, beim Mauerwerk örtliches Know-how zu bewahren und einen Kompromiss zwischen Natur und Planung in einem Gestaltungsprozess zu erreichen, der zu einer wahrhaft neuen Form geführt hat.

Sans ironie, l'architecte écrit : « Ce bâtiment a été conçu comme une montagne artificielle. Le concept dérive du site, de ces plaines entourées de montagnes qui étaient cultivées, il y a peu. » Le développement urbain a entraîné la construction de bâtiments d'administration locale et de nombreuses tours conçues par Ma Qing Yun de Mada SPAM. Selon Wang Shu : « La partie inférieure du musée est un simple carré, tandis que sa partie supérieure est en forme de montagne. Les visiteurs pénètrent dans le musée à partir d'une faille de 30 mètres de long creusée en son milieu. On trouve à l'intérieur trois vallées à grands escaliers – deux à l'intérieur, et un en extérieur –, quatre cavernes situées dans l'entrée, dans le hall d'accueil et sur les deux faces de la pente escarpée de la vallée extérieure, ainsi que quatre cours en forme de tunnel – deux au centre, et deux au calme et à l'écart. L'intérieur et l'extérieur du bâtiment sont habillés de plaques de béton à texture apparente de bambou et plus de vingt types de briques recyclées, matière magnifique et économique entre l'artificiel et le naturel. » Construit sur un terrain de 45 333 mètres carrés, le musée est encore relativement isolé, un peu à la manière d'une montagne solitaire. Cherchant à préserver le savoir-faire de la pierre locale, l'architecte a recherché un compromis entre la nature et les nécessités du projet, tout en donnant naissance à une forme authentiquement originale.

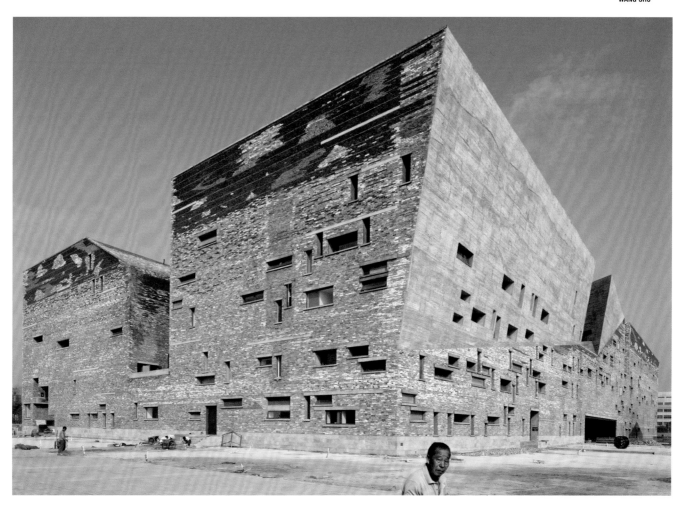

The strong shape of the museum evokes a geological formation—in an architectural interpretation that is certainly unusual.

Die kraftvolle Form des Museums erinnert an eine geologische Formation – in einer sicherlich ungewöhnlichen architektonischen Interpretation.

Les formes puissantes du musée évoquent une formation géologique, dans une interprétation architecturale peu courante.

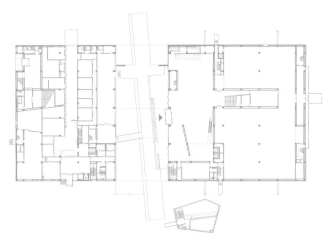

Within a clearly defined rectangle, the architect has carved walkways and openings that allow visitors to explore the rough surfaces of the structure and the vistas that it opens toward the city.

In ein klar begrenztes Rechteck hat der Architekt Wege und Öffnungen eingesetzt, die es den Besuchern ermöglichen, sich mit den rauen Oberflächen des Gebäudes und den Ausblicken zur Stadt auseinanderzusetzen.

À l'intérieur d'un rectangle clairement défini, l'architecte a creusé des passages et des ouvertures qui permettent aux visiteurs d'explorer cette structure de texture brute et de découvrir des perspectives sur la ville.

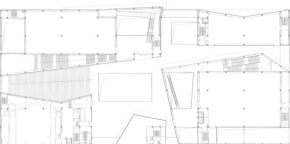

The inner courtyard seen here retains the kind of brute force that is evident in the exterior images.

Der hier sichtbare Innenhof hat etwas von der groben Kraft bewahrt, die auf den Außenansichten erkennbar ist.

La cour intérieure reproduite ici conserve l'impression de force brute ressentie dans les images de l'extérieur.

The interior volume seen above evokes a cavelike form that is in keeping with the geological theme of the museum. Below, a general floor plan shows the irregular paths that pierce the rectangular limits of the building.

Der oben abgebildete Innenraum erinnert an eine Höhle, was dem geologischen Thema des Museums entspricht. Ein Gesamtgrundriss (unten) zeigt die unregelmäßig angeordneten Wege, die durch das rechtwinklig begrenzte Gebäude führen.

Le volume intérieur ci-dessus évoque une caverne, image qui illustre la thématique géologique du musée. Ci-dessous, un plan au sol qui montre les cheminements irréguliers traversant le plan rectangulaire du bâtiment.

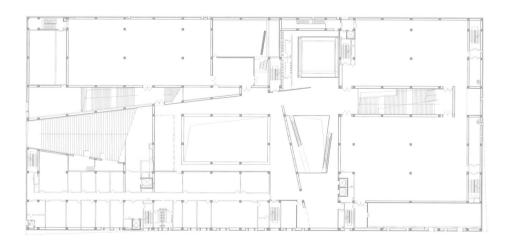

Bamboo growing in an inner courtyard (above), evokes the natural phe-
nomena that are at the origin of the
design. To the right, a canyon-like
inner stair.

Der in einem Innenhof wachsende
Bambus erinnert an die Naturphäno-
mene, die der Planung zugrunde
liegen. Rechts eine schluchtartige
Innentreppe.

La plantation de bambous de cette
cour intérieure (ci-dessus) évoque les
phénomènes naturels à l'origine de
l'inspiration du projet. À droite, un
escalier intérieur dans un « canyon ».

ATELIER ZHANGLEI

AZL Atelier Zhanglei
Architecture Design Institute, NJU
Hankou Road 22
210093 Nanjing, Jiangsu
China

Tel: +86 25 5186 1369
Fax: +86 25 5186 1367
E-mail: atelierzhanglei@163.com

ZHANG LEI was born in 1964 in Jiangsu province, China, whose major city is Nanjing. From 1981 to 1985, he studied architecture at the Nanjing Institute of Technology, and then went on to complete postgraduate studies at the ETH in Zurich (1992–93). He created his own office, Atelier Zhanglei, in 2000, and presently has 14 employees. He has been a Professor of Architectural Design at Nanjing University since 2000, and has also taught at the ETH and the University of Hong Kong. His major projects include the Student Dormitory, Nantong Foreign Language School (Nantong, 1998–99); the Pottery Studio of Nanjing Normal University (2001); the Taoyuan 02 Graduate Student Dormitory, Nanjing University (Nanjing, 2001–03); the office building for the Xinhua Construction Company (Xinhua, 2002–03); the Office & Lab Building of the Model Animal Genetic Research Center (Nanjing, 2002–03); the Staff Residence of Dongguan Institute of Technology (Dongguan, 2002–04); the Jianye Sport Mansion (Nanjing, 2004–05); the Cross Show Room (Qingpu, Shanghai, 2005); No. 4 House, CIPEA (Nanjing, 2005–06); and the Split House (Nanjing, 2006). More recent work includes the N-Park, Jiangsu Software Park (Nanjing, 2006–07); and the N4A Museum (Liyang, 2006–07, published here), all in China.

ZHANG LEI wurde 1964 in der Provinz Jiangsu, China, geboren, deren größte Stadt Nanjing ist. Von 1981 bis 1985 studierte er an der Technischen Hochschule in Nanjing Architektur und absolvierte danach ein Postgraduate-Studium an der Eidgenössischen Technischen Hochschule (ETH) in Zürich (1992–93). 2000 gründete er das Atelier Zhanglei, das heute 14 Mitarbeiter beschäftigt. Seit 2000 ist er Professor für architektonisches Entwerfen an der Universität Nanjing und hat auch an der ETH Zürich und der Universität Hongkong gelehrt. Zu seinen bedeutenden Projekten zählen das Studentenwohnheim der Fremdsprachenschule Nantong (Nantong, 1998–99), das Keramikatelier der Nanjing Normal University (2001), das Graduate-Studentenwohnheim Taoyuan 02 der Universität Nanjing (Nanjing, 2001–03), ein Bürogebäude für die Baufirma Xinhua (Xinhua, 2002–03), das Büro- und Laboratoriumsgebäude des Model Animal Genetic Research Center (Nanjing, 2002–03), Wohnungen für den Lehrkörper der Technischen Hochschule Dongguan (Dongguan, 2002–04), Jianye Sport Mansion (Nanjing, 2004–05), Cross Show Room (Qingpu, Shanghai, 2005), No. 4 House, CIPEA (Nanjing, 2005–06) und das Split House (Nanjing, 2006). Neuere Bauten sind der N-Park, Jiangsu Software Park (Nanjing, 2006–07) und das N4A Museum (Liyang, 2006–07, hier veröffentlicht), alle in China.

ZHANG LEI est né en 1964 dans la province du Jiangsu (Chine), dont la capitale est Nankin. De 1981 à 1985, il a étudié l'architecture à l'Institut de technologie de Nankin, puis a poursuivi ses études supérieures à l'ETH de Zurich (1992–93). Il a créé son agence, Atelier Zhanglei, en 2000, et emploie aujourd'hui quatorze personnes. Il est professeur de conception architecturale à l'université de Nankin depuis 2000, et a également enseigné à l'ETH et à l'université de Hong Kong. Parmi ses principales réalisations, toutes en Chine : le dortoir pour étudiants de l'École des langues étrangères de Nantong (Nantong, 1998–99) ; le studio de poterie de l'École normale supérieure de Nankin (2001) ; le dortoir pour étudiants Taoyuan 02 de l'université de Nankin (2001–03) ; un immeuble de bureaux pour l'entreprise de constructions Xinhua (Xinhua, 2002–03) ; l'immeuble de bureaux et de laboratoires du Centre de recherche génétique sur le génome animal (Nankin, 2002–03) ; la résidence du personnel de l'Institut de technologie de Dongguan (Dongguan, 2002–04) ; la résidence du sport Jianye (Nankin, 2004–05) ; le Cross Show Room (Qingpu, Shanghaï, 2005) ; la maison N° 4, CIPEA (Nankin, 2005–06) et la Split House (Nankin, 2006). Plus récemment, il a réalisé le N-Park, dans le parc du logiciel informatique du Jiangsu (Nankin, 2006–07) et le musée N4A (Liyang, 2006–07), publié ici.

N4A MUSEUM

Liyang, China, 2006–07

Address: Shuixi village, Liyang, Jiangsu Province, China, +86 519 8781 8918, www.n4ajnzhb.com
Area: 3800 m². Client: Liyang City Cultural Bureau. Cost: €900 000

Liyang is a city located 70 kilometers southeast of Nanjing. The New 4th Army, established in 1937, was one of the main forces of the Chinese Communist Party, active south of the Yangtze River from the 1930s on. The New 4th Army Jiangnan Headquarters Exhibition Hall was built in memory of this organization. Badges worn by Army members on their shoulder carried the acronym N4A, whence the name of this new institution. Fragmented granite is used here as a façade cladding. The architect states: "The pure cubic volume expresses the very strong, monumental function of this project. The courtyard turns from internal volume to external façade, and exposes itself in dramatic red section, presenting its revolutionary feature." Indeed, the structure is powerful, or perhaps willfully enigmatic and monolithic. Its style is quite unlike that of modern museums found elsewhere, expressing the originality of Zhang Lei and, indeed, of a part of recent contemporary Chinese architecture. This concrete building is located on a 7100-square-meter site and has three floors.

Die Stadt Liyang liegt 70 km südöstlich von Nanjing. Die hier 1937 begründete Neue 4. Armee war eine der Hauptkräfte der Kommunistischen Partei Chinas und seit den 1930er-Jahren südlich des Jangtse im Einsatz. Die Ausstellungshalle des Jiangnan-Hauptquartiers der Neuen 4. Armee wurde zum Gedenken an diese Einheit errichtet. Der Name des Gebäudes stammt vom Akronym N4A, das die Armeeangehörigen auf der Schulter trugen. Granitbruch wurde zur Verkleidung des Gebäudes genutzt. Der Architekt erklärt: „Das klare, kubische Volumen betont die starke, monumentale Funktion des Projekts. Der Hof verwandelt sich von einem inneren Volumen zur Außenfassade und drückt als dramatisches, rotes Bauteil den revolutionären Charakter aus." Das Bauwerk ist in der Tat kraftvoll oder vielleicht bewusst geheimnisvoll und monolithisch, im Stil völlig verschieden von anderen modernen Museen; es ist Ausdruck von Zhang Leis Originalität und durchaus auch der zeitgenössischen chinesischen Architektur. Dieser Betonbau steht auf einem 7100 m² großen Grundstück und hat drei Geschosse.

La ville de Liyang se trouve à soixante-dix kilomètres au sud-est de Nankin. La Nouvelle 4ème armée, créée en 1937, était l'une des principales forces militaires du Parti communiste, active au sud du Yang-Tsé-Kiang depuis les années 30. Le musée du siège de la Nouvelle 4ème armée a été édifié en souvenir de son histoire. Des badges portés sur l'épaule par ses membres montraient le sigle N4A, d'où le nom du musée. Les façades sont revêtues de granite fragmenté. « Les volumes cubiques expriment la très forte fonction monumentale de ce projet. La cour passe du statut de volume intérieur à celui de façade extérieure, et s'expose dans une spectaculaire section de couleur rouge révolutionnaire. » Ce bâtiment en béton de trois niveaux sur un terrain de 7100 mètres carrés est d'une architecture puissante, monolithique, voire énigmatique. Son style est assez différent de celui d'autres musées actuels. Il exprime l'originalité de Zhang Lei et appartient résolument à la nouvelle architecture contemporaine.

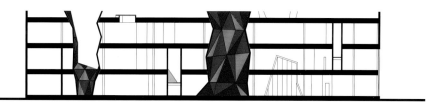

The N4A Museum stands like a regular, but fragmented block. Its openings are clearly visible in the section drawing above.

Das Museum N4A steht da wie ein gleichmäßiger, aber zerklüfteter Block. Seine Einschnitte sind im Schnitt (oben) deutlich erkennbar.

Le musée N4A se dresse à la manière d'un énorme bloc de forme régulière mais fragmentée. Ses ouvertures apparaissent clairement dans le dessin de coupe ci-dessus.

Seen through a traditional gateway
(left), the museum has a striking,
palace- or temple-like presence.

Beim Blick durch einen traditionellen
Torbogen (links) wirkt das Museum
wie ein Palast oder ein Tempel.

Aperçu à travers une porte traditionnelle (à gauche), le musée possède
une présence qui évoque celle d'un
palais ou d'un temple.

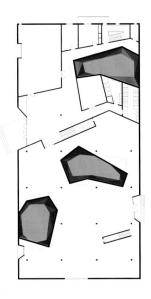
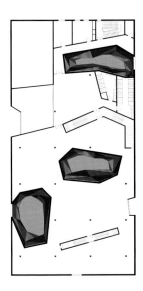
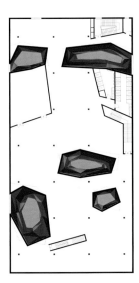

Floor plans show how the architect
adds irregular interior volumes
to the slightly notched rectangular
structure.

Die Grundrisse zeigen, wie der Architekt ungleichmäßige Innenräume im
leicht eingeschnittenen, rechtwinkligen Volumen untergebracht hat.

Les plans au sol montrent comment
l'architecte a inséré des volumes
intérieurs de forme irrégulière dans
un volume rectangulaire légèrement
indenté.

Fore

INDEX OF ARCHITECTS, BUILDINGS, AND PLACES

0–9

21_21 Design Sight, Tokyo, Japan — 009, 022, 036
21st-Century Museum of Contemporary Art, Kanazawa, Japan — 016, 030, 044

A

Abe, Hitoshi — 048
Abu Dhabi Maritime Museum, Abu Dhabi, UAE — 009, 022
Acebo X Alonso Arquitectos — 056
Albury Library Museum, Albury, New South Wales, Australia — 082
Altes Museum, Museum Island, Berlin, Germany — 006, 019, 033
Adjaye, David — 010, 023, 037
Aires Mateus — 015, 028, 042, 064
Ando, Tadao — 009, 022–023, 036–037
Aoki, Jun — 070
Aomori Museum of Art, Aomori, Japan — 072
Archeology Museum of Álava, Vitoria, Spain — 226
ARM — 080
Arp Museum, Rolandseck, Germany — 234
Art Gallery of Ontario Expansion, Toronto, ON, Canada — 008, 021, 035, 142
Art Institute of Chicago, Modern Wing, Chicago, IL, USA — 007, 020, 034, 302
Art Museum, Central Academy of Fine Arts, Beijing, China — 200
Australia
Albury, New South Wales, Albury Library Museum — 082
Austria
Neuhaus/Suha, Carinthia, Liaunig Museum — 310

B

Ban, Shigeru — 012–014, 026–027, 040–041, 086
Behnisch Architekten — 015, 024, 028, 042, 092
Bellevue Art Museum, Seattle, WA, USA — 011, 024, 038
Berkel, Ben van — 011, 024, 038
BMW Welt, Munich, Germany — 015, 028, 042
Bragança Contemporary Art Museum, Bragança, Portugal — 350
Brandhorst Museum, Munich, Germany — 322
Brazil
São Paulo, São Paulo, Brazilian Museum of Sculpture — 015, 029, 043
São Paulo, São Paulo, Portuguese Language Museum — 024, 029, 043, 240
Brazilian Museum of Sculpture, São Paulo, São Paulo, Brazil — 015, 029, 042
Breuer, Marcel — 006, 019, 033

C

CaixaForum, Madrid, Spain — 008, 021, 035–036
Calatrava, Santiago — 008, 021, 035, 038
California Academy of Sciences, San Francisco, CA, USA — 007, 020, 034
Canada
Toronto, ON, Art Gallery of Ontario Expansion — 008, 021, 035, 142
Centre Pompidou,
Paris, France — 007, 009, 013, 016, 020, 022, 026–027, 029, 034, 040, 043
Centre Pompidou-Metz,
Metz, France — 011, 013–014, 024, 026, 038, 041, 088
Chichu Art Museum, Naoshima, Japan — 009, 022, 036
China
Beijing, Art Museum, Central Academy of Fine Arts — 200
Hangzhou, Liangzhu Culture Museum — 108
Liyang, N4A Museum — 015, 030, 043, 408
Ningbo, Ningbo History Museum — 012, 026, 040, 398
Shenzhen, OCT Art & Design Gallery — 390
Taiyuan, Taiyuan Museum of Art — 114
Tangshan, Tangshan Urban Planning Museum — 386
Chipperfield, David — 011–012, 025, 038, 100
Clark Art Institute, Williamstown, MA, USA — 009, 022, 036
Clément, Gilles — 009, 022, 036
Cohen, Preston Scott — 112
Coop Himmelb(l)au — 008, 014, 021, 027, 041–042, 122
Cornerstone Arts Centre, Didcot, Oxfordshire, UK — 136

D

Delugan Meissl Associated Architects — 014–015, 028, 042, 126
Denmark
Copenhagen, Ordrupgaard Museum Extension — 168
De Young Museum, San Francisco, CA, USA — 008, 021, 035
DIA Beacon, OpenOffice, Beacon, New York, USA — 013, 027, 041
Diller Scofidio + Renfro — 016, 029, 043

E

Egypt
Giza, Grand Eqyptian Museum — 014, 028, 041–042
Eiffel Tower, Paris, France — 009, 022, 036
Ellis Williams — 134

F
Finsterwalder, Rudolf   336
Forest of Tombs Museum, Kumamoto, Japan   009, 022, 036
Foster, Norman   008–009, 012, 022, 025, 035–036
France
Lens, Louvre-Lens   011, 014, 016, 024, 027, 030, 038, 041, 318
Lyon, Musée des Confluences   014, 027, 041, 124
Metz, Centre Pompidou-Metz   011, 013–014, 024, 026, 038, 041, 088
Paris, Centre Pompidou
            007, 009, 013, 016, 020, 022, 026–027, 029, 034, 040, 043
Paris, Eiffel Tower   009, 022, 036
Paris, Grand Louvre   006–007, 013, 016, 020, 022, 029, 034, 040, 043
Paris, Louvre Pyramid   017, 031, 047
Paris, Quai Branly Museum   009, 022, 036
Sabres, Museum of the Landes de Gascogne   214
Frost Art Museum, Miami, FL, USA   194

G
Gehry, Frank O.
    006–014, 017, 019–021, 025–027, 031, 033, 037, 039–041, 045, 140
Germany
Berlin, Altes Museum, Museum Island   006, 019, 033
Berlin, Neue Nationalgalerie   006, 019, 033
Berlin, Neues Museum, Museum Island   011, 025, 038, 102
Berlin, Reichstag, New German Parliament   012, 025, 039
Halle, Saale, Moritzburg Museum Extension   268
Munich, BMW Welt   015, 028, 042
Munich, Brandhorst Museum   322
Neuss-Hombroich, Hombroich Museum   338
Rolandseck, Arp Museum   234
Stralsund, Ozeaneum, German Oceanographic Museum
            011, 015, 024, 028, 038, 042, 094
Stuttgart, Mercedes-Benz Museum   015, 028, 042
Stuttgart, Porsche Museum   015, 028, 042, 128
Waiblingen, Stihl Art Gallery and Art School   330
Getty Center, Los Angeles, CA, USA   045, 232
González de León, Teodoro   017, 030, 044, 146
GRAFT   154
Grand Egyptian Museum, Giza, Egypt   014, 028, 041–042

Grand Louvre, Paris, France 006–007, 013, 016, 020, 022, 029, 034, 040, 043
Greece
Athens, The New Acropolis Museum   368
Grenchen Art Museum Extension, Grenchen, Switzerland   356
Grimshaw, Nicholas   015, 029, 038, 042, 160
Guggenheim Bilbao, Bilbao, Spain
        006–008, 012–014, 017, 019, 025, 027, 031, 033–035, 039–041
Guggenheim Museum, New York, NY, USA   008, 021, 035

H
Hadid, Zaha   011–012, 024–026, 038–039, 166
Heneghan.Peng.Architects   014, 028, 042
Herzog & de Meuron 008–010, 013, 019, 021–023, 027, 035–037, 041, 182
HOK   192
Holl, Steven   011, 024, 038
Hombroich Museum, Neuss-Hombroich, Germany   338
Horno 3: Museo del Acero, Monterrey, Mexico
                011, 015, 024, 029, 038, 042, 162

I
Institute of Contemporary Art, Boston, MA, USA   016, 030, 043
Isozaki, Arata   008, 021, 198
Israel
Tel Aviv, Tel Aviv Museum of Art   118
Italy
Bolzano, Museion, Museum of Modern and Contemporary Art   208
Rome, MAXXI, National Museum of 21st-Century Arts
                012, 025–026, 039, 178
Venice, Palazzo Grassi   009, 022, 036
Venice, Punta della Dogana   009, 022, 036–037

J
Japan
Aomori, Aomori Museum of Art   072
Izumo, Shimane Museum of Ancient Izumo   220
Kanazawa, 21st-Century Museum of Contemporary Art   016, 030, 044
Kumamoto, Forest of Tombs Museum   009, 022, 036
Matsudai, Matsudai Cultural Village Center   262
Naoshima, Chichu Art Museum   009, 022, 036

Osaka, Suntory Museum — 009, 022, 036

Shiogama, Kanno Museum — 050

Tokyo, 21_21 Design Sight — 009, 022, 036

Towada City, Towada Art Center — 282

K

Kanno Museum, Shiogama, Japan — 050

Koolhaas, Rem — 011, 024, 038

KSV Krüger Schuberth Vandreike — 206

L

Liangzhu Culture Museum, Hangzhou, China — 108

Liaunig Museum, Neuhaus/Suha, Carinthia, Austria — 310

Los Angeles County Museum of Art, Los Angeles, CA, USA — 011, 024, 038

Louvre, Abu Dhabi, UAE — 009, 013, 022, 036, 040

Louvre-Lens, Lens, France — 011, 014, 016, 024, 027, 030, 038, 041, 044, 318

Louvre Pyramid, Paris, France — 017, 031, 047

M

Mader, Bruno — 212

Madinat al-Zahra Museum and Research Center, Córdoba, Spain — 274

Maki, Fumihiko — 218

Mangado, Francisco — 224

Matsudai Cultural Village Center, Matsudai, Japan — 262

MAXXI, National Museum of 21st-Century Arts, Rome, Italy — 012, 025–026, 039, 178

Meier, Richard — 010, 023, 037, 232

Mendes da Rocha, Paulo — 015, 029, 038, 043, 238

Mercedes-Benz Museum, Stuttgart, Germany — 015, 028

Metropolitan Museum of Art, New York, NY, USA — 006, 010, 016, 019, 023, 037, 043

Mexico

Monterrey, Horno 3: Museo del Acero — 011, 015, 024, 029, 038, 042, 162

Mexico City, University Museum for Contemporary Art (UNAM) — 017, 030, 044, 146

Mies van der Rohe, Ludwig — 006, 019, 033

Milwaukee Art Museum, WI, USA — 010, 024, 038

Mobile Art, Chanel Contemporary Art Container — 011, 024, 038, 174

Modern Art Museum of Fort Worth, Fort Worth, TX, USA — 009, 022, 036

Moneo, Rafael — 010, 023, 037, 244

Mori, Toshiko — 252

Moritzburg Museum Extension, Halle, Saale, Germany — 268

Musée des Confluences, Lyon, France — 014, 027, 041, 124

Museion, Museum of Modern and Contemporary Art, Bolzano, Italy — 208

Museum of Contemporary Art/Denver, Denver, CO, USA — 010, 023, 037

Museum of Human Evolution, Burgos, Spain — 012, 026, 040

Museum of Islamic Art, Doha, Qatar — 006–007, 020, 034, 294

Museum of Middle East Modern Art (MOMEMA), Khor Dubai, UAE — 378

Museum of Modern Art (MoMA), New York, NY, USA — 012, 014–015, 023, 025, 027, 037, 039, 041, 043

Museum of the Landes de Gascogne, Sabres, France — 214

Museum of the Roman Theater, Cartagena, Spain — 246

MVRDV — 009, 022, 036, 260

N

N4A Museum, Liyang, China — 015, 030, 043, 408

National Gallery of Art, Washington D. C., USA — 006–007, 019, 029, 033–034

National Museum of Science and Technology (MUNCYT), A Coruña, Spain — 058

Neue Nationalgalerie, Berlin, Germany — 006, 019, 033

Neues Museum, Museum Island, Berlin, Germany — 011, 025, 038, 102

New Acropolis Museum, Athens, Greece — 368

New German Parliament, Reichstag, Berlin, Germany — 012, 025, 039

New Museum of Contemporary Art, New York, NY, USA — 016, 030, 043

Nieto Sobejano — 266

Ningbo History Museum, Ningbo, China — 012, 026, 040, 398

Nishizawa, Ryue — 014, 016, 027, 030, 040, 043–044, 280, 316

Norway

Alstahaug, Nordland, Petter Dass Museum — 344

Nouvel, Jean — 009, 012–013, 022, 026, 036, 040

O

Olgiati, Valerio — 286

Ordrupgaard Museum Extension, Copenhagen, Denmark — 168

Ozeaneum, German Oceanographic Museum, Stralsund, Germany — 011, 015, 024, 028, 038, 042, 094

P

Palazzo Grassi, Venice, Italy — 009, 022, 036

Pei, I. M. — 006–007, 017, 019, 031, 034, 045–047, 292

Petter Dass Museum, Alstahaug, Nordland, Norway — 344

Piano, Renzo — 007–013, 017, 022, 025–026, 031, 034–038, 040, 045, 300

Portugal

Bragança, Bragança Contemporary Art Museum — 350

Cascais, Santa Maria Lighthouse Museum — 011, 015, 024, 028, 038, 042, 066

Portuguese Language Museum, São Paulo, São Paulo, Brazil — 024, 029, 240

Porsche Museum, Stuttgart, Germany — 015, 028, 042, 128

Prado, Madrid, Spain — 010, 023, 037

Prix, Wolf D. — 014, 028, 041

Pulitzer Foundation for the Arts, Saint Louis, MO, USA — 009, 022, 036

Punta della Dogana, Venice, Italy — 009, 022, 036–037

Q

Qatar

Doha, Museum of Islamic Art — 006–007, 020, 034, 294

Quai Branly Museum, Paris, France — 009, 022, 036

Querkraft — 308

R

Reichstag, New German Parliament, Berlin, Germany — 012, 025, 039

Rogers, Richard — 007, 011, 013, 020, 025–026, 034, 038, 040

Russia

Moscow, The Russian Jewish Museum of Tolerance — 156

Russian Jewish Museum of Tolerance, Moscow, Russia — 156

S

SANAA — 014, 016, 027, 030, 040, 043–044, 316

Santa Maria Lighthouse Museum, Cascais, Portugal
011, 015, 024, 028, 038, 042, 066
Sauerbruch Hutton 320
Schinkel, Karl Friedrich 006, 019, 033
Schneider, Hartwig N. 328
Sejima, Kazuyo 014, 016, 027, 030, 040, 043–044, 316
Shimane Museum of Ancient Izumo, Izumo, Shimane, Japan 220
Siza Vieira, Álvaro 336
Snøhetta 342
Souto de Moura, Eduardo 348
Spain
A Coruña, National Museum of Science and Technology (MUNCYT) 058
Bilbao, Guggenheim Bilbao
006–008, 012–014, 017, 019, 021, 025, 033, 035, 039
Burgos, Museum of Human Evolution 012, 026, 040
Cartagena, Museum of the Roman Theater 246
Córdoba, Madinat al-Zahra Museum and Research Center 274
Madrid, CaixaForum 008, 021, 035
Madrid, Prado 010, 023, 037
Santa Cruz de Tenerife, Canary Islands, Tenerife Espacio de las Artes (TEA)
008–009, 022, 036, 184
Vitoria, Archeology Museum of Álava 226
SSM Architekten 354
Stihl Art Gallery and Art School, Waiblingen, Germany 330
Stout, Randall 360
Suntory Museum, Osaka, Japan 009, 022, 036
Swiss National Park Visitor Center, Zernez, Switzerland 288
Switzerland
Grenchen, Grenchen Art Museum Extension 356
Zernez, Swiss National Park Visitor Center 288

T
Taiyuan Museum of Art, Taiyuan, China 114
Tangshan Urban Planning Museum, Tangshan, China 386
Taniguchi, Yoshio 010, 012, 023, 025, 037, 039
Tate Gallery, London, UK 008, 013, 016, 021, 026, 035, 040, 043
Tate Modern, London, UK 008, 013, 021, 027, 035, 040
Taubman Museum of Art, Roanoke, VA, USA 362
Tel Aviv Museum of Art, Tel Aviv, Israel 118
Tenerife Espacio de las Artes (TEA), Santa Cruz de Tenerife,
Canary Islands, Spain 008–009, 022, 036, 184
Towada Art Center, Towada City, Aomori, Japan 282
Transforming Tate Modern, London, UK 008, 021, 035
Tschumi, Bernard 366

U
University Museum for Contemporary Art (UNAM),
Mexico City, Mexico 017, 030, 044, 146
United Arab Emirates
Abu Dhabi, Abu Dhabi Maritime Museum 009, 022, 036
Abu Dhabi, Louvre 009, 013, 022, 036, 040
Khor Dubai, Museum of Middle East Modern Art (MOMEMA) 378
United Kingdom
Didcot, Oxfordshire, Cornerstone Arts Center 136

London, Tate Gallery 008, 013, 016, 021, 026, 029, 035, 040, 043
London, Tate Modern 008, 013, 021, 027, 035, 041
London, Transforming Tate Modern 008, 021, 035
UNStudio 011, 015, 024, 028, 042, 376
United States
Beacon, NY, OpenOffice, DIA Beacon 013, 027, 041
Boston, MA, Institute of Contemporary Art 016, 030, 043
Buffalo, NY, Visitor Center for Frank Lloyd Wright's Darwin D. Martin House 254
Chicago, IL, Art Institute of Chicago, Modern Wing 006, 020, 034, 302
Denver, CO, Museum of Contemporary Art/Denver 010, 023, 037
Fort Worth, TX, Modern Art Museum of Fort Worth 009, 022, 036
Los Angeles, CA, The Getty Center 010, 023, 037
Los Angeles, CA, Los Angeles County Museum 011, 024, 038
Miami, FL, Frost Art Museum 194
Milwaukee, WI, Milwaukee Art Museum 010, 024, 038
Minneapolis, MN, Walker Art Center 008, 021, 035
New York, NY, Guggenheim Museum 008, 021, 035
New York, NY, Metropolitan Museum of Art
006, 010, 015, 019, 023, 037, 043
New York, NY, Museum of Modern Art (MoMA)
012, 014–015, 023, 025, 029, 041, 043
New York, NY, New Museum of Contemporary Art 016, 030, 043
New York, NY, Whitney Museum of Modern Art 006, 011, 019, 038
Roanoke, VA, Taubman Museum of Art 362
Saint Louis, MO, Pulitzer Foundation for the Arts 009, 022, 036
San Francisco, CA, California Academy of Sciences 007, 020, 034
San Francisco, CA, De Young Museum 008, 021, 035
Seattle, WA, Bellevue Art Museum 008, 024, 038
Washington D. C., National Gallery of Art
006–007, 019, 029, 033–034
Williamstown, MA, Clark Art Institute 009, 022, 036
URBANUS Architecture & Design 384

V
Visitor Center for Frank Lloyd Wright's Darwin D. Martin House,
Buffalo, NY, USA 254

W
Walker Art Center, Minneapolis, MN, USA 008, 021, 035
Wang, Shu 012, 026, 040, 396
West8 014, 028, 042
Whitney Museum of Modern Art, New York, NY, USA 006, 011, 019, 038

Z
Atelier Zhanglei 406
Zhang, Lei 015, 030, 043

CREDITS

PHOTO CREDITS — 2 © Hertha Hurnaus / **7** © Jose Fuste Raga/Corbis / **9** © Roland Halbe / **10** © Ed Reeve / **11** © Alan Karchmer / **12** © Ateliers Jean Nouvel/ **13** © Shigeru Ban Architects Europe / **15** © Roland Halbe / **16** © Nic Lehoux / **17** © Pedro Hiriart / **20** © Renzo Piano Building Workshop / **21** © Duccio Malagamba / **22** © Mitsuo Matsuoka / **23** © Timothy Hursley / **24** © Roland Halbe / **25 left** © SMB/Zentralarchiv / **25 right** © Christian Richters / **28** © Leonardo Finotti / **29** © Christian Richters / **30** © AZL Atelier Zhanglei / **31** © Dean Kaufman / **34** © Nic Lehoux / **35** © Roland Halbe / **37** © Shigeo Ugawa / **38** © Paúl Rivera/archphoto.com / **39** © Leonardo Finotti / **40** © Iwan Baan / **42** © Ari Marcopoulos / **43** © Nelson Kon / **44** © Kanazawa Museum / **45** © Lindsay Hebberd/Corbis / **47** © artur/Artedia / **48** © Atelier Hitoshi Abe / **49–55** © Daici Ano / **49–55** © **56** © Victoria Acebo y Ángel Alonso Arquitectos / **57–63** © SANTOS-DÍEZ/FABPICS / **64** © Francisco Aires Mateus Arquitectos / **65–69** © Leonardo Finotti / **70** © Yoshiaki Tsutsui / **71–79** © Daici Ano / **80** © ARM / **81–85** © John Gollings/Arcaid / **86** © Shigeru Ban Architects / **87–89 top, 90 bottom–91** © Shigeru Ban Architects Europe / **89 bottom, 90 top** Chantier du Centre Pompidou-Metz, septembre 2009 © Shigeru Ban Architects Europe et Jean de Gastines / Metz Métropole / Centre Pompidou-Metz / Photo Olivier H. Dancy / **92** © David Matthiessen / **93–99** © Roland Halbe / **100** © Nick Knight / **101, 105, 106 top left and right, bottom left, 107, 109–111** © Christian Richters / **102–103** © SPK/DCA, Foto: Jörg von Bruchhausen / **106 bottom right** © SPK/DCA, Foto: Ute Zscharnt / **112** © Maurice Weiss/OSTKREUZ / **122** © Ivo Kocherscheidt / **126** © Delugan Meissl Associated Architects / **127–133** © Roland Halbe / **134** © Ellis Williams Architects / **135–139** © Daniel Hopkins/Arcaid / **140** © Courtesy of Gehry Partners LLP / **141–142, 144 bottom, 145** © Image Coutesy of Gehry Partners LLP / **143 bottom left, top, 144 top** © Thomas Mayer/thomasmayerarchive.de / **146** © Bernardo Arcos / **147–153** © Pedro Hiriart / **154** © Ricky Ridecos / **160** © Ben Johnson / **161–165** © Paúl Rivera/archphoto.com / **166** © Steve Double / **167, 170–171 left** © FS GUERRA/FABPICS / **168–169** © Roland Halbe / **171 right, 179–180** © Hélène Binet / **172–173** © Cristóbal Palma / **175** © John Linden / **176 top, 176 bottom left, 177 top left** © Virgile Simon Bertrand / **174, 176 bottom right, 177 bottom** © Toshio Kaneko / **177 top right** © Marc Gerritsen / **178–181** © Roland Halbe / **182** © Adriano A. Biondo / **183, 188–189 top** © Roland Halbe / **184, 185 top, 190–191** © Iwan Baan / **185 bottom, 186–187, 189 bottom** © Duccio Malagamba / **192** © HOK / **193–197** © Moris Moreno, courtesy by HOK / **198** © Hong Kong RIHAN International Culture Co., Ltd. / **199–205** © Iwan Baan / **206** © Werner Huthmacher / **207–211** © Paolo Riolzi / **212** © Agence Mader / **213** © Serge Demailly / **214, 216–217** © Gaston F. Bergeret / **215** © Agence Mader / **218** © Maki and Associates / **219–223** © Toshiharu Kitajima / **224** © Pablo Neustadt / **225–231** © Roland Halbe / **232** © Richard Phibbs / **233** © Roland Halbe / **234–237** © Roland Halbe / **238** © Paulo Mendes da Rocha / **239–243** © Leonardo Finotti / **244** © Rafael Moneo / **245–251** © Duccio Malagamba / **252** © Yanai Yechiel / **253–257 top, 258–259** © Paul Warchol / **257 bottom** © Biff Henrich/Keystone Film Prod., Inc. / **260–265** © Rob 't Hart/www.rob-thart.nl / **266** © Ralf Lehmann/BILD Halle / **267, 269–279** © Roland Halbe / **280** © Takashi Okamoto / **281–285** © Christian Richters / **286** © Archive Olgiati / **287–291** © Javier Miguel Verme / **292** © Victor Zbigniew / **293–299** © Morley von Sternberg / **300** © Renzo Piano Building Workshop – ph. Stefano Goldberg / **301–302, 303 bottom, 306–307** © Nic Lehoux / **303 top, 305** © Christian Richters / **306** © Querkraft - Hertha Hurnaus / **307–315** © Querkraft - Lisa Rastl / **316** © Takashi Okamoto / **320** © Wilfried Dechau / **321** © Andreas Lechtape / **322, 323 bottom left and right, 326–327** © Annette Kisling / **323 top** © Rainer Viertlböck / **325** © Noshe / **325** © Jannis Kounellis / **326** © Cy Twombly, 2009 / **327** © 2009 The Andy Warhol Foundation for the Visual Arts, Inc. / Artists Rights Society (ARS, New York) / **328** © Hartwig N. Schneider / **329–335** © Christian Richters / **336** © Rudolf Finsterwalder / **337–341** © FS GUER-RA/FABPICS / **342** © Snøhetta / **343–347** © Aake E. Lindman / **348–353** © Luis Ferreira Alves / **354** © Jürg Stäuble, SSM Architekten / **355–359** © Antje Quiram / **360** © Randall Stout Architects © **361–365** © Timothy Hursley / **366** © Bernard Tschumi Architects / **367–375** © Peter Maus/Esto / **376** © Peter Guenzel / **384** © Jin Qiang/URBANUS Architecture & Design / **385–389** © Yang Chaoying/URBANUS Architecture & Design / **390–395** © Jin Qiang/URBANUS Architecture & Design / **396** © Wang Shu/Amateur Architecture Studio / **397–398, 400–402 top, 403–405** © Iwan Baan / **399, 402 bottom** © Wang Shu/Amateur Architecture Studio / **406** © AZL Atelier Zhanglei / **407, 410** © Lu Hengzhong / **409, 411** © Jia Fang

CREDITS FOR PLANS / DRAWINGS / CAD DOCUMENTS — 8 © Herzog & de Meuron and Hayes Davidson / **14** © heneghan.peng.architects / **26** © Zaha Hadid / **27** © COOP HIMMELB(L)AU / **36** © Ateliers Jean Nouvel / **41** © SANAA / **53, 55** © Atelier Hitoshi Abe / **59** © Victoria Acebo y Ángel Alonso Arquitectos / **66, 69** © Francisco Aires Mateus Arquitectos / **74** © Jun Aoki & Associates / **82, 85** © ARM / **89–90** © Shigeru Ban Architects / **95–96, 98** © Behnisch Architekten / **104, 108** © David Chipperfield Architects / **113–121** © Courtesy of Preston Scott Cohen, Inc. / **123–125** © COOP HIMMELB(L)AU / **129, 131, 133** © Delugan Meissl Associated Architects / **144** © Courtesy of Gehry Partners LLP / **149, 151** © Pedro Hiriart/Teodoro González de León Arquitectos / **155–159** © Graft / **162, 165** © Grimshaw / **171–173, 181 bottom right** © Courtesy of Zaha Hadid Architects / **191** © Herzog & de Meuron / **196** © HOK / **201, 203** © Arata Isozaki & Associates / **208–209** © KSV Krüger Schuberth Vandreike / **215, 217** © Bruno Mader / **221** © Courtesy of Maki and Associates /**229** © Francisco Mangado / **235–236** © Richard Meier / **240** © Paulo Mendes da Rocha / **248** © Rafael Moneo / **257, 259** © Toshiko Mori Architect / **262, 264** © MVRDV / **268, 272–273, 276, 279** © Nieto Sobejano / **285** © Office of Ryue Nishizawa / **288, 290** © Archive Olgiati / **294, 295, 298** © I.M. Pei Architect / **302, 304, 306–307** © Renzo Piano Building Workshop / **310, 312–313** © Querkraft / **317–319** © SANAA / **324, 326** © Sauerbruch Hutton / **332** © Hartwig N. Schneider / **341** © Álvaro Siza Arquitecto / **346** © Snøhetta / **351, 353** © Souto de Moura Arquitectos / **357, 359** © SSM Architekten / **364** © Randall Stout Architects / **371, 373–374** © Bernard Tschumi Architects / **377–383** © UNStudio / **386, 389, 391, 393–394** © URBANUS Architecture & Design / **399–400, 403** © Wang Shu/Amateur Architecture Studio / **409–410** © AZL Atelier Zhanglei